THE RANDOM HOUSE READER

edited by

FREDERICK CREWS

University of California, Berkeley

THE RANDOM HOUSE READER

FOR MY PARENTS

First Edition
98765432
 Published in the United States by Random House, Inc., and simultaneously in Canada by Random House of Canada Limited, Toronto.

Library of Congress Cataloging in Publication Data
Main entry under title:

The Random House reader.

Includes index.
1. College readers. I. Crews, Frederick C.
PE1122.R29 808'.0427 80–23079
ISBN 0–394–32268–1

Manufactured in the United States of America

Cover design: Carol Grube

PERMISSIONS ACKNOWLEDGMENTS

Shana Alexander, "Judy Garland," from *Talking Woman,* by Shana Alexander. Copyright © 1976 by Shana Alexander. Reprinted by permission of Delacorte Press.

Roger Angell, "The Cool Bubble," from *The Summer Game,* by Roger Angell. Copyright © 1966 by Roger Angell. Reprinted by permission of *The New Yorker* and Viking Penguin, Inc.

Maya Angelou, from *I Know Why the Caged Bird Sings,* pp. 180–189. Copyright © 1969 by Maya Angelou. Reprinted by permission of Random House, Inc.

James Baldwin, "Stranger in the Village," from *Notes of a Native Son,* by James Baldwin. Copyright © 1955 by James Baldwin. Reprinted by permission of Beacon Press.

Sissela Bok, "Deceptive Social Science Research," from *Lying: Moral Choice in Public and Private Life,* by Sissela Bok. Copyright © 1978 by Sissela Bok. Reprinted by permission of Pantheon Books, a Division of Random House, Inc.

Daniel Boorstin, abridged from "From News Gathering to News Making: A Flood of Pseudo-Events," in *The Image,* by Daniel J. Boorstin. Copyright © 1961 by Daniel J. Boorstin. Reprinted by permission of Atheneum Publishers.

Vladimir Bukovsky, (retitled: "Life Behind Bars") from *To Build A Castle: My Life as a Dissenter,* by Vladimir Bukovsky. Translated by Michael Scammell. Copyright © 1978

Permissions Acknowledgments Continued on Page 406

TO THE INSTRUCTOR

The primary organization of this book rests not only on a succession of modes, but also on an effort to form a close relation between student reading and student writing. Each of my twelve secondary headings corresponds to a typical and constructive writing assignment. Within **Telling** I have grouped the sets of four essays under *Recalling One's Early Self, Presenting a Character, Capturing Immediate Experience,* and *Narrating an Action.* **Explaining** contains four examples each of *Illustrating a Generalization, Analyzing Parts and Functions, Showing Causes and Effects,* and *Comparing and Contrasting.* And finally, **Arguing** offers selections divided among *Arguing from Experience, Establishing a Principle, Questioning Received Opinion,* and *Arguing by Implication.* Each set of four essays is arranged in order of increasing difficulty of comprehension, so that under a given heading you can easily locate the pieces that are most readily grasped or most challenging.

If you prefer to assign essays connected thematically rather than by rhetorical principles, you should consult the Contents Arranged by Subject Area on page x. Note, too, that each selection is followed by Study Questions that can direct attention to the essay's chief thematic and rhetorical traits.

Beth Goldman, Ann Van Sant, and I have written an unusually thorough *Instructor's Guide,* intended as a day-by-day aid in the classroom use of this *Reader.* (The Teacher's Edition of the *Reader* contains a representative segment of the *Guide* in its back pages.) The *Guide* ranks all selections by degree of accessibility to students, so that the book can be adapted to courses with diverse levels of expectation. Further, for each essay the *Guide* proposes a sampling of vocabulary to be mastered or reviewed; discusses possible answers to all of the Study Questions; suggests writing projects ranging in length from one or two paragraphs to a full essay; mentions potential opportunities and problems that an instructor may face; specifies other essays that could be effectively paired with this one; and highlights points of connection to the rhetorical principles explained in a companion text, *The Random House Handbook.* Instructors already acquainted with the *Handbook* will not only meet some familiar authors in the *Reader,* but also find suggestions in the *Guide* for combining reading assignments from the two books. At the same time, non-users of the *Handbook* should find the *Reader* fully compatible with other composition texts.

ACKNOWLEDGMENTS

For expert consultation and collaboration from the beginning, and for constant support and encouragement, I am deeply indebted to Ann Van Sant and Beth Goldman. Richard Garretson has been a sustaining presence at Random House, as have Seibert Adams, David Follmer, Christine Pellicano, June Smith, and Elizabeth Stern. Anna Marie Muskelly has been my extremely capable and agreeable project editor. Ingrid Crews expertly typed the lengthy *Instructor's Guide.* And for valuable advice I would like to thank James B. Carothers, University of Kansas; John Clifford, University of North Carolina, Wilmington; Elizabeth Crews; Richard L. Larson, Herbert H. Lehman College; Robert Lescher; T. Jeff Evans, University of Maine, Orono; Ron Fortune, Ohio State University; E. D. Hirsch, Jr., University of Virginia; Robert Mundhenk, Northamton Community College; Nancy Sommers; John Trimble, University of Texas, Austin; and Karl Zender, University of California, Davis.

CONTENTS

CONTENTS ARRANGED BY SUBJECT AREA

In the following fifteen lists, every selection appears at least twice. The headings are by no means exhaustive, but they do indicate strong clusters of subject matter that might be obscured by the primary rhetorical ordering of contents. Instructors can devise a sequence of readings within one list, and students, when asked to discuss or write about a given essay, can consult other essays within that essay's lists as a means of developing pertinent comparisons and contrasts.

---

1. American Places

2. A Changing Culture

6. Adapting

7. Processes

8. Sports/Recreation/Entertainment

9. Prejudice

10. Violence

11. Ordeals

12. Obligations

13. Rights

14. Behind Appearances

15. The Nonhuman World

INTRODUCTION

This is a book of readings for apprentice writers. I have chosen its forty-eight essays to meet the two requirements of such readings, that they stimulate thought and discussion and that their rhetorical features be worth imitating. I offer neither a parade of early masterpieces to be admired from afar nor, at the other extreme, a collection of snippets illustrating such isolated maneuvers as definition and classification. Young writers, I believe, are best served by exposure to lively, accessible, effective prose showing the range of plausible occasions for employing different voices and strategies. I have therefore favored contemporary American essays representing diverse approaches to tasks that a student, too, might be expected to perform.

The three main headings under which I have grouped the selections, **Telling**, **Explaining**, and **Arguing**, modify the traditional fourfold division of essay modes into description, narration, exposition, and argument. My relatively simple and comprehensible terms emphasize a writer's activity rather than supposedly fixed essay types.

The crucial discriminating factor in my scheme is the writer's degree of distance from immediate physical experience. **Telling**, which acknowledges the *presentational* similarity between description and narration, calls chiefly for faithfulness to the physical actuality of a recounted experience. In **Explaining**, a writer aims primarily not to depict an experience, but to reveal the nature, function, causes, or effects of something, often by contrast with something else. And **Arguing** marks a further abstraction from the immediate experience that was presented in the first mode and analyzed in the second. Now the writer's concern is neither to show us some part of the world nor to explain it to us, but to convince us that a certain view or policy is preferable to another.

If you think of **Telling** as a ring enclosing immediate experience, you can imagine **Explaining** and **Arguing** as wider rings, implying greater distance from the sense data of experience and, in many essays, an incorporation of a smaller area:

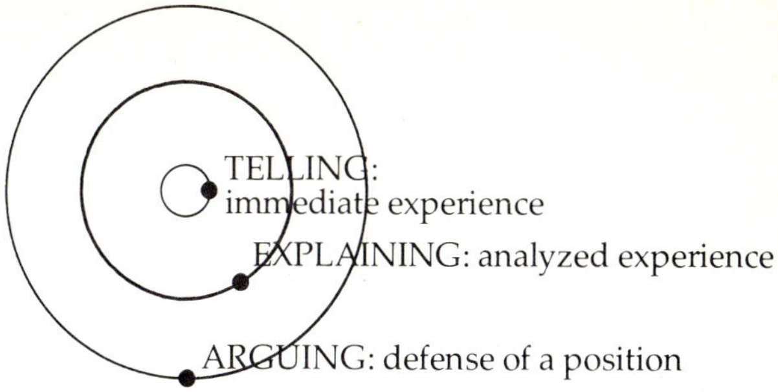

Thus, an essay of explaining will almost certainly contain some telling; a writer has to present something before proceeding to analyze it. Similarly, someone constructing an argument must do some explaining, for explanations make up the reasons why the argumentative thesis deserves to be believed. Many essays in a "wider" mode are engaging and convincing precisely because they have been refreshed by elements of a "narrower" one. Although the process sometimes works in reverse, with explanation or even argument surfacing within a story, readers are least surprised when a relatively immediate kind of writing serves as grounding for relatively abstract conclusions.

Essays, then, quite regularly display a mixture of modes. The choice of calling a given essay an instance of Telling, Explaining, or Arguing often borders on the arbitrary. That fact would be vexing if we conceived of the modes as classic forms bound by ironclad rules. But since our modes are nothing more than a range of the essayist's typical activities, we can acknowledge what the selections to follow amply demonstrate: that the essay is an extraordinarily open genre.

PART I

TELLING

RECALLING ONE'S EARLY SELF

Maxine Hong Kingston

Maxine Hong Kingston was raised in Stockton, California, where her Chinese-speaking parents were in the laundry business. She received a B.A. from the University of California, Berkeley, in 1962 and now does her writing from her home in Honolulu. She has written a book about her forebears, *China Men,* and an autobiographical volume, *The Woman Warrior* (1976), from which this selection is taken. The setting of "Talk!" is Stockton in the early 1950s.

"TALK!"*

1 My mouth went permanently crooked with effort, turned down on the left side and straight on the right. How strange that the emigrant villagers are shouters, hollering face to face. My father asks, "Why is it I can hear Chinese from blocks away? Is it that I understand the language? Or is it they talk loud?" They turn the radio up full blast to hear the operas, which do not seem to hurt their ears. And they yell over the singers that wail over the drums, everybody talking at once, big arm gestures, spit flying. You can see the disgust on American faces looking at women like that. It isn't just the loudness. It is the way Chinese sounds, chingchong ugly, to American ears, not beautiful like Japanese sayonara° words with the consonants and vowels as regular as Italian. We make guttural peasant noise and have Ton Duc Thang names you can't remember. And the Chinese can't hear Americans at all; the language is too soft and western music unhearable. I've watched a Chinese audience laugh, visit, talk-story, and holler during a piano recital, as if the musician could not hear them. A Chinese-American, somebody's

---

*Title chosen by editor

[1] **sayonara:** (Jap.) farewell

son, was playing Chopin,° which has no punctuation, no cymbals, no gongs. Chinese piano music is five black keys. Normal Chinese women's voices are strong and bossy. We American-Chinese girls had to whisper to make ourselves American-feminine. Apparently we whispered even more softly than the Americans. Once a year the teachers referred my sister and me to speech therapy, but our voices would straighten out, unpredictably normal, for the therapists. Some of us gave up, shook our heads, and said nothing, not one word. Some of us could not even shake our heads. At times shaking my head no is more self-assertion than I can manage. Most of us eventually found some voice, however faltering. We invented an American-feminine speaking personality, except for that one girl who could not speak up even in Chinese school.

2 She was a year older than I and was in my class for twelve years. During all those years she read aloud but would not talk. Her older sister was usually beside her; their parents kept the older daughter back to protect the younger one. They were six and seven years old when they began school. Although I had flunked kindergarten, I was the same age as most other students in our class; my parents had probably lied about my age, so I had had a head start and came out even. My younger sister was in the class below me; we were normal ages and normally separated. The parents of the quiet girl, on the other hand, protected both daughters. When it sprinkled, they kept them home from school. The girls did not work for a living the way we did. But in other ways we were the same.

3 We were similar in sports. We held the bat on our shoulders until we walked to first base. (You got a strike only when you actually struck at the ball.) Sometimes the pitcher wouldn't bother to throw to us. "Automatic walk," the other children would call, sending us on our way. By fourth or fifth grade, though, some of us would try to hit the ball. "Easy out," the other kids would say. I hit the ball a couple of times. Baseball was nice in that there was a definite spot to run to after hitting the ball. Basketball confused me because when I caught the ball I didn't know whom to throw it to. "Me. Me," the kids would be yelling. "Over here." Suddenly it would occur to me I hadn't memorized which ghosts° were on my team and which were on the other. When the kids said, "Automatic walk," the girl who was quieter than I kneeled with one end of the bat in each hand and placed it carefully on the plate. Then she dusted her hands as she walked to first base, where she rubbed her hands softly, fingers spread. She always got tagged out before second base. She would whisper-read but not talk. Her whisper was as soft as if she had no muscles. She seemed to be breathing from a distance. I heard no anger or tension.

---

[1] **Chopin:** Frédéric Chopin (1810–1849), Polish composer and pianist

[3] **ghosts:** In Kingston's Chinese family, the name for Caucasians

4 I joined in at lunchtime when the other students, the Chinese too, talked about whether or not she was mute, although obviously she was not if she could read aloud. People told how *they* had tried *their* best to be friendly. *They* said hello, but if she refused to answer, well, they didn't see why they had to say hello anymore. She had no friends of her own but followed her sister everywhere, although people and she herself probably thought I was her friend. I also followed her sister about, who was fairly normal. She was almost two years older and read more than anyone else.

5 I hated the younger sister, the quiet one. I hated her when she was the last chosen for her team and I, the last chosen for my team. I hated her for her China doll hair cut. I hated her at music time for the wheezes that came out of her plastic flute.

6 One afternoon in the sixth grade (that year I was arrogant with talk, not knowing there were going to be high school dances and college seminars to set me back), I and my little sister and the quiet girl and her big sister stayed late after school for some reason. The cement was cooling, and the tetherball poles made shadows across the gravel. The hooks at the rope ends were clinking against the poles. We shouldn't have been so late; there was laundry work to do and Chinese school to get to by 5:00. The last time we had stayed late, my mother had phoned the police and told them we had been kidnapped by bandits. The radio stations broadcast our descriptions. I had to get home before she did that again. But sometimes if you loitered long enough in the schoolyard, the other children would have gone home and you could play with the equipment before the office took it away. We were chasing one another through the playground and in and out of the basement, where the playroom and lavatory were. During air raid drills (it was during the Korean War, which you knew about because every day the front page of the newspaper printed a map of Korea with the top part red and going up and down like a window shade), we curled up in this basement. Now everyone was gone. The playroom was army green and had nothing in it but a long trough with drinking spigots in rows. Pipes across the ceiling led to the drinking fountains and to the toilets in the next room. When someone flushed you could hear the water and other matter, which the children named, running inside the big pipe above the drinking spigots. There was one playroom for girls next to the girls' lavatory and one playroom for boys next to the boys' lavatory. The stalls were open and the toilets had no lids, by which we knew that ghosts have no sense of shame or privacy.

7 Inside the playroom the lightbulbs in cages had already been turned off. Daylight came in x-patterns through the caging at the windows. I looked out and, seeing no one in the schoolyard, ran outside to climb the fire escape upside down, hanging on to the metal stairs with fingers and toes.

8 I did a flip off the fire escape and ran across the schoolyard. The

day was a great eye, and it was not paying much attention to me now. I could disappear with the sun; I could turn quickly sideways and slip into a different world. It seemed I could run faster at this time, and by evening I would be able to fly. As the afternoon wore on we could run into the forbidden places—the boys' big yard, the boys' playroom. We could go into the boys' lavatory and look at the urinals. The only time during school hours I had crossed the boys' yard was when a flatbed truck with a giant thing covered with canvas and tied down with ropes had parked across the street. The children had told one another that it was a gorilla in captivity; we couldn't decide whether the sign said "Trail of the Gorilla" or "Trial of the Gorilla." The thing was as big as a house. The teachers couldn't stop us from hysterically rushing to the fence and clinging to the wire mesh. Now I ran across the boys' yard clear to the Cyclone fence and thought about the hair that I had seen sticking out of the canvas. It was going to be summer soon, so you could feel that freedom coming on too.

9 I ran back into the girls' yard, and there was the quiet sister all by herself. I ran past her, and she followed me into the girls' lavatory. My footsteps rang hard against cement and tile because of the taps I had nailed into my shoes. Her footsteps were soft, padding after me. There was no one in the lavatory but the two of us. I ran all around the rows of twenty-five open stalls to make sure of that. No sisters. I think we must have been playing hide-and-go-seek. She was not good at hiding by herself and usually followed her sister; they'd hide in the same place. They must have gotten separated. In this growing twilight, a child could hide and never be found.

10 I stopped abruptly in front of the sinks, and she came running toward me before she could stop herself, so that she almost collided with me. I walked closer. She backed away, puzzlement, then alarm in her eyes.

11 "You're going to talk," I said, my voice steady and normal, as it is talking to the familiar, the weak, and the small. "I am going to make you talk, you sissy-girl." She stopped backing away and stood fixed.

12 I looked into her face so I could hate it close up. She wore black bangs, and her cheeks were pink and white. She was baby soft. I thought that I could put my thumb on her nose and push it bonelessly in, indent her face. I could poke dimples into her cheeks. I could work her face around like dough. She stood still, and I did not want to look at her face anymore; I hated fragility. I walked around her, looked her up and down the way the Mexican and Negro girls did when they fought, so tough. I hated her weak neck, the way it did not support her head but let it droop; her head would fall backward. I stared at the curve of her nape. I wished I was able to see what my own neck looked like from the back and sides. I hoped it did not look like hers; I wanted a stout neck. I grew my hair long to hide it in case it was a flower-stem neck. I walked around to the front of her to hate her face some more.

13 I reached up and took the fatty part of her cheek, not dough, but meat, between my thumb and finger. This close, and I saw no pores. "Talk," I said. "Are you going to talk?" Her skin was fleshy, like squid out of which the glassy blades of bones had been pulled. I wanted tough skin, hard brown skin. I had callused my hands; I had scratched dirt to blacken the nails, which I cut straight across to make stubby fingers. I gave her face a squeeze. "Talk." When I let go, the pink rushed back into my white thumbprint on her skin. I walked around to her side. "Talk!" I shouted into the side of her head. Her straight hair hung, the same all these years, no ringlets or braids or permanents. I squeezed her other cheek. "Are you? Huh? Are you going to talk?" She tried to shake her head, but I had hold of her face. She had no muscles to jerk away. Her skin seemed to stretch. I let go in horror. What if it came away in my hand? "No, huh?" I said, rubbing the touch of her off my fingers. "Say 'No,' then," I said. I gave her another pinch and a twist. "Say 'No.' " She shook her head, her straight hair turning with her head, not swinging side to side like the pretty girls'. She was so neat. Her neatness bothered me. I hated the way she folded the wax paper from her lunch; she did not wad her brown paper bag and her school papers. I hated her clothes—the blue pastel cardigan, the white blouse with the collar that lay flat over the cardigan, the homemade flat, cotton skirt she wore when everybody else was wearing flared skirts. I hated pastels; I would wear black always. I squeezed again, harder, even though her cheek had a weak rubbery feeling I did not like. I squeezed one cheek, then the other, back and forth until the tears ran out of her eyes as if I had pulled them out. "Stop crying," I said, but although she habitually followed me around, she did not obey. Her eyes dripped; her nose dripped. She wiped her eyes with her papery fingers. The skin on her hands and arms seemed powdery-dry, like tracing paper, onion skin. I hated her fingers. I could snap them like breadsticks. I pushed her hands down. "Say 'Hi,' " I said. " 'Hi.' Like that. Say your name. Go ahead. Say it. Or are you stupid? You're so stupid, you don't know your own name, is that it? When I say, 'What's your name?' you just blurt it out, o.k.? What's your name?" Last year the whole class had laughed at a boy who couldn't fill out a form because he didn't know his father's name. The teacher sighed, exasperated, and was very sarcastic, "Don't you notice things? What does your mother call him?" she said. The class laughed at how dumb he was not to notice things. "She calls him father of me," he said. Even we laughed, although we knew that his mother did not call his father by name, and a son does not know his father's name. We laughed and were relieved that our parents had had the foresight to tell us some names we could give the teachers. "If you're not stupid," I said to the quiet girl, "what's your name?" She shook her head, and some hair caught in the tears; wet black hair stuck to the side of the pink and white face. I reached up (she was taller than I) and took a strand of hair. I pulled it. "Well, then, let's honk your hair," I said. "Honk. Honk."

Then I pulled the other side—"ho-o-n-nk"—a long pull; "ho-o-n-n-nk"—a longer pull. I could see her little white ears, like white cutworms° curled underneath the hair. "Talk!" I yelled into each cutworm.

14 I looked right at her. "I know you talk," I said. "I've heard you." Her eyebrows flew up. Something in those black eyes was startled, and I pursued it. "I was walking past your house when you didn't know I was there. I heard you yell in English and in Chinese. You weren't just talking. You were shouting. I heard you shout. You were saying, 'Where are you?' Say that again. Go ahead, just the way you did at home." I yanked harder on the hair, but steadily, not jerking. I did not want to pull it out. "Go ahead. Say, 'Where are you?' Say it loud enough for your sister to come. Call her. Make her come help you. Call her name. I'll stop if she comes. So call. Go ahead."

15 She shook her head, her mouth curved down, crying. I could see her tiny white teeth, baby teeth. I wanted to grow big strong yellow teeth. "You do have a tongue," I said. "So use it." I pulled the hair at her temples, pulled the tears out of her eyes. "Say, 'Ow,' " I said. "Just 'Ow.' Say, 'Let go.' Go ahead. Say it. I'll honk you again if you don't say, 'Let me alone.' Say, 'Leave me alone,' and I'll let you go. I will. I'll let go if you say it. You can stop this anytime you want to, you know. All you have to do is tell me to stop. Just say, 'Stop.' You're just asking for it, aren't you? You're just asking for another honk. Well then, I'll have to give you another honk. Say, 'Stop.' " But she didn't. I had to pull again and again.

16 Sounds did come out of her mouth, sobs, chokes, noises that were almost words. Snot ran out of her nose. She tried to wipe it on her hands, but there was too much of it. She used her sleeve. "You're disgusting," I told her. "Look at you, snot streaming down your nose, and you won't say a word to stop it. You're such a nothing." I moved behind her and pulled the hair growing out of her weak neck. I let go. I stood silent for a long time. Then I screamed, "Talk!" I would scare the words out of her. If she had had little bound feet, the toes twisted under the balls, I would have jumped up and landed on them—crunch!—stomped on them with my iron shoes. She cried hard, sobbing aloud. "Cry, 'Mama,' " I said. "Come on. Cry, 'Mama.' Say, 'Stop it.' "

17 I put my finger on her pointed chin. "I don't like you. I don't like the weak little toots you make on your flute. Wheeze. Wheeze. I don't like the way you don't swing at the ball. I don't like the way you're the last one chosen. I don't like the way you can't make a fist for tetherball. Why don't you make a fist? Come on. Get tough. Come on. Throw fists." I pushed at her long hands; they swung limply at her sides. Her fingers were so long, I thought maybe they had an extra joint. They couldn't possibly make fists like other people's. "Make a fist," I said.

---

13 **cutworms:** caterpillars

"Come on. Just fold those fingers up; fingers on the inside, thumbs on the outside. Say something. Honk me back. You're so tall, and you let me pick on you.

18 "Would you like a hanky? I can't get you one with embroidery on it or crocheting along the edges, but I'll get you some toilet paper if you tell me to. Go ahead. Ask me. I'll get it for you if you ask." She did not stop crying. "Why don't you scream, 'Help'?" I suggested. "Say, 'Help.' Go ahead." She cried on. "O.K. O.K. Don't talk. Just scream, and I'll let you go. Won't that feel good? Go ahead. Like this." I screamed, not too loudly. My voice hit the tile and rang it as if I had thrown a rock at it. The stalls opened wider and the toilets wider and darker. Shadows leaned at angles I had not seen before. It was very late. Maybe a janitor had locked me in with this girl for the night. Her black eyes blinked and stared, blinked and stared. I felt dizzy from hunger. We had been in this lavatory together forever. My mother would call the police again if I didn't bring my sister home soon. "I'll let you go if you say just one word," I said. "You can even say, 'a' or 'the,' and I'll let you go. Come on. Please." She didn't shake her head anymore, only cried steadily, so much water coming out of her. I could see the two duct holes where the tears welled out. Quarts of tears but no words. I grabbed her by the shoulder. I could feel bones. The light was coming in queerly through the frosted glass with the chicken wire embedded in it. Her crying was like an animal's—a seal's—and it echoed around the basement. "Do you want to stay here all night?" I asked. "Your mother is wondering what happened to her baby. You wouldn't want to have her mad at you. You'd better say something." I shook her shoulder. I pulled her hair again. I squeezed her face. "Come on! Talk! Talk! Talk!" She didn't seem to feel it anymore when I pulled her hair. "There's nobody here but you and me. This isn't a classroom or a playground or a crowd. I'm just one person. You can talk in front of one person. Don't make me pull harder and harder until you talk." But her hair seemed to stretch; she did not say a word. "I'm going to pull harder. Don't make me pull anymore, or your hair will come out and you're going to be bald. Do you want to be bald? You don't want to be bald, do you?"

19 Far away, coming from the edge of town, I heard whistles blow. The cannery was changing shifts, letting out the afternoon people, and still we were here at school. It was a sad sound—work done. The air was lonelier after the sound died.

20 "Why won't you talk?" I started to cry. What if I couldn't stop, and everyone would want to know what happened? "Now look what you've done," I scolded. "You're going to pay for this. I want to know why. And you're going to tell me why. You don't see I'm trying to help you out, do you? Do you want to be like this, dumb (do you know what dumb means?), your whole life? Don't you ever want to be a cheerleader? Or a pompon girl? What are you going to do for a living? Yeah, you're going to have to work because you can't be a housewife. Somebody has to marry

you before you can be a housewife. And you, you are a plant. Do you know that? That's all you are if you don't talk. If you don't talk, you can't have a personality. You'll have no personality and no hair. You've got to let people know you have a personality and a brain. You think somebody is going to take care of you all your stupid life? You think you'll always have your big sister? You think somebody's going to marry you, is that it? Well, you're not the type that gets dates, let alone gets married. Nobody's going to notice you. And you have to talk for interviews, speak right up in front of the boss. Don't you know that? You're so dumb. Why do I waste my time on you?" Sniffling and snorting, I couldn't stop crying and talking at the same time. I kept wiping my nose on my arm, my sweater lost somewhere (probably not worn because my mother said to wear a sweater). It seemed as if I had spent my life in that basement, doing the worst thing I had yet done to another person. "I'm doing this for your own good," I said. "Don't you dare tell anyone I've been bad to you. Talk. Please talk."

21 I was getting dizzy from the air I was gulping. Her sobs and my sobs were bouncing wildly off the tile, sometimes together, sometimes alternating. "I don't understand why you won't say just one word," I cried, clenching my teeth. My knees were shaking, and I hung on to her hair to stand up. Another time I'd stayed too late, I had had to walk around two Negro kids who were bonking each other's head on the concrete. I went back later to see if the concrete had cracks in it. "Look. I'll give you something if you talk. I'll give you my pencil box. I'll buy you some candy. O.K.? What do you want? Tell me. Just say it, and I'll give it to you. Just say, 'yes,' or, 'O.K.,' or, 'Baby Ruth.' " But she didn't want anything.

22 I had stopped pinching her cheek because I did not like the feel of her skin. I would go crazy if it came away in my hands. "I skinned her," I would have to confess.

23 Suddenly I heard footsteps hurrying through the basement, and her sister ran into the lavatory calling her name. "Oh, there you are," I said. "We've been waiting for you. I was only trying to teach her to talk. She wouldn't cooperate, though." Her sister went into one of the stalls and got handfuls of toilet paper and wiped her off. Then we found my sister, and we walked home together. "Your family really ought to force her to speak," I advised all the way home. "You mustn't pamper her."

STUDY QUESTIONS

1. In reconstructing her childhood self, Kingston has to set aside a good deal of knowledge and opinion she has acquired since then. What are the "childish" aspects of young Kingston's sense of

things, and how does she let us know that she has gotten beyond that sense by now? Consider the "Americanization" question.

2. Consider how the first five paragraphs of this selection affect the way we read the story that properly begins at paragraph 6. What would Kingston have sacrificed by beginning at paragraph 6?
3. In language and sentence structure, "Talk!" is one of the "simplest" essays in this collection. Yet careful readers will not be likely to accuse Kingston of simple-mindedness. Why has she chosen a relatively simple-looking manner, and how do you know that her mind is sophisticated?
4. Although Kingston tells us that she hated the "quiet sister," there are signs that show more complex feelings. What are those signs?
5. In reading this narrative, do you feel sorry for Maxine as well as for the girl she torments? If so, look for specific passages that make you inclined to be sympathetic.
6. Although Kingston's story has no explicit thesis, or main idea, it does have an air of unity and purpose. See if you can come up with an implied (unstated) thesis for the story.
7. It might seem surprising that the four girls walk home together at the end. What does this ending tell us about young Maxine's feelings from the start?

Maya Angelou

Maya Angelou grew up in Arkansas, Missouri, and California. She has involved herself in theater, dance, and politics as well as in writing for newspapers and television. In addition to *I Know Why the Caged Bird Sings* (1969), from which this selection is taken, her books include *Just Give Me a Cool Drink of Water . . . 'Fore I Die, Gather Together in My Name, Oh Pray My Wings Are Gonna Fit Me Well,* and *Singin' and Swingin' and Gettin' Merry Like Christmas.*

THE EXTRACTION*

1 The Angel of the candy counter° had found me out at last, and was exacting excruciating penance for all the stolen Milky Ways, Mounds, Mr. Goodbars and Hersheys with Almonds. I had two cavities that were

---

*Title chosen by editor

1 **the Angel of the candy counter:** the "Balancing Angel" (end of this paragraph), who presumably sees to it that bad actions receive their exact degree of required punishment

rotten to the gums. The pain was beyond the bailiwick of crushed aspirins or oil of cloves. Only one thing could help me, so I prayed earnestly that I'd be allowed to sit under the house and have the building collapse on my left jaw. Since there was no Negro dentist in Stamps,° nor doctor either, for that matter, Momma° had dealt with previous toothaches by pulling them out (a string tied to the tooth with the other end looped over her fist), pain killers and prayer. In this particular instance the medicine had proved ineffective; there wasn't enough enamel left to hook a string on, and the prayers were being ignored because the Balancing Angel was blocking their passage.

2 I lived a few days and nights in blinding pain, not so much toying with as seriously considering the idea of jumping in the well, and Momma decided I had to be taken to a dentist. The nearest Negro dentist was in Texarkana,° twenty-five miles away, and I was certain that I'd be dead long before we reached half the distance. Momma said we'd go to Dr. Lincoln, right in Stamps, and he'd take care of me. She said he owed her a favor.

3 I knew there were a number of whitefolks in town that owed her favors. Bailey° and I had seen the books which showed how she had lent money to Blacks and whites alike during the Depression, and most still owed her. But I couldn't aptly remember seeing Dr. Lincoln's name, nor had I ever heard of a Negro's going to him as a patient. However, Momma said we were going, and put water on the stove for our baths. I had never been to a doctor, so she told me that after the bath (which would make my mouth feel better) I had to put on freshly starched and ironed underclothes from inside out. The ache failed to respond to the bath, and I knew then that the pain was more serious than that which anyone had ever suffered.

4 Before we left the Store, she ordered me to brush my teeth and then wash my mouth with Listerine. The idea of even opening my clamped jaws increased the pain, but upon her explanation that when you go to a doctor you have to clean yourself all over, but most especially the part that's to be examined, I screwed up my courage and unlocked my teeth. The cool air in my mouth and the jarring of my molars dislodged what little remained of my reason. I had frozen to the pain, my family nearly had to tie me down to take the toothbrush away. It was no small effort to get me started on the road to the dentist. Momma spoke to all the passers-by, but didn't stop to chat. She ex-

1 **Stamps:** small town in Arkansas where Angelou lived as a girl

Momma: Angelou's paternal grandmother, with whom she and her brother lived during much of their childhood. Their father lived in Los Angeles, their mother in St. Louis, Los Angeles, and San Francisco.

2 **Texarkana:** the name of two conjoined but politically independent towns on the border of Texas and Arkansas

3 **Bailey:** Angelou's brother, one year older than she

plained over her shoulder that we were going to the doctor and she'd "pass the time of day" on our way home.

5 Until we reached the pond the pain was my world, an aura that haloed me for three feet around. Crossing the bridge into whitefolks' country, pieces of sanity pushed themselves forward. I had to stop moaning and start walking straight. The white towel, which was drawn under my chin and tied over my head, had to be arranged. If one was dying, it had to be done in style if the dying took place in whitefolks' part of town.

6 On the other side of the bridge the ache seemed to lessen as if a whitebreeze blew off the whitefolks and cushioned everything in their neighborhood—including my jaw. The gravel road was smoother, the stones smaller and the tree branches hung down around the path and nearly covered us. If the pain didn't diminish then, the familiar yet strange sights hypnotized me into believing that it had.

7 But my head continued to throb with the measured insistence of a bass drum, and how could a toothache pass the calaboose,° hear the songs of the prisoners, their blues and laughter, and not be changed? How could one or two or even a mouthful of angry tooth roots meet a wagonload of powhitetrash° children, endure their idiotic snobbery and not feel less important?

8 Behind the building which housed the dentist's office ran a small path used by servants and those tradespeople who catered to the butcher and Stamps' one restaurant. Momma and I followed that lane to the backstairs of Dentist Lincoln's office. The sun was bright and gave the day a hard reality as we climbed up the steps to the second floor.

9 Momma knocked on the back door and a young white girl opened it to show surprise at seeing us there. Momma said she wanted to see Dentist Lincoln and to tell him Annie was there. The girl closed the door firmly. Now the humiliation of hearing Momma describe herself as if she had no last name to the young white girl was equal to the physical pain. It seemed terribly unfair to have a toothache and a headache and have to bear at the same time the heavy burden of Blackness.

10 It was always possible that the teeth would quiet down and maybe drop out of their own accord. Momma said we would wait. We leaned in the harsh sunlight on the shaky railings of the dentist's back porch for over an hour.

11 He opened the door and looked at Momma. "Well, Annie, what can I do for you?"

12 He didn't see the towel around my jaw or notice my swollen face.

---

[7] **calaboose:** jail

powhitetrash: "poor white trash," or the poorest of uneducated southern white people

13 Momma said, "Dentist Lincoln. It's my grandbaby here. She got two rotten teeth that's giving her a fit."

14 She waited for him to acknowledge the truth of her statement. He made no comment, orally or facially.

15 "She had this toothache purt' near four days now, and today I said, 'Young lady, you going to the Dentist.' "

16 "Annie?"

17 "Yes, sir, Dentist Lincoln."

18 He was choosing words the way people hunt for shells. "Annie, you know I don't treat nigra, colored people."

19 "I know, Dentist Lincoln. But this here is just my little grandbaby, and she ain't gone be no trouble to you . . ."

20 "Annie, everybody has a policy. In this world you have to have a policy. Now, my policy is I don't treat colored people."

21 The sun had baked the oil out of Momma's skin and melted the Vaseline in her hair. She shone greasily as she leaned out of the dentist's shadow.

22 "Seem like to me, Dentist Lincoln, you might look after her, she ain't nothing but a little mite. And seems like maybe you owe me a favor or two."

23 He reddened slightly. "Favor or no favor. The money has all been repaid to you and that's the end of it. Sorry, Annie." He had his hand on the doorknob. "Sorry." His voice was a bit kinder on the second "Sorry," as if he really was.

24 Momma said, "I wouldn't press on you like this for myself but I can't take No. Not for my grandbaby. When you come to borrow my money you didn't have to beg. You asked me, and I lent it. Now, it wasn't my policy. I ain't no moneylender, but you stood to lose this building and I tried to help you out."

25 "It's been paid, and raising your voice won't make me change my mind. My policy . . ." He let go of the door and stepped nearer Momma. The three of us were crowded on the small landing. "Annie, my policy is I'd rather stick my hand in a dog's mouth than in a nigger's."

26 He had never once looked at me. He turned his back and went through the door into the cool beyond. Momma backed up inside herself for a few minutes. I forgot everything except her face which was almost a new one to me. She leaned over and took the doorknob, and in her everyday soft voice she said, "Sister, go on downstairs. Wait for me. I'll be there directly."

27 Under the most common of circumstances I knew it did no good to argue with Momma. So I walked down the steep stairs, afraid to look back and afraid not to do so. I turned as the door slammed, and she was gone.

28 *Momma walked in that room as if she owned it. She shoved that silly nurse aside with one hand and strode into the dentist's office. He was sitting in his chair, sharpening his mean instruments and putting extra sting into his medicines. Her eyes were blazing*

like live coals and her arms had doubled themselves in length. He looked up at her just before she caught him by the collar of his white jacket.

29 *"Stand up when you see a lady, you contemptuous scoundrel." Her tongue had thinned and the words rolled off well enunciated. Enunciated and sharp like little claps of thunder.*

30 *The dentist had no choice but to stand at R.O.T.C. attention. His head dropped after a minute and his voice was humble. "Yes, ma'am, Mrs. Henderson."*

31 *"You knave, do you think you acted like a gentleman, speaking to me like that in front of my granddaughter?" She didn't shake him, although she had the power. She simply held him upright.*

32 *"No, ma'am, Mrs. Henderson."*

33 *"No, ma'am, Mrs. Henderson, what?" Then she did give him the tiniest of shakes, but because of her strength the action set his head and arms to shaking loose on the ends of his body. He stuttered much worse than Uncle Willie.° "No, ma'am, Mrs. Henderson, I'm sorry."*

34 *With just an edge of her disgust showing, Momma slung him back in his dentist's chair. "Sorry is as sorry does, and you're about the sorriest dentist I ever laid my eyes on." (She could afford to slip into the vernacular because she had such eloquent command of English.)*

35 *"I didn't ask you to apologize in front of Marguerite,° because I don't want her to know my power, but I order you, now and herewith. Leave Stamps by sundown."*

36 *"Mrs. Henderson, I can't get my equipment . . ." He was shaking terribly now.*

37 *"Now, that brings me to my second order. You will never again practice dentistry. Never! When you get settled in your next place, you will be a vegetarian caring for dogs with the mange, cats with the cholera and cows with the epizootic.° Is that clear?"*

38 *The saliva ran down his chin and his eyes filled with tears. "Yes, ma'am. Thank you for not killing me. Thank you, Mrs. Henderson."*

39 *Momma pulled herself back from being ten feet tall with eight-foot arms and said, "You're welcome for nothing, you varlet, I wouldn't waste a killing on the likes of you."*

40 *On her way out she waved her handkerchief at the nurse and turned her into a crocus sack° of chicken feed.*

41 Momma looked tired when she came down the stairs, but who wouldn't be tired if they had gone through what she had. She came close to me and adjusted the towel under my jaw (I had forgotten the toothache; I only knew that she made her hands gentle in order not to awaken the pain). She took my hand. Her voice never changed. "Come on, Sister."

42 I reckoned we were going home where she would concoct a brew to eliminate the pain and maybe give me new teeth too. New teeth that would grow overnight out of my gums. She led me toward the drug-

---

[33] **Uncle Willie:** Momma's son, crippled since babyhood

[35] **Marguerite:** Angelou herself, who is about twelve or thirteen in this episode

[37] **epizootic:** a parasitic disease of animals

[40] **crocus sack:** burlap bag

store, which was in the opposite direction from the Store. "I'm taking you to Dentist Baker in Texarkana."

43 I was glad after all that that I had bathed and put on Mum and Cashmere Bouquet talcum powder. It was a wonderful surprise. My toothache had quieted to solemn pain, Momma had obliterated the evil white man, and we were going on a trip to Texarkana, just the two of us.

44 On the Greyhound she took an inside seat in the back, and I sat beside her. I was so proud of being her granddaughter and sure that some of her magic must have come down to me. She asked if I was scared. I only shook my head and leaned over on her cool brown upper arm. There was no chance that a dentist, especially a Negro dentist, would dare hurt me then. Not with Momma there. The trip was uneventful, except that she put her arm around me, which was very unusual for Momma to do.

45 The dentist showed me the medicine and the needle before he deadened my gums, but if he hadn't I wouldn't have worried. Momma stood right behind him. Her arms were folded and she checked on everything he did. The teeth were extracted and she bought me an ice cream cone from the side window of a drug counter. The trip back to Stamps was quiet, except that I had to spit into a very small empty snuff can which she had gotten for me and it was difficult with the bus humping and jerking on our country roads.

46 At home, I was given a warm salt solution, and when I washed out my mouth I showed Bailey the empty holes, where the clotted blood sat like filling in a pie crust. He said I was quite brave, and that was my cue to reveal our confrontation with the peckerwood° dentist and Momma's incredible powers.

47 I had to admit that I didn't hear the conversation, but what else could she have said than what I said she said? What else done? He agreed with my analysis in a lukewarm way, and I happily (after all, I'd been sick) flounced into the Store. Momma was preparing our evening meal and Uncle Willie leaned on the door sill. She gave her version.

48 "Dentist Lincoln got right uppity. Said he'd rather put his hand in a dog's mouth. And when I reminded him of the favor, he brushed it off like a piece of lint. Well, I sent Sister downstairs and went inside. I hadn't never been in his office before, but I found the door to where he takes out teeth, and him and the nurse was in there thick as thieves. I just stood there till he caught sight of me." Crash bang the pots on the stove. "He jumped just like he was sitting on a pin. He said, 'Annie, I done tole you, I ain't gonna mess around in no niggah's mouth.' I said, 'Somebody's got to do it then,' and he said, 'Take her to Texarkana to the colored dentist' and that's when I said, 'If

---

46 **peckerwood:** poor white (lit. "woodpecker")

you paid me my money I could afford to take her.' He said, 'It's all been paid.' I tole him everything but the interest been paid. He said ''Twasn't no interest.' I said ''Tis now. I'll take ten dollars as payment in full.' You know, Willie, it wasn't no right thing to do, 'cause I lent that money without thinking about it.

49 "He tole that little snippity nurse of his'n to give me ten dollars and make me sign a 'paid in full' receipt. She gave it to me and I signed the papers. Even though by rights he was paid up before, I figger, he gonna be that kind of nasty, he gonna have to pay for it."

50 Momma and her son laughed and laughed over the white man's evilness and her retributive sin.

51 I preferred, much preferred, my version.

STUDY QUESTIONS

1. Locate some passages revealing how the child in this narrative views the white world. In what ways does the child's perspective differ from that of the mature author? Think, for example, about the figure of the dentist as seen (a) by the child and (b) by ourselves as readers.
2. Angelou describes the painfulness of the toothache with comic exaggeration. Why does she report her experience in this way? Think of this exaggeration in tandem with later overstatements. What connections and significant differences do you perceive?
3. The dentist's "policy" (paragraph 20) is brutally insulting to Momma and the child, but it also indicates more about his own mentality than he might want anyone to know. In what senses does his "policy" reflect on his character and personality?
4. Look closely at the italicized passage (paragraphs 28–40) constituting the child's version of Momma's private confrontation with the dentist. Isolate some words that typify the level of diction used in that passage. In what way is such diction appropriate to Angelou's purpose? What does it tell us about the young heroine?
5. What are Momma's chief traits of character, and how does Angelou bring them out?
6. Do you feel at the end that Momma has played fair? Why, or why not? And is her victory complete? In this regard, be sure to take the concluding sentence into account.
7. Why do you suppose we have chosen the title "The Extraction" for this episode from *I Know Why the Caged Bird Sings?*

Andrew Ward

The humorist Andrew Ward, who now lives in New Haven, Connecticut, has also worked as a photographer and teacher. "Pencils Down" appears in *Fits and Starts: The Premature Memoirs of Andrew Ward* (1978).

PENCILS DOWN

1 Everything will be going fine and then suddenly I will have that dream again, the one in which I am walking across a campus and a classmate runs by me, waving his arms and shouting, "Come on! You're late!"

2 "Late?" I call after him. "Late for what?"

3 *"Late for what?!"* he exclaims. "Late for Bretko's final!"

4 In spite of myself, I begin to lope after him. "Bretko? Who's Bretko?"

5 "Jesus Christ!" he says as we dash toward the classroom building, "where have you *been* all semester?"

6 It is just when we reach the classroom, where the final in a course I have never heard of on a subject I know nothing about is already in progress, that I wake up in a tangle of bedding, my eyes bulging like eggs.

7 The first real test I remember taking was at a solemn little pedagogic enterprise called the Lab School, to which the faculty of the University of Chicago sent its children and in which it tested out some of its educational theories. I spent four years guinea-pigging my way through the Lab School, but I don't remember very much about it. I do remember a wide, saintly kindergarten teacher who cured my stuttering ("Now, take your time, Andy," she would say as I stammered before her, "we have all the time in the world."). And I remember Miss Mums, a siren° of a second-grade teacher with a flamboyant bust who used to hop up and down whenever one of us answered her correctly. I still think the University was on to something when it hired Miss Mums; most of us did our best to keep her perpetually hopping before us.

8 In any case, sometime during the second grade a group of pale young men with attaché cases arrived at the school and established themselves in a little room which was usually devoted to hearing tests. We were called in one by one "to have a little fun," as Miss Mums put

---

[7] **siren:** seductively beautiful or charming woman

it, "with some nice big men." Some of us didn't want to have a little fun. One boy, whose mother made him wear some sort of prophylactic powder in his hair, fainted in the hallway when his turn came, and had to spend the rest of the day with the nurse.

9 When it came my turn, I walked down to the testing room and stood silently in the doorway, waiting to be noticed, which was my way of announcing myself in those days. I was finally beckoned in by a man with thick glasses that made his eyes look like fish suspended in ice.

10 "Now, Mark," he said brightly, "if you'll just take your seat right here, we can all start playing with blocks."

11 Much too polite to correct him about my name, I took my seat at a table around which four men with note pads loomed attentively. I was given six red plastic cubes and told, with many winks and nods, to do whatever I felt like doing with them. In truth, I didn't feel like doing anything with them. I was old enough to know that you couldn't build anything with six cubes. But the men looked so eager that I decided to do what I could, which was to line them all up into a row, then into two rows of three, then into three rows of two. The three rows of two seemed to go over very big. I could see out of the corner of my eye that they had begun to jot furiously, nodding to themselves as if entire life philosophies were being confirmed before their eyes.

12 I shoved the blocks around a while longer and finally leaned back. There was a pause, and then suddenly one of the men rose to his feet agitatedly and jabbed his pencil into the fish-eyed man's ribs.

13 "See?" he exclaimed. "See? What did I tell you?"

14 "You never told me *anything!*" the fish-eyed man hissed back, shoving the pencil aside. There was a scene, and in the confusion I got down off my chair and made my way back to Miss Mums' room. "Now," she asked me as I sat down at my desk, "wasn't that fun?"

15 "Yes," I said, and she gave a little hop.

16 My parents seemed to have had me down for college *in utero.*° I remember working on a geography report about Bolivia when I was in the third grade and my mother standing over me with an anxious look and declaring, "They're going to count this for college."

17 As far as she was concerned, they were going to count everything for college. She used college in her disciplinary warnings the way some mothers used Santa Claus. This had the effect of simultaneously trivializing and exalting my academic labors. On the one hand, I could not believe that my knowledge that Bolivia was the only country in the world to lynch two successive heads of state from the same lamp post was going to count for anything in college. On the other hand, I could

---

[16] **in utero:** (Lat.) in the womb

sometimes imagine a tweedy admissions officer leaning back and asking, "By the way, Andrew, what country was it that lynched two successive heads of state from the same lamp post?"

18 "I believe that was Bolivia, sir."

19 "Excellent! Oh, excellent! Andrew, I believe you and Harvard are going to get along very nicely."

20 I never did very well in school; in fact, the further along I got the worse I did, until by senior year in high school I was just squeaking through. I ascribe this to a difficulty I've always had with admitting to ignorance. It is hard to learn anything when you are constantly trying to look as though you know it already. I would rarely ask a question, for instance, unless it was designed to demonstrate a precocious knowledge of the subject under discussion. I would always start off my questions with, "Wouldn't you say that . . .," knowing full well that the teacher would, and congratulate me for my insight. In what were known as bullshit courses, this worked in my favor. In math and science it got me nowhere.

21 My parents were perplexed by my performance in high school, to the point of commissioning a university testing center in New York City to determine what my problem was. Every Saturday for four weeks I made my way into the Village to undergo batteries of five or six tests at a sitting. I went in with my parents the first day, and we all sat around with a cheerful man who kept asking me what I thought of myself. I told him I wanted to be an artist, and had trouble studying. He smiled indulgently and said we would see about that.

22 I guess I've blocked out a lot of the tests I took in the following weeks. One of them was to check out my suitability for cost accounting. Another consisted of a series of paintings depicting ambiguous scenes which I was to interpret using multiple choice.

23 "The man and woman in the picture above have just:

A. Had an argument.
B. Made love.
C. Poisoned themselves.
D. Filed a joint return."

24 Another was a tricky test for artistic ability. There would be four drawings of, say, a circle placed in a square. In one the circle would be centered, in another it would be to one side, in another it would be to another side, and so on. The idea was to select the one which was most sound compositionally. I say this was tricky because at the time every artistic convention was up for grabs, and I could have whipped up a convincing aesthetic argument for any one of them. I decided, however, that the centered circle was most likely to suit the testing center's artistic soul, and my high score bore this out.

25 One of the exams was an oral I.Q. test. The tester was an earnest man in shirt sleeves who repeatedly told me to relax. "We're just going

to kick around a few things," he said. "There's absolutely nothing to be afraid of."

26 He had me push blocks through holes, do something simple with some checkers, and perform various other tasks, and then we came to a part of the test where I was to explain to him the derivation of different sayings. This proved a bumpier ride than he had expected, because I had never heard a lot of the sayings he read to me. "One swallow does not make a summer," for instance, troubled me deeply. I had never heard it, knew nothing about ornithology, and stammered along for several minutes, operating on the theory that he meant the act of swallowing. I think I said something about the wine of life and the flask of spring, and I could see from the way my tester fidgeted that he had not been provided with contingencies covering my interpretation.

27 I can't say I didn't get anything out of all this. I was given some instruction on the ukelele by an old man in Washington Square during a testing break, and discovered a newsstand near the subway where I could buy *Gent* and *Nugget* without raising an eyebrow. When my parents and I were called back to hear the results, we were told that I was sharp as a tack, had trouble motivating myself to study, and should consider art as a profession. The cheerful man accepted my father's check for $125.00, and we all silently rode the train back to where I'd started.

28 I did pretty well on my English and history College Boards, and miserably in math and science, as was my pattern. My parents had me sign up for every testing date there was, and I swung at the ball in such varying locales as Danbury State Teachers' College, Tom's School of Business Success, and most of the high school auditoriums in southwestern Connecticut. One day, my mother saw an ad in the back of the *Times* for a College Board preparation class at a private school in the city, and in no time I was commuting again. It turned out that I was the only one in the class who did not come from midtown Manhattan, and the only male who didn't wear a yarmulke.° The course turned out to be a fraud. The teacher, a shaky old fellow in gold framed bifocals, started off by informing us that there was no secret to doing well on College Boards, went on to talk a little about a sister of his who was about to undergo surgery, and then had us spend the rest of the time taking mock College Boards in exercise books we bought from the school for five dollars apiece.

29 Oberlin College° was my first choice, naturally enough, because my parents went there, and my brother, and all my aunts and uncles,

---

28 **yarmulke:** in Judaism, a man's skullcap, worn esp. during prayer and religious study

29 **Oberlin College:** private college in Ohio

because my grandfather was head of its art department, and my father was one of its trustees. Oberlin had strict admissions standards in those days, and there was considerable doubt on my parents' part that I would gain admittance.

30 When I had my admissions interview in a hotel suite in New York, I had just received a D in chemistry, a course I had to pass in order to meet the science requirement, since I had all but flunked biology the year before. After several genial inquiries as to my family's health and whereabouts, the admissions officer proved remarkably encouraging. He hinted that I would be admitted under what he called Oberlin's "Tom Sawyer Program," which permitted students with "asymmetrical aptitudes," as he put it, to get in. He could not keep from wincing as his eyes descended row upon row of D's and C's in my high-school record, but he emphasized and reemphasized the positive side: high marks in art and English, soloist in the chorus, good attendance; and as the interview drew to a close, I got the impression that he was even more eager for me to go to Oberlin College than I was. As he waited with me for the elevator in the foyer outside his suite, he held my coat for me as I attempted, in vain, to get my second arm into its sleeve. We waltzed around in this way for some time, and as I finally stepped into the elevator, still lunging about for my elusive sleeve, he looked at me with the game, pained expression of a man at a dinner party who must smack his lips over something repugnant.

31 Oberlin didn't turn out to be quite what I had in mind, and vice versa. As I went along, I had more and more trouble getting to class, until eventually I lost all track of where I was supposed to be, and when. Sometimes I would catch a glimpse of someone dimly familiar and follow him to his next class, in the hope that it would turn out to be one of my own. It never did turn out to be one of my own, but in this way I attended some fascinating lectures on subjects ranging from a historical review of the Albanian nation-state to the topical poetry of Po Chü-i.°

32 I was well into my third, last-ditch semester at Oberlin College before I finally managed to pinpoint my problem. I couldn't read. Not that I couldn't have stood up before a Wednesday Assembly and read aloud from my geology text in a clear, authoritative voice, making myself heard unto the last rows of Finney Chapel. It was just that to my own ears I wouldn't have been making any sense.

33 As finals week approached, I tried to overcome this disability by locking myself into my room in the dormitory, laying out my study materials in the lone beam of my Tensor desk lamp, and sitting there,

[31] **Po Chü-i:** Chinese poet (A.D. 772–846)

hunched over my open textbook with a yellow felt-tip pen ready to underline important passages. I sat that way for hours at a time, waiting for the words over which my eyes passed to form phrases, sentences, ideas, and managing only an occasional flicker of recognition, enough to link perhaps twenty words together—"The exercise begins a rather extensive study to be continued in later sections of Chapter XXI"—never enough to gain me a foothold.

34 I was reduced to hoping that it was all penetrating my mind subconsciously, and I would tidily underline what I could only assume was important—headings, captions, opening and closing sentences, numbers, anything resembling a list, and sometimes a central sentence, a few of which, I figured, were probably important, too.

35 Underlining accomplished several purposes. It gave me something to do, it demarcated the pages I had already gone through (I had no other way of knowing), and it hid from whoever might duck into my room the fact that I was, in effect, an illiterate, and had no business being in college in the first place.

36 My last final at Oberlin was in Geology I, a course I took because it was touted to have been designed for the scientifically inept. This touting did not, however, seem to have originated with the Geology Department. If there is more to know about rocks than was included in Geology I, I don't want to hear about it. By the time I took the final, I had missed all but seven of my classes, and had received an F on my research paper, a study of the Greenwich, Connecticut, reservoir system which I had based on a water company comic book starring a character made out of drain-pipe named Wally Water.

37 I took the exam with some fifty other geology cadets in a dark, gothic room overlooking Tappan Square. The proctor, a work-booted geology major, handed out the test sheet and the bluebooks, and, stop-watch raised, signalled to us to begin.

38 The questions must have been mimeographed minutes before, because the ink still smelled sweet and dizzying. The first and second questions rang no bells at all, and as I read them my pen felt icy and useless in my fingers. In the third question I could barely make out the following: ". . . bituminous coal and discuss its suitability as a fuel. Use illustrations to explain your answer where necessary."

39 It was as if I had stumbled into someone else's identity. I didn't know anything about rocks. I didn't know anything about science. Why were they asking me these things? I stared up at the blackboard, where the proctor was already chalking up how much time we had left. He squinted back at me with suspicion, and I swerved my gaze ceilingward, as if searching for the appropriate phrasing with which to set down my brimming knowledge.

40 Coal. What did I know about coal? I thought of black lung, carbon paper, the heap of coal in my parents' basement in Chicago. Then, for

a moment, a phrase sprang to my mind from an eighth-grade science text: "Coal results from the deterioration and mineralization of prehistoric tropical rainforests."

41 Quickly, before it sank back out of reach, I opened my bluebook and began to write. "Coal results from the deterioration and mineralization of prehistoric tropical rainforests. Coal deposits are apt to be found in those places where prehistoric tropical rainforests once stood. Thus, coal mines in present use are located in these places.

42 "Coal," I continued boldly, "contains some of the chemical elements of prehistoric tropical rainforests, but usually not all of them. Those that remain are those which have survived and, in a sense, resulted from, the deterioration and mineralization of prehistoric tropical rainforests."

43 That got me through three pages of large, loopy script. All around me, my classmates were filling one bluebook after another. One girl across the room wrote the ink out of one ballpoint, hurled it to the floor, and furiously scrawled on with another. All I could hear in the room was the steady scrape of pens and the rapid flutter of pages.

44 To drive home my point, I decided to deliver on a few illustrations. Carefully, but with a certain graphic flair, I drew:

1. a rainforest with arrows pointing to "trees," "scrub vegetation," "sun," and "topsoil,"
2. a rainforest deteriorating,
3. a deteriorated rainforest making its way underground,
4. a coal mine in full operation labelled "Thousands of years later," and,
5. a black lump labelled "resultant coal ore fragment."

45 These led to another drawing illustrating the chemical breakup of coal. I drew a circle and divided it into three parts, labelled "sulfur," "carbon," and "other." Coal was suitable as a fuel, I noted, because it burned.

46 As I underlined all my headings and captions I wondered about my alternatives. I could claim that I had overdosed on NoDoz, that I was reeling, hallucinating, unable to think. I could hand in a blank bluebook, copy out a C-level set of answers in another bluebook that evening, hand it in the next morning, and elegantly apologize for the mixup. I could feign a fainting spell or an epileptic fit or psychosomatic paralysis of my right hand. I could accuse the earnest, chalk-faced girl beside me of cheating and storm out the door, or punch out the proctor in a rebellious frenzy, becoming, overnight, a campus legend.

47 But it gradually became obvious to me that the college simply wanted me to answer these questions. Otherwise, I reasoned, they would not be asking them. And it was just as obvious that if I couldn't answer their questions, I had no business being there.

Somehow, in the rustle of the testing room, this hit me like a revelation. I wanted to get up then, find the professor, and exclaim, "Say, sir, I didn't *realize* any of this." He would understand. It must have happened before.

48 I looked at two of my friends a few rows away, both busily writing. At these times my friends seemed distant and unfamiliar. They were each into their third or fourth bluebooks. What in God's name were they writing about?

49 The hinge of my jaw ached and trembled and as I yawned, the floor took on a soft, inviting look. I put down my pen and stretched out my legs and wondered if it would be all right if I just curled up for a little while on the scuffed, hardwood floor, closed my eyes, and slept.

50 "Pencils down," the proctor commanded, chopping at the air with his hand.

51 A resolute, perspiring girl in the front row raised her hand and asked if she could "just finish one last sentence."

52 The proctor nodded and a score of heads and hands ducked back down to finish sentences. I sat still for a moment, and then scribbled one last sentence, "Coal remains one of the most popular forms of fuel in use today."

53 "All right, that's it," the proctor declared, and everyone groaned and stretched and stacked their bluebooks. I signed mine with a bold hand, but glancing over my five pages I knew it was at last all over for me at Oberlin College. All that remained was one last explosion of red-inked exclamations expressing regrets, alarm, and grave concern for my future.

STUDY QUESTIONS

1. What does the title "Pencils Down" signify? Is it appropriate to the content of this essay in more than one way?
2. At what point (disregarding the headnote that identifies Ward as a humorist) did you become aware that this would be a humorous essay? What element of style or emphasis made Ward's humorous intent clear to you?
3. Look through the essay for extremes of formal and informal diction, and list some examples. Note that Ward has achieved part of his humorous effect by contrasting "high" and "low" language. How do such contrasts work thematically?
4. Do you completely trust the account Ward gives of his early self? Why, or why not? Locate passages that bear on your answer.
5. Does "Pencils Down," despite its light tone and seemingly haphazard organization, have a serious point to make? If so, what is that point? Do you find that the essay has a purposeful structure after all?

Frank Conroy

Frank Conroy is a professional writer who lives on the Massachusetts island of Nantucket. His one book to date is the widely acclaimed, somewhat fictionalized autobiography *Stop-time* (1967), from which this selection is an excerpt. At the time of this episode, Frank is in early adolescence, living in Fort Lauderdale, Florida, with his mother and stepfather.

CONQUERING THE UNIVERSE*

1 The common yo-yo is crudely made, with a thick shank between two widely spaced wooden disks. The string is knotted or stapled to the shank. With such an instrument nothing can be done except the simple up-down movement. My yo-yo, on the other hand, was a perfectly balanced construction of hard wood, slightly weighted, flat, with only a sixteenth of an inch between the halves. The string was not attached to the shank, but looped over it in such a way as to allow the wooden part to spin freely on its own axis. The gyroscopic effect thus created kept the yo-yo stable in all attitudes.

2 I started at the beginning of the book and quickly mastered the novice, intermediate, and advanced stages, practicing all day every day in the woods across the street from my house. Hour after hour of practice, never moving to the next trick until the one at hand was mastered.

3 The string was tied to my middle finger, just behind the nail. As I threw—with your palm up, make a fist; throw down your hand, fingers unfolding, as if you were casting grain—a short bit of string would tighten across the sensitive pad of flesh at the tip of my finger. That was the critical area. After a number of weeks I could interpret the condition of the string, the presence of any imperfections on the shank, but most importantly the exact amount of spin or inertial energy left in the yo-yo at any given moment—all from that bit of string on my fingertip. As the throwing motion became more and more natural I found I could make the yo-yo "sleep" for an astonishing length of time—fourteen or fifteen seconds—and still have enough spin left to bring it back to my hand. Gradually the basic moves became reflexes. Sleeping, twirling, swinging, and precise aim. Without thinking, without even looking, I could run through trick after trick involving various combinations of the elemental skills, switching from one to the other in a smooth continuous

---

*Title chosen by editor

flow. On particularly good days I would hum a tune under my breath and do it all in time to the music.

4 Flicking the yo-yo expressed something. The sudden, potentially comic extension of one's arm to twice its length. The precise neatness of it, intrinsically soothing, as if relieving an inner tension too slight to be noticeable, the way a man might hitch up his pants simply to enact a reassuring gesture. It felt good. The comfortable weight in one's hand, the smooth, rapid descent down the string, ending with a barely audible snap as the yo-yo hung balanced, spinning, pregnant with force and the slave of one's fingertip. That it was vaguely masturbatory seems inescapable. I doubt that half the pubescent boys in America could have been captured by any other means, as, in the heat of the fad, half of them were. A single Loop-the-Loop might represent, in some mysterious way, the act of masturbation, but to break down the entire repertoire into the three stages of throw, trick, and return representing erection, climax, and detumescence seems immoderate.

5 The greatest pleasure in yo-yoing was an abstract pleasure—watching the dramatization of simple physical laws, and realizing they would never fail if a trick was done correctly. The geometric purity of it! The string wasn't just a string, it was a tool in the enactment of theorems. It was a line, an idea. And the top was an entirely different sort of idea, a gyroscope, capable of storing energy and of interacting with the line. I remember the first time I did a particularly lovely trick, one in which the sleeping yo-yo is swung from right to left while the string is interrupted by an extended index finger. Momentum carries the yo-yo in a circular path around the finger, but instead of completing the arc the yo-yo falls on the taut string between the performer's hands, where it continues to spin in an upright position. My pleasure at that moment was as much from the beauty of the experiment as from pride. Snapping apart my hands I sent the yo-yo into the air above my head, bouncing it off nothing, back into my palm.

6 I practiced the yo-yo because it pleased me to do so, without the slightest application of will power. It wasn't ambition that drove me, but the nature of yo-yoing. The yo-yo represented my first organized attempt to control the outside world. It fascinated me because I could see my progress in clearly defined stages, and because the intimacy of it, the almost spooky closeness I began to feel with the instrument in my hand, seemed to ensure that nothing irrelevant would interfere. I was, in the language of jazz, "up tight" with my yo-yo, and finally free, in one small area at least, of the paralyzing sloppiness of life in general.

7 The first significant problem arose in the attempt to do fifty consecutive Loop-the-Loops. After ten or fifteen the yo-yo invariably started to lean and the throws became less clean, resulting in loss of control. I almost skipped the whole thing because fifty seemed excessive. Ten made the point. But there it was, written out in the book. To qualify as an expert you had to do fifty, so fifty I would do.

8 It took me two days, and I wouldn't have spent a moment more. All those Loop-the-Loops were hard on the strings. Time after time the shank cut them and the yo-yo went sailing off into the air. It was irritating, not only because of the expense (strings were a nickel each, and fabricating your own was unsatisfactory), but because a random element had been introduced. About the only unforeseeable disaster in yo-yoing was to have your string break, and here was a trick designed to do exactly that. Twenty-five would have been enough. If you could do twenty-five clean Loop-the-Loops you could do fifty or a hundred. I supposed they were simply trying to sell strings and went back to the more interesting tricks.

9 The witty nonsense of Eating Spaghetti, the surprise of The Twirl, the complex neatness of Cannonball, Backwards round the World, or Halfway round the World—I could do them all, without false starts or sloppy endings. I could do every trick in the book. Perfectly.

10 The day was marked on the kitchen calendar (God Gave Us Bluebell Natural Bottled Gas). I got on my bike and rode into town. Pedaling along the highway I worked out with the yo-yo to break in a new string. The twins were appearing at the dime store.

11 I could hear the crowd before I turned the corner. Kids were coming on bikes and on foot from every corner of town, rushing down the streets like madmen. Three or four policemen were busy keeping the street clear directly in front of the store, and in a small open space around the doors some of the more adept kids were running through their tricks, showing off to the general audience or stopping to compare notes with their peers. Standing at the edge with my yo-yo safe in my pocket, it didn't take me long to see I had them all covered. A boy in a sailor hat could do some of the harder tricks, but he missed too often to be a serious threat. I went inside.

12 As Ramos and Ricardo performed I watched their hands carefully, noticing little differences in style and technique. Ricardo was a shade classier, I thought, although Ramos held an edge in the showy two-handed stuff. When they were through we went outside for the contest.

13 "Everybody in the alley!" Ramos shouted, his head bobbing an inch or two above the others. "Contest starting now in the alley!" A hundred excited children followed the twins into an alley beside the dime store and lined up against the wall.

14 "Attention all kids!" Ramos yelled, facing us from the middle of the street like a drill sergeant. "To qualify for contest you got to Rock the Cradle. You got to rock yo-yo in cradle four time. Four time! Okay? Three time no good. Okay. Everybody happy?" There were murmurs of disappointment and some of the kids stepped out of line. The rest of us closed ranks. Yo-yos flicked nervously as we waited. "Winner receive grand prize. Special Black Beauty Prize Yo-Yo with Diamonds," said Ramos, gesturing to his brother who smiled and held up the prize,

turning it in the air so we could see the four stones set on each side. ("The crowd gasped . . ." I want to write. Of course they didn't. They didn't make a sound, but the impact of the diamond yo-yo was obvious.) We'd never seen anything like it. One imagined how the stones would gleam as it revolved, and how much prettier the tricks would be. The ultimate yo-yo! The only one in town! Who knew what feats were possible with such an instrument? All around me a fierce, nervous resolve was settling into the contestants, suddenly skittish as racehorses.

15 "Ricardo will show trick with Grand Prize Yo-Yo. Rock the Cradle four time!"

16 With a perfect, fluid movement Ricardo threw down the yo-yo, gathered the string and leisurely rocked the cradle.

17 "One!" cried Ramos.

18 "Two!" the kids joined in.

19 "Three!" It was really beautiful. He did it so slowly you would have thought he had all the time in the world. I counted seconds under my breath to see how long he made it sleep.

20 "Four!" said the crowd.

21 "Thirteen," I said to myself as the yo-yo snapped back into his hand. Thirteen seconds. Excellent time for that particular trick.

22 "Attention all kids!" Ramos announced. "Contest start now at head of line."

23 The first boy did a sloppy job of gathering his string but managed to rock the cradle quickly four times.

24 "Okay." Ramos tapped him on the shoulder and moved to the next boy, who fumbled. "Out." Ricardo followed, doing an occasional Loop-the-Loop with the diamond yo-yo. "Out . . . out . . . okay," said Ramos as he worked down the line.

25 There was something about the man's inexorable advance that unnerved me. His decisions were fast, and there was no appeal. To my surprise I felt my palms begin to sweat. Closer and closer he came, his voice growing louder, and then suddenly he was standing in front of me. Amazed, I stared at him. It was as if he'd appeared out of thin air.

26 "What happen boy, you swarrow bubble gum?"

27 The laughter jolted me out of it. Blushing, I threw down my yo-yo and executed a slow Rock the Cradle, counting the four passes and hesitating a moment at the end so as not to appear rushed.

28 "Okay." He tapped my shoulder. "Good."

29 I wiped my hands on my blue jeans and watched him move down the line. "Out . . . out . . . out." He had a large mole on the back of his neck.

30 Seven boys qualified. Coming back, Ramos called out, "Next trick Backward Round the World! Okay? Go!"

31 The first two boys missed, but the third was the kid in the sailor hat. Glancing quickly to see that no one was behind him, he hunched

up his shoulder, threw, and just barely made the catch. There was some loose string in his hand, but not enough to disqualify him.

32 Number four missed, as did number five, and it was my turn. I stepped forward, threw the yo-yo almost straight up over my head, and as it began to fall pulled very gently to add some speed. It zipped neatly behind my legs and there was nothing more to do. My head turned to one side, I stood absolutely still and watched the yo-yo come in over my shoulder and slap into my hand. I added a Loop-the-Loop just to show the tightness of the string.

33 "Did you see that?" I heard someone say.

34 Number seven missed, so it was between myself and the boy in the sailor hat. His hair was bleached by the sun and combed up over his forehead in a pompadour, held from behind by the white hat. He was a year or two older than me. Blinking his blue eyes nervously, he adjusted the tension of his string.

35 "Next trick Cannonball! Cannonball! You go first this time," Ramos said to me.

36 Kids had gathered in a circle around us, those in front quiet and attentive, those in back jumping up and down to get a view. "Move back for room," Ricardo said, pushing them back. "More room, please."

37 I stepped into the center and paused, looking down at the ground. It was a difficult trick. The yo-yo had to land exactly on the string and there was a chance I'd miss the first time. I knew I wouldn't miss twice. "Can I have one practice?"

38 Ramos and Ricardo consulted in their mother tongue, and then Ramos held up his hands. "Attention all kids! Each boy have one practice before trick."

39 The crowd was silent, watching me. I took a deep breath and threw, following the fall of the yo-yo with my eyes, turning slightly, matador-fashion, as it passed me. My finger caught the string, the yo-yo came up and over, and missed. Without pausing I threw again. "Second time," I yelled, so there would be no misunderstanding. The circle had been too big. This time I made it small, sacrificing beauty for security. The yo-yo fell where it belonged and spun for a moment. (A moment I don't rush, my arms widespread, my eyes locked on the spinning toy. The Trick! There it is, brief and magic, right before your eyes! My hands are frozen in the middle of a deaf-and-dumb sentence, holding the whole airy, tenuous statement aloft for everyone to see.) With a quick snap I broke up the trick and made my catch.

40 Ramos nodded. "Okay. Very good. Now next boy."

41 Sailor-hat stepped forward, wiping his nose with the back of his hand. He threw once to clear the string.

42 "One practice," said Ramos.

43 He nodded.

44 "C'mon Bobby," someone said. "You can do it."

45 Bobby threw the yo-yo out to the side, made his move, and

missed. "Damn," he whispered. (He said "dahyum.") The second time he got halfway through the trick before his yo-yo ran out of gas and fell impotently off the string. He picked it up and walked away, winding slowly.

46 Ramos came over and held my hand in the air. "The winner!" he yelled. "Grand prize Black Beauty Diamond Yo-Yo will now be awarded."

47 Ricardo stood in front of me. "Take off old yo-yo." I loosened the knot and slipped it off. "Put out hand." I held out my hand and he looped the new string on my finger, just behind the nail, where the mark was. "You like Black Beauty," he said, smiling as he stepped back. "Diamond make pretty colors in the sun."

48 "Thank you," I said.

49 "Very good with yo-yo. Later we have contest for whole town. Winner go to Miami for State Championship. Maybe you win. Okay?"

50 "Okay." I nodded. "Thank you."

51 A few kids came up to look at Black Beauty. I threw it once or twice to get the feel. It seemed a bit heavier than my old one. Ramos and Ricardo were surrounded as the kids called out their favorite tricks.

52 "Do Pickpocket! Pickpocket!"

53 "Do the Double Cannonball!"

54 "Ramos! Ramos! Do the Turkish Army!"

55 Smiling, waving their hands to ward off the barrage of requests, the twins worked their way through the crowd toward the mouth of the alley. I watched them moving away and was immediately struck by a wave of fierce and irrational panic. "Wait," I yelled, pushing through after them. "Wait!"

56 I caught them on the street.

57 "No more today," Ricardo said, and then paused when he saw it was me. "Okay. The champ. What's wrong? Yo-yo no good?"

58 "No. It's fine."

59 "Good. You take care of it."

60 "I wanted to ask when the contest is. The one where you get to go to Miami."

61 "Later. After school begins." They began to move away. "We have to go home now."

62 "Just one more thing," I said, walking after them. "What is the hardest trick you know?"

63 Ricardo laughed. "Hardest trick killing flies in air."

64 "No, no. I mean a real trick."

65 They stopped and looked at me. "There is a very hard trick," Ricardo said. "I don't do it, but Ramos does. Because you won the contest he will show you. But only once, so watch carefully."

66 We stepped into the lobby of the Sunset Theater. Ramos cleared his string. "Watch," he said, and threw. The trick started out like a Cannonball, and then unexpectedly folded up, opened again, and as I

watched breathlessly the entire complex web spun around in the air, propelled by Ramos' two hands making slow circles like a swimmer. The end was like the end of a Cannonball.

67 "That's beautiful," I said, genuinely awed. "What's it called?"

68 "The Universe."

69 "The Universe," I repeated.

70 "Because it goes around and around," said Ramos, "like the planets."

. . .

71 I spent the last few days before school in the woods, attempting to re-create the trick Ramos had shown me in the lobby of the Sunset Theater. I'd broken it down into three steps, the world, the solar system, and the galaxies, the sum of which was The Universe. The world and the solar system were within my abilities, but in the galaxies stage the yo-yo would run out of gas or the string would tangle. My strategy was to go back and practice the simple Cannonball for duration, snapping my throws out more and more evenly, trying for perfect balance so the string wouldn't touch the inner walls of the yo-yo. At the same time I speeded up the first two stages, attempting to feel The Universe not so much as three separate maneuvers but as one continuous rhythmic statement. Progress was slow but steady, and had I not been interrupted by the opening of school, I might have learned it in a week.

. . .

72 One late afternoon in the woods everything fell into place. I'd been practicing for an hour, running through the easy tricks abstractedly, the way an expert magician might shuffle cards while waiting for his victims to take their seats, when I began to realize something special was happening. Never had I yo-yoed so effortlessly. Never had the tricks clicked with such mathematical precision. The yo-yo seemed to be playing itself as I stood waving my hands like a conductor before an invisible orchestra. The time was ripe for an assault on The Universe, not only the separate parts, but the whole trick as one unit.

73 Unbelievably, it came on the first try. I was flabbergasted. I'd been trying for weeks—for so long, in fact, I was reconciled to creeping up on it slowly, perhaps over a period of months—and suddenly victory was mine. Breathless, hoping it hadn't been a fluke, I threw again. As I watched the trick unfold, it came to me that a ghost or a spirit was controlling the yo-yo's movements, and that to be really good one had simply to give up one's desire to dominate the yo-yo and instead let the ghost take over. It was as if someone spoke to me through the yo-yo. See how easy, was the implication. Just practice till you get over your clumsiness, practice until you can yo-yo without thinking about it and then let me take over. I threw back my head and laughed. I danced a little dance on the sand and shouted out into the pine trees. I knew that in all of Fort Lauderdale and very probably in all of Florida there was not one other boy who could do what I had just done.

74 I knew I was best. As for what happened, I was no more than moderately disappointed when my supposedly unobtainable Black Beauty went on sale at the five-and-ten for sixty cents. I'd gone as far as one could go on the yo-yo. I'd learned tricks the demonstrators didn't know. So when the final contest arrived and I learned that after one or two extremely easy tricks the choice of champion would be based on the greatest number of consecutive Loop-the-Loops, when I learned that my skill counted for nothing in the eyes of the non-yo-yoing judges, when I found myself screwed once again as my string broke at seventy-three (eleven less than a muscle-bound idiot from the beach who couldn't do a simple Cannonball)—when, to wrap it up, all this reality was finally absorbed by my brain, the knowledge that I was without question the best yo-yo player around kept me from despair. There was no despair, only a mild confusion at the sloppiness of things, and a faint sickness at my own bewilderment.

75 I forgot it easily. That same night, hidden in the greenery under the window, I watched a naked girl let down her long red hair.

STUDY QUESTIONS

1. Why does Conroy begin with a description of the yo-yo rather than an account of his own situation or feelings? Do the descriptions of yo-yoing give us valuable information about young Frank's character and mentality?
2. Many autobiographical writers portray themselves in an especially favorable light, implying that they were born with greater sensitivity or virtue than others. Is Conroy that kind of writer? Pick out passages that could be used to support your answer.
3. Young Frank is obviously in a transitional phase of life. Does the story we are told bring out that fact in significant ways? Does Frank "grow" in the course of the narrated action?
4. In the uncut text of *Stop-time,* the final paragraph of this selection comes as less of a surprise than it does here. Yet even in the present version, that paragraph has at least some appropriateness to the main story. What is that appropriateness? Look for earlier details that make the final paragraph seem thematically "right," even if it *is* a surprise.
5. Suppose this episode had ended with young Frank's winning the town yo-yo championship and then the championship of all Florida. What thematic emphasis would Conroy have had to sacrifice to make room for such a "happy ending"?
6. Disregarding quoted dialogue, make separate lists of relatively "high" and "low" diction in this essay. When you have collected enough examples to establish a general pattern, ask

yourself why Conroy has included such a broad range of terms, from the very informal to the formal. On which side is his language weighted, and why?

7. Why do you suppose we have chosen the title "Conquering the Universe" for this excerpt from *Stop-time?*

PRESENTING A CHARACTER

Ben Funk

Ben Funk is a freelance writer who lives in Florida. The present essay first appeared in the *New York Times Magazine* in 1978.

"MILKING" COBRAS FOR CURES

1 As William E. Haast was walking through the woods in New Jersey, a rabbit hopped casually along in front of him. Haast watched amused, until he spotted a rattlesnake coiled in the path ahead. He clapped his hands and shouted, hoping to frighten the rabbit back into the brush, but he was too late. The serpent struck, burying its fangs into one of the rabbit's legs, and the animal was dead in seconds. "It seemed to me then," Haast recalls, "that such a powerful, destructive force—like atomic energy—could be converted to many good uses, if it were properly controlled."

2 Since then, Haast has developed a method of producing pure, stable snake venom in powdered form and, and as a direct result of his work, the medical profession is using a variety of snake venoms and serums in the treatment of an increasing number of human illnesses, from myasthenia gravis (the nerve disease that killed Aristotle Onassis) to migraine headaches. But Haast's path from that stricken rabbit in the Jersey woods to his contribution to world medicine was long, frightening and exceedingly dangerous.

3 One of Haast's first jobs, as an airline flight engineer in the 1940's, gave him a chance to pursue both his fascination with snakes (at 12, he had kept them as pets) and his theories on the value of venom research. His flights took him to India, where cobras kill 20,000 people a year. During these stopovers he talked with experts—and added to his snake collection, bringing several back to the United States in his suitcases. Pilots brought him more from Africa, Burma and South and Central America. Before long, with the best collection of exotic reptiles in the

country, he quit the airline job and built a serpentarium in Miami to produce venom for scientific research. At that time, he said, "the only cobra venoms available in America were imported and cost $1,500 an ounce. I wanted to work out a way to produce a standard, dependable, lower-priced venom and open the way to unlimited research." Since he was short of money, he enlisted tourists to help him finance the project. On the first day that he hung up a sign, 200 people paid 50 cents each to watch him handle his cobras and extract venom from them. Today, in the completed serpentarium, large circular walls enclose landscaped pits in which the reptiles slither through the grass and among tropical trees or lie motionless in the shrubbery. Along the outer walls, the cobras curl up in air-conditioned compartments. After "milking" the snakes, Haast processes their venom in a spotless laboratory.

4 In the course of his treacherous activities, Haast has been bitten 126 times. Knowing that this would happen, he had, early in the action, begun injecting cobra venom into his system to build immunity. First, he diluted the venom 1,000 times in a saline solution; gradually, he strengthened the doses. At one point, a zoo curator urged him to stop, pointing out that horses injected with venom to produce snakebite serum had died within two years. But Haast went ahead. Eleven months after he began pumping venom into his arms, he was bitten by a cobra. His wife implored him to seek medical aid but he refused. For several hours, he suffered a terrible headache and burning pain around the wound. But he came through all right. In 1949 he was nailed by a Mexican moccasin, whose bite can kill a horse in 20 minutes. The venom is both haemotoxic and neurotoxic, attacking both the bloodstream and the nervous system. Although the injections of cobra venom had made Haast immune to the neurotoxic poison, he was as sensitive to the haemotoxic element as anyone else. Fifteen minutes after he was bitten, he began to vomit and reel with spasms of pain; in his record book he noted the time, 6:40 P.M., and his reaction, then collapsed. Mrs. Haast, almost hysterical, tied on a tourniquet, slashed the wound and applied a suction pump to try to draw out the poison, but the spasms grew worse and by 4 A.M. she was certain her husband was dying. Still, he refused hospitalization. For four more hours he suffered great torture, but at 8 A.M. the pains receded, and Mrs. Haast was able to write "out of danger" in the record.

5 Haast subsequently came even closer to death, through the auspices of a big Siamese cobra. As usual, he had propped up the glass front door of the cobra compartment and prepared to take the snake out for a venom extraction. To a small group of visitors watching him, it was a moment filled with dread as the reptile reared into striking position, its hood spread, at the first hint of motion through the glass. Now Haast started shadow boxing the cobra, his right hand darted back and forth, inches from the cobra's head—inches from death. The hissing reptile swayed with the hand, watching with cold, glassy eyes for a chance to

strike. Haast's strategy is to feint with his right hand, then seize the snake at the back of the head with his left. But this cobra had him figured. In the same split second that Haast's left hand shot in for the capture, the cobra slashed downward at the right forearm, shooting enough venom into Haast's bloodstream to kill 20 humans.

6 After pulling the cobra's fangs out of his arm, Haast went on with the venom extraction. He then returned the snake to its compartment and finally looked to his wound. It was the worst he had ever received, but he did nothing except wash away the blood. He was not afraid, because he had lived through two other cobra bites in the preceding months.

7 This time, however, things began to go wrong—and fast. Within minutes, his throat was sore, his eyes heavy. Breathing became difficult. A growing weakness crept into his legs. An hour later, when it was time for more extractions, he told his wife, Clarita: "I don't know if I can do it." He was seeing double now and only by a great effort could he hold his eyelids open. He managed one more extraction, then headed back toward his office.

8 "He walked like a drunken man," his wife says. "His legs were buckling and I thought he was going to fall. I got him into bed and he began chilling violently. In the next few minutes, his legs became paralyzed and he couldn't speak or open his eyes."

9 This time Haast agreed to call for medical aid. Paralysis was slowly enveloping his throat and lungs, and breathing was becoming almost impossible. By the time his son, Bill Jr., got him to a hospital, Haast was totally paralyzed, as rigid as a board. By the time he was put in an iron lung, breathing had stopped: Death had appeared. His face was black, and he felt "as though my mind had separated from my body. It seemed that I was standing off to one side and seeing everything that happened. Just before that, I had been fighting for breath like a drowning person. Then a great wave of relief swept over me. I think that is the feeling of death."

10 But in the iron lung, he began to breathe again. The nurses pried open his jaws and put a suction tube in his mouth to draw out the gathering saliva. For the next 24 hours, Haast lay seemingly unconscious, but he was aware of everything done to him, and most of all, of a burning pain as the venom ravaged his system. Very slowly, the antibodies in him overcame the effects of the venom. On the second day, he could open his eyes. On the third day, he could breathe without help. When they removed him from the iron lung, he demanded to be taken home. Two days after his hospital release, he was extracting venom from five king cobras.

11 Had Haast's body, in fighting off the effects of the two earlier bites, exhausted its immunity? One doctor believed this to be the case, and warned him that he had probably developed such a sensitivity to venom that another bite would kill him quickly. But Haast ignored the

warning: "There's too much to be done with snake venom. The surface has just been scratched."

12 A few days later, another cobra bit him. "Well," he commented after his recovery, "I guess this knocks the doctor's theory out the window."

13 Haast first attracted the attention of medical researchers in 1949 when, in rapid succession, he was bitten by two cobras. Again, his wife kept the usual record—paralysis, labored breathing, sporadic heart action, soaring temperature. When it was over, Haast studied the record and told Clarita, "That looks just like polio."

14 He hurried to the University of Miami research laboratories, advanced his theory, and was invited to participate in an experiment with rhesus monkeys. Polio virus was injected into all the animals. This was followed immediately by mild shots of detoxified venom in half of the monkeys. The ones who didn't get the venom contracted paralysis and other polio symptoms in the normal time. Those given the venom were not affected until hours later.

15 What had happened, the researchers said, was that an "interference phenomenon" had been created. Scientists had known for many years of such a phenomenon, in which a conflict can be created between two infectious agents, so that the victim can survive without infection from either.

16 The university gave Haast a grant-in-aid and sent him to India to collect more cobras. He was allowed to keep them in his serpentarium. In return, he supplied the university with venom at a low price. The experiments continued and out of them came an exciting promise of a polio cure—just before the Salk vaccine° came onto the scene.

17 Since then, medical laboratories here and abroad have been pursuing research in the use of venom, and the results are increasingly impressive. "Venoms have powerful physiological properties," says Dr. Daniel Drachman of Johns Hopkins University in Baltimore. "Bill Haast realized that, long before scientists did. He foresaw its effects and inspired the opening of a new field in research of the nervous system."

18 Drachman works with venoms supplied by Haast to attack the mysterious disease called myasthenia gravis (M.G.). So far, the experiments have led mainly to a greater understanding of the malady. M.G. was long believed to be caused by the failure of motor nerve endings to produce enough acetycholine, a compound vital to nerve transmissions. But biopsies from human victims showed that the blame could be laid on defects in the nerve receptors themselves. Patients tested had only 20 percent of the normal number of receptors functioning properly.

19 Using extracts of venom from the Taiwan cobra, Drachman and

16 **Salk vaccine:** the first effective vaccine against poliomyelitis, developed by the American physician Jonas E. Salk

others have reduced the breakdown rate of receptors by binding the nerve ends which transmit impulses from one to the other. This has enabled researchers to study the receptor sites and learn more about the functions of the nerves themselves. "The venom extracts have given us a handle on what goes on in myasthenia gravis," says Drachman.

20 Dr. Murray Sanders, head of the Sanders Medical Research Foundation in Boca Raton, Fla., uses venoms to treat "Lou Gehrig's disease," an ailment so-called because it took the life of the famed "iron man" of the New York Yankees. A relentless destroyer of the central nervous system, the malady, amyotrophic lateral sclerosis (A.L.S.), has baffled the medical world.

21 Sanders had been a member of the University of Miami team which did the successful venom experiments in polio treatment. Because the symptoms of polio and A.L.S. are similar, he began to test venom's effect on animals suffering from A.L.S. The results were rewarding, so Sanders, using a mixture of cobra and krait venom, began to treat human victims of A.L.S. To date, he has treated more than 800. Some who came to him paralyzed and helpless are walking again and partially able to take care of themselves. A cure for this terrible disease remains elusive but Sanders says, "The backbone of research in this field is the source of venom. Bill Haast has provided it, and, God knows, he has paid the price."

22 Dr. John H. Laragh of the Cornell Medical Center in New York is using cobra venom to treat patients with high blood pressure, and he says the results have been "extremely promising." At the Howard Hughes Medical Research Foundation in Miami, Dr. Robert A. Nelson discovered that a nontoxic cobra-venom factor, which he calls cobratoxin, prevents rejections of transplants in animals. In Mexico City, Dr. Caroline Molinari has reported encouraging results in the use of Haast's venoms in treatment of both animal and human cancers.

23 A product called cobroxin, which relieves the pain of cancer and migraine headaches when patients become immune to other drugs, has been available for years. Haast supplies the Welcome Foundation of London with viper venom which is used to control bleeding in surgery. Another product, in the experimental stage at Abbott Laboratories in Chicago, dissolves blood clots in the body without danger of hemorrhaging.

24 The effectiveness of venom, particularly in the treatment of diseases of the nervous system, seems somewhat paradoxical, for venom attacks the motor nerve endings, thereby blocking the impulses which govern muscular function. This causes rapid paralysis, hence respiratory failure—and death. But when the venoms are broken down and the toxic elements are removed, the opposite happens. The purified venom fractions go to work to repair the damaged nerve endings from which impulses are translated from one nerve to the other. This impedes the nerve destruction that occurs in Lou Gehrig's disease, myasthenia gravis

and many other afflictions. Since nerves affected by stress are also at the root of such ailments as high blood pressure and migraine headaches, venom is helpful in treating those conditions.

25 Haast has received wide recognition for his work, as well as numerous awards and citations "for unusual service to humanity" and "for heroic contributions to the saving of lives by offering himself as a human guinea pig."

26 By now, Haast's blood is so full of venom antibodies that it has become a perfect serum for snakebite victims. He has given it freely and has saved the lives of 22 people. He has flown, on a moment's notice, to hospitals far from his home in order to donate his blood, which he gives free of charge while footing the bill for his trip.

27 For a man who has done so much to save lives, one recent event has been devastating. It occurred when a visitor to the serpentarium perched his 6-year-old son on the wall of a circular pit which was the home of an African Nile crocodile. When the father turned away for a moment, the boy toppled into the pit and was instantly killed by the beast. It was the only such tragedy that had ever occurred at the serpentarium and Haast was heartbroken. He killed the crocodile, which took 24 shots from a Luger, and buried it on the spot. His grief was so intense that he decided to close the serpentarium and abandon his life's work. But the boy's mother called and urged him to continue. Her family, she said, revered him for his work and did not want him to abandon it because of an accident that was no fault of his own.

28 So Haast is once again back at his absorbing and perilous work. He has flirted with death so many times he is sure he knows exactly what it will be like to die if one of his serpents finally kills him. But the pain and the convulsive struggles for life have only strengthened his dedication.

29 "It's a good feeling to know that I've saved some lives and prevented a lot of suffering," he says. "It's worth all the days of torture. A person should never fear death. I've got much to live for, but I wouldn't be afraid to die. I think I know that when a man dies, the experience isn't a bad one. The feeling is one of great relief, like a badly beaten fighter gets when the bell finally ends the last round."

STUDY QUESTIONS

1. This essay mixes a portrait of William Haast with information about the uses of snake venom. Notice where that information appears (paragraphs 17–24), and then reread the opening and closing paragraphs. Why do you think the author chose to place the strictly medical information where he did?

2. In writing " 'Milking' Cobras for Cures," Funk must have kept his intended audience in mind. The *New York Times Magazine* reaches over a million nonspecialist readers. What precautions has Funk taken against "losing" those readers when he discusses research into the nature and cure of rare diseases?
3. What are Haast's chief traits of character as you see them here? Locate passages that convey those traits.
4. What do you consider the author's attitude toward Haast to be, and how can you tell? How could another writer have used the same information to create a very different picture?

John Leonard

The novelist, essayist, and critic John Leonard has been editor of *The New York Times Book Review.* "The Only Child" appears in a collection of his short essays, *Private Lives in the Imperial City* (1979).

THE ONLY CHILD

1 He is big. He always has been, over six feet, with that slump of the shoulders and tuck in the neck big men in this country often affect, as if to apologize for being above the democratic norm in size. (In high school and at college he played varsity basketball. In high school he was senior class president.) And he looks healthy enough, blue-eyed behind his beard, like a trapper or a mountain man, acquainted with silences. He also grins a lot.

2 Odd, then, to have noticed earlier—at the house, when he took off his shabby coat to play Ping-Pong—that the white arms were unmuscled. The coat may have been a comment. This, after all, is southern California, where every man is an artist, an advertiser of himself; where every surface is painted and every object potted; where even the statues seem to wear socks. The entire population ambles, in polyesters, toward a Taco Bell. To wear a brown shabby cloth coat in southern California is to admit something.

3 So he hasn't been getting much exercise. Nor would the children have elected him president of any class. At the house they avoided him. Or, since he was too big to be avoided entirely, they treated his presence as a kind of odor to pass through hurriedly, to be safe on the other side. They behaved like cats. Of course, he ignored them. But I think they

were up to more than just protecting themselves from his lack of curiosity. Children are expert readers of grins.

4 His grin is intermittent. The dimples twitch on and off; between them, teeth are bared; above them, the blue eyes disappear in a wince. This grin isn't connected to any humor the children know about. It may be a tic. It could also be a function of some metronome made on Mars. It registers inappropriate intervals. We aren't listening to the same music.

5 This is the man who introduced me to the mysteries of mathematical science, the man I could never beat at chess, the man who wrote haiku° and played with computers. Now there is static in his head, as though the mind had drifted off its signal during sleep. He has an attention span of about thirty seconds.

6 I am to take him back to where he lives, in the car I have rented in order to pretend to be a Californian. We are headed for a rooming house in one of the beach cities along a coast of off-ramps and oil wells. It is a rooming house that thinks of itself as Spanish. The ruined-hacienda° look requires a patio, a palm tree and several miles of corrugated tile. He does not expect me to come up to his room, but I insist. I have brought along a six-pack of beer.

7 The room is a slum, and it stinks. It is wall-to-wall beer cans, hundreds of them, under a film of ash. He lights cigarettes and leaves them burning on the windowsill or the edge of the dresser or the lip of the sink, while he thinks of something else—Gupta° sculpture, maybe, or the Sephiroth Tree of the Kabbalah.° The sink is filthy, and so is the toilet. Holes have been burnt in the sheet on the bed, where he sits. He likes to crush the beer cans after he has emptied them, then toss them aside.

8 He tells me that he is making a statement, that this room is a statement, that the landlord will understand the meaning of his statement. In a week or so, according to the pattern, they will evict him, and someone will find him another room, which he will turn into another statement, with the help of the welfare checks he receives on account of his disability, which is the static in his head.

9 There are no books, no newspapers or magazines, no pictures on the wall. There is a television set, which he watches all day long while drinking beer and smoking cigarettes. I am sufficiently familiar with the literature on schizophrenia to realize that this room is a statement he is making about himself. I am also sufficiently familiar with his history to

---

5 **haiku:** a form of evocative Japanese verse employing seventeen syllables per poem

6 **hacienda:** in Spain or Spanish territories, a ranch house

7 **Gupta:** Indian dynasty, A.D. c. 320–550

Sephiroth Tree of the Kabbalah: In Kabbalistic or Jewish mystical doctrine, the Sephiroth are primordial emanations of the Godhead, often diagramed as parts of either a man or a tree.

understand that, along with his contempt for himself, there is an abiding arrogance. He refuses medication. They can't make him take it, any more than they can keep him in a hospital. He has harmed no one. One night, in one of these rooms, he will set himself on fire.

10 He talks. Or blurts: scraps from Oriental philosophers—Lao-tzu,° I think—puns, incantations, obscenities, names from the past. There are conspiracies; I am part of one of them. He grins, winces, slumps, is suddenly tired, wants me to get out almost as much as I want to get out, seems to have lapsed in a permanent parenthesis. Anyway, I have a busy schedule.

11 Well, speed kills slowly, and he fiddled too much with the oxygen flow to his brain. He wanted ecstasy and revelation, the way we grew up wanting a bicycle, a car, a girlfriend. These belonged to us by right, as middle-class Americans. So, then, did salvation belong to us by right. I would like to thank Timothy Leary° and all the other sports of the 1960's who helped make this bad trip possible. I wish R. D. Laing° would explain to me, once again and slowly, how madness is a proof of grace. "The greatest magician," said Novalis,° "would be the one who would cast over himself a spell so complete that he would take his own phantasmagorias as autonomous appearances."

12 One goes back to the rented car and pretending to be a Californian as, perhaps, one had been pretending to be a brother. It is odd, at my age, suddenly to have become an only child.

STUDY QUESTIONS

1. Why does Leonard narrate this story in the present tense? To generate possible answers, read a few paragraphs changing *is* to *was, are* to *were,* and so on, and note the difference in effect.
2. What is Leonard's attitude toward his brother, and in what ways does it come across? Consider the author's manner of writing as well as his direct expressions of opinion.
3. What is the significance of "California" in this piece written by a longtime resident of New York? (You will find relevant material in paragraphs 2, 6, and 12.)
4. What meaning or meanings do you attach to Leonard's title? Who

[10] **Lao-tzu:** Chinese philosopher, sixth century B.C.; supposed to have founded taoism

[11] **Timothy Leary:** former professor who convinced many young people in the 1960s to "tune in, turn on, drop out"

R. D. Laing: influential British psychological theorist who has claimed that society, not the schizophrenic, is truly crazy

Novalis: pen name of Friedrich von Hardenberg (1772–1801), German poet

is "the only child," and how does Leonard's delayed answer to that question produce a strong rhetorical effect?

5. Now that you have finished reading this essay, look again at the opening paragraph. What previously overlooked hints of trouble do you find in Leonard's early remarks about his brother? And why do you think Leonard chose to begin as he did, with superficially "positive" details, instead of immediately revealing that his brother had become schizophrenic?

Edward Hoagland

Edward Hoagland is a novelist, an essayist and a writer of books about nature and travel. Many of his best pieces can be found in *The Edward Hoagland Reader* (1979).

A LOW-WATER MAN

1 Leave the astronauts out of it, and the paratroop teams that free-fall for 10,000 feet or skate down by means of those flattish, maneuverable new parachutes. Leave out the six people who have survived the 220-foot fall from the Golden Gate Bridge, and the divers of Acapulco, who swan-dive 118 feet, clearing outcrops of 21 feet as they plunge past the sea cliff. Leave out even the ordinary high diver, who enters the pool rigid and pointed after a comely jackknife. Come down from such lofty characters to Henri LaMothe—who on his seventieth birthday last April dove from a 40-foot ladder into a play pool of water 12 inches deep.

2 The high diver in his development first increases his height, then crowds more gainers° and twists into his drop, but LaMothe's progress in middle age and since has not involved ascending higher. Rather, he has provided himself with less and less water to land in: an ambition oddly private and untheatrical. Three feet, two feet, twenty inches, sixteen inches, fourteen inches. He strikes, not headfirst or feetfirst, which would be the finish of him, but on the arched ball of his belly. Inevitably, his endeavor over the years has been to manage somehow to jump into no water at all in the end. Since this is impossible, he is designing a break-away plastic pool whose sides will collapse as he hits, so that except for the puddles

---

[2] **gainers:** backward somersaults

remaining on the pavement, he will at least experience the sensation of having done just exactly that.

3 It's as if LaMothe hasn't heard that during his lifetime man has learned to fly, or that he knows that the flying we do is not really flying. In the meantime his posture resembles a flying squirrel's. Apparently nobody else entertains similar ambitions, although one of the old-time carnival thrills was for a stunt man to jump feetfirst from a platform into a very considerably deeper hogshead° of water, doing what divers describe as a tuck° as he entered, then partly somersaulting and scooping madly. As the person dropped, he could steer just a bit by tilting his head—the head being the heaviest mass in the body—but like Henri's feat, this one was gilded with none of the nifty, concise aesthetics of fancy diving: no "points" to be scored, no springboard to bound from, no Hawaiian plunge after the midair contortions into a sumptuous, deep-blue, country-club pool, with a pretty crawl stroke afterwards to carry him out of the way of the next competitor. Such a performer lived on hot dogs and slept with the ticket seller and often received an involuntary enema through the two pairs of trunks that he wore; got sinus and mastoid infections and constant colds from the water forced into his nose.

4 LaMothe dives, however—doesn't jump—into water that scarcely reaches his calves as he stands up, his hands in a Hallelujah gesture. His sailor hat never leaves his head, his back stays dry unless the wash wets him, and yet so bizarre is the sight of a person emerging from water so shallow that one's eye sees him standing there as if with his drawers fallen around his feet. As he plummets, his form is as ugly and poignant as the flop of a frog—nothing less ungainly would enable him to survive —and, watching, one feels witness to something more interesting than a stunt—a leap for life into a fire net, perhaps.

5 He wears a thin white-sleeved bodysuit that looks like a set of long johns (the crowd is likely to titter), and, up on his jointed ladder, huddles into a crouch, holding onto the shafts behind him. Like a man in the window of a burning building, he squats, stares down, hesitating, concentrating, seeming to quail, and finally letting go, puts out his arms in what seems a clumsy gesture, creeping into space between gusts of wind. He sneaks off the top of the ladder, spreading his fingers, reaching out, arching his back, bulging his stomach, cocking his head back, gritting his teeth, never glancing down, and hits in the granddaddy of all bellywhoppers, which flings water twenty feet out.

6 Though one's natural impulse when falling is to ball up to protect one's vitals, he survives precisely by thrusting his vitals *out.* He goes *splat.* And when a microphone is put to him—"How do you do it?"—

---

[3] **hogshead:** a large cask, especially for wine

tuck: a diving move in which the knees are bent and the thighs pulled close to the chest

Henri says, "Guts!" grinning at the pun. "Why do you do it?" asks the reporter. "I get a *bang* out of it!" sez LaMothe, sez that he is "a low-water man." In his long johns, white-haired, in that tremulous hunch forty feet up a guyed-out magnesium ladder that he folds up and wheels about for fees of a few hundred dollars, he's anything but an Evel Knievel. He's from vaudeville, a fire victim, his career a succession of happenstances.

7 In Chicago, growing up pint-sized with the nickname Frenchy—his father, a South Side carpenter, was from Montreal—he dove off coal tipples,° bridges and boxcars, swimming and swaggering at the 76th Street Beach, doing the Four-Mile Swim off Navy Pier. In the winter he swam indoors with a gang that included Johnny Weissmuller, who was already swinging from the girders over the pool. But Henri's hands were too small, his build too slight for competitive swimming. To make a living he drove a cab and posed at the Chicago Art Institute, where he began to draw too. He stayed up late, speeding around town to neighborhood Charleston° contests, four or five in a night—this being the Roaring Twenties—winning up to a hundred dollars an evening. He quit modeling in order to Charleston full time, closing his act with handstands, back bends, and a belly-flop, sliding and rolling across the waxed floor. His girlfriend's specialty was the split; she'd kick him into his belly-flop, do the split over him and "lift" him up with two fingers and dance on his stomach as he leaned over backwards, balancing on his hands. They were local champions, and by and by he invented an Airplane Dance, his arm the propeller—"the Lucky Lindy," for Lindbergh—which he claims was adapted into the Lindy Hop. June Havoc and Gypsy Rose Lee's famously stingy stage mama took him to New York City as one of six "Newsboys" in their hoofer show, but he quit to dance in a musical called *Keep It Clean.* By 1928 he was dancing at the Paramount as "Hotfoot Henri" ("Hotpants" backstage), usually planted among the ushers or as a dummy sax player in the orchestra pit when the show began. The clowning, pat repartee and belly-busters were right up his alley; on occasion he still will flop on his breadbasket into a puddle of beer at home to startle guests, or lie flat and lift his wife Birgit by the strength of his stomach muscles.

8 Although he'd been thankful to dancing for whisking him away from the Windy City and the life of a commercial artist drawing pots and pans for newspaper ads, after the 1929 crash he had to scratch for a job. He designed Chinese menus to pay for his meals, did flyer layouts for theaters and bands, and painted signs. He was art editor of the *Hobo News,* later the *Bowery News,* and tinkered, streamlining the stapler used

---

7 **tipples:** devices that tip a freight car to dump its contents
Charleston: a vigorous dance that typified the "Jazz Age" of the 1920s

everywhere nowadays, and inventing a "Bedroom Mood Meter" to post on the wall, like the ones sold in Times Square novelty shops. He got work drawing advertising for a Long Island plastics company, and actually prospered; even flew his own plane. Mushing down for a landing, he would think of the pratfalls he had performed in the Charleston contests and his belly-flops back on Muscle Beach, clowning his way to popularity.

9 Clowning on the board at the swimming club for the executives, he heard the suggestion that he ought to do it professionally, and so after a stint in a shipyard during World War II he went swimming with Johnny Weissmuller's troupe in Peru. Then he went to Italy with his own water show, the "Aquats," in partnership with two girls, one of whom, a Dane called Birgit Gjessing, became his wife. Birgit had been an actress in Germany during the war, a swimmer before that, and a puppeteer back home in Denmark, marking time after fleeing the collapse of the Reich.° She's a lean lady of fifty-seven with a quick expressive face, a school counselor now, but she remembers playing chess in a wine cellar near Mainz during the worst of the bombing. At one point in 1944 she traded her winter coat for a bicycle, thinking to swim the Rhine while holding it over her head and then peddle on home.

10 Henri would emulate the dives the girls did and mess everything up, or get into a race and be towed through the water, roped to a car. He dressed as Sweet Pea or Baby Snooks° with a curl painted on his forehead. Wheeled to the pool in a buggy by Birgit, dressed in a starchy costume, he would scramble up on the high diving board while his nurse underneath pleaded with him to climb down. She would fall in, and he would pancake on top of her, landing crisscross. He used break-off boards to make his dive doubly abrupt, or wore a pullover sweater fifteen feet long, which would still be unraveling as he stumbled backwards into his fall. In a beret, with his French mustache, he'd put on blue long johns with rolled-up newspapers over his biceps and a great cape and, calling himself Stupor Man, bend "iron" bars and launch himself on a mission of mercy from a high place, only to crash on his belly into the water. He would "drown" and need artificial respiration, but as the girls bent over him, would squirt water at them from his mouth. Then, running to apologize to Birgit, he would trip, belly-whop, and skid into her.

11 He wore low-necked bathing suits through which he could push his bay window, and sometimes to publicize the show would stand on his elbows on a building ledge, drinking coffee, eating a doughnut. Unfortunately it wasn't until both he and the century were into their fifties that

[9] **Reich:** the Third Reich (1933–1945), Hitler's German state

[10] **Sweet Pea, Baby Snooks:** fictitious child characters of comic strip and radio, respectively

his agent had sense enough to tip him off that the dive he was doing anyway as a water comedian would earn more money if done straight, so he speaks of those first twenty years of diving as "wasted." Then it was maybe another two thousand leaps before his seventieth birthday provided a gimmick to get him a *Daily News* centerfold and a spot on a David Frost show. For part of this long period he practiced commercial art in New York, but New Year's Eve would find him in Miami Beach dressed as the Baby New Year, poised in a third-floor hotel window as the clock tolled twelve, diving into "Lake Urine," the kiddie pool. He sprang out of trees, from flagpole yardarms and roofs—once from the ensign standard forty-seven feet up into two feet of water in the Westchester Country Club wading pool. Touring the country clubs, they "ate lentils," says Birgit. And always Henri looked a bit silly as he stood up, the water lapping at his shins: the less water the sillier.

12 Water shows are lumped with ice shows in the lower echelon of show business. The very term has a kiddie ring. Indeed, Birgit still shivers, remembering a week in Quebec when they had to perform in a hockey rink, paired with a skating follies, in water poured into a tank right on top of the ice. She wore a fish costume and executed finny undulations to the *Basin Street Blues,* but otherwise, as always, tried to get herself and the rest of the ballet swimmers out of the water at frequent intervals to remind the audience that they were really human, not fishy, in shape. Ice skaters have no such identity problem. Water, on the other hand, elemental, deep, somber, healing as it is, imparts a nobility to swimming which no ice show can match. With the mysterious oceans behind it, stretching around the world, water can be a powerful ally.

13 But Henri, leaping into a thin film of water, has sacrificed the majesty of the ocean to the bravery of his frog dive. Landing as he does, on the paunch, the craw, the crop, he loses the pretensions to dignity of mankind as well. It's raw, realer than drama, and tremendously poignant; it's his masterpiece, he says, in a life of inventing, which, even when he's been shabbily treated on the show-business scene, nobody has been able to steal away from him. He talks now of diving from the Eiffel Tower or the Leaning Tower of Pisa, combining this with his dream of diving at last into no water at all.

14 He's a short, plump, pigeonlike man who rubs his stomach continually, bends his back and bulges his chest. His look is matter-of-fact, like a man calculating practicalities, yet self-preoccupied, like one who knows pain and catastrophe. Though he dives on an empty stomach with lungs half filled, he lives by the bulge of his stomach. Clapping his hands, he will demonstrate how his arched back is the key to surviving. If air is trapped between the hands the clap is loud, but if one hand is convex the impact is muted. Just so, he explains, an air pocket under his belly would "split me right open." His belly is holding up fine, but his back is decidedly less limber; his scrapbook of photographs testifies to

what a bend he could bring to his work only a decade ago. Offstage he looked the daredevil then, and back in the fifties, his two lady partners would give him a rubdown after his feat. Now, because of the slackening that old age effects on the best of bodies, except for his stern mouth and nose he looks more like a health nut maintaining his youth.

15 He has a fluffy ring of white hair around his bald head, and likes being up on his ladder—says that he's happy up there. His beloved round pool glows like a globe below him, even seeming to expand. He says that a power goes out from him to intimidate the water. "That water is going to take the punishment, not me." Kids always ask whether it hurts. "Why do you care if it hurts?" he asks them. At the Hampton, Virginia boat show, where I watched him leap, his dressing room was the aisle between the showers and toilets. Among other exercises he did his stretching drill holding on to a sink and swinging from the top of a toilet stall. "Coffee's working," he said, because emptying his bowels was part of the ritual so he would feel "clean," ready for the impact. He drank a cup half an hour before he climbed up the ladder, both as a laxative and to bring an alive feeling to his stomach. Women sometimes ask if he wears a jock strap, but "I just put my tail between my legs and go." After the evening act he celebrated with a swig of whisky, rippling his stomach anatomy to help it down as he used to do to amuse the students at the Chicago Art Institute. For five or six hours afterwards in his room at the Holiday Inn he let his nerves unwind with the aid of beer, while concocting a vegetable-fruit mix in his blender and soup pot, the day's one big meal.

16 Once when he was a young man LaMothe swam the St. Lawrence—something his father before him had done—fetching up at a convent, where the nuns hid their eyes. And once he was paid three thousand dollars for a week at the San Antonio HemisFair, "banging my belly." Working shopping malls and sports shows, he carries his pool in a shopping bag; it's a flimsy low roll of fencing with a plastic liner which sways with the waves of the blow. (Again, Henri's agent had to wise him up to the hammy fact that the sides ought to be down as low as the water.) On his ladder he lets all other sights and sounds except the bull's-eye blur out. He crouches, "hoping for" rather than aiming for it, and lets go, putting his froggy arms out as his body falls. A team of accident experts from General Motors has tested him and concluded that he hits with the force of gravity multiplied seventy times; or, with his weight, 10,500 pounds.

17 So he does what the bigger kids couldn't do, long after they have given up their own specialties. And since the death wish of a daredevil who is seventy years old must be fairly well under control, perhaps the best explanation for why he continues is that this is what he is good at. Humiliation is a very good school for clowns, and, watching him, as with certain other notable clowns, one is swept with a tenderness for

him as he lands, God's Fool,° safe and sound and alive once again. As with them, our fascination is enhanced because at the same time that he has sought our applause, he has seemed to try to obscure our appreciation, make the venture difficult for us to understand, and thereby escape our applause—a "low-water man."

STUDY QUESTIONS

1. In what ways does Hoagland's opening paragraph set the tone for the rest of his essay? By what means does the author secure our interest in Henri LaMothe?
2. Once Hoagland begins describing LaMothe, how does he make him vivid and appealing? If you find the portrait *un*appealing in any respects, which passages put you off? On reconsideration, can you guess why Hoagland nevertheless felt that he should include those passages?
3. Characterize the author's attitude toward LaMothe, locating whatever signals you can find.
4. What kind of language does Hoagland use in this essay, and to what effect? Does his diction reveal anything about his general outlook on the world?
5. Carefully reread Hoagland's final sentence, and ask yourself if it could apply to Hoagland himself as well as LaMothe. Is there a sense in which this essay has been the work of a "low-water man"?

---

[17] **God's Fool:** a simple, innocent person who, without caring to protect himself, is protected by God

Shana Alexander

Shana Alexander, who was seen by millions as a commentator on CBS's *Sixty Minutes,* spent twenty years working for *Life* and then *Newsweek* as a columnist and reporter. In addition to writing a book on Patricia Hearst, she has collected many of her pieces in *Talking Woman* (1976), from which this essay is taken. Judy Garland died in 1969, eight years after the first publication of Alexander's portrait of her.

JUDY GARLAND

1 Up a dark alley to the stage door hurries a strange little creature bundled in mink from ears to ankles. In the dim light it looks like a fur shmoo° wearing a topknot of hair curlers.

2 Inside the jampacked theater, tension hangs like a net between the audience and the big orchestra on stage. The overture begins, and one by one all the familiar hoped-for melodies come flooding back. Each time the musicians launch a new one across the footlights, fans send back salvos of applause, and with every volley the emotional pressure inside the hall rises a few more degrees. Finally the vast space above the audience shimmers with visions of clanging trolley cars, men that got away, and birds flying over the rainbow. At this point in the series of identical musical evenings which have taken place recently in fourteen major U.S. cities, a plump little thirty-eight-year-old woman hiding behind furls of dusty curtain knows it is again time to go to work, and to deafening billows of applause that drown out the orchestra's final crashing chords, Miss Judy Garland trots cheerfully to center stage.

3 The uproar subsides, the songs begin. ". . . So keep on smiling, 'cause when you're SMILING . . ." At first the audience cannot believe it will last. "You *go* to my head. . . . I could cry—salty tears—" The big, sobby voice flows out unrestrained across the footlights, rich as caramel, solid as lava. This is the *old* Judy Garland voice. ". . . Who cares what banks *fail* in Yonkers, long as you've got a kiss that CONquers?" She's strutting now, balancing on the slender legs and prancing like a pony. At the end of Act I comes a performance of "San Francisco" so brassy, so sassy, delivered with such a full head of steam that one expects the whole theater to pull away from the levee and start churning downriver under its own power.

4 More than a concert is under way in this hall now; it is a tribal celebration. "I—can't—give—you—anything but love, baby . . ." After the first four notes, everybody recognizes the song at the same instant,

[1] **shmoo:** dumpy, lovable little animal in the late Al Capp's comic strip, *Li'l Abner*

and 4,000 people gasp with pleasure. The hot, solid voice speaks personally to each listener until the entire audience has been hypnotized into one huge multicelled organism. The tribal celebration takes on overtones of a mystical experience. "I'm gonna love you like nobody's loved you . . . I'm gonna *love* you, I'm gonna *love* you . . ." Then the Vesuvius° of torch songs, "Stormy Weather," sung with tears in her voice, her eyes, her throat, running down her neck. By the end of Act II (*"Zing* went the *strings* . . . Clang, clang, clang! Rock-a-bye your bay-BEE! . . ."), she has the crowd on its feet, shouting and swaying down the aisles, reaching up over the footlights to touch her hand. Comes the final heart-stopping cry of innocence and unbearable longing, "Why then, oh why . . . can't I?" and on some nights the true believers come swarming up onto the stage like lemmings.

5 It is over. The tribe staggers homeward to sleep off the magic spell. When they awaken, they are a tribe no longer, just individuals, tinker, tailor, soldier, sailor, and nobody can quite say what the uproar was all about. Yet the next time Judy Garland walks out onstage in another town to face thousands of different people, the same thing will happen again. And if she doesn't appear for five years or ten, they will still remember and still pack the theater in hopes that the magic will come again. And if she can't sing another note, they will stand in the aisles and shout, "We love you, Judy!" and "Just stand there, Judy!" For Judy Garland today is more than the most electrifying entertainer to watch on stage since Al Jolson. She has moved beyond talent and beyond fame to become the rarest phenomenon in all show business: part bluebird, part phoenix,° she is a legend in her own time.

6 Sometimes in the evangelical frenzy of her finale, as the crowds scream hoarsely for "More! More! We love you! We want more!" one gets the feeling that Judy Garland may be about to cut a vein. By temperament she is incapable of holding anything of herself in reserve. This gives her performance an old-fashioned theatrical excitement, as if a shower of Roman candles were coming over the footlights. It is a style marvelously florid in this cool electronic era of entertainment. For Garland fans, her great warmth and responsiveness generate the enormous emotional identification that each listener feels for Judy personally. It is what Spencer Tracy is talking about when he says, "A Garland audience doesn't just listen, they feel. They have their arms around her when she works." It is an all-out, go-for-broke performance that takes everything to give.

7 Seen from backstage, Judy sometimes suggests a Calliope° that has been mortally wounded. At intermission she staggers to her dressing

---

4 **Vesuvius:** active volcano in southwest Italy

5 **phoenix:** mythical bird fabled to burn itself to death every five hundred years and rise from its ashes

7 **Calliope:** in Greek mythology, the Muse of heroic poetry

room, gasping and clutching her middle, panting that she cannot possibly finish the show, she is too exhausted, too hot, there is a dagger in her throat. She tears off her soggy costume and sips a glass of white wine as her hairdresser blows icy air over her heaving back and shoulders with a portable dryer. But ten minutes later, the streaked makeup restored, the limp hairdo repuffed, she is zippered into the next costume and ready to go back to work. Often visitors comment on Judy's powers of physical recovery. "Well, you know, I'm like Rocky Graziano,"° she says amiably, and with a little giggle she scampers back toward the stage.

8 When she comes off at the end of her show, she sometimes must be helped to her dressing room. Sprawled on a couch in her fuzzy blue robe (a sentimental talisman from her daughter, Liza), waiting for enough strength to flow back so that she can dress and make her way through the huge crowd gathering now at the stage door, Judy talks about what it feels like to face the kind of frenzied, revivalist receptions she has been getting.

9 "You stand there in the wings," she reflects, "and sometimes you want to yell because the band sounds so good. Then you walk out and if it's a really great audience, a very strange set of emotions can come over you. You don't know what to do. It's a combination of feeling like Queen Victoria and an absolute ass. Sometimes a great reception—though God knows I've had some great receptions and I ought to be prepared for it by now—can really throw you. It kind of shatters you so that you can lose control of your voice and it takes two or three numbers to get back into your stride. I lift my hand in a big gesture in the middle of my first number and if I *see* it's not trembling then I know I haven't lost my control.

10 "A really great reception makes me feel like I have a great big warm heating pad all over me. People en masse have always been wonderful to me. I truly have a great love for an audience, and I used to want to prove it to them by giving them blood. But I have a funny new thing now, a real determination to make people enjoy the show. I want to give them two hours of just *pow!*"

11 This all-out quality, this determination to give everything she has, is a trait that Judy was born with. It is the secret of her success as a performer and it lies at the heart of the Garland legend. But it has taken a lifetime in show business for Judy to learn how to give a maximum of *pow!* with a minimum of blood, and in the course of her thirty-five-year-long lesson in this difficult art, the woman behind the legend has many times come close to destruction.

Rocky Graziano: American boxer (1922–1974), noted for his punishing middleweight championship fights with Tony Zale

12 Judy, whose real name is Frances Ethel Gumm, has been a professional singer since the night she dashed onstage at the Grand Theatre in Grand Rapids, Minnesota, where her family's small-time vaudeville act was booked for Christmas week, and sang two impromptu choruses of "Jingle Bells." She was two and a half years old, and thereafter she toured as the youngest of the Gumm Sisters. "I had great fun as a little girl," Judy says today. "We played games backstage. Then I went on, sang, took bows, came off, and had my mother do my ringlets up again. People always applauded and it was all rather pleasant."

13 It was very much less pleasant when, at twelve, she became a child movie star at M-G-M. For eleven years, after her triumph in *The Wizard of Oz,* though audiences clung to her image as an innocent child skipping along the yellow brick road without a care in the world, she was in reality keeping pace with the most backbreaking production schedule in Hollywood history. While she was still in her teens, she completed twelve pictures, nearly all of them long, difficult, exhausting song-and-dance extravaganzas. On film the result was wonderful: from *Strike Up the Band* through *For Me and My Gal, Meet Me in St. Louis,* and *Easter Parade,* she was about the nicest, prettiest, most talented minstrel girl a moviegoer could hope to see.

14 But the making of the movie star very nearly crippled the girl. M-G-M was cashing in as fast and as often as it could, and nobody worked harder at becoming a star than Judy herself. By driving herself mercilessly, by loading up with stimulants to keep going and then with sleeping pills to relax, she managed to make thirty movies for her studio, every one of them with a high professional sheen. But between pictures, instead of the vacations she needed, she began having nervous breakdowns. Before she was twenty-three years old, she had had three breakdowns and two marriages, first to bandleader David Rose, then to Director Vincente Minnelli.

15 Under the relentless necessity of laying golden eggs for M-G-M, she became a frazzled song-and-dance zombie. She was difficult, impossible. There was a series of suspensions, recriminations, tears, forgiveness, brief rest periods, then more work, more breakdowns. On June 17, 1950, after she failed to report for a Saturday dance rehearsal with Fred Astaire, the studio suspended her for the third time. Despondent and frantic, M-G-M's prize goose dashed into the bathroom and slashed her neck with a broken water glass, and the golden eggs stopped.

16 A few months later, "for her own best interests," the studio released her from her contract. She was considered unemployable. Her salary had not been high by Hollywood standards, and her frequent breakdowns plus the normal movie star's expenses had taken all she earned. Her second marriage had just fallen apart. She was twenty-eight years old.

17 "After I was thrown out of Metro, I really went to pieces for a while," Judy says today. "All I wanted to do was eat and hide. I lost all

my self-confidence. For ten years I was afraid of stores, planes, cars. When I worked, I suffered agonies of stage fright. People had literally to push me out on stage." The person who did the pushing and at times was able to restore Judy's sagging confidence in herself both as a woman and as a performer was Sid Luft, a onetime test pilot for Douglas Aircraft. Luft became Judy's manager, then her husband.

18 Under Luft's stewardship, Judy began making more comebacks than a yo-yo. Over a period of nearly ten years, she played the Palladium, the Palace,° nightclubs, theaters. Everywhere she went she drew record crowds and large grosses. She and Luft made their own movie, *A Star Is Born,* and some critics called it the finest musical ever to come out of Hollywood. She did a TV show for the biggest audience in history. She already had one daughter, Liza Minnelli, and she and Luft had two more children, Lorna and Joseph.

19 But between the high points came many lows. She was obviously often ill; she couldn't pay her bills; there were rumors that she was a hopeless alcoholic, a drug addict; she didn't show up for work, she collapsed onstage, she lost her voice, she lost her figure, she fought with everybody. But it was during these same years of violent ups and downs that the public image of Garland as the bluebird really began to take wing. The struggles of the woman, no longer hidden by the smoke screen of studio publicity, were the making of the legend.

20 By 1958 and 1959, the Garland yo-yo had begun to lose its resiliency. The great voice had perceptibly begun to fail along with everything else, and though people by the thousands still came to see her, all they saw onstage some nights was a dumpy woman singing a quavery lullaby. Neither Judy nor her public knew then how sick she really was. "Sometimes I felt as if I was performing in a blizzard," she says today. At other times she would suddenly feel nauseated or dizzy in the middle of her performance. This was a new terror. "You are never so *alone* as when you are ill onstage. The most nightmarish feeling in the world is to suddenly feel like throwing up in front of four thousand people."

21 By autumn of 1959, Judy was unable to work at all. She felt frightened, sick, and mentally confused. In late November, she was admitted to a hospital in New York City. She looked awful. Her face was a puffy white mask. Her eyes were glazed, she felt faint, she couldn't remember things. Her whole body was grossly fat and bloated. Her limbs were so stiff and swollen that sometimes she could barely move, and at other times she trembled uncontrollably. She was clapped into bed at once, and batteries of tests were begun.

22 All her alarming symptoms, including the mental ones, turned out to have a real physical basis. The doctors said she had hepatitis and that it was due, at least in part, to the combined effects of certain tranquiliz-

[18] **Palladium, Palace:** respectively a famous London theater; a Broadway theater

ers and diet pills which previous doctors, treating previous breakdowns, had prescribed for her. The new doctors guessed she might have been walking around with hepatitis for as long as three years. The patient admitted she had swallowed a great many drugs over the past fifteen years, careening and ricocheting between sleeping pills and pep pills, diet medicines and nerve tonics, in her struggle for physical and emotional stability.

23 There were many puzzling symptoms to her latest collapse, and as the weeks dragged on, platoons of specialists were summoned to review her case. Finally one day the chief specialist appeared at her bedside. Behind him stood Sid Luft, looking equally grave. "Miss Garland, you are still a young woman and I wish I did not have to tell you this," the doctor said. "But I have no choice. For the rest of your life all your physical activity must be curtailed. Everything you eat and drink must be strictly regulated. You must learn to accept the fact that you are a *permanent* semi-invalid. It goes without saying that under no circumstances can you ever work again."

24 Up to that moment it had been a classic Hollywood bedside scene. Then the patient spoke. "Whoopee!" she cried weakly and fell back among the pillows.

25 After five months of hospital care, she spent four more months convalescing at her home in Beverly Hills. She appeared publicly for the first time in July to campaign for her friend Jack Kennedy, and then rather suddenly she flew off to England alone.

26 This flight was the first sign that Judy Garland might have recovered from something more than hepatitis. Her fear of airplanes had once been so severe that she could not go near an airport without trembling. As Judy herself tells the story today, "When the doctor told me that work was out of the question for me forever, I felt greatly relieved. The pressure was off me for the first time in my life. Physically I recovered rather well because I'm a terribly strong woman, but I knew I had to get out of California. I was liked in California but nobody needed me. The phone never rang. In Hollywood I was somebody who *had been* a movie star."

27 In England Judy told the British press she hoped to settle there permanently. Her husband was detained in the United States but would join her in a few weeks. So would her three children. She took a town house, bought a dog, took steps to enroll the children in English schools, and put her Beverly Hills house up for sale. She shopped in Mayfair and fed the pigeons in Trafalgar Square.° Life as a nonworking semi-invalid was turning out to be every bit as pleasant as she had hoped. She still looked chubby but the unhealthy bloat had almost disappeared.

[27] **Mayfair, Trafalgar Square:** respectively, a fashionable part of London, east of Hyde Park; a large square in downtown London, named after a famous British naval victory

By early autumn of 1960, she was feeling better than she had in years.

28 One sleepless night in London (she still suffered, as she has all her life, from galloping insomnia), she got out of bed, locked herself in the bathroom, turned on the hot shower full blast—both to drown out the sound of her voice and to pamper her long-unused throat with live steam—and began to run through some of her old arrangements. Twenty minutes later, she flung open the door, shook her groggy husband awake and, still steaming faintly, read him a list of some thirty-odd songs. "Are you sure it isn't too much?" he inquired, recalling the doctor's warning.

29 "Too much?" repeated Judy in a newly steamed voice that could carry to the second balcony. "If I die we'll know it's too much! That specialist! Where'd they import *him* from, Transylvania?" It must have been clear to sleepers for blocks around that Judy Garland was ready to go back to work.

30 Judy played her new show at the Palladium on August 28, 1960, and, in her words, "It was a pistol!" She played the show in the provinces thereafter and a few times on the Continent. "My work was not going in any particular direction," she says now, "but I didn't care. I seemed to have a brand-new life." In her new life Judy Garland the performer was for the first time playing second fiddle to a high-spirited housewife with the horrible name of Frances Ethel Gumm Luft. As F.E.G. Luft, "I was terribly happy personally. I immensely enjoyed taking my kids to Battersea Park. I looked forward to the days. It sounds so corny to say it, but I felt reborn."

31 At the same time that Judy was being reborn in England, a Music Corporation of America talent agent in New York named Freddie Fields decided it was time to get reborn himself. Fields cut loose from MCA and went into business on his own as a combination personal manager, business manager, and agent for "a few select clients." Judy Garland, he knew from the show business grapevine, was in England, semiretired, personally happy but professionally drifting. What a challenge for a fledgling impresario! He obtained an appointment with Judy and flew to London.

32 The meeting was a pistol, too. "With Freddie, something clicked," Judy says. "He seemed to know how to do exactly what I could not do: channel my work." Returning to New York, Fields cut back the underbrush of a lifetime of managerial untidiness:

He settled his new client's three-year legal battle with CBS and negotiated a giant new TV spectacular.

He got her a starring role in a big new Hollywood movie, *Judgment at Nuremberg.*

He booked her for a fourteen-city, six-week U.S. concert tour, which was the quickest way simultaneously to prove to both the singer and her public that no one in the business could create as much pure theatrical excitement as Judy Garland, and also to begin paying off a huge pile of old bills.

33 Four months ago in Dallas, the phoenix aspect of the Garland legend was revealed to a U.S. audience for the first time. She gave the same show she had programmed in the shower. It lasted two and a quarter hours, left her shaking with fatigue, earned her two standing ovations and a newspaper review that began, with Texas grandeur and simplicity, "No entertainer has ever given such a show in Dallas . . ." Two nights later in Houston she gave the same show, got four standing ovations and, except for the geographical change, the same review: ". . . unquestionably the greatest show ever given in Houston."

34 Buoyed by Texas, Judy Garland went before a Hollywood camera this spring for the first time in six years to play the most un-Garland role ever invented—a drab little German *Hausfrau*° and onetime victim of Nazi persecution who returns to Nuremberg to testify against her former tormentors. Any actress would think twice before accepting the *Hausfrau* role: it was totally unglamorous, technically demanding and she would be playing against such giants as Spencer Tracy, Burt Lancaster, Richard Widmark, and Maximilian Schell, all of whom had important assignments in the same scene. For Judy in particular, the part seemed an insanity: she would not sing a note, she would be on screen for only nine minutes, and the salary was $50,000, a tiny fraction of what she used to be paid. Yet despite all obstacles, Judy and Fields realized that Hollywood needed fast, dramatic proof that Garland was a dependable, professional actress after all.

35 On her first day on the *Nuremberg* set, in the first scene of the day, *Hausfrau* Garland was required to burst into tears. As the cameras ground away, the actors did the scene once, twice, a third time. Finally in the middle of the sixth take Judy suddenly scowled, stamped her foot angrily and walked off the set. The entire crew froze: so it was just like the old days at M-G-M.

36 But it was not like the old days at all. As Judy explained to Director Kramer, "Damn it, Stanley, I can't do it. I've dried up. I'm too happy today to cry." Kramer called a ten-minute break, Garland retired to her dressing room to discompose herself, and when shooting resumed she was able to weep.

37 The night before she left Hollywood Judy went to a small party given by old friends. During the evening, Kramer telephoned from his office at the studio. He, Tracy, Widmark and screenwriter Abby Mann had just viewed the completed footage of her scenes for the first time. When the sequence ended, Kramer told her, the four men had stood up

---

[34] **Hausfrau:** (Ger.) housewife

all alone in the little projection room and burst into applause. At this news Judy shed her first real tears since coming back to her hometown. She was now completely ready in every way for the brutal but profitable concert tour.

38 Judy's financial objective these days is to pay off her old debts, then establish some trust funds for her three children. Alan Jay Lerner and Richard Rodgers hope to write a Broadway musical version of *Roman Holiday* for her. She is working on an autobiography of her first thirty-eight years, and Capitol Records will soon bring out *Judy At Carnegie Hall.* She will tape a TV spectacular in the fall and has scheduled more concert dates. But that's not all: among those negotiating for her services is, of all companies, M-G-M. Her total earnings for this year should be approximately a million dollars. After taxes, expenses, and old bills are paid, she will begin to see some of what managers call "keeping money" for the first time in years.

39 From then on, the chief beneficiaries of the Garland legend will be the three people in the world who are least interested in that legend and most interested in the woman herself: namely, Liza, Lorna, and Joe. This state of affairs is just fine with Judy, a devoted and skillful parent who, despite her own troubled past, has managed to raise a trio of remarkably untroubled and charming children. Sometimes when work forces her to be away from them, Judy says, "I have *no* ambition to be an actress, *no* ambition to be a singer, I have absolutely no drive. I just want to be a mother." But Judy does not envisage complete retirement, even when her debts are paid and her children provided for. She simply would prefer to work less often and under circumstances that she could control. So far, such control is a luxury she cannot afford.

40 The most grueling form of show business ever invented is the one-night stand, whether the performer is a third-rate juggler or a big star like Judy Garland. As the tour progresses, the physical wear and tear tends to increase. In addition to the intense physical exertion on stage (Judy works so hard that her heavy clothes drop to the dressing-room floor at the end of each act like suits of soggy armor), there are all the normal offstage touring problems of getting star, Manager David Begelman, conductor, three musicians, a hairdresser, and a secretary all transported from city to city every second day, on and off trains, in and out of hotels, taxied back and forth to theaters, seeing that everybody is fed, housed, rehearsed, and paid, and keeping track of a mountain of luggage packed with everything from tom-toms to chicken soup. The logistics of all this are carefully planned well in advance of the tour, and none of it is supposed to worry Judy. Her job is to sing, which is like saying that Sir Edmund Hillary's° job is to climb.

---

[40] **Sir Edmund Hillary:** New Zealand mountain climber who was coleader of the first successful ascent of Mt. Everest

41 Actually she becomes involved in everything. One night when the entourage arrived at the railroad station, a strip of red carpet was stretched across the tobacco-stained marble floor. The proud stationmaster was on hand to greet Miss Garland and invite her to wait in his private office until train time when he would personally escort her to her compartment. Judy said she would be delighted. A short while later the dispatcher wandered by and complained that he was having an awful time announcing trains lately. His throat hurt all the time.

42 "You're probably not using your voice right," Judy said. "Take a deep breath and I'll show you." The mink-coated star took hold of the startled dispatcher and pushed hard against his belly. "Feel it? *That's* where your power comes from." She gave him a light punch in the diaphragm. "And be very careful of those loud *eee* sounds. They'll give you a bleeding throat unless you keep your teeth open."

43 Judy copes with her own professional problems with equal efficiency and not much can happen in front of an audience that will faze her. Musically, she depends on her conductor, Mort Lindsey, and three permanent musicians (a jazz drummer, a bongo player, and a first trumpet) to weld the twenty-five-man local orchestras into a unit during the meticulous six-hour rehearsals that precede every concert. The orchestral surprises that do occur are usually caused by Judy's own sudden, powerful impact on the local musicians.

44 In one city, right in the midst of her blood-vessel-bursting final chorus of "Swanee," the brass section was so astonished by Judy's lung power that several men stopped playing and listened. In Buffalo a musician rose in the middle of a number, opened his coat, focused a camera dangling against his chest, clicked, wound, buttoned up, sat down, and got his viola back under his chin in time for his next passage.

45 If there are surprises during a performance, Judy lives through them. One night during "Over the Rainbow," standing on a blacked-out stage in front of 8,000 people, many of them sniffling audibly, her face illuminated by a single dramatic pin-spot, her eyes brimming with tears, she got as far as ". . . way up high—There's a land that I heard of . . ." when a rather large moth flew into her open mouth. With a flick of her tongue, she tucked the moth into her cheek, sang her way perfectly through the next twenty-eight bars while waiting for the blackout, then coughed, spit and stomped. When the lights came up she was seen bowing and smiling through her tears like a seraph.

46 Naturally enough Judy has occasional sore throats, and she knows from experience that the only balm and restorative is live steam. This commodity being sometimes hard to come by in a hotel room, she travels with a hot plate and a steam kettle for emergency treatments. But if a hotel does have good hot water in its pipes, she likes to take advantage of it. Before a performance, she often spends an hour or more in a steam-filled bathroom, reclining on a pile of sofa pillows like some

small Turkish odalisque,° writing postcards to her children and tidily steaming out her collection of knitted travel outfits which hang from the shower rod like a frieze of misty banners.

47 Her hotel room is also the setting for her continuing and incredibly complex battles with insomnia. The strain of giving people two hours of "just *pow!*" every other night makes it very difficult for Judy to unwind afterward, and her main problem on tour is to get enough rest or, on many nights, to get any sleep at all. Dinner may last until 1 A.M. and there is always *The Late, Late Show* but then, as any insomniac knows, come the desperate hours.

48 On tour Judy is no ordinary insomniac. She cannot take sleeping medicines because, when she awakens, she would be too "down" to perform, and if she then took a pep pill to get "up," her vibrato would go. Sometimes during the desperate hours, despite the steamings, despite all care, she can feel her throat closing up *right now!* What to do? Strong magic is needed. At these times Judy the woman must force herself to become the abject handmaiden of Judy the insomniac singer. Ah-ha, she will take the singer for a nice invigorating walk in the beautiful dawn! She dresses and goes outside. She returns invigorated, almost sleepy, but now hungry too. Suddenly she is positive she could fall asleep if only she had a nice hot bowl of Chinese egg-flower soup. She has arrived at the true black magic stage; she knows it, she has been here before and she is rather niftily prepared.

49 "The main problem when practicing witchcraft in strange hotel rooms," as Judy said later when telling this story, "is not to let room service notice anything unusual." At 6:30 one morning she plugged in her bathroom hot plate, rummaged in her luggage until she found a can of chicken noodle soup, found a beer can opener, and went to work. After half an hour's intense concentration, she got most of the noodles through the holes in the can lid. She sprinkled in some seasoning, also from her luggage, and set the soup to simmer. Now she needed only a raw egg and a soup bowl. This was easy. She telephoned room service and gave a very precise breakfast order: "This is Miss Garland speaking. I would like a glass of orange juice and some dry cereal please. Any kind. No, nothing else . . . Oh, I almost forgot. I like a raw egg in my orange juice, but I will put in the egg *myself.*" When the order arrived, Judy discarded the orange juice (which gives her hives) and the cereal (which she has not tasted in twenty years), assembled her soup, drank it, and drifted off at last to sleep.

50 The amount of sleep she is able to get varies, but the ritual of getting ready for the show does not. By the time she has to leave the hotel for the theater, Judy has already been fed (lamb chops and tea), coiffed (by her traveling hairdresser), meticulously made up (by herself

---

46 **odalisque:** female slave or concubine, frequently depicted in reclining postures

—short, medium, or long eyelashes, depending on the size of the theater), and soothed by a manager who says the acoustics are superb and by a conductor who swears that *this* band really swings. Her secretary has packed the giant suitcase with two complete changes of clothes, several spare pairs of sheer black nylons in the smallest size made, and a stack of towels for mopping up. Another bag holds a sack of ice cubes, tumblers, and a bottle or two of chilled white wine. The only alcohol Judy is now permitted to drink is diluted Liebfraumilch,° and she likes to keep a supply in her dressing room. While she is on stage, a friend stands by in the wings with an emergency glassful in case her throat suddenly should go dry between numbers.

51 By 8:50 P.M. at the theater, the overture is pounding forward and the star is dressed and waiting edgily in the darkened wings, borrowing a drag on somebody's cigaret, nibbling a mint, taking a last sip of Liebfraumilch-on-the-rocks and chattering inanely: "Well, what'll we all *do* for the next two hours?" The orchestra cannonballs toward its climax and just a few feet away the bass drum pounds its portentous rhythm: ". . . the road gets *rougher,* it's lonelier and *tougher . . .*" Without warning, Judy Garland suddenly turns her back on the watchers in the wings, sets her shoulders, takes what seems like a ten-gallon deep breath, and then—astonishingly, as one looks out from the darkness directly into the footlights' glare—she appears to glide away onto the bright-lit stage like a child's pull toy, powered by the rising wave of the applause itself.

STUDY QUESTIONS

1. How does Alexander's portrayal of Judy Garland differ from what we expect to hear about female movie stars?
2. Look through the quotations Alexander has included, and ask yourself what uses they serve. What difference would their absence have made?
3. Note that Alexander frequently refers to Garland in animal terms ("little creature," paragraph 1, "trots," paragraph 2, etc.). What is the function of such language?
4. Reread Alexander's first six paragraphs and then ask yourself why she has begun as she has. What points about Judy Garland come through at once, and how do they work for Alexander in the rest of the essay?
5. In what sense is Alexander's concluding paragraph an appropriate ending to this particular essay? Consider it in relation to the opening paragraph and to the main traits of Judy Garland's that Alexander wants to emphasize.

50 **Liebfraumilch:** a German white wine

CAPTURING IMMEDIATE EXPERIENCE

Jane Jacobs

Jane Jacobs, formerly an associate editor of *Architectural Forum,* is an expert on urban affairs. The essay below, describing her one-time neighborhood in New York City's Greenwich Village, is taken from her influential book *The Death and Life of Great American Cities* (1961).

SIDEWALK BALLET*

1 Under the seeming disorder of the old city, wherever the old city is working successfully, is a marvelous order for maintaining the safety of the streets and the freedom of the city. It is a complex order. Its essence is intricacy of sidewalk use, bringing with it a constant succession of eyes. This order is all composed of movement and change, and although it is life, not art, we may fancifully call it the art form of the city and liken it to the dance—not to a simple-minded precision dance with everyone kicking up at the same time, twirling in unison and bowing off en masse, but to an intricate ballet in which the individual dancers and ensembles all have distinctive parts which miraculously reinforce each other and compose an orderly whole. The ballet of the good city sidewalk never repeats itself from place to place, and in any one place is always replete with new improvisations.

2 The stretch of Hudson Street where I live is each day the scene of an intricate sidewalk ballet. I make my own first entrance into it a little after eight when I put out the garbage can, surely a prosaic occupation, but I enjoy my part, my little clang, as the droves of junior high school students walk by the center of the stage dropping candy wrappers. (How do they eat so much candy so early in the morning?)

3 While I sweep up the wrappers I watch the other rituals of morn-

*Title chosen by editor

ing: Mr. Halpert unlocking the laundry's handcart from its mooring to a cellar door, Joe Cornacchia's son-in-law stacking out the empty crates from the delicatessen, the barber bringing out his sidewalk folding chair, Mr. Goldstein arranging the coils of wire which proclaim the hardware store is open, the wife of the tenement's superintendent depositing her chunky three-year-old with a toy mandolin on the stoop, the vantage point from which he is learning the English his mother cannot speak. Now the primary children, heading for St. Luke's, dribble through to the south; the children for St. Veronica's cross, heading to the west, and the children for P.S. 41, heading toward the east. Two new entrances are being made from the wings: well-dressed and even elegant women and men with brief cases emerge from doorways and side streets. Most of these are heading for the bus and subways, but some hover on the curbs, stopping taxis which have miraculously appeared at the right moment, for the taxis are part of a wider morning ritual: having dropped passengers from midtown in the downtown financial district, they are now bringing downtowners up to midtown. Simultaneously, numbers of women in housedresses have emerged and as they crisscross with one another they pause for quick conversations that sound with either laughter or joint indignation, never, it seems, anything between. It is time for me to hurry to work too, and I exchange my ritual farewell with Mr. Lofaro, the short, thick-bodied, white-aproned fruit man who stands outside his doorway a little up the street, his arms folded, his feet planted, looking solid as earth itself. We nod; we each glance quickly up and down the street, then look back to each other and smile. We have done this many a morning for more than ten years, and we both know what it means: All is well.

4 The heart-of-the-day ballet I seldom see, because part of the nature of it is that working people who live there, like me, are mostly gone, filling the roles of strangers on other sidewalks. But from days off, I know enough of it to know that it becomes more and more intricate. Longshoremen who are not working that day gather at the White Horse or the Ideal or the International for beer and conversation. The executives and business lunchers from the industries just to the west throng the Dorgene restaurant and the Lion's Head coffee house; meat-market workers and communications scientists fill the bakery lunchroom. Character dancers come on, a strange old man with strings of old shoes over his shoulders, motor-scooter riders with big beards and girl friends who bounce on the back of the scooters and wear their hair long in front of their faces as well as behind, drunks who follow the advice of the Hat Council and are always turned out in hats, but not hats the Council would approve. Mr. Lacey, the locksmith, shuts up his shop for a while and goes to exchange the time of day with Mr. Slube at the cigar store. Mr. Koochagian, the tailor, waters the luxuriant jungle of plants in his window, gives them a critical look from the outside, accepts a compliment on them from two passers-by, fingers the leaves on the plane tree

in front of our house with a thoughtful gardener's appraisal, and crosses the street for a bite at the Ideal where he can keep an eye on customers and wigwag across the message that he is coming. The baby carriages come out, and clusters of everyone from toddlers with dolls to teen-agers with homework gather at the stoops.

5 When I get home after work, the ballet is reaching its crescendo. This is the time of roller skates and stilts and tricycles, and games in the lee of the stoop with bottletops and plastic cowboys; this is the time of bundles and packages, zigzagging from the drug store to the fruit stand and back over to the butcher's; this is the time when teen-agers, all dressed up, are pausing to ask if their slips show or their collars look right; this is the time when beautiful girls get out of MG's; this is the time when the fire engines go through; this is the time when anybody you know around Hudson Street will go by.

6 As darkness thickens and Mr. Halpert moors the laundry cart to the cellar door again, the ballet goes on under lights, eddying back and forth but intensifying at the bright spotlight pools of Joe's sidewalk pizza dispensary, the bars, the delicatessen, the restaurant and the drug store. The night workers stop now at the delicatessen, to pick up salami and a container of milk. Things have settled down for the evening but the street and its ballet have not come to a stop.

7 I know the deep night ballet and its seasons best from waking long after midnight to tend a baby and, sitting in the dark, seeing the shadows and hearing the sounds of the sidewalk. Mostly it is a sound like infinitely pattering snatches of party conversation and, about three in the morning, singing, very good singing. Sometimes there is sharpness and anger or sad, sad weeping, or a flurry of search for a string of beads broken. One night a young man came roaring along, bellowing terrible language at two girls whom he had apparently picked up and who were disappointing him. Doors opened, a wary semicircle formed around him, not too close, until the police came. Out came the heads, too, along Hudson Street, offering opinion, "Drunk . . . Crazy . . . A wild kid from the suburbs."*

8 Deep in the night, I am almost unaware how many people are on the street unless something calls them together, like the bagpipe. Who the piper was and why he favored our street I have no idea. The bagpipe just skirled° out in the February night, and as if it were a signal the random, dwindled movements of the sidewalk took on direction. Swiftly, quietly, almost magically a little crowd was there, a crowd that evolved into a circle with a Highland fling inside it. The crowd could be seen on the shadowy sidewalk, the dancers could be seen, but the

*He turned out to be a wild kid from the suburbs. Sometimes, on Hudson Street, we are tempted to believe the suburbs must be a difficult place to bring up children.

[8] **skirled:** played shrilly

bagpiper himself was almost invisible because his bravura was all in his music. He was a very little man in a plain brown overcoat. When he finished and vanished, the dancers and watchers applauded, and applause came from the galleries too, half a dozen of the hundred windows on Hudson Street. Then the windows closed, and the little crowd dissolved into the random movements of the night street.

9 The strangers on Hudson Street, the allies whose eyes help us natives keep the peace of the street, are so many that they always seem to be different people from one day to the next. That does not matter. Whether they are so many always-different people as they seem to be, I do not know. Likely they are. When Jimmy Rogan fell through a plate-glass window (he was separating some scuffling friends) and almost lost his arm, a stranger in an old T shirt emerged from the Ideal bar, swiftly applied an expert tourniquet and, according to the hospital's emergency staff, saved Jimmy's life. Nobody remembered seeing the man before and no one has seen him since. The hospital was called in this way: a woman sitting on the steps next to the accident ran over to the bus stop, wordlessly snatched the dime from the hand of a stranger who was waiting with his fifteen-cent fare ready, and raced into the Ideal's phone booth. The stranger raced after her to offer the nickel too. Nobody remembered seeing him before, and no one has seen him since. When you see the same stranger three or four times on Hudson Street, you begin to nod. This is almost getting to be an acquaintance, a public acquaintance, of course.

10 I have made the daily ballet of Hudson Street sound more frenetic than it is, because writing it telescopes it. In real life, it is not that way. In real life, to be sure, something is always going on, the ballet is never at a halt, but the general effect is peaceful and the general tenor even leisurely. People who know well such animated city streets will know how it is. I am afraid people who do not will always have it a little wrong in their heads—like the old prints of rhinoceroses made from travelers' descriptions of rhinoceroses.

11 On Hudson Street, the same as in the North End of Boston or in any other animated neighborhoods of great cities, we are not innately more competent at keeping the sidewalks safe than are the people who try to live off the hostile truce of Turf° in a blind-eyed city. We are the lucky possessors of a city order that makes it relatively simple to keep the peace because there are plenty of eyes on the street. But there is nothing simple about that order itself, or the bewildering number of components that go into it. Most of those components are specialized in one way or another. They unite in their joint effect upon the sidewalk, which is not specialized in the least. That is its strength.

---

11 **Turf:** urban term for a territory controlled by a youth gang, and hence dangerous ground for members of other gangs

STUDY QUESTIONS

1. Why do you suppose Jacobs puts her review of Hudson Street activities into the present tense? You should be able to find more than one reason.
2. Although Jacobs did not choose the title we have given this excerpt from *The Death and Life of Great American Cities,* it corresponds to the dominant figure of speech she uses. Look through the selection and note ways in which the idea of *ballet* is sustained. What are the advantages and disadvantages of choosing such a metaphor and carrying it through several pages?
3. Apart from the ballet metaphor, what is the main organizing principle in this section? Make note of passages that show this principle being worked out.
4. Jacobs evidently has a strong affection for New York City—and for all city neighborhoods that function well. What is her basic concept of a neighborhood that "works"? Do you find passages in which she seems to have sentimentalized the city?

Frank Rowesome, Jr.

Frank Rowesome, Jr., has been an editor of *Popular Science* and an official in the National Aeronautics and Space Administration. The present essay comes from one of his several books, *The Bright and Glowing Place* (1975).

APPLE AND BEECH, BIRCH AND OAK

1 Woodcutting is full of sensuous and kinesthetic rewards. There is the rhythmic *thock* of the axe, with every second stroke freeing flat-spinning chips of yellowish wood. The special alertness of felling builds up during preliminary notching cuts and rises to a breathless moment when the treetop loses the symmetry of its sway, hovers against the sky for a moment, and then sweeps over with fierce cracking as the trunk thunders to the ground with branches thrashing. When limbs are cut free with diagonal-slicing axe strokes, the ellipses of fresh-cut wood gleam against the bark in the soft forest light. As wood is bucked into carryable lengths, measured multiples of what your fireplace accepts, the saw generates little conical hills of cuttings; coarser than carpentry sawdust, these tiny cubes of pale damp wood creep into boot tops and

pockets. When wood is split in the yard by the woodshed there comes a time when a husky billet of hardwood, almost too big and cross-grained to be axe-splittable, nevertheless responds to a precise blow by dropping apart in two even pieces, their inner faces moist and fragrant at this first exposure to light and air. Toward dusk there is an enjoyably tired feeling as the day's yield is stacked for seasoning, the wedge-sectioned pieces fitted evenly, like a carefully built stone wall; only stovewood is allowed to remain in a tumbled heap.

2 Getting in your own firewood has much to recommend it, if not done of necessity. Felling, limbing, bucking, and splitting are the four basic steps in the process, none difficult to bring off passably and yet none so simple that your technique cannot be bettered. Prodigious exertions are not called for, although it is somewhat more strenuous than golf or other conventional absorbents of leisure. It is work that is likely to blister the hands or crick the back unless undertaken along a gentle slope of habituation. You can do a considerable amount of creative resting in the woods, seated on a log, absently rubbing tired muscles, studying the intricate topography of bark, reading the now-ended calendar of tree rings, smelling the fresh woody fragrances, watching the chipmunk or bluejay come closer to scout the meaning of your silence. Almost alone among outdoor pursuits woodcutting is unaffected by weather, and can be engaged in at all times except drenching cold rain or driving sleet (it is quite magical during a snowstorm). You automatically work at a tempo attuned to the temperature, slowly enough to keep from steaming on a golden day in Indian summer, briskly enough to keep comfortable when north winds icily rake the woods.

3 Unlike many leisure activities, woodcutting delivers a product in return for time and effort, a pile of beautiful well-split hardwood, abounding in promise of bright fires radiating their magic on winter nights. The degree of satisfaction is curiously high. It is not altogether clear why a filled woodshed should be so reassuring, more so than shelves of cans and jars in the cupboard or a freezer chest chocked with frosted parcels. Some shadowy motivation is buried here, something to do with the peripheral rewards of possessions, and with a need for making experience tangible and visible to others.

4 Perhaps a clue can be sensed by considering people whose leisure activities do *not* afford a product. If you observe the cameras carried in such profusion by returning travelers as they flow through customs weirs, it is possible to conclude that the profoundest need filled by vacation photography is documentation. Pictures, studied and shown about, function as a kind of certification of experience, and generally they don't bleach as fast as memory. Returning travelers carry, in addition to luggage and cameras, an extraordinary volume of gifts and bric-a-brac. From the balcony above the arrival pens at an international airport, a jetload of tourists tends to look as if most of them were victims

of besetting generosity or compulsive connoisseurship. The scene suggests that possessions bought abroad and carried home have high value as confirmation of time well spent, proof less evanescent than airline tags left dangling and customs symbols chalked on luggage. People appear to buy knickknacks for the oddest of motives, not the least of which is the conversation that can be casually constructed about them later. Evidently recollection is for many persons simply not sufficient, and a physical thing or simulacrum image supplies welcome additional testimony.

5 As for the filled woodshed, it is true that few countrymen whip out a camera to document the achievement of several cords of beech, but it *is* noticeable that conspicuous supplies of firewood are frequently stacked in an open shed in no way concealed from those driving past. Firewood is after all not as inherently invisible as those parcels in the freezer, and a possession that is invisible is somehow slightly diminished.*

6 Getting in firewood is a many-faceted activity, and not the least of its benefits is a sense of calm. You may stride off to the woods bearing, along with axe and saw, a well-nourished grievance; you are almost certain to return with, if you think of it at all, detached surprise that the matter could have been so troublesome. Woodcutting is a sovereign remedy for a churny mind, a specific for festering concern. It works its spell not so much by substitution—which is what skiing does, it being difficult to cherish a grievance while hurtling downhill in continuous alarm over narrowly averted catastrophe—as by the more subtle method of transference. Using an axe or splitting-sledge is of course a form of sanctioned violence, and it takes only a half-hour's tussle with some mulish hickory to mop up any likely supply of hostility. This is nothing so simple as venting one's spleen on poor harmless trees: it is instead a kind of cancellation, perhaps a physiologic process related to the sensations of using the large muscles.

7 Woodcutting also provides a second form of psychotherapy by presenting a series of small, engrossing, and delightfully soluble problems. A tree is felled exactly where it is supposed to fall, despite a slight lean in another direction; threatened pinching of the saw kerf° is avoided by reordering the natural sequence of bucking cuts; an unsplittably gnarled crotch is finessed by relocation of fireplace lengths. It is not

---

*This peculiar verity was discovered, surely not for the first time, during introduction of air-conditioning for automobiles. Disappointing initial acceptance of this costly extra led some Detroit officials to consider adding conspicuous if unneeded air-intake vents to help a buyer derive a full sense of reward for his purchase. Later it was discovered that the sight of people driving around on sweltering days with windows cranked up did the announcement job, but just to be on the safe side a window decal was also provided. Wearing a sign certifying the ownership of an invisible possession is, when you come to think of it, rather odd behavior.

[7] **kerf:** incision made in wood by sawing

necessary to pretend that these are substantial achievements, nor anything more than routine to a woodsman; it is just that the successful solution of random problems, however small, is tonic to the spirits. Certainly it could not have been by chance that Wilhelm II,° the last of the German emperors, his restlessly proud and never very stable mind corroded by an awareness of a world war disastrously lost, spent time each exiled day in woodcutting.* But it is not necessary to have the Marne, and Verdun,° and the utter ruin of an empire on your mind to find reliable serenity in the woodlot.

8 Of course it doesn't always go well. Sometimes a tree chosen for cutting because it looks peckish, no longer a sturdy member of its company, falls with a distinctively hollow thump and shatters, revealing a punky interior so far gone in corruption as to be worth no more work. (A fireplace fire is contemptuous of punky wood, burning it sullenly, as a reluctant duty.) Occasionally the felling goes awry, from miscalculation of lean or veering of the wind during the wavery moment when a tree has concluded to fall but has not yet fixed on direction. It may maliciously slant off-course and lodge, half fallen, propped by the upper branches of a neighboring tree. This is a woodcutter's embarrassment, impossible to explain to anyone who happens by as something intended, and impossible to abandon, being a deadfall peril. If it cannot be jounced free, the choice is either to fell the second tree too, or to dislodge the hang-up by rolling it or by using a log chain to drag the butt out until the top breaks free. The work is arduous, a little dangerous, and thoroughly frustrating. On these infrequent days when malign spirits flit through the woods to perch on branches near by, all woodcutting can grow cranky. With each bucking cut the trunk rolls to new positions of inconvenience, and the saw binds inexplicably, and the axe glances wickedly, and the footing is precarious while you are trudging with a heavy four-length log on your shoulder. It is prudent to gather your tools and depart on such a day. Don't even stop to split what's been cut: the first piece will simply swallow three wedges, and smile.

---

[7] **Wilhelm II:** "the Kaiser" (1859–1941), exiled to the Dutch village of Doorn after his defeat as the emperor of Germany in World War I

*It should not be thought that the old man at Doorn laid about him in a welter of chips and sweat; his approach was rigidly decorous. Joachim von Kürenberg, a sympathetic biographer, describes the scene: "The day started with a morning service; the Kaiser read the lesson. Breakfast followed and after that, weather permitting, a walk in the park or wood sawing; old Schulz or Vieke would stand by, holding the master's coat, watching this new occupation with astonishment. They had been in the Kaiser's service for more than thirty years." Von Kürenberg, a guest at Doorn, clearly felt that *Der Allgehöchest*° at the woodpile was a monocle-dropping sight.

[7n] **Der Allgehöchest:** (Ger.) the most exalted one

Marne, Verdun: scenes of mass slaughter in World War I

STUDY QUESTIONS

1. In what ways is this piece something more than a tribute to the rewards of woodcutting? Can you infer wider values and attitudes held by the author? Pay special attention to paragraphs 4 and 7.
2. Rowesome's prose is rich in concrete detail. Which senses does his language especially address? Make lists of words that appeal to our sight, hearing, etc.
3. Consider the structure of the sentence in paragraph 2 beginning "You can do a considerable amount. . . ." Why is the sentence formed as it is? Do you see possible connections between Rowesome's manner of writing and his theme? If so, you may also appreciate why Rowesome's paragraphs are as long as they are.
4. Having read through this selection, consider the biographical headnote. Do you find it strange that a man of Rowesome's professional background wrote this piece? Whether or not you do, try to think of ways in which this is *not* the work of someone who makes his daily living out-of-doors.
5. As an excerpt from a book chapter, this selection was not intended to be read as a self-contained essay. What do you notice about it that is not "essayistic"? Can you think of any changes that would make for a more complete effect?

Richard Rhodes

Richard Rhodes, a native and current resident of Kansas, has written books about the Donner Party, the Midwest, and the Ozarks. He has also been a contributing editor of *Harper's,* where "Watching the Animals" appeared in 1970.

WATCHING THE ANIMALS

The loves of flint and iron are naturally a little rougher than those of the nightingale and the rose.

—Ralph Waldo Emerson°

1 I remembered today about this country lake in Kansas where I live: that it is artificial, built at the turn of the century, when Upton Sinclair° was writing *The Jungle,* as an ice lake. The trains with their loads of fresh

epigraph **Ralph Waldo Emerson:** American philosopher and author (1803–1882)

1 **Upton Sinclair:** American novelist, socialist, and reformer (1878–1968). *The Jungle* (1906), a novel about abuses in the meatpacking industry, was his most influential book.

meat from the Kansas City stockyards would stop by the Kaw River, across the road, and ice the cars. "You have just dined," Emerson once told what must have been a shocked Victorian audience, "and however scrupulously the slaughterhouse is concealed in the graceful distance of miles, there is complicity, expensive races°—race living at the expense of race. . . ."

2 The I-D Packing Company of Des Moines, Iowa: a small outfit which subcontracts from Armour the production of fresh pork. It can handle about 450 pigs an hour on its lines. No beef or mutton. No smoked hams or hot dogs. Plain fresh pork. A well-run outfit, with federal inspectors alert on all the lines.

3 The kind of slaughterhouse Upton Sinclair was talking about doesn't exist around here any more. The vast buildings still stand in Des Moines and Omaha and Kansas City, but the operations are gone. The big outfits used to operate on a profit margin of 1.5 per cent, which didn't give them much leeway, did it. Now they are defunct, and their buildings, which look like monolithic enlargements of concentration-camp barracks, sit empty, the hundreds of windows broken, dusty, jagged pieces of glass sticking out of the frames as if the animals heard the good news one day and leaped out the nearest exit. Even the stockyards, miles and miles of rotting, weathered board pens, floors paved fifty years ago by hand with brick, look empty, though I am told cattle receipts are up compared to what they were a few years back. The new thing is small, specialized, efficient houses out where the cattle are, in Denver, in Phoenix, in Des Moines, especially in Texas, where the weather is more favorable to fattening cattle. In Iowa the cattle waste half their feed just keeping warm in the wintertime. But in Iowa or in Texas, the point of meat-packing today is refrigeration. It's cheaper to ship cold meat than live animals. So the packing plants have gone out to the farms and ranches. They are even beginning to buy up the ranches themselves so that they won't have to depend on the irregularities of farmers and cattlemen who bring their animals in only when the price is up or the ground too wet for plowing. Farmhouses stand empty all over America. Did you know that? The city has already won, never mind how many of our television shows still depict the hardy bucolic rural. I may regret the victory, but that's my lookout. We are an urban race now, and meat is something you buy shrink-wrapped at the supermarket.

4 There are no stockyards outside the I-D Packing Company. The pigs arrive by trailer truck from Sioux City and other places. Sometimes a farmer brings in two or three in the back of his pickup. He unloads them into the holding pens, where they are weighed and inspected, goes

---

[1] **expensive races:** Emerson evidently meant *species* that prey on other species

into the office and picks up his check. The men, except on the killing floor, are working on the cooled carcasses of yesterday's kill anyway, so there is time to even out the line. Almost everything in a packing-house operates on a chain line, and for maximum profit that line must be full, 450 carcasses an hour at the I-D Packing Company, perhaps 300 heavies if today is heavies day—sows, overgrown hogs. Boars presumably escape the general fate. Their flesh is flavored with rut and tastes like an unventilated gymnasium locker room.

5 Down goes the tail gate and out come the pigs, enthusiastic after their drive. Pigs are the most intelligent of all farm animals, by actual laboratory test. Learn the fastest, for example, to push a plunger with their foot to earn a reward of pelletized feed. And not as reliable in their instincts. You don't have to call cattle to dinner. They are waiting outside the fence at 4:30 sharp, having arrived as silently as the Viet-cong. But perhaps that is pig intelligence too: let you do the work, laze around until the last minute, and then charge over and knock you down before you can slop the garbage into the trough. Cattle will stroll one by one into a row of stalls and usually fill them in serial order. Not pigs. They squeal and nip and shove. Each one wants the entire meal for himself. They won't stick together in a herd, either. Shoot out all over the place, and you'd damned better have every gate closed or they'll be in your garden and on your lawn and even in your living room, nodding by the fire.

6 They talk a lot, to each other, to you if you care to listen. I am not romanticizing pigs. They always scared me a little on the farm, which is probably why I watched them more closely than the other animals. They do talk: low grunts, quick squeals, a kind of hum sometimes, angry shrieks, high screams of fear.

7 I have great respect for the I-D Packing Company. They do a dirty job and do it as cleanly and humanely as possible, and do it well. They were nice enough to let me in the door, which is more than I can say for the Wilson people in Omaha, where I first tried to arrange a tour. What are you hiding, Wilson people?

8 Once into the holding pen, the pigs mill around getting to know each other. The I-D holding pens are among the most modern in the nation, my spokesman told me. Tubular steel painted tinner's red to keep it from rusting. Smooth concrete floors with drains so that the floors can be washed down hygienically after each lot of pigs is run through.

9 The pigs come out of the first holding pen through a gate that allows only one to pass at a time. Just beside the gate is a wooden door, and behind the door is the first worker the pigs encounter. He has a wooden box beside him filled with metal numbers, the shape of each number picked out with sharp needles. For each lot of pigs he selects a new set of numbers—2473, say—and slots them into a device like a

hammer and dips it in nontoxic purple dye. As a pig shoots out of the gate he hits the pig in the side with the numbers, making a tattoo. The pig gives a grunt—it doesn't especially hurt, pigskin is thick, as you know—and moves on to one of several smaller pens where each lot is held until curtain time. The tattoo, my spokesman told me, will stay on the animal through all the killing and cleaning and cutting operations, to the very end. Its purpose is to identify any animal or lot of animals which might be diseased, so that the seller can be informed and the carcasses destroyed. Rather too proud of his tattooing process, I thought, but then, you know the tattoos I am thinking about.

10 It would be more dramatic, make a better story, if the killing came last, but it comes first. We crossed a driveway with more red steel fencing. Lined up behind it, pressing into it because they sensed by now that all was not well with them, were perhaps a hundred pigs. But still curious, watching us go by in our long white canvas coats. Everyone wore those, and hard plastic helmets, white helmets for the workers, yellow helmets for the foremen. I got to be a foreman.

11 Before they reach their end, the pigs get a shower, a real one. Water sprays from every angle to wash the farm off of them. Then they begin to feel crowded. The pen narrows like a funnel; the drivers behind urge the pigs forward, until one at a time they climb onto a moving ramp. The ramp's sides move as well as its floor. The floor is cleated to give the pigs footing. The sides are made of blocks of wood so that they will not bruise, and they slant inward to wedge the pigs along. Now they scream, never having been on such a ramp, smelling the smells they smell ahead. I do not want to overdramatize, because you have read all this before. But it was a frightening experience, seeing their fear, seeing so many of them go by. It had to remind me of things no one wants to be reminded of anymore, all mobs, all death marches, all mass murders and extinctions, the slaughter of the buffalo, the slaughter of the Indian, the Inferno, Judgment Day, complicity, expensive races, race living at the expense of race. That so gentle a religion as Christianity could end up in Judgment Day. That we are the most expensive of races, able in our affluence to hire others of our kind to do this terrible necessary work of killing another race of creatures so that we may feed our oxygen-rich brains. Feed our children, for that matter.

12 At the top of the ramp, one man. With rubber gloves on, holding two electrodes that looked like enlarged curling irons except that they sported more of those needles. As a pig reached the top, this man jabbed the electrodes into the pig's butt and shoulder, and that was it. No more pain, no more fear, no more mudholes, no more sun in the lazy afternoon. Knocked instantly unconscious, the pig shuddered in a long spasm and fell onto a stainless steel table a foot below the end of the ramp. Up came another pig, and the same result. And another, and another, 450 an hour, 3,600 a day, the belts returning below to coax another ride.

13 The pigs are not dead, merely unconscious. The electrodes are humane, my spokesman said, and, relatively speaking, that is true. They used to gas the pigs—put them on a conveyor belt that ran through a room filled with anesthetic gas. That was humane too. The electrodes are more efficient. Anesthesia relaxes the body and loosens the bowels. The gassed pigs must have been a mess. More efficient, then, to put their bodies in spasm.

14 They drop to the table, and here the endless chain begins. A worker takes the nearest dangling chain by its handle as it passes. The chain is attached at the top to a belt of links, like a large bicycle chain. At the bottom the dangling chain has a metal handle like the handle on a bike. The chain runs through the handle and then attaches to the end of the handle, so that by sliding the handle the worker forms a loop. Into the loop he hooks one of the pig's hind feet. Another worker does the same with the other foot. Each has his own special foot to grab, or the pig would go down the line backwards, which would not be convenient. Once hooked into the line, the pig will stay in place by the force of its own weight.

15 Now the line ascends, lifting the unconscious animal into the air. The pig proceeds a distance of ten feet, where a worker standing on a platform deftly inserts a butcher knife into its throat. They call it "sticking," which it is. Then all hell breaks loose, if blood merely is hell. It gushes out, at about a 45-degree angle downward, thick as a ship's hawser, pouring directly onto the floor. Nothing is so red as blood, an incandescent red and most beautiful. It is the brightest color we drab creatures possess. Down on the floor below, with a wide squeegee on a long handle, a worker spends his eight hours a day squeegeeing that blood, some of it clotted, jellied, now, into an open drain. It is cycled through a series of pipes into a dryer, later to be made into blood meal for animal feed.

16 The line swings around a corner, high above the man with the squeegee, around the drain floor, turns again left at the next corner, and begins to ascend to the floor above. This interval—thirteen seconds, I think my spokesman said, or was it thirty?—so that the carcass may drain completely before further processing. Below the carcass on the ascent is a trough like those lowered from the rear of cement trucks, there to catch the last drainings of blood.

17 Pigs are not skinned, as cattle are, unless you are after the leather, and we are after the meat. But the hair must be taken off, and it must first be scalded loose. Courteously, the line lowers the carcass into a long trough filled with water heated to 180 degrees. The carcass will float if given a chance, fat being lighter than water, so wooden pushers on crankshafts spaced equally along the scalding tank immerse and roll the carcasses. Near the end of the trough, my spokesman easily pulls out a tuft of hair. The line ascends again, up and away, and the carcass goes into a chamber where revolving brushes as tall as a man whisk away the

hair. We pass to the other side of the chamber and find two workers with wide knives scraping off the few patches of hair that remain. The carcasses then pass through great hellish jets of yellowish-blue gas flame to singe the skin and harden it. The last step is polishing: more brushes. Our pig has turned pink and clean as a baby.

18 One of the small mercies of a slaughterhouse: what begins as a live animal loses all similarity as the processing goes on, until you can actually face the packaged meat at the exit door and admire its obvious flavor.

19 The polished carcasses swing through a door closed with rubber flaps, and there, dear friends, the action begins. Saws. Long knives. Butcher knives. Drawknives. Boning knives. Wails from the saws, large and small, that are driven by air like a dentist's drill. Shouts back and forth from the men, jokes, announcements, challenges. The temperature down to 50 degrees, everyone keen. Men start slicing off little pieces of the head right inside the door, each man his special slice, throwing them onto one of several lines that will depart for special bins. A carcass passes me and I see a bare eyeball staring, stripped of its lids. Deft knives drop the head from the neck leaving it dangling by a two-inch strip of skin. Around a corner, up to a platform, and three men gut the carcasses, great tubs of guts, each man taking the third carcass as it goes by. One of them sees me with my tape recorder and begins shouting at us something like "I am the greatest!" A crazy man, grinning and roaring at us, turning around and slipping in the knife, and out comes everything in one great load flopped onto a stainless-steel trough. And here things divide, and so must our attention.

20 My spokesman is proud of his chitterling machine. "I call them chitlins, but they're really chitterlings." It is the newest addition to his line. A worker separates the intestines from the other internal organs and shoves them down a slide, gray and shiny. Another worker finds one end and feeds it onto a steel tube flushed with water. Others trim off connective tissue, webbings, fat. The intestines shimmer along the tube into a washing vat, skinny up to the top of the machine where they are cooled, skinny back down where they are cooled further, and come out the other side ready for the supermarket. A worker drops them into wax buckets, pops on a lid, and packs them into shipping boxes. That is today's chitlin machine. They used to have to cool the chitlins overnight before they could be packaged. Now five men do the work of sixteen, in less time.

21 The remaining organs proceed down a waist-high conveyor; on the other side of the same walkway, the emptied carcasses pass; on a line next to the organ line the heads pass. By now all the meat has been trimmed off each head. A worker sockets them one at a time into a support like a footrest in a shoeshine parlor and a wedge neatly splits them in half. Out come the tongues, out come the brains, and at the end

of the line, out come the pituitaries, each tiny gland being passed to a government inspector in white pants, white shirt, and a yellow hard hat, who looks it over and drops it into a wax bucket. All these pieces, the brain, the tongue, the oddments of sidemeat off the head and carcass, will become "by-products": hot dogs, baloney, sausage. You are what you eat.

22 The loudest noise in the room comes from the big air-saw used to split the carcass in half down the backbone, leaving, again, connections at the butt end and between the shoulders. Other workers trim away interior fat, and then the carcasses proceed down their chain at 50 miles an hour to the blast freezer, 25 below zero and no place for mere mortals, to be chilled overnight.

23 Coming out of the freezer in another part of the room is yesterday's kill, cold and solid and smooth. A worker splits apart the two sides; the hams come off and go onto their own line; the shoulders come off and go onto theirs, to be made into picnics, shoulder roasts, trotters.° Away goes the valuable loin, trimmed out deftly by a worker with a drawknife. Away goes the bacon. Chunks and strips of fat go off from everywhere in buckets carried on overhead hooks to a grinder that spins out worms of fat and blows them through a tube directly to the lard-rendering vats. Who uses lard anymore, I ask my spokesman. I don't know, he says, I think we export most of it.

24 At the end of all these lines men package the component parts of pig into wax-paper-lined cartons, load the cartons onto pallets, forklift the pallets into spotless aluminum trailers socketed right into the walls of the building so that I do not even realize I am inside a truck until my spokesman tells me, and off they go to Armour.

25 Processing an animal is exactly the opposite of processing a machine: the machine starts out with components and ends up put together; the animal starts out put together and ends up components. No clearer illustration of the law of entropy has ever been devised.

26 And that is a tour of a slaughterhouse, as cheerful as I could make it.

27 But the men there. Half of them blacks, some Mexicans, the rest whites. It gets harder and harder to hire men for this work, even though the pay is good. The production line keeps them hopping; they take their breaks when there is a break in the line, so that the killing floor breaks first, and their break leaves an empty space ten minutes long in the endless chain, which, arriving at the gutting operation, allows the men there to break, and so on. Monday morning absenteeism is a problem, I was told. Keeping the men under control can be a problem, too, I sensed: when the line broke down briefly during my tour, the men cheered as convicts might at a

23 **trotters:** "pigs' feet"

state license-plate factory when the stamping machine breaks down. It cannot be heartening to kill animals all day.

28 There is a difference, too, between the men who work with the live animals and hot carcasses and those who cut up the cold meat, a difference I remember from my days of butchering on the farm: the killing unsettles, while the cold cutting is a craft like carpentry or plumbing and offers the satisfactions of craftsmanship. The worker with the electrodes jammed them into the animal with anger and perverse satisfaction, as if he were knocking off the enemy. The worker at the guts acted as if he were wrestling bears. The hot workers talked to themselves, yelled at each other, or else lapsed into that strained silence you meet in deeply angry men; the cold workers said little but worked with deftness and something like pride. They knew they were good, and they showed off a little, zip zip, as we toured by. They used their hands as if they knew how to handle tools, and they did.

29 The technology at the I-D Packing Company is humane by present standards, at least so far as the animals are concerned. Where the workers are concerned, I'm not so sure. They looked to be in need of lulling.

30 Beyond technology is the larger question of attitude. Butchering on the farm when I was a boy had the quality of a ceremony. We would select, say, a steer, and pen it separately overnight. The next morning several of us boys—this was a boys' home as well as a farm—would walk the steer to a large compound and leave it standing, trusting as hell, near the concrete-floored area where we did the skinning and gutting. Then the farm manager, a man of great kindness and reserve, would take aim with a .22 rifle at the crosspoint of two imaginary lines drawn from the horns to the opposite eyes. And hold his bead until the steer was entirely calm, looking at him, a certain shot, because this man did not want to miss, did not want to hurt the animal he was about to kill. And we would stand in a spread-out circle, at a respectful distance, tense with the drama of it, because we didn't want him to miss either.

31 The shot cracked out, the bullet entered the brain, and the animal instantly collapsed. Then the farm manager handed back the rifle, took a knife, ran forward, and cut into the throat. Then we dragged the steer onto the concrete, hooked its back legs through the Achilles tendons to a crosstree, and laboriously winched it into the air with a differential pulley. Four boys usually did the work, two older, two younger. The younger boys were supposed to be learning this skill, and you held your stomach together as best you could at first while the older boys played little tricks like, when they got there in the skinning, cutting off the pizzle° and whipping it around your neck, but even these crudities had their place: they accustomed you to contact with flesh and blood.

---

31 **pizzle:** penis

32 And while the older boys did their work of splitting the halves with a hacksaw, you got to take the guts, which on the farm we did not save except for the liver, the heart, and the sweetbreads, in a wheelbarrow down to the back lane where you built with wood you had probably cut yourself, a most funereal pyre. Then we doused the guts with gasoline, tossed in a match, and Whoosh! off they went. And back on the concrete, the sawing done, the older boys left the sides hanging overnight in the winter cold to firm the meat for cutting.

33 By now it was noon, time for lunch, and you went in with a sort of pride that you had done this important work, and there on the table was meat some other boys had killed on some other ceremonial day. It was bloody work, of course, and sometimes I have wondered how adults could ask children to do such work, but it was part of a coherent way of life, as important as plowing or seeding or mowing or baling hay. It had a context, and I was literary enough even then to understand that burning the guts had a sacrificial significance. We could always have limed them and dumped them into a ditch. Lord knows they didn't burn easily.

34 I never saw our farm manager more upset than the day we were getting ready to butcher five pigs. He shot one through the nose rather than through the brain. It ran screaming around the pen, and he almost cried. It took two more bullets to finish the animal off, and this good man was shaking when he had finished. "I hate that," he said to me. "I hate to have them in pain. Pigs are so damned hard to kill clean."

35 But we don't farm anymore. The coherence is gone. Our loves are no longer the loves of flint and iron, but of the nightingale and the rose, and so we delegate our killing. Our farm manager used to sleep in the sheep barn for nights on end to be sure he was there to help the ewes deliver their lambs, ewes being so absentminded they sometimes stop labor with the lamb only halfway out. You saw the beginning and the end on the farm, not merely the prepackaged middle. Flint and iron, friends, flint and iron. And humility, and sorrow that this act of killing must be done, which is why in those days good men bowed their heads before they picked up their forks.

STUDY QUESTIONS

1. What expectations did you feel when you read Rhodes's title? Think of ways in which that title seems both appropriate and inappropriate to the essay it introduces, and try to reconstruct the author's reasons for preferring it to a more informative title.
2. What do you suppose is the meaning of the epigraph from Emerson, and how does it fit into Rhodes's own thematic emphasis? (Note that Emerson's sentence is partially quoted again in the final paragraph of the essay.)

3. What effect is created by Rhodes's opening paragraph? When you have an answer, consider paragraphs 1 and 2 together, noting their differences of mood and sentence structure. Then ask yourself what qualities of mind and emotion have been suggested by this distinctly mixed way of beginning.
4. Look through the first twelve paragraphs of the essay and collect instances of Rhodes's characterizing the thoughts and feelings of the doomed pigs. What is his attitude toward them, and how is it conveyed?
5. Note that, beginning with paragraph 19, Rhodes shifts attention from the pigs and their carcasses to the men who are processing them. What is his view of those men, and how does it come across to us? In answering this question, you can develop an idea of Rhodes's total attitude—which is never directly stated—toward the business of the slaughterhouse.
6. How would you characterize the tone of the whole essay? Collect specific uses of language that strike you as typifying that tone.
7. In paragraph 10, Rhodes concedes that "It would be more dramatic, make a better story, if the killing came last . . ." If you nevertheless find elements of drama and good storytelling in Rhodes's "undramatic" narrative, try to locate and describe them. Otherwise stated, how does Rhodes keep us engaged through a process that is entirely predictable?
8. What is the effect of the extended flashback, or shifting to an earlier time sequence (paras. 30–35), with which the essay ends?

Tom Wolfe

Tom Wolfe is, among other things, one of the founders of "the new journalism," an emotionally vivid, densely factual kind of reporting. His books include *The Pump-House Gang, The Painted Word, The Right Stuff,* and *The Kandy-Kolored Tangerine-Flake Streamline Baby* (1965), from which the following essay is drawn.

A SUNDAY KIND OF LOVE

1 Love! Attar° of libido in the air! It is 8:45 A.M. Thursday morning in the IRT subway station at 50th Street and Broadway and already two kids are hung up in a kind of herringbone weave of arms and legs, which

---

1 **Attar:** perfume obtained from flowers

proves, one has to admit, that love is not *confined* to Sunday in New York. Still, the odds! All the faces come popping in clots out of the Seventh Avenue local, past the King Size Ice Cream machine, and the turnstiles start whacking away as if the world were breaking up on the reefs. Four steps past the turnstiles everybody is already backed up haunch to paunch for the climb up the ramp and the stairs to the surface, a great funnel of flesh, wool, felt, leather, rubber and steaming alumicron, with the blood squeezing through everybody's old sclerotic arteries in hopped-up spurts from too much coffee and the effort of surfacing from the subway at the rush hour. Yet there on the landing are a boy and a girl, both about eighteen, in one of those utter, My Sin,° backbreaking embraces.

2 He envelops her not only with his arms but with his chest, which has the American teen-ager concave shape to it. She has her head cocked at a 90-degree angle and they both have their eyes pressed shut for all they are worth and some incredibly feverish action going with each other's mouths. All round them, tens, scores, it seems like hundreds, of faces and bodies are perspiring, trooping and bellying up the stairs with arteriosclerotic grimaces past a showcase full of such novel items as Joy Buzzers, Squirting Nickels, Finger Rats, Scary Tarantulas and spoons with realistic dead flies on them, past Fred's barbershop, which is just off the landing and has glossy photographs of young men with the kind of baroque haircuts one can get in there, and up onto 50th Street into a madhouse of traffic and shops with weird lingerie and gray hair-dyeing displays in the windows, signs for free teacup readings and a pool-playing match between the Playboy Bunnies and Downey's Showgirls, and then everybody pounds on toward the Time-Life Building, the Brill Building or NBC.

3 The boy and the girl just keep on writhing in their embroilment. Her hand is sliding up the back of his neck, which he turns when her fingers wander into the intricate formal gardens of his Chicago Boxcar hairdo at the base of the skull. The turn causes his face to start to mash in the ciliated° hull of her beehive hairdo, and so she rolls her head 180 degrees to the other side, using their mouths for the pivot. But aside from good hair grooming, they are oblivious to everything but each other. Everybody gives them a once-over. Disgusting! Amusing! How touching! A few kids pass by and say things like "Swing it, baby." But the great majority in that heaving funnel up the stairs seem to be as much astounded as anything else. The vision of love at rush hour cannot strike anyone exactly as romance. It is a feat, like a fat man crossing the English Channel in a barrel. It is an earnest accomplishment against the

---

1 **My Sin:** a perfume, frequently advertised with a picture of a passionate-looking kiss

3 **ciliated:** having cilia, that is, the hairlike outgrowths that enable protozoans to move. In this sentence the word means *wispy.*

tide. It is a piece of slightly gross heroics, after the manner of those knobby, varicose old men who come out from some place in baggy shorts every year and run through the streets of Boston in the Marathon race. And somehow that is the gaffe against love all week long in New York, for everybody, not just two kids writhing under their coiffures in the 50th Street subway station; too hurried, too crowded, too hard, and no time for dalliance. Which explains why the real thing in New York is, as it says in the song, a Sunday kind of love.

4 There is Saturday, but Saturday is not much better than Monday through Friday. Saturday is the day for errands in New York. More millions of shoppers are pouring in to keep the place jammed up. Everybody is bobbing around, running up to Yorkville to pick up these arty cheeses for this evening, or down to Fourth Avenue to try to find this Van Vechten° book, *Parties,* to complete the set for somebody, or off to the cleaner's, the dentist's, the hairdresser's, or some guy's who is going to loan you his station wagon to pick up two flush doors to make tables out of, or over to some place somebody mentioned that is supposed to have fabulous cuts of meat and the butcher wears a straw hat and arm garters and is colorfully rude.

5 True, there is Saturday night, and Friday night. They are fine for dates and good times in New York. But for the dalliance of love, they are just as stupefying and wound up as the rest of the week. On Friday and Saturday nights everybody is making some kind of scene. It may be a cellar cabaret in the Village where five guys from some place talk "Jamaican" and pound steel drums and the Connecticut teen-agers wear plaid ponchos and knee-high boots and drink such things as Passion Climax cocktails, which are made of apple cider with watermelon balls thrown in. Or it may be some cellar in the East 50's, a discotheque, where the alabaster kids come on in sleeveless minksides jackets, tweed evening dresses and cool-it Modernismus° hairdos. But either way, it's a scene, a production, and soon the evening begins to whirl, like the whole world with the bed-spins, in a montage of taxis, slithery legs slithering in, slithery legs slithering out, worsted, piqué,° grins, eye teeth, glissandos,° buffoondos,° tips, par lamps, doormen, lines, magenta ropes, white dickies, mirrors and bar bottles, pink men and shawl-collared coats, hatcheck girls and neon peach fingernails, taxis, keys, broken lamps and no coat hangers. . . .

---

4 **Van Vechten:** Carl Van Vechten (1880–1964), American author

5 **Modernismus:** (Ger.) modernism, a movement of experiment in various twentieth-century arts

piqué: fabric with raised cords

glissandos: musical passages played by sliding one or more fingers rapidly across piano keys or harp strings

buffoondos: a made-up word suggesting actions fitting a buffoon—i.e., someone who deliberately makes a fool of himself to amuse others

6 And, then, an unbelievable dawning; Sunday, in New York.

7 George G., who writes "Z" ads for a department store, keeps saying that all it takes for him is to smell coffee being made at a certain point in the percolation. It doesn't matter where. It could be the worst death-ball hamburger dive. All he has to do is smell it, and suddenly he finds himself swimming, drowning, dissolving in his own reverie of New York's Sunday kind of love.

8 Anne A.'s apartment was nothing, he keeps saying, and that was the funny thing. She lived in Chelsea.° It was this one room with a cameo-style carving of a bored Medusa° on the facing of the mantelpiece, this one room plus a kitchen, in a brownstone sunk down behind a lot of loft buildings and truck terminals and so forth. Beautiful Chelsea. But on Sunday morning by 10:30 the sun would be hitting cleanly between two rearview buildings and making it through the old no man's land of gas effluvia ducts, restaurant vents, aerials, fire escapes, stairwell doors, clotheslines, chimneys, skylights, vestigial lightning rods, Mansard° slopes, and those peculiarly bleak, filthy and misshapen backsides of New York buildings, into Anne's kitchen.

9 George would be sitting at this rickety little table with an oilcloth over it. How he goes on about it! The place was grimy. You couldn't keep the soot out. The place was beautiful. Anne is at the stove making coffee. The smell of the coffee being made, just the smell . . . already he is turned on. She had on a great terrycloth bathrobe with a sash belt. The way she moved around inside that bathrobe with the sun shining in the window always got him. It was the *at*mosphere of the thing. There she was, moving around in that great fluffy bathrobe with the sun hitting her hair, and they had all the time in the world. There wasn't even one flatulent truck horn out on Eighth Avenue. Nobody was clobbering their way down the stairs in high heels out in the hall at 10 minutes to 9.

10 Anne would make scrambled eggs, plain scrambled eggs, but it was a feast. It was incredible. She would bring out a couple of these little smoked fish with golden skin and some smoked oysters that always came in a little can with ornate lettering and royal colors and flourishes and some Kissebrot bread and black cherry preserves, and then the coffee. They had about a million cups of coffee apiece, until the warmth seemed to seep through your whole viscera. And then cigarettes. The cigarettes were like some soothing incense. The radiator was always making a hissing sound and then a clunk. The sun was shining in and the fire escapes and effluvia ducts were just silhouettes out there some-

---

[8] **Chelsea:** "artistic" quarter, containing many converted industrial buildings, south of Greenwich Village in lower Manhattan

Medusa: in Greek mythology, one of the three Gorgons; a female figure with snakes in her hair

Mansard: a roof with a nearly flat upper slope and a nearly vertical lower one

place. George would tear off another slice of Kissebrot and pile on some black cherry preserves and drink some more coffee and have another cigarette, and Anne crossed her legs under her terrycloth bathrobe and crossed her arms and drew on her cigarette, and that was the way it went.

11 "It was the *torpor,* boy," he says. "It was beautiful. Torpor is a beautiful, underrated thing. Torpor is a luxury. Especially in this stupid town. There in that kitchen it was like being in a perfect cocoon of love. Everything was beautiful, a perfect cocoon."

12 By and by they would get dressed, always in as shiftless a getup as possible. She would put on a big heavy sweater, a raincoat and a pair of faded slacks that gripped her like neopreme rubber. He would put on a pair of corduroy pants, a crew sweater with moth holes and a raincoat. Then they would go out and walk down to 14th Street for the Sunday paper.

13 All of a sudden it was great out there on the street in New York. All those damnable millions who come careening into Manhattan all week weren't there. The town was empty. To a man and woman shuffling along there, torpid, in the cocoon of love, it was as if all of rotten Gotham had improved overnight. Even the people looked better. There would be one of those old dolls with little flabby arms all hunched up in a coat of pastel oatmeal texture, the kind whose lumpy old legs you keep seeing as she heaves her way up the subway stairs ahead of you and holds everybody up because she is so flabby and decrepit . . . and today, Sunday, on good, clean, empty 14th Street, she just looked like a nice old lady. There was no one around to make her look slow, stupid, unfit, unhip, expendable. That was the thing about Sunday. The weasel millions were absent. And Anne walking along beside him with a thready old pair of slacks gripping her like neopreme rubber looked like possibly the most marvelous vision the world had ever come up with, and the cocoon of love was perfect. It was like having your cake and eating it, too. On the one hand, here it was, boy, the prize: New York. All the buildings, the Gotham spires, were sitting up all over the landscape in silhouette like ikons representing all that was great, glorious and triumphant in New York. And, on the other hand, there were no weasel millions bellying past you and eating crullers on the run with the crumbs flaking off the corners of their mouths as a reminder of how much *Angst*° and *Welthustle*° you had to put into the town to get any of that out of it for yourself. All there was was the cocoon of love, which was complete. It was like being inside a scenic Easter Egg where you look in and the Gotham spires

---

[13] **Angst:** (Ger.) anguish, anxiety

Welthustle: a made-up word combining *hustle* with the German word for *world;* hence, "universal hustle"

are just standing there like a little gemlike backdrop.

14 By and by the two of them would be back in the apartment sprawled out on the floor rustling through the Sunday paper, all that even black ink appliquéd on big fat fronds of paper. Anne would put an E. Power Biggs organ record on the hi-fi, and pretty soon the old trammeler's bass chords would be vibrating through you as if he had clamped a diathermy° machine on your solar plexus. So there they would be, sprawled out on the floor, rustling through the Sunday paper, getting bathed and massaged by E. Power Biggs' sonic waves. It was like taking peyote or something. This marvelously high feeling would come over them, as though they were psychedelic, and the most commonplace objects took on this great radiance and significance. It was like old Aldous Huxley° in his drug experiments, sitting there hooking down peyote buttons and staring at a clay geranium pot on a table, which gradually became the most fabulous geranium pot in God's world. The way it curved . . . why, it curved 360 d-e-g-r-e-e-s! And the clay . . . why, it was the color of the earth itself! And the top . . . It had a r-i-m on it! George had the same feeling. Anne's apartment . . . it was hung all over the place with the usual New York working girl's modern prints, the Picasso° scrawls, the Mondrians° curling at the corners . . . somehow nobody ever gets even a mat for a Mondrian print . . . the Toulouse-Lautrecs° with that guy with the chin kicking his silhouette leg, the Klees,° that Paul Klee is cute . . . why, all of a sudden these were the most beautiful things in the whole hagiology° of art . . . the way that guy with the chin k-i-c-k-s t-h-a-t l-e-g, the way that Paul Klee h-i-t-s t-h-a-t b-a-l-l . . . the way that apartment just wrapped around them like a cocoon, with lint under the couch like angel's hair, and the plum cover on the bed lying halfway on the floor in folds like the folds in a Tiepolo° cherub's silks, and the bored Medusa on the mantelpiece looking like the most splendidly, gloriously b-o-r-e-d Medusa in the face of time!

15 "Now, that was love," says George, "and there has never been anything like it. I don't know what happens to it. Unless it's Monday. Monday sort of happens to it in New York."

---

[14] **diathermy:** heat treatment

Aldous Huxley: (1894–1963) British author, an early student of hallucinogenic drugs

Picasso: Pablo Picasso (1881–1973), Spanish painter and sculptor who lived in France

Mondrians: reproductions of works by the Dutch painter Piet Mondrian (1872–1944)

Toulouse-Lautrecs: reproductions of the theatrical posters made by the French painter Henri Toulouse-Lautrec (1864–1901)

Klees: reproductions of works by the Swiss painter Paul Klee (1879–1940)

hagiology: lore about saints

Tiepolo: Giovanni Battista Tiepolo (1696–1770), Italian painter especially noted for his depiction of skies

STUDY QUESTIONS

1. Wolfe's title is also that of an old popular song expressing a yearning for a permanent (presumably married) love, as opposed to passing fancies. Think about the way the phrase "a Sunday kind of love" is used in this essay, and consider the effect Wolfe must have intended by using this title.
2. As you can see from the opening paragraph alone, "A Sunday Kind of Love" contains an extraordinary range of diction, from the slangy to the rare and technical. What is the rhetorical effect of this mixture of levels? Pick several examples of "high" and "low" terms in proximity, and ask yourself in each case what effect Wolfe intends.
3. Details like "Joy Buzzers, Squirting Nickels, Finger Rats . . ." (paragraph 2) must seem at first like distractions from Wolfe's essential story. If, by the end, you have a different view of them, try to formulate and justify that view.
4. After the opening scene of the kiss in the subway station, what expectations do we have about Wolfe's further treatment of amorous couples? Are those expectations fulfilled? If your answer is no, explain what Wolfe gives us instead—and why he does so.
5. Why does paragraph 6 consist of only one sentence, and a fragmentary one at that?
6. Wolfe's sentence structure is as various as his diction. Pick out several extremely elaborate sentences (for example, those ending paragraphs 5 and 8), and ask yourself in each case why the sentence is constructed as it is. If the same information had been delivered in several brief sentences, what effects would have been lost?
7. Despite its sophistication, Wolfe's essay is quite straightforward in structure. What is the main principle of that structure, and how would you group its elements by sets of paragraphs?
8. On the basis of this essay, what kind of person does Wolfe himself appear to be? Be prepared to back up your answer with references to specific passages.

NARRATING AN ACTION

Lois Gould

Lois Gould, formerly executive editor of *Ladies Home Journal,* is a novelist, journalist, and freelance writer. "Letter to a Robber" is taken from her collection of essays, *Not Responsible for Personal Articles* (1978).

LETTER TO A ROBBER

1 Listen, I hope you won't think I'm not grateful for the way you handled it. I mean not killing us or . . . anything. How often does a New York holdup man burst into a brownstone on a quiet Saturday night, tie up a whole family, stuff all their cash and valuables into a couple of jumbo shopping bags, and then quietly sashay out into the rain, breaking stride only to select a nice umbrella from the hall rack? As the police put it, ten minutes after you left, "Count your blessings, folks." We have, we have. So, many thanks from all of us—me and Bob and the kids. We'll never forget you.

2 Did you know you were our first armed robber? Oh, we've had *burglaries.* And both Tony and Roger, who are in their teens, have been shaken down for quarters in the park. But you were absolutely the first person ever to force his way into our house with an actual gun, herd us into an upstairs bedroom, tie us up with pantyhose from my underwear drawer, and spend an hour ransacking the premises, all the while muttering ominously, "Where's the *good* stuff?"

3 So naturally we had no preconceived idea of what you might have planned in the way of an ending.

4 It came as a real surprise, when I finally broke loose from my trussed-chicken pose (in yoga class we call it the bow), that not only had you snuck out like, well, a thief in the night, but that except for the severed phone, the torn pantyhose and the lock you had tried to jimmy before Roger opened the door by mistake, you hadn't *destroyed* a thing.

I mean, I've seen more physical damage done at a dull cocktail party.

5 I don't know what I might have done differently if I had suspected, even for a minute, that we would all live to tell about it. From the instant you appeared in the hall, with the gun cradled in your palm like a Master Charge card, it never occurred to me that you weren't going to kill us. "This is it," I said to myself, with the deadly calm of a recorded announcement. And then I added, "So be it." It never guesses, that kind of an inner voice; it knows.

6 One of the troubles with being a writer is that whenever something unthinkable happens, I can't do anything *but* think about it. It's as if I have no control over the denouement until I get to my typewriter. That night, I realize, the odds were no better than 50–50 that I'd ever make it to my typewriter again. But in the thirty seconds or so that we all stood in the hall like statues, I never thought of *that.* I thought of about a hundred other insanely relevant questions. What made the Jews line up for the gas chamber? Was Hamlet really a simple coward? If I ran for the door, or the telephone, what would you do to Roger, who was standing right next to you? And the more I thought, the more solidly I froze. Could catatonia during a crisis be just a severe form of writer's block? Or was it an elaborate protective device, like an internal Holmes security system? It couldn't stop disaster from striking; it could only keep me from striking back. No heroics. But, you have to admit, no hysterics either. I kept my cool, which kept the children cool, which kept *you* cool. Somehow, some miraculous how, you didn't hurt us. So I must have been doing nothing right. Right?

7 Anyway, while you were taking over our lives, the writer part of my frozen brain was the only part that didn't get taken. Crouched in its insulated corner, biting its ragged nails, it sat there watching, listening, with a perverse and impotent fascination. It was part prisoner, part voyeur. It could make no move to interfere with our fate. It could only fix the nightmare on my inner ear and eye, to be exorcised later—if I ever woke up.

8 Well, that was one theory I had about why I began at once to obey your orders; why I moved so slowly and carefully, as if I were swimming underwater or under deep hypnosis. "Lie down," you said softly. I did —and the children followed me. "Don't look up." I didn't; they didn't. Simon says . . . put your hands behind your back. Simon says . . . keep cool; no crying. Simon says let's not play any games.

9 Of course you didn't tell us to do anything *hard.* You never once forced my hand by threatening, or hurting, the children, by assaulting them or me sexually, by forcing us to help you trap my husband, who was late coming home from an overnight trip to Pittsburgh. And you asked only reasonable questions, in a quiet, reasonable tone. Hypnotic. "Where's your pocketbook?" "Where's your jewelry?" "What airport is your husband coming from?" "Where's the light switch in the closet?"

10 Only once did I even get angry—and you'd never guess what did it. "What does your father do for a living?" you asked the children. Suddenly my liberated female consciousness flared. Talk about irony! There I was, flat on the floor, a living symbol of woman as victim, and all I could think was: "You rotten chauvinist! Couldn't you ask what their *mother* does? It so happens I've got a book coming out next month!"

11 And that, of course, started me brooding about being a dead author on the spring list. Ah. I pictured the somber, lump-in-the-throat publisher's ad, with the heavy black border. I imagined the tender posthumous reviews. Hell, I started *writing* them in my head. One for the daily, one for the Sunday . . . oh, victimhood would have its pitiful rewards. For a few crazy minutes there I forgot all about you, rummaging methodically in the bowels of our house. Rifling my office desk? Scattering papers from Bob's file cabinet? Emptying the children's toy chests? Then suddenly you were back in the bedroom, looming over us. But you'd already *done* the bedroom. You'd searched every last drawer, every closet, under the bed, behind the pictures, looking for the "good stuff." There could be only one thing you'd come back for . . .

12 This is it, I thought, freezing again. This is *really* it. One bullet in the back of each bowed head? The black boots came closer; first the left, then the right, stepped over our prostrate bodies. A single thrill of pure physical terror jolted through my spine. This *is* it!

13 But all you did was step over us to get to the phone and cut the wire. Why hadn't I guessed by now what you were hanging around for? Waiting for Bob! All the time I thought you'd want to *avoid* him. I kept warning you he was due any minute, *over*due; thinking it would scare you into hurrying up and getting out. I guess I'd make a lousy robber. Overcautious. You figured what's another half-hour compared to another full wallet? Besides, it was raining out. I had to think about how I could do something *besides* think. But for the life of me, for the life of all of us, I couldn't.

14 I glanced at Roger, lying there so unnaturally still beside me, his lips chalky with fear. And Tony, a few feet away, seemed half asleep, his small chin buried in the dark carpet. You had taken off his glasses and laid them gently on the floor beside him. But you hadn't hurt him. He and Roger were both alive, and so was I, and you'd left the room again, and maybe, just maybe, the worst was over, and you'd go away, and Bob would be home and it would be tomorrow.

15 "Roger," I whispered idiotically, "don't ever open the door to a stranger." Roger nodded gravely. Less than an hour ago, at the sound of keys in the front door, Roger had opened the door for Daddy. Only it had turned out to be you instead.

16 "Did he cut the phone?" I whispered. Roger couldn't see it. Tony was lying closer to it but he couldn't see it either, without his glasses. "Don't try anything, Mommy," Roger pleaded. "He'll shoot us!" My turn to nod gravely. I gave up struggling with the bonds on my wrists

and ankles. They only pulled tighter when I writhed, anyway, and the tighter they pulled, the more they hurt. You had let me off easy, tying me up like that. I didn't have to feel guilty for *not* trying—though of course I did. The female role! Oh God, I took to it like a born woman!

17 Then I heard your steps behind me again, walking back and forth. Pacing? Nervous? Checking us for false moves? No. You were—I still can't believe this—trying on clothes. *My* clothes. Parading back and forth in front of the full-length mirror. All we could see were different colors of suede and leather pants legs flashing past our heads. If only I'd had the nerve to look up, I might have seen the fashion show of the year. But I didn't have the nerve, so I missed it. I bet you look terrific in the violet sheepskin outfit you chose. And the brown leather pantsuit too. I'm still not sure about the fox coat, though. Well, maybe for evening.

18 "Your husband's kinda late, isn't he?" you said suddenly in that ominously quiet voice. "Uh, yes." I felt a barely controllable urge to start apologizing—"Well, after all, he wasn't expecting you." Or, "Don't feel you have to wait, I'll tell him you were here."

19 I could tell you were getting edgy. I could hear you crackling paper bags—packing up. What if Bob decided to stay another night in Pittsburgh? *Nobody* stays another night in Pittsburgh. Yes, but what if he had to? If he didn't show up, would you blow your cool, finally, and shoot us, after all? There was definitely a testy note to your voice the next time you asked where the safe was, with the "good stuff." "There is no safe," I said for perhaps the fifth time. I still didn't dare point out that the drawerful of jewelry you'd already emptied *was* the good stuff. Not good enough, apparently. Well, at least we had the same taste in clothes.

20 As for cash, there wasn't a cent left in the house except for $3 of Roger's allowance, which he had in his pocket. Unfortunately you finally got around to asking if the kids had any money, say, in a piggy bank. Roger instantly piped up about the $3, and told you which pocket. Now we were all wiped out.

21 And then the doorbell rang. My one chance to throw you off guard! I knew it had to be Bob, but *you* didn't. "Who would that be?" you asked. I was so floored by your syntax that I forgot to lie. "That would be my husband," I parroted like an apt pupil. Judas! Idiot! By the time I realized what I'd done, you were thundering down the stairs to greet him. I heard the two voices—quiet, reasonable, unbelievably controlled—on the landing below. I should have guessed Bob would try to reason with you. A psychiatrist is a psychiatrist even at a time like this. I heard him say, "Maybe I can help you," and I heard you scoff, "How can you help me?" I doubt if any psychiatrist could have come up with the right answer. Seconds later you were both in the bedroom, Bob's hands already tied behind his back. All you had to do was secure his feet, and you were off again. Downstairs? *Gone?* I looked sheepishly at Bob. He was furious. *Furious!* He'd already started struggling violently

against the bindings. He had to do *something*—fight, run, something. The absolute antithesis of me! I would have stayed trussed up for another hour, just to be sure you were safely home in a taxi before I moved. Bob strained so hard to be free—to regain control—that he cut deep gashes in his hands and wrists. "Why?" I cried. "What can you possibly do? The phone is cut. He's still in the house!"

22 "I'll run out!" Bob said. "I'll get help!"

23 "But he's armed," I argued. "What if he's on the stairs? He'll . . ."

24 "I think it's a fake gun." (Did he *really* think that? Then why hadn't he tried to stop you? Maybe he thought the gun was real when you pointed it at him, but then decided it was fake because you hadn't shot it?)

25 I was—and still am—*positive* it was real. Yet I rolled over to help untie Bob's wrists, with the free fingers of my own bound hands. I still don't know why I did that. Because he was so angry? Why *was* he so angry, anyway? Because you had rendered him impotent—unmanned him—with a gun he didn't believe in? You rendered me impotent too—unwomanned me?—but it hadn't made me angry. Certainly not angry enough to risk running into you on a dark staircase.

26 I was thunderstruck by the contrast between our reactions. Bob was a solid mass of rage and movement. I was a blob of passive ice. Both of us locked into sex-role stereotypes. Culturally induced? Innate? My God, was this whole horror story reducible to a feminist issue? Was *everything* reducible to a feminist issue? What does your father do, indeed? He *acts,* while your mother lies there *thinking.*

27 Within five minutes Bob was free and running down the stairs, and I had suddenly come to life—untied my wrists, locked the bedroom door and hobbled to the window—just in time to see him running back into the house. Where were you at that historic moment? None of us knew, but of course you were already gone. Singin', I daresay, in the rain. I never reflected, until days later, on how come I was able to work myself free so fast, *after* Bob did it? Did I feel *protected?* Did I need to have a *man* lead the way? What did that prove about me? About women in general? Nothing, dammit. I know a woman who grappled with a mugger on a dark street and frightened him off. (She also rides a motorcycle.) I consoled myself with the possibility that I might have been braver too (more reckless?) if the children hadn't been there. But how do I know for sure?

28 Anyway, the nightmare is over. We've followed the cops' sage advice and counted our blessings a fair number of times by now. Also we've absorbed some lessons from the experience. What lessons? Well, the children learned not to open the door without asking who's there, even if they're 1,000 percent *sure* who, as the politicians say. Also, they learned that real violence isn't quite the same as in crime stories. As Roger observed the other day, "In a story, we'd have gotten loose just

like that, and sneaked up behind him and given him a karate chop. It sure isn't that easy, is it?"

29 Bob learned that there are some situations even a psychiatrist can't talk his way out of. When I asked him if he'd learned anything else, he said, "Sure. Never come home late from Pittsburgh."

30 As for me, I learned to trust the inside of my head, for perhaps the first time in my life. Whatever madness was going on in there—woman's intuition, writer's block, rank cowardice, maternal instinct, death wish, gallows humor, none or all of the above—I now know that it helped save our lives.

31 I learned that there are feminists in foxholes.

32 And finally I learned that even if a person practices yoga every day, she cannot remain in the bow position for an hour without feeling stiff in the hip joints. *Scared* stiff.

33 P.S. By the way, if you're ever in the neighborhood again, don't forget: *You've already been here.*

STUDY QUESTIONS

1. Since the chances that Gould's robber would actually read her "letter" are slim, why does she choose this form for her essay? Consider the advantages she gains by using the second-person singular *you* instead of writing *about* the intruder.
2. Think about the tone of this essay. How does it differ from the tone of other selections you have read in this book? Why do you suppose Gould chose that tone? Relate your answer both to the form of her essay and to its subject matter.
3. All suspense would seem to be sacrificed in Gould's opening paragraph, which tells us that this robbery turned out rather mildly. Assuming that the author knew what she was doing, try to reconstruct her purpose in beginning this way.
4. In what ways does Gould's career as a writer get involved in the story of the robbery?
5. In paragraph 26 Gould describes herself and her husband as having been "locked into sex-role stereotypes." Go through the entire essay collecting evidence that relates to the question of prescribed sexual roles. Can you make a case for the claim that this question is the real issue in "Letter to a Robber"?
6. In what respects does the robber, as described by Gould, fail to "add up"? Why do you think Gould left his portrait so incomplete?
7. The sentence that constitutes paragraph 31, "I learned that there are feminists in foxholes," paraphrases an old saying, "There are no atheists in foxholes." (In other words, all soldiers under fire ask God for help, even those who previously claimed to disbelieve in God.) What does Gould's version mean, and how does it relate to the original?

E. B. White

E. B. White was for many years an editor and contributor to *The New Yorker.* His books include several collections of essays and the children's classics *Stuart Little* and *Charlotte's Web.* Since 1937 he has been a devoted resident of coastal Maine, the setting of the present essay from *The Second Tree from the Corner* (1954).

DEATH OF A PIG

1 I spent several days and nights in mid-September with an ailing pig and I feel driven to account for this stretch of time, more particularly since the pig died at last, and I lived, and things might easily have gone the other way round and none left to do the accounting. Even now, so close to the event, I cannot recall the hours sharply and am not ready to say whether death came on the third night or the fourth night. This uncertainty afflicts me with a sense of personal deterioration; if I were in decent health I would know how many nights I had sat up with a pig.

2 The scheme of buying a spring pig in blossomtime, feeding it through summer and fall, and butchering it when the solid cold weather arrives, is a familiar scheme to me and follows an antique pattern. It is a tragedy enacted on most farms with perfect fidelity to the original script. The murder, being premeditated, is in the first degree but is quick and skillful, and the smoked bacon and ham provide a ceremonial ending whose fitness is seldom questioned.

3 Once in a while something slips—one of the actors goes up in his lines and the whole performance stumbles and halts. My pig simply failed to show up for a meal. The alarm spread rapidly. The classic outline of the tragedy was lost. I found myself cast suddenly in the role of pig's friend and physician—a farcical character with an enema bag for a prop. I had a presentiment, the very first afternoon, that the play would never regain its balance and that my sympathies were now wholly with the pig. This was slapstick—the sort of dramatic treatment that instantly appealed to my old dachshund, Fred, who joined the vigil, held the bag, and, when all was over, presided at the interment. When we slid the body into the grave, we both were shaken to the core. The loss we felt was not the loss of ham but the loss of pig. He had evidently become precious to me, not that he represented a distant nourishment in a hungry time, but that he had suffered in a suffering world. But I'm running ahead of my story and shall have to go back.

4 My pigpen is at the bottom of an old orchard below the house. The pigs I have raised have lived in a faded building that once was an icehouse. There is a pleasant yard to move about in, shaded by an apple

tree that overhangs the low rail fence. A pig couldn't ask for anything better—or none has, at any rate. The sawdust in the icehouse makes a comfortable bottom in which to root, and a warm bed. This sawdust, however, came under suspicion when the pig took sick. One of my neighbors said he thought the pig would have done better on new ground—the same principle that applies in planting potatoes. He said there might be something unhealthy about that sawdust, that he never thought well of sawdust.

5 It was about four o'clock in the afternoon when I first noticed that there was something wrong with the pig. He failed to appear at the trough for his supper, and when a pig (or a child) refuses supper a chill wave of fear runs through any household, or ice-household. After examining my pig, who was stretched out in the sawdust inside the building, I went to the phone and cranked it four times. Mr. Dameron answered. "What's good for a sick pig?" I asked. (There is never any identification needed on a country phone; the person on the other end knows who is talking by the sound of the voice and by the character of the question.)

6 "I don't know, I never had a sick pig," said Mr. Dameron, "but I can find out quick enough. You hang up and I'll call Henry."

7 Mr. Dameron was back on the line again in five minutes. "Henry says roll him over on his back and give him two ounces of castor oil or sweet oil, and if that doesn't do the trick give him an injection of soapy water. He says he's almost sure the pig's plugged up, and even if he's wrong, it can't do any harm."

8 I thanked Mr. Dameron. I didn't go right down to the pig, though. I sank into a chair and sat still for a few minutes to think about my troubles, and then I got up and went to the barn, catching up on some odds and ends that needed tending to. Unconsciously I held off, for an hour, the deed by which I would officially recognize the collapse of the performance of raising a pig; I wanted no interruption in the regularity of feeding, the steadiness of growth, the even succession of days. I wanted no interruption, wanted no oil, no deviation. I just wanted to keep on raising a pig, full meal after full meal, spring into summer into fall. I didn't even know whether there were two ounces of castor oil on the place.

9 Shortly after five o'clock I remembered that we had been invited out to dinner that night and realized that if I were to dose a pig there was no time to lose. The dinner date seemed a familiar conflict: I move in a desultory society and often a week or two will roll by without my going to anybody's house to dinner or anyone's coming to mine, but when an occasion does arise, and I am summoned, something usually turns up (an hour or two in advance) to make all human intercourse seem vastly inappropriate. I have come to believe that there is in hostesses a special power of divination, and that they deliberately arrange

dinners to coincide with pig failure or some other sort of failure. At any rate, it was after five o'clock and I knew I could put off no longer the evil hour.

10 When my son and I arrived at the pigyard, armed with a small bottle of castor oil and a length of clothesline, the pig had emerged from his house and was standing in the middle of his yard, listlessly. He gave us a slim greeting. I could see that he felt uncomfortable and uncertain. I had brought the clothesline thinking I'd have to tie him (the pig weighed more than a hundred pounds) but we never used it. My son reached down, grabbed both front legs, upset him quickly, and when he opened his mouth to scream I turned the oil into his throat—a pink, corrugated area I had never seen before. I had just time to read the label while the neck of the bottle was in his mouth. It said Puretest. The screams, slightly muffled by oil, were pitched in the hysterically high range of pig-sound, as though torture were being carried out, but they didn't last long: it was all over rather suddenly, and, his legs released, the pig righted himself.

11 In the upset position the corners of his mouth had been turned down, giving him a frowning expression. Back on his feet again, he regained the set smile that a pig wears even in sickness. He stood his ground, sucking slightly at the residue of oil; a few drops leaked out of his lips while his wicked eyes, shaded by their coy little lashes, turned on me in disgust and hatred. I scratched him gently with oily fingers and he remained quiet, as though trying to recall the satisfaction of being scratched when in health, and seeming to rehearse in his mind the indignity to which he had just been subjected. I noticed, as I stood there, four or five small dark spots on his back near the tail end, reddish brown in color, each about the size of a housefly. I could not make out what they were. They did not look troublesome but at the same time they did not look like mere surface bruises or chafe marks. Rather they seemed blemishes of internal origin. His stiff white bristles almost completely hid them and I had to part the bristles with my fingers to get a good look.

12 Several hours later, a few minutes before midnight, having dined well and at someone else's expense, I returned to the pighouse with a flashlight. The patient was asleep. Kneeling, I felt his ears (as you might put your hand on the forehead of a child) and they seemed cool, and then with the light made a careful examination of the yard and the house for sign that the oil had worked. I found none and went to bed.

13 We had been having an unseasonable spell of weather—hot, close days, with the fog shutting in every night, scaling for a few hours in midday, then creeping back again at dark, drifting in first over the trees on the point, then suddenly blowing across the fields, blotting out the world and taking possession of houses, men, and animals. Everyone kept hoping for a break, but the break failed to come. Next day was another hot one. I visited the pig before breakfast and tried to tempt him

with a little milk in his trough. He just stared at it, while I made a sucking sound through my teeth to remind him of past pleasures of the feast. With very small, timid pigs, weanlings, this ruse is often quite successful and will encourage them to eat; but with a large, sick pig the ruse is senseless and the sound I made must have made him feel, if anything, more miserable. He not only did not crave food, he felt a positive revulsion to it. I found a place under the apple tree where he had vomited in the night.

14 At this point, although a depression had settled over me, I didn't suppose that I was going to lose my pig. From the lustiness of a healthy pig a man derives a feeling of personal lustiness; the stuff that goes into the trough and is received with such enthusiasm is an earnest of some later feast of his own, and when this suddenly comes to an end and the food lies stale and untouched, souring in the sun, the pig's imbalance becomes the man's, vicariously, and life seems insecure, displaced, transitory.

15 As my own spirits declined, along with the pig's, the spirits of my vile old dachshund rose. The frequency of our trips down the footpath through the orchard to the pigyard delighted him, although he suffers greatly from arthritis, moves with difficulty, and would be bedridden if he could find anyone willing to serve him meals on a tray.

16 He never missed a chance to visit the pig with me, and he made many professional calls on his own. You could see him down there at all hours, his white face parting the grass along the fence as he wobbled and stumbled about, his stethoscope dangling—a happy quack, writing his villainous prescriptions and grinning his corrosive grin. When the enema bag appeared, and the bucket of warm suds, his happiness was complete, and he managed to squeeze his enormous body between the two lowest rails of the yard and then assumed full charge of the irrigation. Once, when I lowered the bag to check the flow, he reached in and hurriedly drank a few mouthfuls of the suds to test their potency. I have noticed that Fred will feverishly consume any substance that is associated with trouble—the bitter flavor is to his liking. When the bag was above reach, he concentrated on the pig and was everywhere at once, a tower of strength and inconvenience. The pig, curiously enough, stood rather quietly through this colonic carnival, and the enema, though ineffective, was not as difficult as I had anticipated.

17 I discovered, though, that once having given a pig an enema there is no turning back, no chance of resuming one of life's more stereotyped roles. The pig's lot and mine were inextricably bound now, as though the rubber tube were the silver cord.° From then until the time of his death I held the pig steadily in the bowl of my mind; the task of trying to deliver him from his misery became a strong obsession. His suffering

---

[17] **the silver cord:** an imaginary bond tying people's fates together

soon became the embodiment of all earthly wretchedness. Along toward the end of the afternoon, defeated in physicking,° I phoned the veterinary twenty miles away and placed the case formally in his hands. He was full of questions, and when I casually mentioned the dark spots on the pig's back, his voice changed its tone.

18 "I don't want to scare you," he said, "but when there are spots, erysipelas° has to be considered."

19 Together we considered erysipelas, with frequent interruptions from the telephone operator, who wasn't sure the connection had been established.

20 "If a pig has erysipelas can he give it to a person?" I asked.

21 "Yes, he can," replied the vet.

22 "Have they answered?" asked the operator.

23 "Yes, they have," I said. Then I addressed the vet again. "You better come over here and examine this pig right away."

24 "I can't come myself," said the vet, "but McFarland can come this evening if that's all right. Mac knows more about pigs than I do anyway. You needn't worry too much about the spots. To indicate erysipelas they would have to be deep hemorrhagic infarcts."°

25 "Deep hemorrhagic what?" I asked.

26 "Infarcts," said the vet.

27 "Have they answered?" asked the operator.

28 "Well," I said, "I don't know what you'd call these spots, except they're about the size of a housefly. If the pig has erysipelas I guess I have it, too, by this time, because we've been very close lately."

29 "McFarland will be over," said the vet.

30 I hung up. My throat felt dry and I went to the cupboard and got a bottle of whiskey. Deep hemorrhagic infarcts—the phrase began fastening its hooks in my head. I had assumed that there could be nothing much wrong with a pig during the months it was being groomed for murder; my confidence in the essential health and endurance of pigs had been strong and deep, particularly in the health of pigs that belonged to me and that were part of my proud scheme. The awakening had been violent and I minded it all the more because I knew that what could be true of my pig could be true also of the rest of my tidy world. I tried to put this distasteful idea from me, but it kept recurring. I took a short drink of the whiskey and then, although I wanted to go down to the yard and look for fresh signs, I was scared to. I was certain I had erysipelas.

31 It was long after dark and the supper dishes had been put away when a car drove in and McFarland got out. He had a girl with him. I could just make her out in the darkness—she seemed young and pretty.

[17] **physicking:** (obs.) doctoring

[18] **erysipelas:** an infectious, inflammatory skin disease

[24] **hemorrhagic infarcts:** tissue areas destroyed because bleeding deprived them of necessary blood supply

"This is Miss Owen," he said. "We've been having a picnic supper on the shore, that's why I'm late."

32 McFarland stood in the driveway and stripped off his jacket, then his shirt. His stocky arms and capable hands showed up in my flashlight's gleam as I helped him find his coverall and get zipped up. The rear seat of his car contained an astonishing amount of paraphernalia, which he soon overhauled, selecting a chain, a syringe, a bottle of oil, a rubber tube, and some other things I couldn't identify. Miss Owen said she'd go along with us and see the pig. I led the way down the warm slope of the orchard, my light picking out the path for them, and we all three climbed the fence, entered the pighouse, and squatted by the pig while McFarland took a rectal reading. My flashlight picked up the glitter of an engagement ring on the girl's hand.

33 "No elevation," said McFarland, twisting the thermometer in the light. "You needn't worry about erysipelas." He ran his hand slowly over the pig's stomach and at one point the pig cried out in pain.

34 "Poor piggledy-wiggledy!" said Miss Owen.

35 The treatment I had been giving the pig for two days was then repeated, somewhat more expertly, by the doctor, Miss Owen and I handing him things as he needed them—holding the chain that he had looped around the pig's upper jaw, holding the syringe, holding the bottle stopper, the end of the tube, all of us working in darkness and in comfort, working with the instinctive teamwork induced by emergency conditions, the pig unprotesting, the house shadowy, protecting, intimate. I went to bed tired but with a feeling of relief that I had turned over part of the responsibility of the case to a licensed doctor. I was beginning to think, though, that the pig was not going to live.

36 He died twenty-four hours later, or it might have been forty-eight—there is a blur in time here, and I may have lost or picked up a day in the telling and the pig one in the dying. At intervals during the last day I took cool fresh water down to him and at such times as he found the strength to get to his feet he would stand with head in the pail and snuffle his snout around. He drank a few sips but no more; yet it seemed to comfort him to dip his nose in water and bobble it about, sucking in and blowing out through his teeth. Much of the time, now, he lay indoors half buried in sawdust. Once, near the last, while I was attending him I saw him try to make a bed for himself but he lacked the strength, and when he set his snout into the dust he was unable to plow even the little furrow he needed to lie down in.

37 He came out of the house to die. When I went down, before going to bed, he lay stretched in the yard a few feet from the door. I knelt, saw that he was dead, and left him there: his face had a mild look, expressive neither of deep peace nor of deep suffering, although I think he had suffered a good deal. I went back up to the house and to bed, and cried internally—deep hemorrhagic intears. I didn't wake till nearly eight the next morning, and when I looked out the open window the

grave was already being dug, down beyond the dump under a wild apple. I could hear the spade strike against the small rocks that blocked the way. Never send to know for whom the grave is dug, I said to myself, it's dug for thee.° Fred, I well knew, was supervising the work of digging, so I ate breakfast slowly.

38 It was a Saturday morning. The thicket in which I found the gravediggers at work was dark and warm, the sky overcast. Here, among alders and young hackmatacks,° at the foot of the apple tree, Lennie had dug a beautiful hole, five feet long, three feet wide, three feet deep. He was standing in it, removing the last spadefuls of earth while Fred patrolled the brink in simple but impressive circles, disturbing the loose earth of the mound so that it trickled back in. There had been no rain in weeks and the soil, even three feet down, was dry and powdery. As I stood and stared, an enormous earthworm which had been partially exposed by the spade at the bottom dug itself deeper and made a slow withdrawal, seeking even remoter moistures at even lonelier depths. And just as Lennie stepped out and rested his spade against the tree and lit a cigarette, a small green apple separated itself from a branch overhead and fell into the hole. Everything about this last scene seemed overwritten—the dismal sky, the shabby woods, the imminence of rain, the worm (legendary bedfellow of the dead), the apple (conventional garnish of a pig).

39 But even so, there was a directness and dispatch about animal burial, I thought, that made it a more decent affair than human burial: there was no stopover in the undertaker's foul parlor, no wreath nor spray; and when we hitched a line to the pig's hind legs and dragged him swiftly from his yard, throwing our weight into the harness and leaving a wake of crushed grass and smoothed rubble over the dump, ours was a businesslike procession, with Fred, the dishonorable pallbearer, staggering along in the rear, his perverse bereavement showing in every seam in his face; and the post mortem performed handily and swiftly right at the edge of the grave, so that the inwards that had caused the pig's death preceded him into the ground and he lay at last resting squarely on the cause of his own undoing.

40 I threw in the first shovelful, and then we worked rapidly and without talk, until the job was complete. I picked up the rope, made it fast to Fred's collar (he is a notorious ghoul), and we all three filed back up the path to the house, Fred bringing up the rear and holding back every inch of the way, feigning unusual stiffness. I noticed that although he weighed far less than the pig, he was harder to drag, being possessed of the vital spark.

---

[37] **Never send to know . . . :** A mock version of a famous line in a sermon by the English clergyman and poet John Donne (1573–1631), "Never send to know for whom the bell tolls: it tolls for thee."

[38] **hackmatacks:** trees also known as tamaracks

41 The news of the death of my pig travelled fast and far, and I received many expressions of sympathy from friends and neighbors, for no one took the event lightly and the premature expiration of a pig is, I soon discovered, a departure which the community marks solemnly on its calendar, a sorrow in which it feels fully involved. I have written this account in penitence and in grief, as a man who failed to raise his pig, and to explain my deviation from the classic course of so many raised pigs. The grave in the woods is unmarked, but Fred can direct the mourner to it unerringly and with immense good will, and I know he and I shall often revisit it, singly and together, in seasons of reflection and despair, on flagless memorial days of our own choosing.

STUDY QUESTIONS

1. What effect coes White's title have on us as we begin reading and then continue? What does he gain and lose by settling on such a title?
2 Consider the opening sentence of White's essay. What "first impression" of the author does it leave us with? In what ways does it encourage us to keep reading?
3. White's second paragraph mentions a "tragedy" and a "ceremonial ending." Once you have understood what he means by these terms, ask yourself how the story that *he* will tell departs from the pattern established here. Why does he devote a whole paragraph to a "familiar scheme"? Where else in the essay does the idea of *drama* occur?
4. Study the role of the dog Fred in this narrative. Do you believe everything White says about him? In characterizing the dog as he does, what does White reveal to us about himself?
5. By what means does White make the dying pig into a character —a creature whose fate is of interest to us?
6. What would you say is the tone, or general manner, of "Death of a Pig"? Pick out several sentences or passages that seem to sum up that tone. Do you think you might be able to identify another E. B. White essay by recognizing its tone? What features would you look for?
7. What effect is created when, at the end of paragraph 3, White tells us that he is "running ahead of [his] story"? Has he made a careless mistake which will now be corrected? If not, why *has* he "run ahead of his story"?
8. Any story about a dying animal will be suspected of sentimentality, or a cheaply dramatic playing upon the reader's feelings. Do you think White avoids sentimentality here? If not, which passages strike you as sentimental? Insofar as White *has* warded off sentimentality, how has he done so? Look for specific instances to support your answer.

Joan Didion

The novelist and essayist Joan Didion was raised in Sacramento, California, well north of the area described in this essay. Her collections of nonfiction include *The White Album* and *Slouching Towards Bethlehem* (1968), from which "Some Dreamers . . ." is taken.

SOME DREAMERS OF THE GOLDEN DREAM

1 This is a story about love and death in the golden land, and begins with the country. The San Bernardino Valley lies only an hour east of Los Angeles by the San Bernardino Freeway but is in certain ways an alien place: not the coastal California of the subtropical twilights and the soft westerlies off the Pacific but a harsher California, haunted by the Mojave just beyond the mountains, devastated by the hot dry Santa Ana wind that comes down through the passes at 100 miles an hour and whines through the eucalyptus windbreaks and works on the nerves. October is the bad month for the wind, the month when breathing is difficult and the hills blaze up spontaneously. There has been no rain since April. Every voice seems a scream. It is the season of suicide and divorce and prickly dread, wherever the wind blows.

2 The Mormons settled this ominous country, and then they abandoned it, but by the time they left the first orange tree had been planted and for the next hundred years the San Bernardino Valley would draw a kind of people who imagined they might live among the talismanic fruit and prosper in the dry air, people who brought with them Midwestern ways of building and cooking and praying and who tried to graft those ways upon the land. The graft took in curious ways. This is the California where it is possible to live and die without ever eating an artichoke, without ever meeting a Catholic or a Jew. This is the California where it is easy to Dial-A-Devotion, but hard to buy a book. This is the country in which a belief in the literal interpretation of Genesis has slipped imperceptibly into a belief in the literal interpretation of *Double Indemnity,*° the country of the teased hair and the Capris and the girls for whom all life's promise comes down to a waltz-length white wedding dress and the birth of a Kimberly or a Sherry or a Debbi and a Tijuana° divorce and a return to hairdressers' school. "We were

---

2 **Double Indemnity:** a 1936 novel by James M. Cain (paragraph 25), and later a Hollywood murder movie, based on the idea named in its title: the payment of two times the stated value of a life insurance policy

Tijuana: Mexican border city, near San Diego, Calif.

just crazy kids," they say without regret, and look to the future. The future always looks good in the golden land, because no one remembers the past. Here is where the hot wind blows and the old ways do not seem relevant, where the divorce rate is double the national average and where one person in every thirty-eight lives in a trailer. Here is the last stop for all those who come from somewhere else, for all those who drifted away from the cold and the past and the old ways. Here is where they are trying to find a new life style, trying to find it in the only places they know to look: the movies and the newspapers. The case of Lucille Marie Maxwell Miller is a tabloid monument to that new life style.

3 Imagine Banyan Street first, because Banyan is where it happened. The way to Banyan is to drive west from San Bernardino out Foothill Boulevard, Route 66: past the Santa Fe switching yards, the Forty Winks Motel. Past the motel that is nineteen stucco tepees: "SLEEP IN A WIGWAM —GET MORE FOR YOUR WAMPUM." Past Fontana Drag City and the Fontana Church of the Nazarene and the Pit Stop A Go-Go; past Kaiser Steel, through Cucamonga, out to the Kapu Kai Restaurant-Bar and Coffee Shop, at the corner of Route 66 and Carnelian Avenue. Up Carnelian Avenue from the Kapu Kai, which means "Forbidden Seas," the subdivision flags whip in the harsh wind. "HALF-ACRE RANCHES! SNACK BARS! TRAVERTINE[3] ENTRIES! $95 DOWN." It is the trail of an intention gone haywire, the flotsam of the New California. But after a while the signs thin out on Carnelian Avenue, and the houses are no longer the bright pastels of the Springtime Home owners but the faded bungalows of the people who grow a few grapes and keep a few chickens out here, and then the hill gets steeper and the road climbs and even the bungalows are few, and here—desolate, roughly surfaced, lined with eucalyptus and lemon groves—is Banyan Street.

4 Like so much of this country, Banyan suggests something curious and unnatural. The lemon groves are sunken, down a three- or four-foot retaining wall, so that one looks directly into their dense foliage, too lush, unsettlingly glossy, the greenery of nightmare; the fallen eucalyptus bark is too dusty, a place for snakes to breed. The stones look not like natural stones but like the rubble of some unmentioned upheaval. There are smudge pots, and a closed cistern. To one side of Banyan there is the flat valley, and to the other the San Bernardino Mountains, a dark mass looming too high, too fast, nine, ten, eleven thousand feet, right there above the lemon groves. At midnight on Banyan Street there is no light at all, and no sound except the wind in the eucalyptus and a muffled barking of dogs. There may be a kennel somewhere, or the dogs may be coyotes.

---

[3] **TRAVERTINE:** suggestive of an ancient Roman villa

5 Banyan Street was the route Lucille Miller took home from the twenty-four-hour Mayfair Market on the night of October 7, 1964, a night when the moon was dark and the wind was blowing and she was out of milk, and Banyan Street was where, at about 12:30 A.M, her 1964 Volkswagen came to a sudden stop, caught fire, and began to burn. For an hour and fifteen minutes Lucille Miller ran up and down Banyan calling for help, but no cars passed and no help came. At three o'clock that morning, when the fire had been put out and the California Highway Patrol officers were completing their report, Lucille Miller was still sobbing and incoherent, for her husband had been asleep in the Volkswagen. "What will I tell the children, when there's nothing left, nothing left in the casket," she cried to the friend called to comfort her. "How can I tell them there's nothing left?"

6 In fact there was something left, and a week later it lay in the Draper Mortuary Chapel in a closed bronze coffin blanketed with pink carnations. Some 200 mourners heard Elder Robert E. Denton of the Seventh-Day Adventist Church of Ontario speak of "the temper of fury that has broken out among us." For Gordon Miller, he said, there would be "no more death, no more heartaches, no more misunderstandings." Elder Ansel Bristol mentioned the "peculiar" grief of the hour. Elder Fred Jensen asked "what shall it profit a man, if he shall gain the whole world, and lose his own soul?" A light rain fell, a blessing in a dry season, and a female vocalist sang "Safe in the Arms of Jesus." A tape recording of the service was made for the widow, who was being held without bail in the San Bernardino County Jail on a charge of first-degree murder.

7 Of course she came from somewhere else, came off the prairie in search of something she had seen in a movie or heard on the radio, for this is a Southern California story. She was born on January 17, 1930, in Winnipeg, Manitoba, the only child of Gordon and Lily Maxwell, both schoolteachers and both dedicated to the Seventh-Day Adventist Church, whose members observe the Sabbath on Saturday, believe in an apocalyptic Second Coming, have a strong missionary tendency, and, if they are strict, do not smoke, drink, eat meat, use makeup, or wear jewelry, including wedding rings. By the time Lucille Maxwell enrolled at Walla Walla College in College Place, Washington, the Adventist school where her parents then taught, she was an eighteen-year-old possessed of unremarkable good looks and remarkable high spirits. "Lucille wanted to see the world," her father would say in retrospect, "and I guess she found out."

8 The high spirits did not seem to lend themselves to an extended course of study at Walla Walla College, and in the spring of 1949 Lucille Maxwell met and married Gordon ("Cork") Miller, a twenty-four-year-old graduate of Walla Walla and of the University of Oregon dental school, then stationed at Fort Lewis as a medical officer. "Maybe you

could say it was love at first sight," Mr. Maxwell recalls. "Before they were ever formally introduced, he sent Lucille a dozen and a half roses with a card that said even if she didn't come out on a date with him, he hoped she'd find the roses pretty anyway." The Maxwells remember their daughter as a "radiant" bride.

9 Unhappy marriages so resemble one another that we do not need to know too much about the course of this one. There may or may not have been trouble on Guam, where Cork and Lucille Miller lived while he finished his Army duty. There may or may not have been problems in the small Oregon town where he first set up private practice. There appears to have been some disappointment about their move to California: Cork Miller had told friends that he wanted to become a doctor, that he was unhappy as a dentist and planned to enter the Seventh-Day Adventist College of Medical Evangelists at Loma Linda, a few miles south of San Bernardino. Instead he bought a dental practice in the west end of San Bernardino County, and the family settled there, in a modest house on the kind of street where there are always tricycles and revolving credit and dreams about bigger houses, better streets. That was 1957. By the summer of 1964, they had achieved the bigger house on the better street and the familiar accouterments of a family on its way up: the $30,000 a year, the three children for the Christmas card, the picture window, the family room, the newspaper photographs that showed "Mrs. Gordon Miller, Ontario Heart Fund Chairman. . . ." They were paying the familiar price for it. And they had reached the familiar season of divorce.

10 It might have been anyone's bad summer, anyone's siege of heat and nerves and migraine and money worries, but this one began particularly early and particularly badly. On April 24 an old friend, Elaine Hayton, died suddenly; Lucille Miller had seen her only the night before. During the month of May, Cork Miller was hospitalized briefly with a bleeding ulcer, and his usual reserve deepened into depression. He told his accountant that he was "sick of looking at open mouths," and threatened suicide. By July 8, the conventional tensions of love and money had reached the conventional impasse in the new house on the acre lot at 8488 Bella Vista, and Lucille Miller filed for divorce. Within a month, however, the Millers seemed reconciled. They saw a marriage counselor. They talked about a fourth child. It seemed that the marriage had reached the traditional truce, the point at which so many resign themselves to cutting both their losses and their hopes.

11 But the Millers' season of trouble was not to end that easily. October 7 began as a commonplace enough day, one of those days that sets the teeth on edge with its tedium, its small frustrations. The temperature reached 102° in San Bernardino that afternoon, and the Miller children were home from school because of Teachers' Institute. There

was ironing to be dropped off. There was a trip to pick up a prescription for Nembutal,° a trip to a self-service dry cleaner. In the early evening, an unpleasant accident with the Volkswagen: Cork Miller hit and killed a German shepherd, and afterward said that his head felt "like it had a Mack truck on it." It was something he often said. As of that evening Cork Miller was $63,479 in debt, including the $29,637 mortgage on the new house, a debt load which seemed oppressive to him. He was a man who wore his responsibilities uneasily, and complained of migraine headaches almost constantly.

12 He ate alone that night, from a TV tray in the living room. Later the Millers watched John Forsythe and Senta Berger in *See How They Run,* and when the movie ended, about eleven, Cork Miller suggested that they go out for milk. He wanted some hot chocolate. He took a blanket and pillow from the couch and climbed into the passenger seat of the Volkswagen. Lucille Miller remembers reaching over to lock his door as she backed down the driveway. By the time she left the Mayfair Market, and long before they reached Banyan Street, Cork Miller appeared to be asleep.

13 There is some confusion in Lucille Miller's mind about what happened between 12:30 A.M., when the fire broke out, and 1:50 A.M., when it was reported. She says that she was driving east on Banyan Street at about 35 m.p.h. when she felt the Volkswagen pull sharply to the right. The next thing she knew the car was on the embankment, quite near the edge of the retaining wall, and flames were shooting up behind her. She does not remember jumping out. She does remember prying up a stone with which she broke the window next to her husband, and then scrambling down the retaining wall to try to find a stick. "I don't know how I was going to push him out," she says. "I just thought if I had a stick, I'd push him out." She could not, and after a while she ran to the intersection of Banyan and Carnelian Avenue. There are no houses at that corner, and almost no traffic. After one car had passed without stopping, Lucille Miller ran back down Banyan toward the burning Volkswagen. She did not stop, but she slowed down, and in the flames she could see her husband. He was, she said, "just black."

14 At the first house up Sapphire Avenue, half a mile from the Volkswagen, Lucille Miller finally found help. There Mrs. Robert Swenson called the sheriff, and then, at Lucille Miller's request, she called Harold Lance, the Millers' lawyer and their close friend. When Harold Lance arrived he took Lucille Miller home to his wife, Joan. Twice Harold Lance and Lucille Miller returned to Banyan Street and talked to the Highway Patrol officers. A third time Harold Lance returned alone, and when he came back he said to Lucille Miller, "O.K. . . . you don't talk any more."

---

[11] **Nembutal:** brand name of a common tranquilizer, phenobarbitol

15 When Lucille Miller was arrested the next afternoon, Sandy Slagle was with her. Sandy Slagle was the intense, relentlessly loyal medical student who used to baby-sit for the Millers, and had been living as a member of the family since she graduated from high school in 1959. The Millers took her away from a difficult home situation, and she thinks of Lucille Miller not only as "more or less a mother or a sister" but as "the most wonderful character" she has ever known. On the night of the accident, Sandy Slagle was in her dormitory at Loma Linda University, but Lucille Miller called her early in the morning and asked her to come home. The doctor was there when Sandy Slagle arrived, giving Lucille Miller an injection of Nembutal. "She was crying as she was going under," Sandy Slagle recalls. "Over and over she'd say, 'Sandy, all the hours I spent trying to save him and now what are they trying to *do* to me?' "

16 At 1:30 that afternoon, Sergeant William Paterson and Detectives Charles Callahan and Joseph Karr of the Central Homicide Division arrived at 8488 Bella Vista. "One of them appeared at the bedroom door," Sandy Slagle remembers, "and said to Lucille, 'You've got ten minutes to get dressed or we'll take you as you are.' She was in her nightgown, you know, so I tried to get her dressed."

17 Sandy Slagle tells the story now as if by rote, and her eyes do not waver. "So I had her panties and bra on her and they opened the door again, so I got some Capris on her, you know, and a scarf." Her voice drops. "And then they just took her."

18 The arrest took place just twelve hours after the first report that there had been an accident on Banyan Street, a rapidity which would later prompt Lucille Miller's attorney to say that the entire case was an instance of trying to justify a reckless arrest. Actually what first caused the detectives who arrived on Banyan Street toward dawn that morning to give the accident more than routine attention were certain apparent physical inconsistencies. While Lucille Miller had said that she was driving about 35 m.p.h. when the car swerved to a stop, an examination of the cooling Volkswagen showed that it was in low gear, and that the parking rather than the driving lights were on. The front wheels, moreover, did not seem to be in exactly the position that Lucille Miller's description of the accident would suggest, and the right rear wheel was dug in deep, as if it had been spun in place. It seemed curious to the detectives, too, that a sudden stop from 35 m.p.h.—the same jolt which was presumed to have knocked over a gasoline can in the back seat and somehow started the fire—should have left two milk cartons upright on the back floorboard, and the remains of a Polaroid camera box lying apparently undisturbed on the back seat.

19 No one, however, could be expected to give a precise account of what did and did not happen in a moment of terror, and none of these inconsistencies seemed in themselves incontrovertible evidence of criminal intent. But they did interest the Sheriff's Office, as did Gordon

Miller's apparent unconsciousness at the time of the accident, and the length of time it had taken Lucille Miller to get help. Something, moreover, struck the investigators as wrong about Harold Lance's attitude when he came back to Banyan Street the third time and found the investigation by no means over. "The way Lance was acting," the prosecuting attorney said later, "they thought maybe they'd hit a nerve."

20 And so it was that on the morning of October 8, even before the doctor had come to give Lucille Miller an injection to calm her, the San Bernardino County Sheriff's Office was trying to construct another version of what might have happened between 12:30 and 1:50 A.M. The hypothesis they would eventually present was based on the somewhat tortuous premise that Lucille Miller had undertaken a plan which failed: a plan to stop the car on the lonely road, spread gasoline over her presumably drugged husband, and, with a stick on the accelerator, gently "walk" the Volkswagen over the embankment, where it would tumble four feet down the retaining wall into the lemon grove and almost certainly explode. If this happened, Lucille Miller might then have somehow negotiated the two miles up Carnelian to Bella Vista in time to be home when the accident was discovered. This plan went awry, according to the Sheriff's Office hypothesis, when the car would not go over the rise of the embankment. Lucille Miller might have panicked then—after she had killed the engine the third or fourth time, say, out there on the dark road with the gasoline already spread and the dogs baying and the wind blowing and the unspeakable apprehension that a pair of headlights would suddenly light up Banyan Street and expose her there—and set the fire herself.

21 Although this version accounted for some of the physical evidence —the car in low because it had been started from a dead stop, the parking lights on because she could not do what needed doing without some light, a rear wheel spun in repeated attempts to get the car over the embankment, the milk cartons upright because there had been no sudden stop—it did not seem on its own any more or less credible than Lucille Miller's own story. Moreover, some of the physical evidence did seem to support her story: a nail in a front tire, a nine-pound rock found in the car, presumably the one with which she had broken the window in an attempt to save her husband. Within a few days an autopsy had established that Gordon Miller was alive when he burned, which did not particularly help the State's case, and that he had enough Nembutal and Sandoptal° in his blood to put the average person to sleep, which did: on the other hand Gordon Miller habitually took both Nembutal and Fiorinal (a common headache prescription which contains Sandoptal), and had been ill besides.

---

[21] **Sandoptal:** a tranquilizer

22 It was a spotty case, and to make it work at all the State was going to have to find a motive. There was talk of unhappiness, talk of another man. That kind of motive, during the next few weeks, was what they set out to establish. They set out to find it in accountants' ledgers and double-indemnity clauses and motel registers, set out to determine what might move a woman who believed in all the promises of the middle class—a woman who had been chairman of the Heart Fund and who always knew a reasonable little dressmaker and who had come out of the bleak wild of prairie fundamentalism to find what she imagined to be the good life—what should drive such a woman to sit on a street called Bella Vista and look out her new picture window into the empty California sun and calculate how to burn her husband alive in a Volkswagen. They found the wedge they wanted closer at hand than they might have at first expected, for, as testimony would reveal later at the trial, it seemed that in December of 1963 Lucille Miller had begun an affair with the husband of one of her friends, a man whose daughter called her "Auntie Lucille," a man who might have seemed to have the gift for people and money and the good life that Cork Miller so noticeably lacked. The man was Arthwell Hayton, a well-known San Bernardino attorney and at one time a member of the district attorney's staff.

23 In some ways it was the conventional clandestine affair in a place like San Bernardino, a place where little is bright or graceful, where it is routine to misplace the future and easy to start looking for it in bed. Over the seven weeks that it would take to try Lucille Miller for murder, Assistant District Attorney Don A. Turner and defense attorney Edward P. Foley would between them unfold a curiously predictable story. There were the falsified motel registrations. There were the lunch dates, the afternoon drives in Arthwell Hayton's red Cadillac convertible. There were the interminable discussions of the wronged partners. There were the confidantes ("I knew everything," Sandy Slagle would insist fiercely later. "I knew every time, places, everything") and there were the words remembered from bad magazine stories ("Don't kiss me, it will trigger things," Lucille Miller remembered telling Arthwell Hayton in the parking lot of Harold's Club in Fontana after lunch one day) and there were the notes, the sweet exchanges: "Hi Sweetie Pie! You are my cup of tea!! Happy Birthday—you don't look a day over 29!! Your baby, Arthwell."

24 And, toward the end, there was the acrimony. It was April 24, 1964, when Arthwell Hayton's wife, Elaine, died suddenly, and nothing good happened after that. Arthwell Hayton had taken his cruiser, *Captain's Lady,* over to Catalina° that weekend; he called home at nine o'clock Friday night, but did not talk to his wife because Lucille Miller an-

---

24 **Catalina:** island off the coast of southern California

swered the telephone and said that Elaine was showering. The next morning the Haytons' daughter found her mother in bed, dead. The newspapers reported the death as accidental, perhaps the result of an allergy to hair spray. When Arthwell Hayton flew home from Catalina that weekend, Lucille Miller met him at the airport, but the finish had already been written.

25 It was in the breakup that the affair ceased to be in the conventional mode and began to resemble instead the novels of James M. Cain,° the movies of the late 1930's, all the dreams in which violence and threats and blackmail are made to seem commonplaces of middle-class life. What was most startling about the case that the State of California was preparing against Lucille Miller was something that had nothing to do with law at all, something that never appeared in the eight-column afternoon headlines but was always there between them: the revelation that the dream was teaching the dreamers how to live. Here is Lucille Miller talking to her lover sometime in the early summer of 1964, after he had indicated that, on the advice of his minister, he did not intend to see her any more: "First, I'm going to go to that dear pastor of yours and tell him a few things. . . . When I do tell him that, you won't be in the Redlands Church any more. . . . Look, Sonny Boy, if you think your reputation is going to be ruined, your life won't be worth two cents." Here is Arthwell Hayton, to Lucille Miller: "I'll go to Sheriff Frank Bland and tell him some things that I know about you until you'll wish you'd never heard of Arthwell Hayton." For an affair between a Seventh-Day Adventist dentist's wife and a Seventh-Day Adventist personal-injury lawyer, it seems a curious kind of dialogue.

26 "Boy, I could get that little boy coming and going," Lucille Miller later confided to Erwin Sprengle, a Riverside contractor who was a business partner of Arthwell Hayton's and a friend to both the lovers. (Friend or no, on this occasion he happened to have an induction coil attached to his telephone in order to tape Lucille Miller's call.) "And he hasn't got one thing on me that he can prove. I mean, I've got concrete —he has nothing concrete." In the same taped conversation with Erwin Sprengle, Lucille Miller mentioned a tape that she herself had surreptitiously made, months before, in Arthwell Hayton's car.

27 "I said to him, I said 'Arthwell, I just feel like I'm being used.' . . . He started sucking his thumb and he said 'I love you. . . . This isn't something that happened yesterday. I'd marry you tomorrow if I could. I don't love Elaine.' He'd love to hear that played back, wouldn't he?"

28 "Yeah," drawled Sprengle's voice on the tape. "That would be just a little incriminating, wouldn't it?"

---

[25] **James M. Cain:** American novelist who specialized in sensational crime stories such as *The Postman Always Rings Twice* (1934) and *Double Indemnity* (1936).

29 "Just a *little* incriminating," Lucille Miller agreed. "It really *is.*"

30 Later on the tape, Sprengle asked where Cork Miller was.

31 "He took the children down to the church."

32 "You didn't go?"

33 "No."

34 "You're naughty."

35 It was all, moreover, in the name of "love"; everyone involved placed a magical faith in the efficacy of the very word. There was the significance that Lucille Miller saw in Arthwell's saying that he "loved" her, that he did not "love" Elaine. There was Arthwell insisting, later, at the trial, that he had never said it, that he may have "whispered sweet nothings in her ear" (as her defense hinted that he had whispered in many ears), but he did not remember bestowing upon her the special seal, saying the word, declaring "love." There was the summer evening when Lucille Miller and Sandy Slagle followed Arthwell Hayton down to his new boat in its mooring at Newport Beach and untied the lines with Arthwell aboard, Arthwell and a girl with whom he later testified he was drinking hot chocolate and watching television. "I did that on purpose," Lucille Miller told Erwin Sprengle later, "to save myself from letting my heart do something crazy."

36 January 11, 1965, was a bright warm day in Southern California, the kind of day when Catalina floats on the Pacific horizon and the air smells of orange blossoms and it is a long way from the bleak and difficult East, a long way from the cold, a long way from the past. A woman in Hollywood staged an all-night sit-in on the hood of her car to prevent repossession by a finance company. A seventy-year-old pensioner drove his station wagon at five miles an hour past three Gardena poker parlors and emptied three pistols and a twelve-gauge shotgun through their windows, wounding twenty-nine people. "Many young women become prostitutes just to have enough money to play cards," he explained in a note. Mrs. Nick Adams said that she was "not surprised" to hear her husband announce his divorce plans on the Les Crane Show, and, farther north, a sixteen-year-old jumped off the Golden Gate Bridge and lived.

37 And, in the San Bernardino County Courthouse, the Miller trial opened. The crowds were so bad that the glass courtroom doors were shattered in the crush, and from then on identification disks were issued to the first forty-three spectators in line. The line began forming at 6 a.m., and college girls camped at the courthouse all night, with stores of graham crackers and No-Cal.

38 All they were doing was picking a jury, those first few days, but the sensational nature of the case had already suggested itself. Early in December there had been an abortive first trial, a trial at which no evidence was ever presented because on the day the jury was seated the San Bernardino *Sun-Telegram* ran an "inside" story quoting Assistant

District Attorney Don Turner, the prosecutor, as saying, "We are looking into the circumstances of Mrs. Hayton's death. In view of the current trial concerning the death of Dr. Miller, I do not feel I should comment on Mrs. Hayton's death." It seemed that there had been barbiturates in Elaine Hayton's blood, and there had seemed some irregularity about the way she was dressed on that morning when she was found under the covers, dead. Any doubts about the death at the time, however, had never gotten as far as the Sheriff's Office. "I guess somebody didn't want to rock the boat," Turner said later. "These were prominent people."

39 Although all of that had not been in the *Sun-Telegram*'s story, an immediate mistrial had been declared. Almost as immediately, there had been another development: Arthwell Hayton had asked newspapermen to an 11 a.m. Sunday morning press conference in his office. There had been television cameras, and flash bulbs popping. "As you gentlemen may know," Hayton had said, striking a note of stiff bonhomie, "there are very often women who become amorous toward their doctor or lawyer. This does not mean on the physician's or lawyer's part that there is any romance toward the patient or client."

40 "Would you deny that you were having an affair with Mrs. Miller?" a reporter had asked.

41 "I would deny that there was any romance on my part whatsoever."

42 It was a distinction he would maintain through all the wearing weeks to come.

43 So they had come to see Arthwell, these crowds who now milled beneath the dusty palms outside the courthouse, and they had also come to see Lucille, who appeared as a slight, intermittently pretty woman, already pale from lack of sun, a woman who would turn thirty-five before the trial was over and whose tendency toward haggardness was beginning to show, a meticulous woman who insisted, against her lawyer's advice, on coming to court with her hair piled high and lacquered. "I would've been happy if she'd come in with it hanging loose, but Lucille wouldn't do that," her lawyer said. He was Edward P. Foley, a small, emotional Irish Catholic who several times wept in the courtroom. "She has a great honesty, this woman," he added, "but this honesty about her appearance always worked against her."

44 By the time the trial opened, Lucille Miller's appearance included maternity clothes, for an official examination on December 18 had revealed that she was then three and a half months pregnant, a fact which made picking a jury even more difficult than usual, for Turner was asking the death penalty. "It's unfortunate but there it is," he would say of the pregnancy to each juror in turn, and finally twelve were seated, seven of them women, the youngest forty-one, an assembly of the very peers—housewives, a machinist, a truck driver, a grocery-store manag-

er, a filing clerk—above whom Lucille Miller had wanted so badly to rise.

45 That was the sin, more than the adultery, which tended to reinforce the one for which she was being tried. It was implicit in both the defense and the prosecution that Lucille Miller was an erring woman, a woman who perhaps wanted too much. But to the prosecution she was not merely a woman who would want a new house and want to go to parties and run up high telephone bills ($1,152 in ten months), but a woman who would go so far as to murder her husband for his $80,000 in insurance, making it appear an accident in order to collect another $40,000 in double indemnity and straight accident policies. To Turner she was a woman who did not want simply her freedom and a reasonable alimony (she could have had that, the defense contended, by going through with her divorce suit), but wanted everything, a woman motivated by "love and greed." She was a "manipulator." She was a "user of people."

46 To Edward Foley, on the other hand, she was an impulsive woman who "couldn't control her foolish little heart." Where Turner skirted the pregnancy, Foley dwelt upon it, even calling the dead man's mother down from Washington to testify that her son had told her they were going to have another baby because Lucille felt that it would "do much to weld our home again in the pleasant relations that we used to have." Where the prosecution saw a "calculator," the defense saw a "blabbermouth," and in fact Lucille Miller did emerge as an ingenuous conversationalist. Just as, before her husband's death, she had confided in her friends about her love affair, so she chatted about it after his death, with the arresting sergeant. "Of course Cork lived with it for years, you know," her voice was heard to tell Sergeant Paterson on a tape made the morning after her arrest. "After Elaine died, he pushed the panic button one night and just asked me right out, and that, I think, was when he really—the first time he really faced it." When the sergeant asked why she had agreed to talk to him, against the specific instructions of her lawyers, Lucille Miller said airily, "Oh, I've always been basically quite an honest person. . . . I mean I can put a hat in the cupboard and say it cost ten dollars less, but basically I've always kind of just lived my life the way I wanted to, and if you don't like it you can take off."

47 The prosecution hinted at men other than Arthwell, and even, over Foley's objections, managed to name one. The defense called Miller suicidal. The prosecution produced experts who said that the Volkswagen fire could not have been accidental. Foley produced witnesses who said that it could have been. Lucille's father, now a junior-high-school teacher in Oregon, quoted Isaiah to reporters: *"Every tongue that shall rise against thee in judgment thou shalt condemn."* "Lucille did wrong, her affair," her mother said judiciously. "With her it was love. But with some I guess it's just passion." There was Debbie, the Millers' fourteen-year-old, testifying in a steady voice about how she and her mother had gone to a supermarket to buy the gasoline can the week before the

accident. There was Sandy Slagle, in the courtroom every day, declaring that on at least one occasion Lucille Miller had prevented her husband not only from committing suicide but from committing suicide in such a way that it would appear an accident and ensure the double-indemnity payment. There was Wenche Berg, the pretty twenty-seven-year-old Norwegian governess to Arthwell Hayton's children, testifying that Arthwell had instructed her not to allow Lucille Miller to see or talk to the children.

48 Two months dragged by, and the headlines never stopped. Southern California's crime reporters were headquartered in San Bernardino for the duration: Howard Hertel from the *Times,* Jim Bennett and Eddy Jo Bernal from the *Herald-Examiner.* Two months in which the Miller trial was pushed off the *Examiner*'s front page only by the Academy Award nominations and Stan Laurel's death. And finally, on March 2, after Turner had reiterated that it was a case of "love and greed," and Foley had protested that his client was being tried for adultery, the case went to the jury.

49 They brought in the verdict, guilty of murder in the first degree, at 4:50 p.m. on March 5. "She didn't do it," Debbie Miller cried, jumping up from the spectators' section. "She didn't *do* it." Sandy Slagle collapsed in her seat and began to scream. "Sandy, for God's sake please *don't,*" Lucille Miller said in a voice that carried across the courtroom, and Sandy Slagle was momentarily subdued. But as the jurors left the courtroom she screamed again: "You're murderers. . . . Every last one of you is a *murderer.*" Sheriff's deputies moved in then, each wearing a string tie that read "1965 SHERIFF'S RODEO," and Lucille Miller's father, that sad-faced junior-high-school teacher who believed in the word of Christ and the dangers of wanting to see the world, blew her a kiss off his fingertips.

50 The California Institution for Women at Frontera, where Lucille Miller is now, lies down where Euclid Avenue turns into country road, not too many miles from where she once lived and shopped and organized the Heart Fund Ball. Cattle graze across the road, and Rainbirds° sprinkle the alfalfa. Frontera has a softball field and tennis courts, and looks as if it might be a California junior college, except that the trees are not yet high enough to conceal the concertina wire around the top of the Cyclone fence. On visitors' day there are big cars in the parking area, big Buicks and Pontiacs that belong to grandparents and sisters and fathers (not many of them belong to husbands), and some of them have bumper stickers that say "SUPPORT YOUR LOCAL POLICE."

51 A lot of California murderesses live here, a lot of girls who somehow misunderstood the promise. Don Turner put Sandra Garner here

---

50 **Rainbirds:** watering machines for irrigation

(and her husband in the gas chamber at San Quentin) after the 1959 desert killings known to crime reporters as "the soda-pop murders." Carole Tregoff is here, and has been ever since she was convicted of conspiring to murder Dr. Finch's wife in West Covina, which is not too far from San Bernardino. Carole Tregoff is in fact a nurse's aide in the prison hospital, and might have attended Lucille Miller had her baby been born at Frontera; Lucille Miller chose instead to have it outside, and paid for the guard who stood outside the delivery room in St. Bernardine's Hospital. Debbie Miller came to take the baby home from the hospital, in a white dress with pink ribbons, and Debbie was allowed to choose a name. She named the baby Kimi Kai. The children live with Harold and Joan Lance now, because Lucille Miller will probably spend ten years at Frontera. Don Turner waived his original request for the death penalty (it was generally agreed that he had demanded it only, in Edward Foley's words, "to get anybody with the slightest trace of human kindness in their veins off the jury"), and settled for life imprisonment with the possibility of parole. Lucille Miller does not like it at Frontera, and has had trouble adjusting. "She's going to have to learn humility," Turner says. "She's going to have to use her ability to charm, to manipulate."

52 The new house is empty now, the house on the street with the sign that says

PRIVATE ROAD
BELLA VISTA
DEAD END

The Millers never did get it landscaped, and weeds grow up around the fieldstone siding. The television aerial has toppled on the roof, and a trash can is stuffed with the debris of family life: a cheap suitcase, a child's game called "Lie Detector." There is a sign on what would have been the lawn, and the sign reads "ESTATE SALE." Edward Foley is trying to get Lucille Miller's case appealed, but there have been delays. "A trial always comes down to a matter of sympathy," Foley says wearily now. "I couldn't create sympathy for her." Everyone is a little weary now, weary and resigned, everyone except Sandy Slagle, whose bitterness is still raw. She lives in an apartment near the medical school in Loma Linda, and studies reports of the case in *True Police Cases* and *Official Detective Stories.* "I'd much rather we not talk about the Hayton business too much," she tells visitors, and she keeps a tape recorder running. "I'd rather talk about Lucille and what a wonderful person she is and how her rights were violated." Harold Lance does not talk to visitors at all. "We don't want to give away what we can sell," he explains pleasantly; an attempt was made to sell Lucille Miller's personal story to *Life,* but *Life* did not want to buy it. In the district attorney's offices they are prosecuting other murders now, and do not see why the Miller trial attracted so much attention. "It wasn't a very interesting murder as murders go," Don Turner says laconically. Elaine Hayton's death is no longer under investigation. "We know everything we want to know," Turner says.

53 Arthwell Hayton's office is directly below Edward Foley's. Some people around San Bernardino say that Arthwell Hayton suffered; others say that he did not suffer at all. Perhaps he did not, for time past is not believed to have any bearing upon time present or future, out in the golden land where every day the world is born anew. In any case, on October 17, 1965, Arthwell Hayton married again, married his children's pretty governess, Wenche Berg, at a service in the Chapel of the Roses at a retirement village near Riverside. Later the newlyweds were feted at a reception for seventy-five in the dining room of Rose Garden Village. The bridegroom was in black tie, with a white carnation in his buttonhole. The bride wore a long white *peau de soie*° dress and carried a shower bouquet of sweetheart roses with stephanotis° streamers. A coronet of seed pearls held her illusion veil.

STUDY QUESTIONS

1. What effect did Didion's opening sentence have on you when you first read it, and how does it strike you now that you have read the whole essay? In what ways does that sentence make a suitable beginning to the story of Lucille Miller?
2. What is the tone or mood of the first paragraph as a whole? Pick out several uses of language that contribute to that tone, and make note of the way Didion has lent a psychological quality to physical details. Has she "overdone it"?
3. Read through Didion's second paragraph again. Why has she crowded that paragraph with details? What effect do you think she is trying to create in her readers' minds?
4. What is the effect of the sentence that ends paragraph 4? How is that effect connected to Didion's thematic emphasis throughout the essay?
5. Consider Didion's first six paragraphs as a unit leading to the information that Lucille Miller was charged with having murdered her husband. What effect does Didion gain by delaying that information? How have our sympathies been influenced in advance of learning about the trial and its outcome?
6. Although the characters in Didion's story do and say some surpris-

---

53 **peau de soie:** (Fr. "skin of silk") Japanese silk
stephanotis: white flowers often used in floral crowns

ing things, they do not seem like especially interesting people. Why do you think Didion found them worth writing about at such length?

7. Review the essay to see how much "hard" evidence of Lucille Miller's guilt has been presented. Is the case resolved to your satisfaction?
8. At what points in the essay do we learn information that decisively affects our sense of Lucille's character? Why do you suppose Didion wished to withhold that information for so long?
9. Look at the long sentence in paragraph 22 beginning "They set out to find it. . . ." How would you characterize the structure of that sentence? What kinds of authorial control does it suggest, and what is its intended effect?
10. What does Didion mean by saying (paragraph 25) that "the dream was teaching the dreamers how to live"? What is Didion's implied attitude, here and elsewhere, toward the "golden dream"?
11. In Didion's final paragraph, why does her emphasis fall where it does? If this is a "surprise ending" to an essay about an alleged murder, in what ways is it nevertheless appropriate to everything that has come before it?
12. If you have already thought about Questions 2, 3, and 4 above, you have been thinking about *symbolism,* or language that bears a special thematic appropriateness beyond its literal (factual) meaning. Pick out several further examples of such language, and be prepared to discuss their intended effects.

Mary McCarthy

Mary McCarthy has been a leading American novelist and essayist since the 1940s. Her works of fiction include *The Company She Keeps* and *The Groves of Academe.* "The Blackguard" is drawn from an autobiography, *Memories of a Catholic Girlhood* (1957).

THE BLACKGUARD°

1 Were he living today, my Protestant grandfather would be displeased to hear that the fate of his soul had once been the occasion of intense theological anxiety with the Ladies of the Sacred Heart. While

title **blackguard:** (pronouned *blag'ärd*) scoundrel, person of weak morals

his mortal part, all unaware, went about its eighteen holes of golf, its rubber of bridge before dinner at the club, his immortal part lay in jeopardy with us, the nuns and pupils of a strict convent school set on a wooded hill quite near a piece of worthless real estate he had bought under the impression that Seattle was expanding in a northerly direction. A sermon delivered at the convent by an enthusiastic Jesuit had disclosed to us his danger. Up to this point, the disparity in religion between my grandfather and myself had given me no serious concern. The death of my parents, while it had drawn us together in many senses, including the legal one (for I became his ward), had at the same time left the gulf of a generation between us, and my grandfather's Protestantism presented itself as a natural part of the grand, granite scenery on the other side. But the Jesuit's sermon destroyed this ordered view in a single thunderclap of doctrine.

2 As the priest would have it, this honest and upright man, a great favorite with the Mother Superior, was condemned to eternal torment by the accident of having been baptized. Had he been a Mohammedan, a Jew, a pagan, or the child of civilized unbelievers, a place in Limbo° would have been assured him; Cicero and Aristotle and Cyrus the Persian might have been his companions, and the harmless souls of unbaptized children might have frolicked about his feet. But if the Jesuit were right, all baptized Protestants went straight to Hell. A good life did not count in their favor. The baptismal rite, by conferring on them God's grace, made them also liable to His organizational displeasure. That is, baptism turned them Catholic whether they liked it or not, and their persistence in the Protestant ritual was a kind of asseverated apostasy. Thus my poor grandfather, sixty years behind in his Easter duty, actually reduced his prospects of salvation every time he sat down in the Presbyterian church.

3 The Mother Superior's sweet frown acknowledged me, an hour after the sermon, as I curtsied, all agitation, in her office doorway. Plainly, she had been expecting me. Madame MacIllvra, an able administrator, must have been resignedly ticking off the names of the Protestant pupils and parents all during the concluding parts of the morning's service. She had a faint worried air, when the conversation began, of depreciating the sermon: doctrinally, perhaps, correct, it had been wanting in delicacy; the fiery Jesuit, a missionary celebrity, had lived too long among the Eskimos. This disengaged attitude encouraged me to hope. Surely this lady, the highest authority I knew, could find a way out for my grandfather. She could see that he was a special case, outside the brutal rule of thumb laid down by the Jesuit. It was she, after all, in the convent, from whom all exemptions flowed, who created arbitrary holi-

---

[2] **Limbo:** according to some Catholics, a region between hell and heaven reserved for unbaptized infants, righteous people who died before the coming of Christ, and others whose final fate is questionable

days (called *congés* by the order's French tradition); it was she who permitted us to get forbidden books from the librarian and occasionally to receive letters unread by the convent censor. (As a rule, all slang expressions, violations of syntax, errors of spelling, as well as improper sentiments, were blacked out of our friends' communications, so unless we moved in a circle of young Addisons° or Burkes,° the letters we longed for came to us as fragments from which the original text could only be conjectured.) To my twelve-year-old mind, it appeared probable that Madame MacIllvra, our Mother Superior, had the power to give my grandfather *congé,* and I threw myself on her sympathies.

4 How could it be that my grandfather, the most virtuous person I knew, whose name was a byword among his friends and colleagues for a kind of rigid and fantastic probity—how could it be that this man should be lost, while I, the object of his admonition, the despair of his example—I, who yielded to every impulse, lied, boasted, betrayed—should, by virtue of regular attendance at the sacraments and the habit of easy penitence, be saved?

5 Madame MacIllvra's full white brow wrinkled; her childlike blue eyes clouded. Like many headmistresses, she loved a good cry, and she clasped me to her plump, quivering, middle-aged bosom. She understood; she was crying for my grandfather and the injustice of it too. She and my grandfather had, as a matter of fact, established a very amiable relation, in which both took pleasure. The masculine line and firmness of his character made an aesthetic appeal to her, and the billowy softness and depth of the Mother Superior struck him favorably, but, above all, it was their difference in religion that salted their conversations. Each of them enjoyed, whenever they met in her straight, black-and-white little office, a sense of broadness, of enlightenment, of transcendent superiority to petty prejudice. My grandfather would remember that he wrote a check every Christmas for two Sisters of Charity who visited his office; Madame MacIllvra would perhaps recall her graduate studies and Hume.° They had long, liberal talks which had the tone of *performances,* virtuoso feats of magnanimity were achieved on both sides. Afterward, they spoke of each other in nearly identical terms: "A very fine woman," "A very fine man."

6 All this (and possibly the suspicion that her verdict might be repeated at home) made Madame MacIllvra's answer slow. "Perhaps God," she murmured at last, "in His infinite mercy . . ." Yet this formulation satisfied neither of us. God's infinite mercy we believed in, but its manifestations were problematical. Sacred history showed us that it was more likely to fall on the Good Thief or the Woman Taken in

---

3 **Addisons:** people resembling Joseph Addison (1672–1719), British essayist and poet
Burkes: people resembling Edmund Burke (1729–1797), Irish statesman, orator, and author

5 **Hume:** David Hume (1711–1776), skeptical Scottish philosopher

Adultery than on persons of daily virtue and regular habits, like my grandfather. Our Catholic thoughts journeyed and met in a glance of alarmed recognition. Madame MacIllvra pondered. There were, of course, she said finally, other loopholes. If he had been improperly baptized . . . a careless clergyman . . . I considered this suggestion and shook my head. My grandfather was not the kind of man who, even as an infant, would have been guilty of a slovenly baptism.

7 It was a measure of Madame MacIllvra's intelligence, or of her knowledge of the world, that she did not, even then, when my grandfather's soul hung, as it were, pleadingly between us, suggest the obvious, the orthodox solution. It would have been ridiculous for me to try to convert my grandfather. Indeed, as it turned out later, I might have dropped him into the pit with my innocent traps (the religious books left open beside his cigar cutter, or "Grandpa, won't you take me to Mass this Sunday? I am so tired of going alone"). "Pray for him, my dear," said Madame MacIllvra, sighing, "and I will speak to Madame Barclay. The point may be open to interpretation. She may remember something in the Fathers of the Church. . . ."°

8 A few days later, Madame MacIllvra summoned me to her office. Not only Madame Barclay, the learned prefect of studies, but the librarian and even the convent chaplain had been called in. The Benedictine view, it seemed, differed sharply from the Dominican, but a key passage in Saint Athanasius° seemed to point to my grandfather's safety. The unbeliever, according to this generous authority, was not to be damned unless he rejected the true Church with sufficient knowledge and full consent of the will. Madame MacIllvra handed me the book, and I read the passage over. Clearly, he was saved. Sufficient knowledge he had not. The Church was foreign to him; he knew it only distantly, only by repute, like the heathen Hiawatha, who had heard strange stories of missionaries, white men in black robes who bore a Cross. Flinging my arms about Madame MacIllvra, I blessed for the first time the insularity of my grandfather's character, the long-jawed, shut face it turned toward ideas and customs not its own. I resolved to dismantle at once the little altar in my bedroom at home, to leave off grace before meals, elaborate fasting, and all ostentatious practices of devotion, lest the light of my example shine upon him too powerfully and burn him with sufficient knowledge to a crisp.

9 Since I was a five-day boarder, this project had no time to grow stale, and the next Sunday, at home, my grandfather remarked on the change in me, which my feeling for the dramatic had made far from

---

[7] **Fathers of the Church:** early Christian writers whose works are the main sources for the history, doctrines, and observances of the Catholic Church through the Middle Ages

[8] **St. Athanasius:** (c. 296–373) bishop of Alexandria and author of the Athanasian Creed, a central dogma of Catholicism

unobtrusive. "I hope," he said in a rather stern and ironical voice, "that you aren't using the *irreligious* atmosphere of this house as an excuse for backsliding. There will be time enough when you are older to change your beliefs if you want to." The unfairness of this rebuke delighted me. It put me solidly in the tradition of the saints and martyrs; Our Lord had known something like it, and so had Elsie Dinsmore° at the piano. Nevertheless, I felt quite angry and slammed the door of my room behind me as I went in to sulk. I almost wished that my grandfather would die at once, so that God could furnish him with the explanation of my behavior—certainly he would have to wait till the next life to get it; in this one he would only have seen in it an invasion of his personal liberties.

10 As though to reward me for my silence, the following Wednesday brought me the happiest moment of my life. In order to understand my happiness, which might otherwise seem perverse, the reader must yield himself to the spiritual atmosphere of the convent. If he imagines that the life we led behind those walls was bare, thin, cold, austere, sectarian, he will have to revise his views; our days were a tumult of emotion. In the first place, we ate, studied, and slept in that atmosphere of intrigue, rivalry, scandal, favoritism, tyranny, and revolt that is common to all girls' boarding schools and that makes "real" life afterward seem a long and improbable armistice, a cessation of the true anguish of activity. But above the tinkling of this girlish operetta, with its clink-clink of changing friendships, its plot of smuggled letters, notes passed from desk to desk, secrets, there sounded in the Sacred Heart convent heavier, more solemn strains, notes of a great religious drama, which was also all passion and caprice, in which salvation was the issue and God's rather sultanlike and elusive favor was besought, scorned, despaired of, connived for, importuned. It was the paradoxical element in Catholic doctrine that lent this drama its suspense. The Divine Despot we courted could not be bought, like a piece of merchandise, by long hours at the *prie-dieu,*° faithful attendance at the sacraments, obedience, reverence toward one's superiors. These solicitations helped, but it might well turn out that the worst girl in the school, whose pretty, haughty face wore rouge and a calm, closed look that advertised even to us younger ones some secret knowledge of men, was in the dark of her heart another Mary of Egypt,° the strumpet saint in our midst. Such notions furnished a strange counterpoint to discipline; surely the Mother Superior never could have expelled a girl without recalling, with a shade of perplexity,

---

9 **Elsie Dinsmore:** "goody-goody" heroine of many popular novels by the nineteenth-century American writer Martha Farquharson Finley

10 **prie-dieu:** (Fr. "pray-God") piece of furniture for kneeling on during prayer

Mary of Egypt: fifth-century penitent saint, thought to have been converted after packing a lifetime's-worth of sin into her adolescent years

the profligate youth of Saint Augustine° and of Saint Ignatius of Loyola.°

11 This dark-horse doctrine of salvation, with all its worldly wisdom and riddling charm, was deep in the idiom of the convent. The merest lay sister° could have sustained with spiritual poise her end of a conversation on the purification through sin with Mr. Auden, Herr Kafka, or *Gospodin* Dostoevski; ° and Madame MacIllvra, while she would have held it bad taste to bow down, like Father Zossima, before the murder in Dmitri Karamazov's° heart, would certainly have had him in for a series of long, interesting talks in her office.

12 Like all truly intellectual women, these were in spirit romantic desperadoes. They despised organizational heretics of the stamp of Luther and Calvin, but the great atheists and sinners were the heroes of the costume picture they taught as a subject called history. Marlowe, Baudelaire—above all, Byron—glowed like terrible stars above their literature courses. Little girls of ten were reciting "The Prisoner of Chillon" and hearing stories of Clare Clairmont, Caroline Lamb, the Segatti, and the swim across the Hellespont.° Even M. Voltaire° enjoyed a left-handed popularity. The nuns spoke of him with horror and admiration mingled: "A great mind, an unconquerable spirit—and what fearful use they were put to." In Rousseau,° an unbuttoned, middle-class figure, they had no interest whatever.

13 These infatuations, shared by the pupils, were brought into line with official Catholic opinion by a variety of strategems. The more highly educated nuns were able to accept the damnation of these great Luciferian spirits. A simple young nun, on the other hand, who played baseball and taught arithmetic to the sixth and seventh grades, used to tell her pupils that she personally was convinced that Lord Byron in his last hours must have made an act of contrition.°

14 It was not, therefore, unusual that a line from the works of this dissipated author should have been waiting for us on the blackboard of

---

St. Augustine: (354–430) bishop of Hippo in North Africa, a key father of the Catholic Church. His *Confessions* tell of a wild youth followed by a conversion.

St. Ignatius of Loyola: (1491–1556) Spanish soldier and ecclesiastic, founder of the Society of Jesus (Jesuits)

11 **lay sister** a woman who has taken religious vows and habit but is employed in her order chiefly in manual labor

Father Zossima, Dmitri Karamazov: characters in Dostoevski's masterpiece *The Brothers Karamazov* (1879–1880)

Mr. Auden, Herr Kafka, and Gospodin Dostoevski: writers concerned variously with religious conversion, punishment, and guilt

12 **"The Prisoner of Chillon" . . . the swim across the Hellespont:** in the career of George Gordon, Lord Byron (1788–1824), a poem, several amorous entanglements, and a famous feat of daring

Voltaire, Rousseau: freethinking eithteenth-century French philosophers and authors

13 **act of contrition:** a ritual confession ("Oh, my God, I am heartily sorry for having offended Thee . . .") which supposedly enables even a notorious sinner to become eligible for salvation

the eighth-grade rhetoric classroom when we filed in that Wednesday morning which remains still memorable to me. *"Zoe mou, sas agapo"*°: the words of Byron's last assurance to the Maid of Athens° stood there in Madame Barclay's French-looking script, speaking to us of the transiency of the passions. To me, as it happened, it spoke a twice-told tale. I had read the poem before, alone in my grandfather's library; indeed, I knew it by heart, and I rather resented the infringement on my private rights in it, the democratization of the poem which was about to take place. Soon, Madame Barclay's pointer was rapping from word to word: "My . . . life . . . I . . . love . . . you," she sharply translated. When the pointer started back for its second trip, I retreated into hauteur and began drawing a picture of the girl who sat next to me. Suddenly the pointer cracked across my writing tablet.

15 "You're just like Lord Byron, brilliant but unsound."

16 I heard the pointer being set down and the drawing being torn crisply twice across, but I could not look up. I had never felt so flattered in my life. Throughout the rest of the class, I sat motionless, simulating meekness, while my classmates shot me glances of wonder, awe, and congratulation, as though I had suddenly been struck by a remarkable disease, or been canonized, or transfigured. Madame Barclay's pronouncement, which I kept repeating to myself under my breath, had for us girls a kind of final and majestic certainty. She was the severest and most taciturn of our teachers. Her dark brows met in the middle; her skin was a pure olive; her upper lip had a faint mustache; she was the iron and authority of the convent. She tolerated no infractions, overlooked nothing, was utterly and obdurately fair, had no favorites; but her rather pointed face had the marks of suffering, as though her famous discipline had scored it as harshly as one of our papers. She had a bitter and sarcastic wit, and had studied, it was said, at the Sorbonne. Before this day, I had once or twice dared to say to myself that Madame Barclay liked me. Her dark, quite handsome eyes would sometimes move in my direction as her lips prepared an aphorism or a satiric gibe. Yet hardly had I estimated the look, weighed and measured it to store it away in my memory book of requited affections, when a stinging penalty would recall me from my dream and I could no longer be sure. Now, however, there was no doubt left. The reproof was a declaration of love as plain as the sentence on the blackboard, which shimmered slightly before my eyes. My happiness was a confused exaltation in which the fact that I was Lord Byron and the fact that I was loved by Madame Barclay, the most puzzling nun in the convent, blended in a Don Juanesque triumph.

"Zoe mou, sas agapo": (Gr.) "My life, I love you"

the Maid of Athens: Teresa Macri, celebrated in Byron's poem "Maid of Athens, Ere We Part," each stanza of which ends with the Greek refrain just quoted

17 In the refectory that noon, publicity was not wanting to enrich this moment. Insatiable, I could hardly wait for the week end, to take Madame Barclay's words home as though they had been a prize. With the generosity of affluence, I spoke to myself of sharing this happiness, this honor, with my grandfather. Surely, *this* would make up to him for any worry or difficulty I had caused him. At the same time, it would have the practical effect of explaining me a little to him. Phrases about my prototype rang in my head: "that unfortunate genius," "that turbulent soul," "that gifted and erratic nature."

18 My grandfather turned dark red when he heard the news. His forehead grew knotty with veins; he swore; he looked strange and young; it was the first time I had ever seen him angry. Argument and explanation were useless. For my grandfather, history had interposed no distance between Lord Byron and himself. Though the incestuous poet° had died forty years before my grandfather was born, the romantic perspective was lacking. That insularity of my grandfather's that kept him intimate with morals and denied the reality of the exotic made him judge the poet as he judged himself or one of his neighbors—that is, on the merit of his actions. He was on the telephone at once, asking the Mother Superior in a thundering, courtroom voice what right one of her sisters had to associate his innocent granddaughter with that degenerate blackguard, Byron. On Monday, Madame Barclay, with tight-drawn lips, told her class that she had a correction to make: Mary McCarthy did not resemble Lord Byron in any particular; she was neither brilliant, loose-living, nor unsound.

19 The interviews between my grandfather and Madame MacIllvra came to an end. To that remarkable marriage of minds the impediment had at last been discovered. But from this time on, Madame Barclay's marks of favor to me grew steadily more distinct, while the look of suffering tightened on her face, till some said she had cancer (a theory supported by the yellowness of her skin) and some said she was being poisoned by an antipathy to the Mother Superior.

STUDY QUESTIONS

1. After reading the first paragraph of this essay, which character did you assume to be the "blackguard" of the title? In view of the whole essay, see if you can make a case for a different identification of the blackguard.
2. McCarthy tells us that she was twelve years old at the time of

---

[18] **the incestuous poet:** Byron was alleged to have had sexual relations with his half-sister.

these events. In what ways does the girl-self that she portrays typify the attitudes and limited knowledge of a twelve-year-old?

3. How does McCarthy reveal to us that she no longer harbors the attitudes she held as a twelve-year-old? Locate passages that evidence a psychological distancing from the narrated events.
4. In some respects "The Blackguard" is intended as a comic essay. Its comedy, however, is subtle and easily missed. Locate passages that you consider humorous in intent, and try to explain the source of humor in each case.
5. This essay is distinctly ironical; that is, it creates expectations that are undercut by opposite developments. What ironies can you detect, and how do they operate?
6. At the beginning of paragraph 9, McCarthy refers to her "feeling for the dramatic." How is this feeling demonstrated (a) in the reported events of the story, and (b) in the structure of that story as McCarthy tells it?
7. In her final paragraph, McCarthy echoes Shakespeare's Sonnet 116: "Let me not to the marriage of true minds/Admit impediments." Shakespeare's line in turn echoes the marriage service of the Church of England: "If any of you know cause or just impediment why these persons should not be joined together. . . ." It is clear that no literal marriage between McCarthy's grandfather and Madame MacIllvra is at issue. What, then, is McCarthy referring to? What *is* the impediment, and in what sense could the two characters be regarded as a couple?

PART II

EXPLAINING

ILLUSTRATING A GENERALIZATION

George F. Will

George F. Will is a journalist, a nationally syndicated columnist, and a political commentator. The essay below is taken from his book *The Pursuit of Happiness and Other Sobering Thoughts* (1978).

ON HER OWN IN THE CITY

1 When police, responding to her call, arrived at her East Harlem tenement, she was hysterical: "The dog ate my baby." The baby girl had been four days old, twelve hours "home" from the hospital. Home was two rooms and a kitchen on the sixth floor, furnished with a rug, a folding chair, and nothing else, no bed, no crib.

2 "Is the baby dead?" asked an officer. "Yes," the mother said, "I saw the baby's insides." Her dog, a German shepherd, had not been fed for five days. She explained: "I left the baby on the floor with the dog to protect it." She had bought the dog in July for protection from human menaces.

3 She is twenty-four. She went to New York three years ago from a small Ohio community. She wanted to be on her own. She got that wish.

4 She was employed intermittently, until the fifth month of her pregnancy, which she says was the result of a rape she did not report to the police. She wanted the baby. She bought child-care books, and had seven prenatal checkups at Bellevue Hospital. Although she rarely called home or asked for money, she called when the baby was born. Her mother mailed twenty-five dollars for a crib. It arrived too late.

5 When labor began she fed the dog with the last food in the apartment and went alone to the hospital. The baby was born on Wednesday. When she left Bellevue Sunday evening, the hospital office holding her welfare payment was closed. With six dollars in her pocket and a baby in her arms, she took a cab home. The meter said four dollars and the

driver demanded a dollar tip. When she asked his assistance in getting upstairs, he drove off.

6 The hospital had given her enough formula for three feedings for the baby. Rather than spend her remaining dollar that night on food for herself and the dog, she saved it for the bus ride back to Bellevue to get her welfare money. Having slept with the baby on a doubled-up rug, she left the baby and dog at 7 A.M. It was 53 degrees, too cold she thought to take the baby. She had no warm baby clothes and she thought the hospital had said the baby was ailing. She got back at 8:30 A.M. Then she called the police.

7 Today the forces of law and order and succor are struggling to assign "blame" in order to escape it. Her attorney and Bellevue are arguing about how she was released, or expelled, on Sunday evening. Welfare officials are contending with charges that they are somehow culpable for her failure to receive a crib before giving birth, and for her living conditions. (She was receiving payment of $270 a month; her rent was $120.) She has been arraigned on a charge of negligent homicide, but no one seems anxious to prosecute.

8 Late in New York's U.S. Senate primary, Daniel P. Moynihan, talking like a senator prematurely, said that this case dramatizes weaknesses of the welfare system, and indicated that it also dramatizes the need for him in Washington. Perhaps.

9 But because cities are collections of strangers, they are, inevitably, bad places to be poor. Not that there are good places, but cities, being kingdoms of the strong, are especially hellish for the poor.

10 Cities have their indispensable purposes, and their charms, not the least of which is that you can be alone in a crowd. But that kind of living alone is an acquired taste, and not for the weak or unfortunate. They are apt to learn that no city's institutions can provide protective supports like those of an extended family or real community. No metropolis can provide a floor of support solid enough to prevent the bewildered—like the woman from Ohio—from falling through the cracks.

11 Through those cracks you get an occasional glimpse of what George Eliot° meant: "If we had a keen vision and feeling of all ordinary human life, it would be like hearing the grass grow and the squirrel's heartbeat, and we should die of that roar which lies on the other side of silence."

---

[11] **George Eliot:** pen name of Mary Ann Evans (1819–1880), British novelist

STUDY QUESTIONS

1. Why do you suppose Will mentions neither the name nor the race of the woman whose unfortunate story he tells?
2. In paragraph 1, Will puts quotation marks around the word *home,* and in paragraph 7 he does the same with the word *blame.* What is the significance of those quotation marks? How do they serve Will's main purpose as you can infer it?
3. This essay falls neatly into two parts. Where does the break occur? Can you characterize the relation between the first and second segments?
4. The brevity of "On Her Own in the City" was dictated by the space requirements of a magazine column. Nevertheless, Will turns it to advantage by employing *understatement,* or the taking of a mild or neutral tone when "the facts" seem to call for more excitement. Find several instances of understatement in Will's essay, and be prepared to discuss their effect. Consider not only what Will says, but also the structure of his sentences.
5. What do you think is the meaning and effect of Will's concluding quotation from George Eliot?
6. Will tells a shocking story, not for its own sake, but in order to make a point. What sentence in the essay most nearly states its thesis or main idea?
7. Could this essay, classified here as an instance of explaining, also be considered an instance of telling or arguing? Be prepared to explain your answer.

Abigail Zuger

Abigail Zuger published the following essay in *Harper's* in 1975, when she was a senior at Radcliffe and managing editor of the *Harvard Independent.*

ACROPHOBIA° IN THE IVORY TOWER

1 My father, who has not set foot in a college classroom in almost fifty years, occasionally wakes up in the middle of the night in a cold

title **acrophobia:** fear of high places, esp. with the obsessional thought that one is going to fall

breakfast he tells us that he was somewhere on his college campus, racing blindly up a walk, two hours late for an exam and stark naked. Someone has taken all the knobs off his bureau drawers, and he has spent two frantic hours looking for his clothes. Stomach churning, he pounds on the door of the exam building. His advisor has told him that the outcome of this exam is crucial to his professional career. The door remains locked, however; the jeers of the passersby resound in his ears, and his professor peers out of an upstairs window, face convulsed in laughter. Fifty years have done nothing to quell the horror of this dream.

2 In 1973 *Harvard Magazine,* a bulletin for Harvard alumni, published a short article on pre-exam nightmares and received a staggering number of congratulatory letters. Harvard men of all ages wrote in that their subconscious minds still regularly treated them to these dreams. Graying businessmen found themselves seated for an art-history exam without ever having taken the course. Feeble doctors habitually galloped across the campus searching for a Bio. 1 exam no one seemed to have heard of. Lawyers by the score showed up for freshman English and found the exam written in Chinese. To a man they seemed to be saying that to live through these dreams was a thousand times more grueling than anything they had experienced since leaving college.

3 The ivory tower, as college students—and psychiatrists—across the country will testify, is not nearly so pleasant an abode as it appears from the outside. It shelters its inhabitants from some of life's pedestrian difficulties, but at the same time creates new traumas and problems, which take on, in such closed quarters, an importance of which the real world cannot conceive. The legendary tower of learning is not a stable structure: it is buffeted by the high winds of exam periods, by the gales of preprofessional competition; it shakes with the constant underground rumblings of adolescent crises. What shall I be? What shall I do? Will I succeed? At times it sways so forebodingly that the unfortunate standing on top sees his future in a heap of broken bones and ivory rubble.

4 Every student has his own mechanism for coping with the panic which invades even the most sedate college existence. It is a kind of panic difficult to describe except by example, a panic of which there is no real equivalent in the nonacademic world. It comes after forty-eight hours of sleepless labor, with the realization that the paper must be completely reorganized; or on the day before the exam, with the realization that a human being cannot read 5,000 pages in one day; or on the Friday before the Monday, with the realization that an academically respectable job on the given topic is the work of a lifetime, and not a weekend. It is the lucky student who can internalize his worries and

convert them into an occasional nightmare. Others resort to desperate means.

5 When the federal law giving students the right to see their own records went into effect last fall, colleges across the country began to sort painstakingly through student files for confidential letters of recommendation, which must be returned to the writer for a signature before being released to the student. At Harvard, several professors received letters of recommendation they had never written, urging that a student named [deleted]° be considered for admission to various medical schools, for Phi Beta Kappa, for a highly desirable scholarship. Admitting to the forgeries,———was requested to leave the school.

6 His saddened coworkers in the lab announced they were forced to question the validity of experimental work he had done; his friends were baffled. He had been an enormously talented, straight-A student, had celebrated promising lab results over champagne with Dr. James D. Watson,° could probably have gotten into any medical school in the country. The recommendations he had written for himself, it was whispered across Harvard, were couched in far less glowing terms than the recommendations other professors had written for him. ———, accounting for his "highly regrettable acts," explained that he had lost all perspective on his life and his work. "Almost constant pressure . . . , spending excessive time in the laboratory, and a demanding course load," he admitted, "caused me to see events in desperate terms."

7 ———'s desperation is only an ironic exaggeration of the desperation that pervades college campuses in other forms. It is at the root of the notorious pre-med gangsterism, of the flourishing term-paper companies, of the waiting lists in college psychiatric facilities, of the occasional sad college suicide that never makes the front page. Some students survive their college traumas with enough equanimity to mold it all, under the benign influence of time, into part of the best years of their lives. The others wince as they remember, and dream unsettling dreams.

---

[5] **[deleted]:** The student's name appears in Zuger's original essay but has been editorially omitted from this and three later sentences.

[6] **Dr. James D. Watson:** American geneticist who won a Nobel Prize in 1962 for his part in discovering the molecular structure of DNA

STUDY QUESTIONS

1. In what ways does Zuger's opening paragraph constitute an appropriate and engaging introduction to the rest of her essay? Think of the different effect that would have been created by an immediate statement of her thesis.
2. What *is* Zuger's thesis, or main idea, and where is it stated?
3. How would you characterize the structure of this essay? Look for key transitions. By what means has Zuger kept a sense of unity through the several parts of her essay?
4. Examine the metaphor of the ivory tower in paragraph 3. How has Zuger given life to the cliché (overused expression) *ivory tower,* and how does her extended metaphor serve her main purpose? What is the relation between this metaphor and Zuger's title?
5. Consider the case of the student who forged his letters of recommendation (paragraphs 5–6). How does his case illustrate Zuger's thesis? Incidentally, do you think it was proper or improper for us to omit his name from the present text of Zuger's essay? What would be the main arguments for and against such an omission?
6. "Acrophobia in the Ivory Tower" emphasizes the anxieties of college life without mentioning any of its possible advantages. Judging from Zuger's own essay, in what ways do you suppose that she herself benefited from her college education?

Alison Lurie

Alison Lurie, who currently teaches children's literature at Cornell University, is the author of several novels, including *Real People* and *The War Between the Tates.* The essay below was first published in *Harper's* in 1979.

VULGAR, COARSE, AND GROTESQUE

1 Imagine an ideal suburban or small-town elementary schoolyard at recess. Sunshine, trees, swings: children playing tag or jumping rope —a scene of simplicity and innocence. Come nearer; what are those nice little girls chanting as they turn the rope?

Fudge, fudge, tell the judge,
Mama has a baby.
It's a boy, full of joy,
Papa's going crazy.

Wrap it up in toilet paper,
Send it down the elevator.

2 Soon the school bell will sound and the children will file into assembly. Gazing up at the American flag on the stage, they will lift their young voices in patriotic song:

My country's tired of me,
I'm going to Germany,
To see the king.
His name is Donald Duck,
He drives a garbage truck,
He taught me how to———.
Let freedom ring.

3 Adults who have forgotten their childhood may be shocked by these verses; but anyone who has recently read *Tom Sawyer, Alice's Adventures in Wonderland,* or any of a number of other classics should not be surprised. Most of the lasting works of juvenile literature are thoroughly subversive in one way or another: they express feelings not generally approved of or even recognized by grown-ups; they make fun of honored figures and piously held beliefs; and they view social pretenses with clear-eyed directness, remarking—as in Andersen's° famous tale—that the emperor has no clothes.

4 I am not speaking here of run-of-the-mill children's books, which in all eras, including our own, tend to support the *status quo.* Bookshops today are full of such stories, often well-told and charmingly illustrated. There are delightful picture-books in which good little bears and raccoons visit grandma or the doctor, are naughty or frightened, but are forgiven and comforted by kind, wise mummy and daddy bears or raccoons. For older children there are entertaining tales in which the (often suburban) world is temporarily disrupted by magic or by some exciting natural adventure (the escape of animals from a zoo, a flood, a robbery, and so on). Jokes are played, mysteries abound, crises occur; but virtue triumphs and the basic institutions of society hold firm. There is no doubt that these stories give much pleasure, but they are not the ones that will survive.

5 Nor, necessarily, will many of the books that win prizes for excellence: those stylistically admirable, beautifully produced volumes with their serious moral messages. Here brave and resourceful boys and girls learn to survive in the wilderness, or cope with such real-life problems as the death of parents, racial prejudice, handicapped siblings, and foster homes. I respect these books, but I have never yet met a child who listed one of them among his or her favorites, or wanted to read them over and over again. Children are not influenced by awards; they make their own choices. Over the years, with or without the help of parents,

---

[3] **Andersen:** Hans Christian Andersen (1805–1875), Danish author of many fairy tales

teachers, and librarians, they have made some books into classics—and these books, more often than not, mock the existing order.

6 Mark Twain's *Adventures of Tom Sawyer,* for instance, is not the kind of story authorities of the period recommended for children. It was, in fact, written in irritable reaction against what Twain described as "goody-goody boys' books"—the improving tales that were distributed in tremendous numbers by religious and educational institutions of the time. The standard plot of these works was that known to folklorists as "Kind and Unkind." It is perhaps most familiar to laymen from Hogarth's° series of prints depicting the lives of the Good and Bad Apprentices: the enterprising one practices every virtue and rises to riches and honor, while his lazy, thieving companion dies penniless.

7 In *Tom Sawyer* Twain deliberately turned this plot on its head. Tom lies, steals, swears, smokes, plays hooky, and wins a Sunday School prize by fraud. He ends up with a small fortune in gold, the admiration of the whole town, and the love of Becky Thatcher—while his goody-goody brother Sid is last seen being literally kicked and cuffed out the door.

8 Twain's portrait of his home town, Hannibal, Missouri (which appears in the book as St. Petersburg), is equally seditious. Its adult citizens are shown as vindictive, credulous, and overawed by wealth, and their most respected local institutions are empty shams. The Temperance Tavern shelters thieves and outlaws, and sells whiskey in its back room. Church is a place of excruciating weekly boredom where "the choir always tittered and whispered all through service" and the entire congregation is delighted when the sermon is disrupted by a yelping dog. School is even worse: the teacher is a petty tyrant who shames and beats his students, while laboriously training the more docile ones to recite bad poetry and even worse original compositions.

9 How, especially in 1876, did Twain get away with it? Partly, of course, because he was a genius; but partly, too, because, as he declared in his preface, *Tom Sawyer* was "intended mainly for the entertainment of boys and girls," that is, not to be taken seriously. *Huckleberry Finn,* which was issued without this assurance, ran into trouble at once: it was called "vulgar" and "coarse" by critics, and banned by the Concord Library.

10 The greatest British juvenile author of the late nineteenth century, Lewis Carroll, was just as subversive as Twain, but in a more subtle way: it is appropriate that the original title of his first children's book was *Alice's Adventures Underground.* Modern critics have tended to see Carroll's heroine as exploring the inner world of the unconscious; but it is also possible to read *Alice's Adventures in Wonderland* and *Through the Looking-*

---

[6] **Hogarth:** William Hogarth (1697–1764), British painter and engraver

Glass as underground literature in the social and political sense. The Walrus and the Carpenter can be seen as caricatures of the rival politicians Disraeli and Gladstone,° deceiving and devouring the innocent oysters, or voters, but in different styles—a view supported by Sir John Tenniel's illustrations, in which the Walrus sports Disraeli's elegant dress and luxuriant moustache, while the Carpenter has the square jaw and untidy clothes of Gladstone.

11 Even more easily, the courts of the Queen of Hearts and the Red Queen with their pompous formality and arbitrary laws of etiquette can be seen as a grotesque version of the very proper court of Queen Victoria, who also surrounded herself with extensive rose gardens and bowing courtiers. The King of Hearts, like Prince Albert,° takes second place to his consort; while the Red King and the White King, though essential to the chess game upon which *Through the Looking-Glass* is based, hardly appear at all. (Carroll, unlike most of his contemporaries, was by no means awed by Queen Victoria. After *Alice's Adventures in Wonderland* had made him famous, the Queen graciously signified that he might dedicate his next book to her. Carroll followed the letter rather than the spirit of this request, which by prevailing standards was equivalent to a royal command: his next book, *Some Considerations on Determinants,* by Charles Dodgson, Tutor in Mathematics of Christ Church, Oxford, was duly inscribed to Queen Victoria. *Through the Looking-Glass,* as it should have been, was dedicated to Alice Liddell, to whom the story had originally been told.)

12 As one might expect from an Oxford don, the most thoroughgoing satirical attacks in *Alice* are directed at education. The Caterpillar, like a Victorian schoolmaster, asks unanswerable questions and demands that Alice repeat nonsense verses. Humpty-Dumpty, in the manner of some professors, asserts that he "can explain all the poems that ever were invented—and a good many that haven't been invented just yet." He also arranges the sense of statements to suit himself ("When *I* use a word . . . it means just what I choose it to mean"). The Red Queen, like a strict governess, puts Alice through a nightmare oral exam ("What's one and one and one and one and one and one and one and one and one and one?"). The books are full of parodies of the moral verses found in contemporary school readers, and of the rote question-and-answer method of teaching. The "regular course" of instruction followed by the Mock Turtle includes Ambition, Distraction, Uglification, and Derision, while the Gryphon goes to "the Classical master" to study Laughing and Grief—all the subjects that a child in the nineteenth century—or today—must learn in

---

[10] **Disraeli, Gladstone:** Benjamin Disraeli (1804–1881), Tory British prime minister 1867, 1874–1880; William Gladstone (1809–1898), Liberal prime minister four times between 1868 and 1894

[11] **Prince Albert:** (1819–1861) husband of Queen Victoria of England

order to grow up and enter the adult world that Carroll hated.

13 Most radical of all at the time, though difficult to appreciate now, is the unconventional character of Alice herself. Except for her proper manners, she is by no means a good little girl in mid-Victorian terms. She is not gentle, timid, and docile, but active, brave, and impatient; she is highly critical of her surroundings and of the foolish or cruel adults she meets. At the end of both books she fights back, reducing the Queen of Hearts' court to a pack of playing cards and the Red Queen to a kitten, crying "Who cares for *you?*" and "I can't stand this any longer!"

14 Both Twain and Carroll were split personalities in the social if not the technical sense of the term. As Samuel Clemens, Twain was a sentimental, bourgeois *paterfamilias,* a would-be industrial magnate (he financed the manufacture of a typesetting machine and lost $50,000), and a pillar of the community. Under the name of Mark Twain he was a restless adventurer and a bitterly sardonic critic of the proper world his other self inhabited. "Civilization is a shabby poor thing," he wrote, "and full of cruelties, vanities, arrogances, meanness and hypocrisies." Charles Dodgson the Oxford don was prim, devout, obsessive, and painfully shy; occasionally he even refused to accept mail addressed to Lewis Carroll, the affectionate and witty friend of little girls.

15 Many other authors of juvenile classics, though not so strikingly divided in personality, have had the ability to look at the world from below and note its less respectable aspects, just as little children playing on the floor can see the chewing gum stuck to the underside of polished mahogany tables and the hems of silk dresses held up with safety pins. Such writers' instinctive sympathy, like Twain's, is with the rebel, the defier of convention. Toad in Kenneth Grahame's *Wind in the Willows,* for instance, is foolish, rash, and boastful as well as incorrigibly criminal—a kind of Edwardian upper-class juvenile delinquent, with a passion for flashy clothes and fast cars. Yet at the end of the book, only slightly chastened, Toad is restored to his ancestral home and given a triumphal banquet by his friends. Grahame, who was Secretary of the Bank of England, lived a quiet and respectable life, but it is hard not to suspect that in imagination he was on the side of "Toad the motor-car snatcher, the prison-breaker, the Toad who always escapes!"

16 In some cases the anti-establishment message is concealed behind a screen of conventional morality that may fool adults but not their juniors and betters. Beatrix Potter, whose books owe some of their charm to the illustrations that are drawn from a child's-eye view, often appears to be recommending restraint and conformity. After his exciting adventures in Mr. McGregor's garden, Peter Rabbit is sent to bed in disgrace, while good little Flopsy, Mopsy, and Cottontail have "bread and milk and blackberries for supper." But when I asked a class full of young students which character in the book they would have preferred to be, they voted unanimously for Peter, recognizing the concealed

moral of the story: that disobedience and exploration are more fun than good behavior, and not really all that dangerous, whatever mothers may say.

17 Opinions and attitudes that are not currently in style in the adult media often find expression in children's books of the time. In the early years of this century, when Britain was going through a period of material luxury and political smugness, E. Nesbit wrote in *The Five Children and It* that "London is like prison for children, especially if their relations are not rich," and went on in a sequel, *The Story of the Amulet,* to point out that many London adults are also in prison. By magic, the Queen of Babylon is transported to Edwardian England, where four of the Five Children take her on a sightseeing tour. She adores the Tower and the Thames,° but is appalled by the condition of the populace:

18 *"But how badly you keep your slaves. How wretched and poor and neglected they seem," she said, as the cab rattled along the Mile End Road.*

19 *"They aren't slaves; they're working-people," said Jane.*

20 *"Of course they're working-people. That's what slaves are. Don't you tell me. Do you suppose I don't know a slave's face when I see it? Why don't their masters see that they're better fed and better clothed? . . . You'll have a revolt of your slaves if you're not careful," said the Queen.*

21 *"Oh, no," said Cyril; "you see they have votes—that makes them safe not to revolt. It makes all the difference. Father told me so."*

22 *"What is this vote?" asked the Queen. "Is it a charm? What do they do with it?"*

23 *"I don't know," said the harassed Cyril; "it's just a vote, that's all! They don't do anything particular with it."*

24 *"I see," said the Queen; "a sort of plaything."*

25 More recently, during World War II, when "pacifist" was a dirty word, one of the more popular picture books for American children was Munro Leaf's *Ferdinand,* the story of a gentle, noncombative—though very large and strong—bull who lives in Spain. All the other bulls "would fight each other all day . . . butt each other and stick each other with their horns. . . . But not Ferdinand." What he wants is to sit quietly under a tree and smell the flowers. Taken to the bull ring in Madrid, Ferdinand steadfastly refuses to fight and finally has to be sent home again, where he lives happily ever after. (According to experts, this cheerful outcome would be unlikely in reality; insufficiently aggressive bulls are usually killed in the ring. And, of course, conscientious objectors in World War II often went to jail—but one can dream.)

26 In some famous books, the subversive message operates in private rather than public lives. More or less openly, the author takes the side of the child against his or her parents, who are portrayed as at best silly

---

[17] **the Tower, the Thames:** the Tower of London, where state prisoners were imprisoned and/or executed; the Thames is a river that flows past London

and needlessly anxious, at worst selfish and stupid. In James Barrie's *Peter Pan,* Mrs. Darling is charming but light-headed, while Mr. Darling is a bully and a hypocrite. Mr. and Mrs. Banks, the parents in P. L. Travers's *Mary Poppins,* are helpless and incompetent to manage their own household without their magical nanny. At the start of *Mary Poppins Comes Back,* things have got so bad that they are on the verge of separation:

27 *"I don't know what's come over this house," Mr. Banks said. "Nothing ever goes right—hasn't for ages! . . . I am going!" he said. "And I don't know that I shall ever come back."*

28 Mrs. Banks, exhausted, sits on the stairs weeping while the servants (the Bankses are only middle-class, but this is 1935) drop trays of china and set the kitchen chimney on fire and the children scream and squabble in the nursery. When their mother's misery and helplessness is called to their attention, their reaction is cool and detached:

29 *"Children! Children!" Mrs. Banks was wringing her hands in despair. "Be quiet or I shall Go Mad!"*

30 *There was silence for a moment as they stared at her with interest. Would she really? They wondered. And what would she be like if she did?*

31 Throughout the four volumes, it is clear that their real love and concern are for Mary Poppins.

32 A particularly elegant putdown of parental authority occurs in the books of A. A. Milne. In reality, Christopher Robin is a small child in a world of adults; but in *Winnie-the-Pooh* he rules over—and physically towers over—a society most of whose inhabitants are his own toys. Among them are two who seem to represent parents: Kanga, the kind, fussy mother, with her continual "We'll see, dear," and lack of interest in anything except her domestic and maternal duties; and Owl, the pompous pedant who turns out to be unable to spell his own name. As a child, Milne writes, he believed that his father, the headmaster of a boys' school, "knew everything there was to know"; but later on "I formed the opinion that, even if Father knew everything, he knew most of it wrong." Surely part of the universal appeal of the Pooh books is due to the delight any child must experience in imagining himself larger, wiser, and more powerful than the adults who surround him.

33 Of course, not all famous children's books are overtly or even covertly subversive. Rudyard Kipling's *Jungle Books* support the rule of law and order, though it is the law and order of the jungle: each wild beast knows its place, and the duty of Mowgli the Wolf-Cub is to learn from his elders wisdom, courage, and the skills of survival. Like the British Empire, of which Kipling was a strong supporter, *The Jungle Books* created an exciting, exotic world in which properly educated men could exercise authority over the "lesser breeds without the Law." It is not by chance that Mowgli ends up as a game warden under British authority.

34 F. L. Baum's *Wizard of Oz* also contains no criticism of the status quo, even though Baum, as a failed South Dakota newspaper editor, must have been well acquainted with the hard times, low farm prices, and rise in freight rates that had ground down prairie families like Dorothy's. Instead, geography and climate are blamed for the fact that Aunt Em, once a "young, pretty wife," is "thin and gaunt, and never smiled, now," while Uncle Henry "worked hard from morning till night and did not know what joy was." It is true that the Wizard himself combines the appearance of a Gilded Age° politician with that of a medicine-show huckster, and that in the central episode Dorothy and her friends expose him as a humbug whose powers and promises are as full of hot air as the balloon that eventually carries him back to Omaha, Nebraska. But Baum is sympathetic to his hero, who, as he says himself, is "really a very good man" though "a very bad Wizard." He allows the Wizard to give the Scarecrow a brain, the Tin Woodman a heart, and the Cowardly Lion courage—or rather, by a sort of benevolent hocus-pocus, to convince them that they are receiving what they already obviously have. There is a place in American society for the self-improvement merchant, even if his magic is mere hocus-pocus, Baum is telling us—a truth hundreds of entrepreneurs of wealth, health, and happiness from Dale Carnegie to Werner Erhard° were subsequently to prove.

35 Time and social change mute the revolutionary message of other children's classics. A hundred years later, Jo of *Little Women* no longer seems so radical a tomboy: her untidiness, literary ambition, enthusiasm for "romps," and mild boyish slang ("Christopher Columbus!") appear tame. Girls who love Louisa May Alcott's books today tend to be more quiet, feminine, and domestic than the average; their more active peers prefer *Harriet the Spy* and *Nancy Drew,* or *Pippi Longstocking,*° who can lick the circus strong man in a wrestling match. But for at least five generations of girls, Jo was a rebel and an ideal; and they found Alcott's understanding of their own impatience with contemporary models of female behavior ("I hate affected, niminy-piminy chits!" as Jo puts it) nothing less than miraculous.

36 It is the particular gift of some writers to remain in one sense children all their lives: to continue to see the world as boys and girls see it, and take their side instinctively. One author who carries on this

---

34 **Gilded Age:** the wealthy, corrupt period following the end of the American Civil War in 1865

Dale Carnegie, Werner Erhard: respectively, an American promoter of schemes for self-improvement and success; a contemporary American promoter of self-confidence; founder of est

34 **Harriet the Spy, Nancy Drew, Pippi Longstocking:** respectively, a girls' story (1964) by Louise Fitzhugh (1928–1974); the first in a series of girls' stories published 1930–1969 by Harriet Adams under the pseudonym Carolyn Keene; and a girls' story (1945, trans. from Swedish in 1950) by Astrid Lindgren.

tradition today in America is Dr. Seuss, who like Twain and Carroll has adopted a separate literary personality (under his real name, Theodore Geisel, he has been an editorial cartoonist, advertising artist, and screenwriter). Seuss's picture books, though extremely popular with children, have yet to be recognized as classics; they are not even mentioned in many surveys of the "best" children's books. Seuss is in good company here: *The Wizard of Oz* was similarly neglected for more than fifty years, and Maurice Sendak's brilliant *Where the Wild Things Are*—which suggests that children sometimes have violent aggressive impulses toward their parents—was at first condemned as "too frightening" (For whom? one wants to ask).

37 From *And to Think That I Saw It on Mulberry Street* (1937) onward, Dr. Seuss has not only celebrated the power and richness of the child's imagination, but suggested that children may do well to conceal their flights of fancy, and possibly other things, from their elders. The boy and girl in his best-known book, *The Cat in the Hat,* shut indoors on a rainy day, completely wreck the house with the help of the devilish-looking cat, then tidy it up again just before their mother gets home to ask

"Did you have any fun?
Tell me. What did you do?"
And Sally and I did not know
What to say.
Should we tell her
The things that went on there
that day?
Should we tell her about it?
Now, what should we do?

Well . . .
What would YOU do
If your mother asked you?

The implication is that mother will never find out what went on in her absence—and just as well, too.

38 Grown-ups reading this story aloud may feel uneasy; we prefer to think of children as ingenuous and confiding. Usually, too, we like to believe that everything is all right in our immediate world, and that the opinions and attitudes expressed in the popular media represent the full range of possible opinions and attitudes. When we go into shops before Christmas we tend to buy the new children's books that have been recommended by authorities—attractive, well-written books that, though full of adventure and excitement, do not question our basic assumptions. But if we really want to please our kids—or if we want to know what they are really up to—we would do well to look at the classic children's books and listen to the rhymes being sung on school playgrounds.

STUDY QUESTIONS

1. Twice within the first paragraph of her essay, Lurie issues a direct command to her readers. What do you suppose is the purpose of that tactic? Does it succeed?
2. Consider Lurie's first two paragraphs as a unit. What is the function of that unit in the essay as a whole? Why doesn't Lurie state her thesis (main idea) right away?
3. Study the role in this essay of the children's books that do *not* receive Lurie's strong approval. Where are they discussed, and why does Lurie bother with them?
4. What is the significance, for Lurie's position, of the word *Underground* in Lewis Carroll's original title for *Alice's Adventures in Wonderland* (paragraph 10)? And how do Carroll's mock names for mathematical operations and classical languages (paragraph 12) help Lurie to make her main point?
5. How do paragraphs 33–35 bear on Lurie's thesis? Should she have omitted the material in those paragraphs? Why, or why not?
6. Judging from this essay, what would you say is Lurie's general view of children? What is their typical relation to adults, and what is the main reason for that relation?
7. How does Lurie's final paragraph give her essay a sense of conclusion? (If you think it fails to do so, be prepared to say where you think it goes wrong.)

Daniel S. Greenberg

Daniel S. Greenberg, formerly head of the news department of *Science* magazine, is currently the editor and publisher of *Science and Government Report.* The essay below was first published in 1976.

SCIENTISTS WANTED—PIONEERS NEEDN'T APPLY; CALL AD 2000

1 Science continues to mold our future, but what of the future of science itself? It seems impossible to predict what the most exciting frontiers of physics or biology will be in another quarter of a century, but we can be surprisingly confident of what life will be like in the American scientific community. With a very unscientific time machine, we can collect two eminent scientists from the last turn of the century

and transport them into this future, letting their experiences define the changes.

2 The first scientist, a young man with a mediocre academic record, used good family connections to obtain a job in the Swiss Patent Office in 1902. A one-time high school dropout who had been told by a teacher that "You will never amount to anything," he had relied heavily on borrowed lecture notes to get his undergraduate degree. But he had aspirations beyond patent applications.

3 Now imagine the time machine has transported him to the last quarter of this century. Envision the young clerk anxiously opening a letter from a foundation to which he had applied for a graduate fellowship to study physics. Disappointment shrouds his face as he reads the response:

4 Dear Mr. Einstein:

> We are in receipt of your application for financial assistance to pursue graduate studies in physics. Having examined your academic record and references from former teachers, we regret to inform you that your preparation is inadequate for the rigorous requirements of the course of study that you wish to follow. Therefore, we are unable to act favorably on your application.
>
> Sincerely,
> The Graduate Fellowship Committee

5 To meet a second time-traveler, turn back to 1900. An Army surgeon holds the unorthodox notion that yellow fever, then epidemic in an American protectorate, Cuba, is transmitted by mosquitoes. Since there is no way to test this hunch on animals, he proposes to test it on humans. Suddenly he, too, finds himself in the final quarter of this century. Submitting his plan to his superiors, he is rewarded with the following memorandum:

From: Surgeon General, U.S. Army
To: Dr. Walter Reed
Subject: Human Experimentation, Regulations Concerning

6 As we are sure you are aware, any experimentation involving human subjects must conform to the informed-consent regulations that the Department of the Army has adopted from the Department of Health, Education and Welfare in accordance with directives of the Federal Council for Science and Technology. As a preliminary step toward fulfilling the requirements for application for issuance of a

human-experimentation permit, it will be necessary for you to submit a detailed protocol of animal studies. In conjunction with regulations concerning animal welfare, it will also be necessary for you to provide evidence that the preliminary studies cannot be accomplished without the use of animals.

7 Failure to comply with this memorandum will result in disciplinary action.

8 The addressees are real, but the correspondence, of course, is mythical. Patent Clerk Albert Einstein was spared any such rebuff when he sought a graduate fellowship. Working at theoretical physics in his spare time, he quickly published five papers, including the special theory of relativity,[8] and was awarded a doctorate by the University of Zurich.

9 And Dr. Walter Reed simply followed the honorable tradition of using himself and his research-team colleagues as experimental subjects, without encountering the present-day committees that are concerned with animal-welfare regulations and informed consent of human subjects. Some of his co-workers died, but Reed proved his point. The mosquitoes were eradicated and the number of yellow fever cases dropped to zero.

10 Our heroes of the past thrived in what might be called the frontier days of scientific research. Vast and open territories of the scientific unknown lay before any investigator, and virtually all that was required for plunging ahead was the wit and the will to do so, plus relatively minor sums for equipment and supplies. How different it is today, and how much more so it will be tomorrow!

11 Peering ahead to the turn of the century, I see a crowd of people concerned with science—but surprisingly few of them are wearing lab coats.

12 The crowd is mainly composed of legislators, lawyers, economists, diplomats, budget planners, aptitude testers, bookkeepers, labor union officials, technology assessors and lots of anxious citizens. Few of them can distinguish an electron microscope from an automatic olive pitter. Their presence in the heart of the scientific enterprise signifies the blossoming of a theme that is already with us: namely, science is too potent, costly, dangerous and valuable to be wholly entrusted to mere scientists.

13 During the next quarter of a century, research will thrive in terms of expenditures, scientists and technicians at work, ambitious projects and costly facilities. But it will do so as a tightly reined captive of the surrounding society, and in an atmosphere of caution and thrift. Most important, opportunities for scientific research will no longer be judged

---

[8] **special theory of relativity:** the part of Einstein's theory of relativity that applies only to observers whose relative motion is constant; Einstein (1879–1955) put the theory forward in 1905.

in the traditional terms of knowledge being a desirable goal in itself regardless of the purposes to which it might be applied.

14 Scientists and research administrators will find that whole regions of research and technological application have been declared off limits, shunned as economically unworthy of pursuit or legally prohibited as too dangerous to be entrusted to frail humans and their unpredictable social and political institutions.

15 Research in many, if not most, fields will be actively encouraged, for the thickening problems of mankind on a crowded globe will demand scientific and technological solutions. But the choice of what to research will not be left entirely to the people who perform the research. Rather, it will receive the scrutiny and require the approval of a wide-ranging assortment of nonscientists who are concerned with costs, priorities, social impact, public safety and political significance. The "Everest Complex"° will no longer be sufficient reason for undertaking many research projects. Scientists will find that "because it's there" isn't a convincing argument to use on the keepers of the administrative cage in which science is confined.

16 The next 25 years will also produce further changes in the internal affairs of the scientific community, largely as the result of the progressive mechanization of scientific research. The conduct of most kinds of research is impossible without the use of highly expensive facilities—computers, particle accelerators, space satellites, oceanographic vessels, huge banks of experimental animals. There is and always will be a market for the breakthrough genius, but without the assistance of sophisticated apparatus, genius will be to science as expert archery is to modern military affairs—admirable, but ineffective by itself. Theoreticians may still use their traditional tools, paper and pencil, but to test their work they like to have a powerful computer which can race through calculations that would require weeks, even years, of hand computation.

17 Big science thus means big organizations. The machinery of modern science spawns a cast of characters that includes budget planners, technicians, maintenance people, and so forth. Schedule makers reign supreme when the lineup of would-be users overwhelms the available time on a machine. Big organizations mean layers of administrators, divisions of labor, and tendencies to assign people to preconceived duties rather than permit them to flourish according to their individual abilities.

18 When a few test tubes and a microscope constituted a "labora-

[15] **"Everest Complex":** the feeling that a challenge must be met simply because it exists. The name refers to the comment of the mountaineer George Leigh Mallory, who, whenever he was asked why he wanted to conquer Mt. Everest, would reply, "because it is there." (He died "there" in 1924 without having reached the summit.)

tory," research could be done in a spare room as a spare-time occupation. (Our patent clerk did his research on a kitchen table!) But when the tools required for research are million-dollar rockets and atom smashers, the number of persons who are professionally capable of using the tools will always be in surplus supply; patent clerks with abysmal academic records need not apply. These conditions will be particularly onerous to the freewheeling pioneers who people the history of science and technology. Charles Lindbergh picked himself to fly the Atlantic, but committees of physicians and psychologists selected the astronauts who went to the moon. The turn-of-the-century scientist will have to harmonize with his societal and professional setting. To put it bluntly, the scientist will, with rare exception, be a member of a scientific and technological proletariat, well trained and competent, but no more distinguished from the mass of his colleagues than is, for example, an automobile assembly worker of today.

19 How confident can we be of this scenario? Very, because the changes are already taking place. The aspects of science and technology that we have been considering are governed by a powerful inertia; as we move into the last quarter of the century, the forces of change are gradually gathering momentum. Among people who feel that science and technology are at least as much a bane as a blessing, there is an axiom that says the products of research tend to take on a life of their own, that they almost inevitably spread through society and elude control. (Often cited as an example of this is the airplane, which, for the convenience of a few, creates a nuisance for the many.) What does not get much attention is the fact that in recent years some rather serious curbs have been applied. Decisions on technical projects have been increasingly made for political, economic or at least nontechnical reasons.

20 Consider the American effort to build a supersonic transport. Technically, it was a manageable task—as the Anglo-French and Soviet SSTs demonstrate. We could have done it, but we didn't. And the reason we didn't turn thousands of scientists, engineers, and technicians loose on the task was simply that Congress and the public concluded that the SST was a poor investment. So here we see politics and business determining that something that can be done should not be done. There have been other cases along these lines (drilling into the Earth's mantle, manned flight to Mars) and as the outsiders tighten their grip on science and technology, there will be more of them.

21 Consider the case of nuclear explosives for peaceful earth-moving purposes. Known as Project Plowshare, the peaceful use of nuclear devices is described by advocates as a safe, highly economical and unmatchable technique for digging canals, moving mountains and loosening mineral and gas resources from deep inside the earth. Though a few small tests have been conducted, the method is politically taboo and is unlikely ever to come into large-scale use in the United States. This

is not only because Plowshare runs the risk of releasing radioactivity in violation of the atmospheric nuclear test ban treaty to which the United States is a party; it is also because public fears of nuclear power are so extensive that no matter how great the benefits and minuscule the risks, peaceful explorations are—at least for now—politically out of bounds.

22 For another example of politics thwarting what is scientifically and technically doable, consider biological, or germ, warfare. Waging war with microorganisms is such a chancy business that both the United States and the Soviet Union probably felt they had little to lose when they formally renounced biological warfare under the Biological Weapons Convention that went into effect last year.° (The United States, in fact, gave it up unilaterally in 1969.) Prior to the renunciations, however, a large and amply supported community of biological warfare researchers filled a major Army laboratory at Fort Detrick, Maryland. As far as they were concerned, biological weapons merited a serious and continuing research effort, and there can be little doubt that if the decision had been left to them, they would still be at it.

23 These cases all involve the inhibition of science and technology by outside forces. What also must be considered is a relatively new, but rapidly expanding, process of the scientific and technical communities attempting to stay one step ahead of societal restraint by setting limitations for themselves. Last year, genetics researchers from several nations voluntarily agreed to an unprecedented moratorium; they were afraid certain gene transplantation experiments might result in highly dangerous disease-producing strains. The moratorium was partially lifted earlier this year following agreement on safety procedures and the development of microorganisms that are said to be unable to survive outside a controlled laboratory environment. The significance of this episode in voluntary scientific restraint cannot be exaggerated. For the principal figures in the story are all basic researchers, and, historically, if there is any basic tenet to basic science, it is that all of nature's secrets are fair game. The temporary moratorium did not conflict with that rule, but it did have the effect of delaying a good many research projects for social rather than scientific reasons. And that's something new in the life of science.

24 Along these lines, a blend of inside and outside concerns has produced uncertainty and turbulence over the use of human subjects in experimentation. The maze of regulations that has ensued from these concerns would astonish Dr. Walter Reed—just as they often astonish, and thwart, many of his scientific descendants today. What it all adds up to is that in response to pressures from the outside world, the scientific community is now seriously restricted when it wants to test phar-

---

[22] **last year:** 1975

maceutical drugs and other substances on human beings, even when those human beings want to serve as test subjects.

25 Recommendations that are likely to have a profound effect on the conduct of research over coming decades are now being drafted by the National Commission for the Protection of Human Subjects of Biomedical and Behavioral Research. The commission, which advises Congress and the Department of Health, Education and Welfare, has already provided the advice that the Secretary of HEW followed in changing rules for experimentation on fetuses. The moratorium on fetal research instituted by Congress in July 1974 was lifted in August 1975 after guidelines for the conduct of such research were tightened in response to commission recommendations. Now it is looking at the problems involved in experimenting on institutionalized mental patients, children and prisoners. One step ahead of the commission, however, the U.S. Bureau of Prisons has banned the use of prisoners in medical research on the grounds that the potential for abuse and manipulation is too great when a prisoner is invited to "volunteer" to take part in an experiment. The irony of it is that in testimony before the commission prisoners have insisted that they wish to retain the option to take part in experiments. They say they like the financial and psychological rewards that accompany participation. Drug researchers say that the ban will impede the development of valuable pharmaceuticals, since prisoners, living in environments where nutrition and other factors can be controlled, are ideal experimental subjects.

26 Many scientists support the new rules, but many others feel that society is clumsily imposing rules that will ultimately be to the detriment of society. All agree, however, that the days are gone when such matters were exclusively the business of science.

27 Today the federal government pays for about half of all the research and development performed in the United States. Over the first three decades of the postwar period, the amount of federal money for research and development grew so rapidly—from $918 million in 1946 to $24 billion in 1976—that it really was an era in which the doable usually stood a very good chance of getting done. This was a period in which the Air Force spent over $1 billion in a futile effort to construct a nuclear-powered airplane, oblivious of warnings that the weight of the shielding on the reactor would result in a plane that would be huge and slow, and of little military use. Because of the ever-present danger of a crash that would almost certainly spread radioactivity, the plane would not have been permitted to fly over populated areas. Nevertheless, more than a billion dollars was put into the venture and more would have followed if the Kennedy Administration had not stopped it in 1962.

28 From today's perspective, the striking aspect of the atomic aircraft project was that it got under way and flourished with virtually no public notice and scant congressional attention. Today, the scientific landscape

in Washington is dotted with organizations that scrutinize research projects. Private organizations on the periphery of government, such as the Arms Control Association and the Federation of American Scientists, bring together prestigious scientists and engineers to examine the Defense Department's research programs and testify about them in Congress. Laden with Nobel laureates and former high-level officials of the department itself, they work in close alliance with the press and several-score congressmen and senators to throw light on weapons planning. Their main objective is arms control, which means they tend to be naysayers—definitely a minority position on military research and development. But their effect has been powerful in getting the issues out in the open and making the Defense Department less free-wheeling in its weapons programs. For example, the department has been trying for years to obtain funds for the production of a new type of poison gas projectile known as a "binary" in which two gases, nontoxic themselves, are joined to become a lethal weapon at the critical moment. Congress, mainly at the urgings of nongovernment critics of the weapon, has so far refused to put up the money.

29 The Congress itself has taken the unusual step of setting up its own organization, the Office of Technology Assessment, to attempt to look over the horizon and anticipate the impact of scientific and technological developments. OTA went into operation in 1974 and, though still a fledgling, has conducted a wide assortment of studies, ranging from the environmental effects of offshore drilling to the effectiveness of pharmaceutical drugs.

30 Meanwhile, government is increasingly relying on the use of impact statements to attempt to foresee the consequences of federal projects. The widest and best known use is in environmental matters. Before any federal agency can turn a spade of soil, it must now carefully analyze the cost effectiveness of its plans, the available alternatives and the environmental consequences. In effect, it must serve up reams of material that can be used by opponents of the project, which is one reason that the development of nuclear power in the United States is tied up in legal knots. The environmental impact statements have been cited in the court proceedings as evidence that the projects are unsafe, environmentally unsound or uneconomical.

31 In other nations, nuclear power plants are built where the nuclear power authorities choose to build them, with virtually no interference from dissenting parties. This process once prevailed in the United States, but today outsiders have a powerful say.

32 While the government's research programs have come under a variety of constraints, research conducted by private industry is also going through a transformation that is likely to extend for decades. Perhaps the most striking aspect of this transformation is that American industry—once the world's pioneer in innovation—has become ex-

tremely cautious about investing its money in research and development, so much so that some economists are expressing concern about where the new products will come from to spur the economy of the 1980s and 1990s. The increasing corporate timidity about research comes from a number of factors, among them the high costs and uncertainties of getting new products on the market, consumer conservatism in an inflationary period, and a tangle of government regulations concerning product safety. E. I. duPont de Nemours & Co., traditionally a pioneer in turning research into profitable products, typifies the new development. Irving S. Shapiro, chairman and chief executive of the giant chemical company, recently noted the changed attitude toward research projects when he said, "Where we had 24 a couple of years ago, I feel more comfortable with, say, five or six." Other industrial executives say that their firms have concluded that it is safer and more profitable to refine existing products than it is to start from the ground up with new ones.

33 The effect of this caution is likely to spread throughout the entire research enterprise, starting with university training of scientists and engineers. If industry pulls back from innovation, its manpower requirements will have to be changed accordingly. With the academic job market already saturated and offering few employment opportunities for teachers, the trend is already toward warning prospective students that the future may be grim in many scientific and engineering specialties. Thus, a committee of the National Academy of Sciences last year recommended that university astronomy departments carefully advise interested students that the job market in astronomy has virtually collapsed. Even the medical profession is facing the possibility of saturation in some specialties; another Academy committee, studying the problem at the request of Congress, concluded that the United States has an oversupply of surgeons.

34 The maturing° of the American scientific and technical communities has also been accompanied by several developments that would have been considered utterly remote just a decade ago. With employment opportunities declining and job security weakening, union membership is no longer a novelty among university scientists and engineers. Meanwhile, professional scientific societies have departed from their traditionally exclusive concern with substantive professional matters and have organized to protect their members' jobs. The American Chemical Society, for example, has established a legal defense fund to provide low-cost loans for members who feel their rights have been violated. The American Association for the Advancement of Science is

---

[34] **maturing:** used in the technical economic sense of reaching a supply equal to or surpassing the demand

in the process of encouraging its approximately 200 constituent societies to set up committees to protect the "scientific freedom and responsibility" of their members.

35 What, then, will the life of the scientific community be like in, say, 1998? My expectation is that it will be cautious in what it goes about researching; many possibilities will arise for researching this or that, but the final choices will be filtered through scrutiny processes that will examine costs, societal value, potential benefits and hazards. The researchers will enter the profession through a fine-screen selection process and their performance will be closely monitored. The situation is not likely to be favorable for late bloomers or innovators who need a decade to produce results.

36 The situation I foresee is not especially attractive in comparison with the frontier days of science. It is heavily organized, bureaucratized, reasonably productive, relatively safe and probably quite dull in its ultimate output.

37 The Albert Einsteins and Walter Reeds of the next turn of the century won't like it.

STUDY QUESTIONS

1. Greenberg's title is a parody version of a want ad. In what ways is it appropriate as an introduction to what follows? How does it compare in effectiveness to, say, "Future Constraints on Scientific Innovation"?
2. What use does Greenberg make of his "time machine" in the first nine paragraphs? Why does he wait to identify the Swiss patent clerk and the army surgeon?
3. Which of the following statements comes closest to capturing the thesis, or main idea, of Greenberg's essay?
   (a) There will be no room for scientific geniuses in the latter years of this century.
   (b) In the latter years of this century, scientists will play a relatively small part in deciding which investigative projects will be carried through.
   (c) Scientists should be allowed more freedom to decide for themselves which investigative projects will be carried through.

   Be prepared to say why you rejected the two other versions.
4. What kinds of evidence does Greenberg assemble to make his point? Be prepared to discuss representative instances of each kind you have located.
5. How would you characterize the tone of this essay? Given Green-

berg's thesis as you have determined it (question 3), how is that tone appropriate?

6. What is Greenberg's point in mentioning that genetics researchers in 1975 "voluntarily agreed to an unprecedented moratorium" (paragraph 23) on gene transplantation experiments? How does this fact support his thesis?
7. What is the effect of Greenberg's brief final paragraph? How does it serve to unify his essay?

ANALYZING PARTS AND FUNCTIONS

Robert M. Pirsig

Robert M. Pirsig has held many jobs, from day laborer to university professor. His one book to date, *Zen and the Art of Motorcycle Maintenance* (1974), has become something of a classic. There he mixes the story of a long motorcycle trip with autobiographical flashbacks and reflections on subjects as various as attitudes toward machinery and the merits of various philosophical systems. The selection below illustrates what Pirsig calls the classic (or analytic) attitude toward objects, as opposed to the romantic attitude, which favors feelings and impressions instead of "underlying form." Both attitudes have their proper place in this author's scheme of values.

THE RATIONALITY OF REPAIR*

1 This morning I talked about hierarchies of thought—the system. Now I want to talk about methods of finding one's way through these hierarchies—logic.

2 Two kinds of logic are used, inductive and deductive. Inductive inferences start with observations of the machine and arrive at general conclusions. For example, if the cycle goes over a bump and the engine misfires, and then goes over another bump and the engine misfires, and then goes over another bump and the engine misfires, and then goes over a long smooth stretch of road and there is no misfiring, and then goes over a fourth bump and the engine misfires again, one can logically conclude that the misfiring is caused by the bumps. That is induction: reasoning from particular experiences to general truths.

3 Deductive inferences do the reverse. They start with general knowledge and predict a specific observation. For example, if, from

*Title chosen by editor

reading the hierarchy of facts about the machine, the mechanic knows the horn of the cycle is powered exclusively by electricity from the battery, then he can logically infer that if the battery is dead the horn will not work. That is deduction.

4 Solution of problems too complicated for common sense to solve is achieved by long strings of mixed inductive and deductive inferences that weave back and forth between the observed machine and the mental hierarchy of the machine found in the manuals. The correct program for this interweaving is formalized as scientific method.

5 Actually I've never seen a cycle-maintenance problem complex enough really to require full-scale formal scientific method. Repair problems are not that hard. When I think of formal scientific method an image sometimes comes to mind of an enormous juggernaut, a huge bulldozer—slow, tedious, lumbering, laborious, but invincible. It takes twice as long, five times as long, maybe a dozen times as long as informal mechanic's techniques, but you know in the end you're going to *get* it. There's no fault isolation problem in motorcycle maintenance that can stand up to it. When you've hit a really tough one, tried everything, racked your brain and nothing works, and you know that this time Nature has really decided to be difficult, you say, "Okay, Nature, that's the end of the *nice* guy," and you crank up the formal scientific method.

6 For this you keep a lab notebook. Everything gets written down, formally, so that you know at all times where you are, where you've been, where you're going and where you want to get. In scientific work and electronics technology this is necessary because otherwise the problems get so complex you get lost in them and confused and forget what you know and what you don't know and have to give up. In cycle maintenance things are not that involved, but when confusion starts it's a good idea to hold it down by making everything formal and exact. Sometimes just the act of writing down the problems straightens out your head as to what they really are.

7 The logical statements entered into the notebook are broken down into six categories: (1) statement of the problem, (2) hypotheses as to the cause of the problem, (3) experiments designed to test each hypothesis, (4) predicted results of the experiments, (5) observed results of the experiments and (6) conclusions from the results of the experiments. This is not different from the formal arrangement of many college and high-school lab notebooks but the purpose here is no longer just busywork. The purpose now is precise guidance of thoughts that will fail if they are not accurate.

8 The real purpose of scientific method is to make sure Nature hasn't misled you into thinking you know something you don't actually know. There's not a mechanic or scientist or technician alive who hasn't suffered from that one so much that he's not instinctively on guard. That's the main reason why so much scientific and mechanical information sounds so dull and so cautious. If you get careless or go romanticizing

scientific information, giving it a flourish here and there, Nature will soon make a complete fool out of you. It does it often enough anyway even when you don't give it opportunities. One must be extremely careful and rigidly logical when dealing with Nature: one logical slip and an entire scientific edifice comes tumbling down. One false deduction about the machine and you can get hung up indefinitely.

9 In Part One of formal scientific method, which is the statement of the problem, the main skill is in stating absolutely no more than you are positive you know. It is much better to enter a statement "Solve Problem: Why doesn't cycle work?" which sounds dumb but is correct, than it is to enter a statement "Solve Problem: What is wrong with the electrical system?" when you don't absolutely *know* the trouble is *in* the electrical system. What you should state is "Solve Problem: What is wrong with cycle?" and *then* state as the first entry of Part Two: "Hypothesis Number One: The trouble is in the electrical system." You think of as many hypotheses as you can, then you design experiments to test them to see which are true and which are false.

10 This careful approach to the beginning questions keeps you from taking a major wrong turn which might cause you weeks of extra work or can even hang you up completely. Scientific questions often have a surface appearance of dumbness for this reason. They are asked in order to prevent dumb mistakes later on.

11 Part Three, that part of formal scientific method called experimentation, is sometimes thought of by romantics as all of science itself because that's the only part with much visual surface. They see lots of test tubes and bizarre equipment and people running around making discoveries. They do not see the experiment as part of a larger intellectual process and so they often confuse experiments with demonstrations, which look the same. A man conducting a gee-whiz science show with fifty thousand dollars' worth of Frankenstein equipment is not doing anything scientific if he knows beforehand what the results of his efforts are going to be. A motorcycle mechanic, on the other hand, who honks the horn to see if the battery works is informally conducting a true scientific experiment. He is testing a hypothesis by putting the question to nature. The TV scientist who mutters sadly, "The experiment is a failure; we have failed to achieve what we had hoped for," is suffering mainly from a bad scriptwriter. An experiment is never a failure solely because it fails to achieve predicted results. An experiment is a failure only when it also fails adequately to test the hypothesis in question, when the data it produces don't prove anything one way or another.

12 Skill at this point consists of using experiments that test only the hypothesis in question, nothing less, nothing more. If the horn honks, and the mechanic concludes that the whole electrical system is working, he is in deep trouble. He has reached an illogical conclusion. The honking horn only tells him that the battery and horn are working. To design

an experiment properly he has to think very rigidly in terms of what directly causes what. This you know from the hierarchy. The horn doesn't make the cycle go. Neither does the battery, except in a very indirect way. The point at which the electrical system *directly* causes the engine to fire is at the spark plugs, and if you don't test here, at the output of the electrical system, you will never really know whether the failure is electrical or not.

13 To test properly the mechanic removes the plug and lays it against the engine so that the base around the plug is electrically grounded, kicks the starter lever and watches the spark-plug gap for a blue spark. If there isn't any he can conclude one of two things: (a) there is an electrical failure or (b) his experiment is sloppy. If he is experienced he will try it a few more times, checking connections, trying every way he can think of to get that plug to fire. Then, if he can't get it to fire, he finally concludes that *a* is correct, there's an electrical failure, and the experiment is over. He has proved that his hypothesis is correct.

14 In the final category, conclusions, skill comes in stating no more than the experiment has proved. It hasn't proved that when he fixes the electrical system the motorcycle will start. There may be other things wrong. But he does know that the motorcycle isn't going to run until the electrical system is working and he sets up the next formal question: "Solve problem: what is wrong with the electrical system?"

15 He then sets up hypotheses for these and tests them. By asking the right questions and choosing the right tests and drawing the right conclusions the mechanic works his way down the echelons of the motorcycle hierarchy until he has found the exact specific cause or causes of the engine failure, and then he changes them so that they no longer cause the failure.

16 An untrained observer will see only physical labor and often get the idea that physical labor is mainly what the mechanic does. Actually the physical labor is the smallest and easiest part of what the mechanic does. By far the greatest part of his work is careful observation and precise thinking. That is why mechanics sometimes seem so taciturn and withdrawn when performing tests. They don't like it when you talk to them because they are concentrating on mental images, hierarchies, and not really looking at you or the physical motorcycle at all. They are using the experiment as part of a program to expand their hierarchy of knowledge of the faulty motorcycle and compare it to the correct hierarchy in their mind. They are looking at underlying form.

STUDY QUESTIONS

1. "The Rationality of Repair" forms part of what Pirsig calls a *chautauqua*, or an adult-education enterprise that travels around the country. In other words, Pirsig imagines himself as lecturing to fellow citizens who lack a formal academic background or specialized knowledge. What is the tone of this selection, and how does it fit the imagined occasion? Be prepared to point to specific uses of language that convey Pirsig's tone.
2. The points that Pirsig wants to make about method are extremely general and abstract. Unrelieved generality and abstraction, however, are usually tedious. How does Pirsig combat this difficulty? Locate passages that support your answer.
3. What connotations, or overtones of meaning, do you associate with motorcycles? What do you take Pirsig's view of motorcycles to be? In what ways, if any, does his prose put motorcycles in a new light for you?
4. What relation does scientific method have to motorcycle repair as described by Pirsig? Does he conceive of the mechanic as a scientist?
5. Pirsig attacks the common idea that science and experimentation are the same thing. What is the basis of his criticism? And what is his point (paragraph 11) about experiments that fail to achieve predicted results?
6. What does Pirsig mean by his last two words, *underlying form?* Is the underlying form of a motorcycle something different from its working parts?

Aaron Copland

Aaron Copland is an eminent American composer, noted for combining symphonic and folk elements. "How We Listen" first appeared in his book *What to Listen for in Music* (1939).

HOW WE LISTEN

1 We all listen to music according to our separate capacities. But, for the sake of analysis, the whole listening process may become clearer if we break it up into its component parts, so to speak. In a certain sense we all listen to music on three separate planes. For lack of a better

terminology, one might name these: (1) the sensuous plane, (2) the expressive plane, (3) the sheerly musical plane. The only advantage to be gained from mechanically splitting up the listening process into these hypothetical planes is the clearer view to be had of the way in which we listen.

2 The simplest way of listening to music is to listen for the sheer pleasure of the musical sound itself. That is the sensuous plane. It is the plane on which we hear music without thinking, without considering it in any way. One turns on the radio while doing something else and absent-mindedly bathes in the sound. A kind of brainless but attractive state of mind is engendered by the mere sound appeal of the music.

3 You may be sitting in a room reading this book. Imagine one note struck on the piano. Immediately that one note is enough to change the atmosphere of the room—proving that the sound element in music is a powerful and mysterious agent, which it would be foolish to deride or belittle.

4 The surprising thing is that many people who consider themselves qualified music lovers abuse that plane in listening. They go to concerts in order to lose themselves. They use music as a consolation or an escape. They enter an ideal world where one doesn't have to think of the realities of everyday life. Of course they aren't thinking about the music either. Music allows them to leave it, and they go off to a place to dream, dreaming because of and apropos of the music yet never quite listening to it.

5 Yes, the sound appeal of music is a potent and primitive force, but you must not allow it to usurp a disproportionate share of your interest. The sensuous plane is an important one in music, a very important one, but it does not constitute the whole story.

6 There is no need to digress further on the sensuous plane. Its appeal to every normal human being is self-evident. There is, however, such a thing as becoming more sensitive to the different kinds of sound stuff as used by various composers. For all composers do not use that sound stuff in the same way. Don't get the idea that the value of music is commensurate with its sensuous appeal or that the loveliest sounding music is made by the greatest composer. If that were so, Ravel would be a greater creator than Beethoven. The point is that the sound element varies with each composer, that his usage of sound forms an integral part of his style and must be taken into account when listening. The reader can see, therefore, that a more conscious approach is valuable even on this primary plane of music listening.

7 The second plane on which music exists is what I have called the expressive one. Here, immediately, we tread on controversial ground. Composers have a way of shying away from any discussion of music's expressive side. Did not Stravinsky himself proclaim that his music was an "object," a "thing," with a life of its own, and with no other meaning than its own purely musical existence? This intransigent attitude of

Stravinsky's may be due to the fact that so many people have tried to read different meanings into so many pieces. Heaven knows it is difficult enough to say precisely what it is that a piece of music means, to say it definitely, to say it finally so that everyone is satisfied with your explanation. But that should not lead one to the other extreme of denying to music the right to be "expressive."

8 My own belief is that all music has an expressive power, some more and some less, but that all music has a certain meaning behind the notes and that that meaning behind the notes constitutes, after all, what the piece is saying, what the piece is about. This whole problem can be stated quite simply by asking, "Is there a meaning to music?" My answer to that would be, "Yes." And "Can you state in so many words what the meaning is?" My answer to that would be, "No." Therein lies the difficulty.

9 Simple-minded souls will never be satisfied with the answer to the second of these questions. They always want music to have a meaning, and the more concrete it is the better they like it. The more the music reminds them of a train, a storm, a funeral, or any other familiar conception the more expressive it appears to be to them. This popular idea of music's meaning—stimulated and abetted by the usual run of musical commentator—should be discouraged wherever and whenever it is met. One timid lady once confessed to me that she suspected something seriously lacking in her appreciation of music because of her inability to connect it with anything definite. That is getting the whole thing backward, of course.

10 Still, the question remains, How close should the intelligent music lover wish to come to pinning a definite meaning to any particular work? No closer than a general concept, I should say. Music expresses, at different moments, serenity or exuberance, regret or triumph, fury or delight. It expresses each of these moods, and many others, in a numberless variety of subtle shadings and differences. It may even express a state of meaning for which there exists no adequate word in any language. In that case, musicians often like to say that it has only a purely musical meaning. They sometimes go farther and say that *all* music has only a purely musical meaning. What they really mean is that no appropriate word can be found to express the music's meaning and that, even if it could, they do not feel the need of finding it.

11 But whatever the professional musician may hold, most musical novices still search for specific words with which to pin down their musical reactions. That is why they always find Tschaikovsky easier to "understand" than Beethoven. In the first place, it is easier to pin a meaning-word on a Tschaikovsky piece than on a Beethoven one. Much easier. Moreover, with the Russian composer, every time you come back to a piece of his it almost always says the same thing to you, whereas with Beethoven it is often quite difficult to put your finger right on what he is saying. And any musician will tell you that that is why Beethoven

is the greater composer. Because music which always says the same thing to you will necessarily soon become dull music, but music whose meaning is slightly different with each hearing has a greater chance of remaining alive.

12 Listen, if you can, to the forty-eight fugue° themes of Bach's *Well Tempered Clavichord.* Listen to each theme, one after another. You will soon realize that each theme mirrors a different world of feeling. You will also soon realize that the more beautiful a theme seems to you the harder it is to find any word that will describe it to your complete satisfaction. Yes, you will certainly know whether it is a gay theme or a sad one. You will be able, in other words, in your own mind, to draw a frame of emotional feeling around your theme. Now study the sad one a little closer. Try to pin down the exact quality of its sadness. Is it pessimistically sad or resignedly sad; is it fatefully sad or smilingly sad?

13 Let us suppose that you are fortunate and can describe to your own satisfaction in so many words the exact meaning of your chosen theme. There is still no guarantee that anyone else will be satisfied. Nor need they be. The important thing is that each one feel for himself the specific expressive quality of a theme or, similarly, an entire piece of music. And if it is a great work of art, don't expect it to mean exactly the same thing to you each time you return to it.

14 Themes or pieces need not express only one emotion, of course. Take such a theme as the first main one of the *Ninth Symphony,*° for example. It is clearly made up of different elements. It does not say only one thing. Yet anyone hearing it immediately gets a feeling of strength, a feeling of power. It isn't a power that comes simply because the theme is played loudly. It is a power inherent in the theme itself. The extraordinary strength and vigor of the theme results in the listener's receiving an impression that a forceful statement has been made. But one should never try to boil it down to "the fateful hammer of life," etc. That is where the trouble begins. The musician, in his exasperation, says it means nothing but the notes themselves, whereas the nonprofessional is only too anxious to hang on to any explanation that gives him the illusion of getting closer to the music's meaning.

15 Now, perhaps, the reader will know better what I mean when I say that music does have an expressive meaning but that we cannot say in so many words what that meaning is.

16 The third plane on which music exists is the sheerly musical plane. Besides the pleasurable sound of music and the expressive feeling that it gives off, music does exist in terms of the notes themselves and of their manipulation. Most listeners are not sufficiently conscious of this

---

[12] **fugue:** a musical composition of several simultaneous voices, in which the melody in one voice becomes the accompaniment in other voices

[14] **Ninth Symphony:** Beethoven's late symphony, the first ever to use singers and a chorus

third plane. It will be largely the business of this book to make them more aware of music on this plane.

17 Professional musicians, on the other hand, are, if anything, too conscious of the mere notes themselves. They often fall into the error of becoming so engrossed with their arpeggios and staccatos° that they forget the deeper aspects of the music they are performing. But from the layman's standpoint, it is not so much a matter of getting over bad habits on the sheerly musical plane as of increasing one's awareness of what is going on, in so far as the notes are concerned.

18 When the man in the street listens to the "notes themselves" with any degree of concentration, he is most likely to make some mention of the melody. Either he hears a pretty melody or he does not, and he generally lets it go at that. Rhythm is likely to gain his attention next, particularly if it seems exciting. But harmony and tone color° are generally taken for granted, if they are thought of consciously at all. As for music's having a definite form of some kind, that idea seems never to have occurred to him.

19 It is very important for all of us to become more alive to music on its sheerly musical plane. After all, an actual musical material is being used. The intelligent listener must be prepared to increase his awareness of the musical material and what happens to it. He must hear the melodies, the rhythms, the harmonies, the tone colors in a more conscious fashion. But above all he must, in order to follow the line of the composer's thought, know something of the principles of musical form. Listening to all of these elements is listening on the sheerly musical plane.

20 Let me repeat that I have split up mechanically the three separate planes on which we listen merely for the sake of greater clarity. Actually, we never listen on one or the other of these planes. What we do is to correlate them—listening in all three ways at the same time. It takes no mental effort, for we do it instinctively.

21 Perhaps an analogy with what happens to us when we visit the theater will make this instinctive correlation clearer. In the theater, you are aware of the actors and actresses, costumes and sets, sounds and movements. All these give one the sense that the theater is a pleasant place to be in. They constitute the sensuous plane in our theatrical reactions.

22 The expressive plane in the theater would be derived from the feeling that you get from what is happening on the stage. You are moved to pity, excitement, or gayety. It is this general feeling, generated aside from the particular words being spoken, a certain emotional some-

---

[17] **arpeggios, staccatos:** respectively, the sounding of the notes of chords in rapid succession instead of simultaneously; abruptly disconnected notes

[18] **tone color:** the characteristic quality of sound; timbre

thing which exists on the stage, that is analogous to the expressive quality in music.

23 The plot and plot development is equivalent to our sheerly musical plane. The playwright creates and develops a character in just the same way that a composer creates and develops a theme. According to the degree of your awareness of the way in which the artist in either field handles his material will you become a more intelligent listener.

24 It is easy enough to see that the theatergoer never is conscious of any of these elements separately. He is aware of them all at the same time. The same is true of music listening. We simultaneously and without thinking listen on all three planes.

25 In a sense, the ideal listener is both inside and outside the music at the same moment, judging it and enjoying it, wishing it would go one way and watching it go another—almost like the composer at the moment he composes it; because in order to write his music, the composer must also be inside and outside his music, carried away by it and yet coldly critical of it. A subjective and objective attitude is implied in both creating and listening to music.

26 What the reader should strive for, then, is a more *active* kind of listening. Whether you listen to Mozart or Duke Ellington, you can deepen your understanding of music only by being a more conscious and aware listener—not someone who is just listening, but someone who is listening *for* something.

STUDY QUESTIONS

1. The structure of Copland's essay is extremely simple and clear. What is that structure, and why do you suppose Copland chose it? Think of the nature of his subject matter in relation to his intended audience.
2. What does Copland have against people who "go to concerts in order to lose themselves" (paragraph 4)? Your answer should give you insight into the dominant value or ideal that lies behind this essay.
3. What tone does Copland take toward his readers? Be prepared to cite examples. In what way is that tone appropriate or inappropriate to Copland's evident purpose?
4. Why does Copland feel obliged to deal with the point that a piece of music can "mean" different things to different listeners? How does he deal with that point? (See paragraphs 7–15.)
5. In saving "the sheerly musical plane" for the final part of his essay, what is Copland implying about that plane?
6. What is the point of Copland's contrast between Tschaikovsky and Beethoven (paragraph 11)? What standard of musical value

lies behind that contrast? Do you share Copland's standard?
7. Why does Copland devote paragraphs 21–24 to a discussion of the theater? Is he digressing ("changing the subject")?

Robin Lakoff

Robin Lakoff is a professor of linguistics at the University of California, Berkeley. "Making a Lady of Her" is drawn from her book, *Language and Woman's Place* (1975).

MAKING A LADY OF HER*

1 When a word acquires a bad connotation by association with something unpleasant or embarrassing, people may search for substitutes that do not have the uncomfortable effect—that is, euphemisms. Since attitudes toward the original referent are not altered by a change of name, the new name itself takes on the adverse connotations, and a new euphemism must be found. It is no doubt possible to pick out areas of particular psychological strain or discomfort—areas where problems exist in a culture—by pinpointing items around which a great many euphemisms are clustered. An obvious example concerns the various words for that household convenience into which human wastes are eliminated: toilet, bathroom, rest room, comfort station, lavatory, water closet, loo, and all the others.

2 In the case of women, it may be encouraging to find no richness of euphemism; but it is discouraging to note that at least one euphemism for "woman" does exist and is very much alive. The word, of course, is "lady," which seems to be replacing "woman" in a great many contexts. Where both exist, they have different connotations; where only one exists, there is usually a reason, to be found in the context in which the word is uttered.

3 Related to the existence of euphemistic terms for "woman" is the existence of euphemistic terms for woman's principal role, that of "housewife." Most occupational terms do not have coexisting euphemisms: these seem to come into being only when the occupation is considered embarrassing or demeaning. Thus there is no euphemism for "pro-

*Title chosen by editor

fessor," "doctor," "bank president"; but we do find "mortician" and "funeral director" for "undertaker"; "custodian" and "sanitary engineer" for "janitor"; "domestic" for "cleaning woman"; and so forth. Similarly one keeps running into hopeful suggestions, principally in the pages of women's magazines, that the lot of the housewife would be immeasurably improved if she thought of herself as "homemaker," "household executive," "household engineer," or any of several others. I am not sure what to make of the fact that none of these (unlike the bona fide occupational euphemisms) have taken hold: is it because the "housewife" doesn't consider her status demeaning? Then why the search for euphemisms? Or does she feel that there is no escape through a change in nomenclature, or lack pride in her job to such an extent that she doesn't feel up to making the effort? This is a question for the sociologist.

4 It may be objected that *lady* has a masculine counterpart, namely *gentleman,* occasionally shortened to *gent.* But I don't think this is a fair comparison. *Lady* is much more common than *gent(leman),* and, since *gent* exists, the reason is not ease of pronunciation. *Lady* is really a euphemism for *woman,* but *gentleman* is not nearly frequent enough to classify as a euphemism for *man.* Just as we do not call whites "Caucasian-Americans," there is no felt need to refer to men commonly as "gentlemen." And just as there is a need for such terms as "Afro-Americans," there is similarly a felt need for "lady." One might even say that when a derogatory epithet exists, a parallel euphemism is deemed necessary. (The term WASP, white Anglo-Saxon Protestant, may occur to the reader as a possible derogatory term which has no parallel euphemism. But in fact, WASP is not parallel in usage to *nigger, polack,* or *yid.* One can refer to himself as a WASP, as one cannot refer to himself as a *nigger* without either a total lack of self-pride or bitter sarcasm. Thus one can say: "Sure I'm a WASP, and proud of it!" but probably not: "Sure I'm a nigger, and proud of it!" without special sarcastic inflection in the voice suggesting that it is an imitation of the addressee.) To avoid having to resort to terms like "Afro-American," we need only get rid of all expressions like "nigger"; to banish "lady" in its euphemistic sense from the vocabulary of English, we need only first get rid of "broad" and its relations. But of course, as already pointed out, we cannot achieve this commendable simplification of the lexicon unless we somehow remove from our minds the idea that blacks *are* niggers, and that women *are* broads. The presence of the words is a signal that something is wrong, rather than (as too often interpreted by well-meaning reformers) the problem itself. The point here is that, unless we start feeling more respect for women and, at the same time, less uncomfortable about them and their roles in society in relation to men, we cannot avoid *ladies* any more than we can avoid *broads.*

5 In the past, some ethnic groups that today are relatively respectable were apparently considered less so. And in looking at reports of the

terms used to describe those groups at the earlier time, we find two interesting facts: first, there is a much greater incidence of derogatory epithets for that group (as might be expected); and second (which one might not be led to expect automatically), there exist euphemistic terms for that group that are no longer in general use. One can only conclude that euphemisms vanish as they are no longer needed. The example I have in mind is that of the words used to describe Jews. Aside from the uncomplimentary epithets which still exist today, though not encountered very often, one finds, in reading novels written and set more than half a century ago, a number of euphemisms that are not found any more, such as "Hebrew gentleman" and "Israelite." The disappearance of the euphemisms concurrently with the derogatory terms suggests that women will be *ladies* until some more dignified status can be found for them.

6 It might also be claimed that *lady* is no euphemism because it has exactly the same connotations as *woman,* is usable under the same semantic and contextual conditions. But a cursory inspection will show that this is not always the case. The decision to use one term rather than the other may considerably alter the sense of a sentence. The following are examples:

(a) A (woman) that I know makes amazing things out of
(lady)
shoelaces and old boxes.
(b) A (woman) I know works at Woolworth's.
(lady)
(c) A (woman) I know is a dean at Berkeley.
(lady)

(These facts are true for some speakers of English. For others, *lady* has taken over the function of *woman* to such an extent that *lady* can be used in all these sentences.)

7 In my speech, the use of *lady* in *(c)* imparts a frivolous or nonserious tone to the sentence: the matter under discussion is one of not too great moment. In this dialect, then, *lady* seems to be the more colloquial word: it is less apt to be used in writing, or in discussing serious matters. Similarly in *(a),* using *lady* would suggest that the speaker considered the "amazing things" not to be serious art, but merely a hobby or an aberration. If *woman* is used, she might be a serious (pop art)[7] sculptor.

8 Related to this is the use of *lady* in job terminology. For at least some speakers, the more demeaning the job, the more the person holding it (if female, of course) is likely to be described as a *lady.* Thus, *cleaning lady* is at least as common as *cleaning woman, saleslady* as *saleswoman.* But one says, normally, *woman doctor.* To say *lady doctor* is to be very

---

[7] **pop art:** British and American movement of the 1950s and '60s focusing artistic attention on such common objects as soup cans, flags, and comic strips

condescending: it constitutes an insult. For men, there is no such dichotomy. *Garbageman* or *salesman* is the only possibility, never **garbage gentleman.*° And of course, since in the professions the male is unmarked, we never have **man (male) doctor.*

9 Numerous other examples can be given, all tending to prove the same point: that if, in a particular sentence, both *woman* and *lady* might be used, the use of the latter tends to trivialize the subject matter under discussion, often subtly ridiculing the woman involved. Thus, for example, a mention in the San Francisco *Chronicle* of January 31, 1972, of Madalyn Murray O'Hair as the "lady atheist" reduces her position to that of scatterbrained eccentric, or at any rate, one who need not be taken seriously. Even *woman atheist* is scarcely defensible: first, because her sex is irrelevant to her philosophical position, and second, because her name makes it clear in any event. But *lady* makes matters still worse. Similarly a reference to a *woman sculptor* is only mildly annoying (since there is no term **male sculptor,* the discrepancy suggests that such activity is normal for a man, but not for a woman), but still it could be used with reference to a serious artist. *Lady sculptor,* on the other hand, strikes me as a slur against the artist, deliberate or not, implying that the woman's art is frivolous, something she does to fend off the boredom of suburban housewifery, or at any rate, nothing of moment in the art world. Serious artists have shows, not dilettantes. So we hear of *one-woman shows,* but never *one-lady shows.*

10 Another realm of usage in which *lady* contrasts with *woman* is in titles of organizations. It seems that organizations of women who have a serious purpose (not merely that of spending time with one another) cannot use the word *lady* in their titles, but less serious ones may. Compare the *Ladies' Auxiliary* of a men's group, or the *Thursday Evening Ladies Browning and Garden Society,* with **Ladies' Lib* or **Ladies Strike for Peace.*

11 What is curious about this split is that *lady* is, as noted, in origin a euphemism for *woman.* What kind of euphemism is it that subtly denigrates the people to whom it refers, suggests that they are not to be taken seriously, are laughing stocks? A euphemism, after all, is supposed to put a better face on something people find uncomfortable. But this is not really contradictory. What a euphemism is supposed to do, actually, is to remove from thought *that part* of the connotations of a word that creates the discomfort. So each of the euphemisms for toilet, starting with *toilet,* seems to be trying to get further from the notion of excrement, by employing successively more elegant terminology that seems designed to suggest that the piece of furniture in question has really other primary uses, for performing one's toilette, for washing, for comfort, for resting, but never for those other things. Perhaps the notion

---

[8] ***garbage gentleman:** Like other linguists, Lakoff places asterisks before expressions that fall outside normal expected use.

of the nonseriousness of women is not the thing that makes men—the devisers of euphemism—as well as women, uncomfortable. Perhaps it is some other aspect of the man-woman relationship. How can we determine whether this is in fact the case?

12 One way of identifying the precise source of discomfort is, perhaps, by looking at the derogatory terms for something. Many of the terms for blacks refer to their physical characteristics. And the latest euphemism for blacks, *Afro-Americans,* seems to be a specific attempt to get away from color names. (The term *black* is not a euphemism, but rather an attempt to confront the issue squarely and make color into a source of pride.) And as has often been noted, derogatory terms for women are very often overtly sexual: the reader will have no difficulty recalling what I allude to here.

13 The distinction between *lady* and *woman,* in those dialects of American English in which it is found, may be traceable to other causes than the sexual connotations present in *woman.* Most people who are asked why they have chosen to use *lady* where *woman* would be as appropriate will reply that *lady* seemed more polite. The concept of politeness thus invoked is the politeness used in dignifying or ennobling a concept that normally is not thought of as having dignity or nobility. It is this notion of politeness that explains why we have *cleaning lady,* but not, normally, *lady doctor.* A doctor does not need to be exalted by conventional expressions: she has dignity enough from her professional status. But a cleaning woman is in a very different situation, in which her occupational category requires ennobling. Then perhaps we can say that the very notion of womanhood, as opposed to manhood, requires ennobling since it lacks inherent dignity of its own: hence the word *woman* requires the existence of a euphemism like *lady.* Besides or possibly because of being explicitly devoid of sexual connotation, *lady* carries with it overtones recalling the age of chivalry: the exalted stature of the person so referred to, her existence above the common sphere. This makes the term seem polite at first, but we must also remember that these implications are perilous: they suggest that a "lady" is helpless, and cannot do things for herself. In this respect the use of a word like *lady* is parallel to the act of opening doors for women—or ladies. At first blush it is flattering: the object of the flattery feels honored, cherished, and so forth; but by the same token, she is also considered helpless and not in control of her own destiny. Women who protest that they *like* receiving these little courtesies, and object to being liberated from them, should reflect a bit on their deeper meaning and see how much they like *that.*

STUDY QUESTIONS

1. Lakoff writes not only as a linguist, but also as a woman. What do you take her attitude toward "women's place" to be? How does that attitude affect her choice of evidence? Be prepared to support your answer by discussing Lakoff's specific points.
2. Although we have classified "Making a Lady of Her" as an essay of explaining, it might plausibly be considered an argument as well. What would be the thesis, or main idea, of Lakoff's argument?
3. In the essay as a whole, what function is served by paragraphs 4 and 6?
4. What is Lakoff's logic in saying (paragraph 4) that in order to banish *lady* as a euphemism, we need only get rid of *broad* and its relations?
5. What relevance does the *historical* study of euphemisms (paragraph 5) have to Lakoff's case about contemporary uses of *lady?*
6. What does Lakoff mean in saying (paragraph 8) that "in the professions the male is unmarked"? Why is this a significant observation?
7. How does Lakoff deal with the apparent contradiction that *lady,* a euphemism for *woman,* often makes a more insulting impression than the term it replaces?
8. In her final paragraph Lakoff asserts that "the very notion of womanhood . . . requires ennobling since it lacks inherent dignity of its own." Can you reconcile this seemingly damaging concession with the main emphasis of the essay?

Peter Marsh and Rom Harré

Peter Marsh and Rom Harré both teach at Oxford University. Marsh is the author of *Aggro: The Illusion of Violence* and coauthor of *The Rules of Disorder* (1978), which reports at length on the research behind the present essay. Harré is a philosopher of science. "The World of Football Hooligans" first appeared in 1978.

THE WORLD OF FOOTBALL HOOLIGANS

1 There is a widespread belief in Britain that certain soccer fields are scenes of chaos, random violence, and bloody fights that make them

only barely distinguishable from battlefields. A sample of headlines from the daily papers reflects this view:

SOCCER HOOLIGANS RUN RIOT
FENCE THEM IN
SMASH THESE THUGS
CLOBBER BOYS ON THE RAMPAGE

2 The rhetoric is typically British, but the mixed images of anarchy, mindlessness, and complete opposition to public order are as likely to appear in Europe, South America, or the United States. So is the pervasive tone of fear and moral outrage—as if the famous juvenile delinquents of the 1950s were about to explode into violent characters out of *A Clockwork Orange,*° or more likely into sheer savagery.

3 This is not the place to speculate on the ultimate historical significance or moral value of soccer riots. But the prevalent view that they are chaotic, irrational, and extremely dangerous is wrong in every respect.

4 Young people have reasons for what they are doing. They interpret what is happening around them, and the events that we view as disordered and irrational have a very different meaning for those involved. Our work has revealed a social orderliness of a remarkable kind. Among these supposedly wild adolescents, we have found clear directions for the attainment of ambitions and personal worth that they feel are impossible to realize within official institutions. These youths, in short, follow rules; and to say so is neither to approve nor to sentimentalize their behavior. The rules are simply there to be discovered.

5 The complex society of aggressive young soccer (called football in Britain) fans is mostly made up of adolescents for whom the weekday world of school, and sometimes of work, provides no opportunities for the development of a sense of worth, dignity, and personal value. Thus school and football "hooliganism" can be seen as closely related. Young working-class students often find themselves written off as uneducable by the age of 12. To a great extent their state schools, like many ghetto schools in the United States, become mere warehouses.

6 To most of the fans we talked with, school seemed to be a waste of time—an institution imposed on them from above. Too often, teachers and school officials impressed these students (all on a nonacademic, working-class track) as being soft, arrogant, contemptuous, cowardly, unfair, incompetent, or indifferent. And so the students "mess about" in school, lock their teachers in closets, and generally raise hell. These classroom disorders are also more orderly than critics commonly assume, but the rules are not quite the same as those we have studied among "football hooligans."

---

[2] **A Clockwork Orange:** a novel (and later a movie) by the British writer Anthony Burgess, dealing with an extremely violent society of the future

7 What happens when these adolescents get together away from an institution like school, which was made *for* them, and find a place where they can construct institutions for themselves? That is the fascination of the football terraces[7]; for on the terraced concrete grandstands overlooking soccer fields there flourishes a complex society of the adolescents' making, and one in which teachers (good, bad, or indifferent) hold no power. Here boys—never girls—see the chance of becoming men and of carving out careers in which they stand some chance of success and prestige.

8 "Ends"—the spectators' stands behind the goals—may look quite unremarkable to outsiders. But to the dedicated adolescent males we are describing, these terraces are sacred territories to which only they, as members of larger fan groups, are admitted access. It is on these slabs of concrete, which are now surrounded throughout much of Britain by fences, moats, and policemen, that collections of hooligans have created their microsocieties.

9 Fans who eventually become what we shall call Rowdies enter the soccer-terrace culture as Novices, or what older fans call "little kids," when they are as young as nine or 10. Attracted by the noisy spectacle, excitement, and possible danger, they congregate on the edges of the main body of fans. They are there to learn what being a Rowdy is all about, and they spend most of their time watching the activities of their elders instead of the game. Their models are easily identified by a style of dress, synchronized chanting and hand clapping, and from time to time, various forms of ritualized aggression. These older lads are known collectively in the outside world as hooligans. But since the word hooligan is used somewhat differently by insiders, we have preferred to call them Rowdies, a term that they themselves use.

10 Becoming a Rowdy is the first upward step in the terrace structure, because until a boy has gained acceptance in this group, there are no status positions of any kind available. Fortunately for the aspiring Novice, there are no initiation rites and no painful tests to pass. He has simply to demonstrate knowledge of the appropriate songs and chants, to wear appropriate gear, to support the right team, and to be "one of the lads." The gear, for those who have never watched a British football game, changes with the fashions. But while we were studying the society of the terraces, gear included such items as denim jackets and blue jeans, baggy white trousers, heavy boots, thin shirts even in the depths of winter, and colorful silk scarves tied around the neck or to the wrists. As we will see later, various subtleties of dress, which are well understood by the Rowdies themselves, make it clear that we are dealing with a small society and not just a bunch of deranged individuals.

---

[7] **terraces:** stands

11 It is sometimes possible to join the Rowdies without passing through the Novice stage. For example, a lad of 13 or 14 who is already known to the older boys may, after a short apprenticeship, stand on the terrace with his mates. After that, the potential for an ambitious Rowdy is great. Among the roles available to him (all of which afford a special kind of personal value) are those of Chant Leader, Aggro Leader, Organizer, and Hooligan. There is even the chance of recognition as a Nutter.

12 Aggro Leaders are Rowdies who have established a reputation for being constantly involved in battles with the fans of the opposing team. A 17-year-old boy named Phil had this to say about his role as an Aggro Leader:

13 "Lots of the smaller kids really look up to you. . . . They look up to you and think you're a good fighter."

14 "And are you a good fighter?"

15 "Yes—well . . . used to be quite a bit. If people start some trouble or something like that, then I'll be in there. If you live up on the Leys [a fairly rough housing development] then you have to fight or else people piss you about and think you're a bit soft or something. . . . So I'm in there making them run—that's what you're trying to do—and make them feel small. So we're round outside after the game and down the road after them. But I don't go around thumping people all the time. You don't have to. People know who you are."

16 Phil was known as a "hard man" on the terraces and he later ended up in jail for cashing fraudulent checks. A hard Aggro Leader, however, is not to be confused with a good fighter. Aggro (the word comes from "aggravation," not "aggression," but the coincidence is convenient) has more to do with ritual displays of aggression than with acts of physical violence. There is a lot of show and verbal abuse, accompanied by gestures of hostility and defiance. Occasions on which rival fans actually come to blows are, despite widespread opinion to the contrary, rare. The Aggro Leader might never have to fight anybody in his whole career. To be accepted in his role, though, he must convince his peers that if a fight arose, he would be man enough to win it. He must be seen to stand his ground when rivals threaten to invade his territory. And when visiting fans are forced to retreat to their buses at the end of a match, he must be in the vanguard. In general, an Aggro Leader has to show a distinct sense of fearlessness. He has to be a kind of "hard case." But his lack of fear must not be too great; for total, unreasonable fearlessness is the prerogative of the Nutter.

17 Fans are in no doubt as to where bravery ends and sheer lunacy begins, and Nutters are individuals whose actions are seen by other fans to fall outside the boundaries of acceptable conduct. They "go crazy" and do "nutty" things like attempting to beat some poor rival fan to a pulp. If given free rein, they can inflict serious injury on themselves and others. Because the social order to which virtually all Rowdies subscribe requires the restraint of such injuries, Nutters are held back, for in-

stance, in their almost suicidal attempts to take on, single-handed, large groups of rivals. The Nutters confirm the existence of a certain social order among the fans. If all were anarchy and chaos on the terraces, Nutters would be unremarkable and unidentified. But in fact they are deviants within the terrace culture, and like their counterparts in other social worlds, they confirm the majority's notions of what is proper and prescribed.

18 To call a fan a Nutter is not to use a term of abuse. It is simply to make a comment on his style of doing things. Blackpool fans even have a chant that runs: "We are the Nutters—we come from the sea." The implication is that rivals had better watch out because Rowdies from Blackpool might not be restricted by normal conventions. The chant "There's gonna be a Nasty Accident" expresses a similar sentiment. Fortunately, the implied devastation is never fully realized.

19 A Chant Leader has a straightforward role. His task is to initiate songs, chants, and patterns of hand clapping at appropriate times. If the rival club is chanting its team's name—for example, "Chelsea! Chelsea!" —the Chant Leader may try to sabotage that chant by interposing some four-letter word between each "Chelsea." A simple ploy, but upsetting to Chelsea. The leader must be familiar with the entire repertoire.

20 The task has its hazards. A Chant Leader can get the timing wrong. And to sing out the starting line of a chant and find that nobody follows means a loss of dignity and prestige. One needs confidence as well as competence and a degree of social skill that takes some time to acquire. (Being tall and having a loud voice are also helpful.)

21 The successful Chant Leader becomes a kind of conductor of terrace rituals—a focus for collective and unifying activity. As such, he figures strongly as a central character in the informal football hierarchy. He is also much in evidence on the buses that are hired to transport fans to away matches. On these, the repertoire of ritual insults and chants aimed at instilling fear in the opposition is refined and rehearsed. Good Chant Leaders are expected to come up with new variations of old themes and to turn items of topical interest into witty songs.

22 Of course the wit is pretty rough. Like the insults used in the fans' everyday lives, the chants rely heavily on scatology and the implication that the enemy is unmanly, effeminate, or actually female. Goalkeepers have to suffer the accusation that they are homosexuals. Forwards all seem to have cerebral palsy. Masturbation is an almost universal theme: "Swindon Boys, Wank, Wank, Wank"° is typical of chants among the fans of Oxford United. Naturally the Oxford fans characterize their own players as tough guys:

---

22 **wank:** (Brit. slang) masturbate

Oxford boys, we are here,
Shag° your women and drink your
beer.

A recent self-serving chant refers to one's own players as "bionic." And sometimes the insults of the opposition are class conscious rather than sexual. One Rowdy song goes:

In their slums,
In their Nottingham slums,
They look in the dustbin for
something to eat,
They find a dead cat and they think
it's a treat,
In their Nottingham slums.

23 The responsibility of arranging buses for away games falls on the shoulders of Organisers. Not all football terraces have such figures, but those that have them benefit considerably. Organisers arrange the hire of transport, collect the money for it, and enlist others to help in limiting damage and vandalism. The need for such a role is most pressing when the official fan clubs refuse to allow anybody under the age of 18 to join or to use their travel facilities. Thus the Rowdies, most of whom are under 18, have to look after themselves. Organisers may also be called on to arrange petitions or to lead protests against club officials. These protests are almost always ineffectual, but they help to confirm a sense of collective identity on the terraces.

24 The last major role, that of Hooligan, may be the most interesting. The word hooligan comes from an antisocial family named Houlihan that lived in East London during the 19th Century. (For years press dispatches out of the Soviet Union have mentioned Russians arrested for hooliganism, as if it were some sort of catch-all antisocial crime.) But it was not until about 1970 that young people in Britain began being called hooligans by journalists and magistrates. Before that, some football fans might have been labeled ruffians or tearaways.° The increased use of "hooligan" marks a distinct stage in a process of media amplification and goes hand in hand with horror stories of "carnage," "mob rule," and "animal savagery."

25 Terms that begin as labels of abuse or disapproval often become used by the targets of censure to mean something quite different. Thus football Rowdies have incorporated "hooligan" into their own vocabulary and use it to refer to boys who commit acts worthy of special praise within the terrace microculture. Such acts might involve minor damage to property or disruption of certain routine social events. The main characteristic, however, is not the act itself but the manner in which it

---

22 **shag:** (Brit. slang) have sexual intercourse with

24 **tearaways:** (Brit. slang) uncontrollable mischief makers

is carried out. In particular, it has to be funny. Hooligans are actors of wit and style; they are entertainers. Anybody, for example, can steal the billboards or wastepaper baskets outside a newsstand. But not everybody can do an elaborate waltz with them up and down the street before returning them—and without getting caught by the infuriated owner.

26 Hooligans gain honor from such escapades. For a season at Oxford United a 16-year-old named Geoff was famous for his "wicked acts." One day a rival fan threw a lump of dog feces at him. In retaliation Geoff climbed up onto a terrace overlooking the offender and his friends, who were drinking tea, and urinated on them—onto their "heads and into their tea and all over," according to one of Geoff's comrades, "and it's raining a bit as well so they don't notice. Me and some others, we run down and were watching this and we're killing ourselves. But Geoff, he don't shout out or anything—he just waits for a bit till they finish their tea and then he shouts out 'Enjoy your tea then,' and as they look up he pisses a bit more and they go barmy."°

27 An unedifying scene, perhaps. And yet around these roles is woven a network of well-defined social relationships. Beyond these roles, moreover, are the unwritten but cogent rules of being a football Rowdy.

28 These rules fall into two categories: interpretive and prescriptive. First, certain regular events must be given specific kinds of meaning. What constitutes a challenge to fight? What are "bundles," "riots," and acts of "provocation" on the part of the police, and when is a piece of territory "violated" by the "illegitimate" entry of rival Rowdies? These matters have to be quickly resolved by reference to a set of guidelines; for only when fans can decide the question "What is happening?" can the second, prescriptive question "What should be done?" be answered. Having used rules to define the situation, Rowdies call on rules for action to maintain the peculiar order of their collective behavior.

29 These prescriptive rules play a vital role because their major function is to keep social action within distinct boundaries. They stop fans from going too far in fights and attacks on rivals. In listening to the accounts of fans and through closely observing their actions, we have found that those who flout the rules or "go over the top" are subject to severe moral sanctions and social control. Their activities will be declared "out of order" or they will be viewed as Nutters and subsequently will be kept well in check by their peers. Throughout the accounts we have collected are references to actions that are "not right," "going too far," "not on," "out of order," "not playing the game," and "breaking the code." Even references to unwritten rules crop up in the Rowdies' everyday talk.

---

[26] **barmy:** (Brit. slang) crazy

30 The mapping of these sets of rules is a task that is amenable to the interactive principles of a social psychology that regards behavior as largely the result of self-monitoring and self-direction instead of as the outcome of environmental pressures. With this approach it is possible to develop a reasonably systematic discovery procedure that has been shown to be applicable to a variety of other settings. The first stage of such a procedure can begin before any accounts have been obtained from the participants, as long as the activities in question are easily visible. The use of film and video recordings can be of considerable value in these cases.

31 If you look at a disruption or a fight on the terraces, it is easy to imagine that something very bloody and dangerous is happening. One sees fists and boots flying and a surging mass of fans pouring over fences and barriers. It looks like mayhem and is described as such whenever television crews capture the incidents. But if you look very closely at films of these events, some remarkable things appear. Time after time the actual motor patterns of fighting seem to be tailor-made to cause only minimal injury. Straight punches or kicks to sensitive areas of the body are much rarer than are bent-arm blows to nonsensitive areas and kicks that connect with nothing at all. We have films of Rowdies who are lying on the ground, apparently being kicked senseless by five or six rivals—and at the end of such attacks the victim has picked himself up, dusted himself off, and walked away with only a few bruises.

32 The fact that there are rules against murderous assaults can be established in other ways than by examining films. More important, we have interviewed a great many Rowdies at length. Once one penetrates their vocabulary and understands how much exaggeration it contains, the rules against excessive violence become clear. In fact, we have not accepted anything as a real rule unless we found complete consensus on the matter among Rowdies. The following exchange is typical:

33 Questioner: What do you do when you put the boot in?

34 Fan A: You kicks 'em in the head, don't you? . . . Strong boots with metal toecaps on and that.

35 Questioner: And what happens then?

36 (Quizzical look from Fan A)

37 Questioner: Well, what happens to the guy you've kicked?

38 Fan A: He's dead.

39 Fan B: Nah—he's all right—usually anyway.

40 Here is another revealing interview:

41 Questioner: Do you think that when people are going into fights or "getting mad," they aren't deliberately trying to hurt other people very much?

42 Mike: Oh, Yes.

43 Questioner: Do you mean they are actually setting out to hurt them?

44 Mike: Yes—well, you're just swinging around and when it's packed out and everybody's pushing to get at the same people—you can't really take any swings at anybody—it's, well, just feeble efforts really.

45 When pressed, Rowdies usually become realistic. Exaggeration, of course, is one of the rules of the game. And underlying these exaggerations are other rules. Even when a thousand fans are chanting, "You're gonna get your fucking head kicked in," physical violence may not follow—although that chant does convey a grave message of rising hostility. (Usually the chant follows a goal by the rival team—a warning that if the rival team wins the game, a fight will be justified.)

46 Aside from the rules implicit in fights between rivals and in the roles of Aggro Leader, Hooligan, Nutter, and so on, we found other rules governing: the level of challenge implicit in various insults, the goals of fighting, the termination of fights, and much more. To call someone a "cunt," for example, is much more provocative than to call him a "wanker." The goals of a fight include much more than the infliction of physical pain; if the enemy flees, the fight is won, and that is a sign to end it. In a one-on-one confrontation, certain displays of submission are usually enough to end hostilities. And this orderliness pervades a good deal of the lives of Rowdies on football day. For instance, virtually everyone we interviewed would follow an invariable sequence each Saturday when a game was scheduled: dressing in his special aggro gear (after getting up late); hanging around and "doing nothing" until about 1:30 in the afternoon; arriving at the soccer grounds between 1:30 and 2:00; achieving the critical Rowdy density on the terraces between 2:15 and 2:30; "seeing off" the visiting Rowdies after the game, between about 4:40 and 5:30; and then proceeding on to discos, pubs, and more hanging around.

47 One other way in which we established the existence of rules, limits, and other shared interpretations of behavior was by experiment. One of these experiments involved the meanings of the clothes Rowdies wear. We commissioned a series of 21 watercolor paintings depicting a single fan dressed in various combinations of the typical aggro gear we had found in a careful study of our films. Then we showed these paintings to a group of Rowdies and asked them what kinds of people the paintings depicted and how they were likely to behave. Their interpretations were not entirely consistent, but among experienced Rowdies (as distinguished from Novices) certain statistical patterns emerged from a computerized analysis.

48 Denim jackets made the models look "harder" than those without denim jackets. Club scarves, naturally, were a sign of "loyalty." (These terms are the Rowdies', not ours.) Scarves on the wrist rather than around the neck indicated exceptional loyalty *and* hardness. Fans wearing such combinations as scarf, flag, T-shirt, and white baggy pants

struck many boys as "right Hooligans," but they did not seem as hard as most of the other models. Jeans, boots, and denim jacket *without* a scarf pointed to hardness without loyalty, while models without scarves and who were otherwise dressed rather conventionally in casual jacket, trousers, and shoes seemed both hard and loyal. Why the latter interpretation? Because in the context of Rowdies, these more conventionally dressed fans looked like recent graduates of the Rowdy subculture, a type of fan called Town Boys, whose toughness and loyalty have already been proven.

49 Another experiment points up certain tacit rules not only of interpretation but of action. We took a true and typical story of a minor confrontation between two rival Rowdies and then changed some of its elements. After that we told the story and its variants to a series of Rowdies to see if they found anything wrong with it. Most of them agreed with what was right, what was wrong, and why.

50 The true story was simple. An Oxford Rowdy taunts a Sheffield Wednesday Rowdy. A fight ensues. Then a Town Boy intervenes and breaks it up. Everyone we told this story to found it commonplace and hardly worth talking about. But when we gave the story a new denouement—in which the Sheffield Wednesday fan calls over some of his mates, who then give the Oxford Rowdy a kicking—the boys objected. One commented: "You don't get your mates into it like that—well, only when there's too many of them or something and you're going to get kicked about or something like that. He could have just stood up or something and maybe they'd have had a go at each other. But nothing would have come of it 'cos the police are always around there [near the half-time tea stall where the incident was said to have taken place] and they'd soon move in. He's from Sheffield—I don't know—but he shouldn't get his mates in just for that—Oxford would get mad for that." This is a fairly subtle series of interpretations, and it was shared by others.

51 We changed the story again so that it ended with the Sheffield Wednesday fan simply walking away from his confrontation with the taunting Oxford Rowdy. A fan commented: "You can't just walk off like that. He ought to have done something. . . . If I was in there I'd just —well I'd just turn round and maybe have a bit of a go or something. . . . You shouldn't walk off like that so that he can think he's big like."

52 Our Rowdies generally agreed in their interpretations of these stories. If life on the terraces was truly disordered—anarchic, anomic,°—the Rowdies would see nothing surprising however the story ended.

---

52 **anomic:** lacking social norms and values; savage, unpredictable

53 We must say again that even if social order, rather than anarchy, is the rule of the football terraces, there may still be something wrong with the whole phenomenon. A minisociety that looks coherent from the inside—and in fact is coherent—hardly guarantees that all is well. From time to time people are hurt and property is damaged.

54 But given the fact that over half a million people are at football games every Saturday, it would be remarkable if this were not so. Rules on the terraces, like rules in any other area of society, do get broken. Moreover, since we can gain satisfaction and prestige at some relatively peaceful combination of work and play, there is no need for us to seek some alternative like the life of a football Rowdy, with its exaggerations, its machismo, and its frequent lack of a future. And yet to look at the terrace life from the inside is to see it much more clearly than outsiders commonly see it, and by looking at it from the inside we can understand its larger social functions and its value to those who participate in that life. It seems obvious to us, for one thing, that the Rowdies gain glory and excitement on the terraces that they cannot gain in the drab weekday world of home, school, work, and welfare. The normal society is not truly theirs, nor does it supply them with the satisfactions that orderly society is famous for. And so they have invented their own order. It may strike some people as barbaric, but it serves the Rowdies' purposes.

55 The outraged public often contrasts the orderly world of well-behaved spectators with the supposedly anarchic world of the Rowdies. They would do better to contrast the dull world of working-class youths headed for an even duller adulthood with the much more interesting world of the terraces. They would do well, too, to compare that terrace world with their own. Both societies include hierarchies, rules, standards, roles, careers, communities, and chances of achieving prestige. Both societies are similar in that they differ from collections of people in which all these rituals and institutions are absent and in which rules are arbitrary or nonexistent—and in which people are truly dehumanized, as they are by certain modern forms of war and propaganda. Although Rowdies and other subcultures of the young do not represent a problem of that order, they do indicate that some adolescents are abandoning the general social order in favor of another. And that should give us pause.

STUDY QUESTIONS

1. What is the function of Marsh and Harré's first two paragraphs?
2. Where is the thesis, or main idea, of this essay stated? In what way have the authors decided to limit the scope of that thesis?

3. What would be your first reaction to a film showing Rowdies in action against one another? If, having read through this essay, you would now have a different reaction, which aspects of the authors' presentation have changed your attitude?
4. How do these two British authors, writing for an American magazine *(Human Nature)*, show that they are keeping their audience in mind? Be ready to cite specifics.
5. What part does *definition* play in the authors' attempt to give us a picture of Rowdies "from the inside"?
6. On what kinds of evidence have Marsh and Harré relied in drawing their conclusions? What precautions have they taken against "finding" only what they expected to find?
7. This essay contains some language that is rough by any standard. Should the authors have excluded it? Should *we* have excluded it? Think of arguments on both sides of the issue.
8. Why do the authors, having first mentioned "Nutters" in paragraph 11, wait until paragraph 17 to define the term?
9. The authors write as social scientists, not as casual personal observers. How does their identity as scientific investigators affect their tone? Pick out expressions that strike you as demonstrating a sociological point of view.
10. In the "story experiments" explained in paragraphs 49–52, why did Marsh and Harré feel obliged to change the original story?
11. In the essay as a whole, what is the function of paragraph 53?
12. Despite its striving for impersonal objectivity, this essay does convey feelings toward Rowdies. What are those feelings, and where do you find indications of them?
13. What is the meaning of the authors' concluding sentence? Are they writing as sociologists there?

SHOWING CAUSES AND EFFECTS

Marie Winn

Marie Winn is a freelance social commentator and the author of numerous books for parents and children. The present selection is excerpted from *The Plug-In Drug: TV and the American Family* (1977).

THE PLUG-IN DRUG*

1 A quarter of a century after the introduction of television into American society, a period that has seen the medium become so deeply ingrained in American life that in at least one state the television set has attained the rank of a legal necessity, safe from repossession in case of debt along with clothes, cooking utensils, and the like, television viewing has become an inevitable and ordinary part of daily life. Only in the early years of television did writers and commentators have sufficient perspective to separate the activity of watching television from the actual content it offers the viewer. In those early days writers frequently discussed the effects of television on family life. However, a curious myopia afflicted those early observers: almost without exception they regarded television as a favorable, beneficial, indeed, wondrous influence upon the family.

2 "Television is going to be a real asset in every home where there are children," predicts a writer in 1949.

3 "Television will take over your way of living and change your children's habits, but this change can be a wonderful improvement," claims another commentator.

4 "No survey's needed, of course, to establish that television has

*Title chosen by editor

brought the family together in one room," writes *The New York Times* television critic in 1949.

5 Each of the early articles about television is invariably accompanied by a photograph or illustration showing a family cozily sitting together before the television set, Sis on Mom's lap, Buddy perched on the arm of Dad's chair, Dad with his arm around Mom's shoulder. Who could have guessed that twenty or so years later Mom would be watching a drama in the kitchen, the kids would be looking at cartoons in their room, while Dad would be taking in the ball game in the living room?

6 Of course television sets were enormously expensive in those early days. The idea that by 1975 more than 60 percent of American families would own two or more sets was preposterous. The splintering of the multiple-set family was something the early writers could not foresee. Nor did anyone imagine the number of hours children would eventually devote to television, the common use of television by parents as a child pacifier, the changes television would effect upon child-rearing methods, the increasing domination of family schedules by children's viewing requirements—in short, the *power* of the new medium to dominate family life.

7 After the first years, as children's consumption of the new medium increased, together with parental concern about the possible effects of so much television viewing, a steady refrain helped to soothe and reassure anxious parents. "Television always enters a pattern of influences that already exist: the home, the peer group, the school, the church and culture generally," write the authors of an early and influential study of television's effects on children. In other words, if the child's home life is all right, parents need not worry about the effects of all that television watching.

8 But television does not merely influence the child; it deeply influences that "pattern of influences" that is meant to ameliorate its effects. Home and family life have changed in important ways since the advent of television. The peer group has become television-oriented, and much of the time children spend together is occupied by television viewing. Culture generally has been transformed by television. Therefore it is improper to assign to television the subsidiary role its many apologists (too often members of the television industry) insist it plays. Television is not merely one of a number of important influences upon today's child. Through the changes it has made in family life, television emerges as *the* important influence in children's lives today.

The Quality of Family Life

9 Television's contribution to family life has been an equivocal one. For while it has, indeed, kept the members of the family from dispersing, it has not served to bring them *together.* By its domination of the time

families spend together, it destroys the special quality that distinguishes one family from another, a quality that depends to a great extent on what a family *does,* what special rituals, games, recurrent jokes, familiar songs, and shared activities it accumulates.

10 "Like the sorcerer of old," writes Urie Bronfenbrenner,° "the television set casts its magic spell, freezing speech and action, turning the living into silent statues so long as the enchantment lasts. The primary danger of the television screen lies not so much in the behavior it produces—although there is danger there—as in the behavior it prevents: the talks, the games, the family festivities and arguments through which much of the child's learning takes place and through which his character is formed. Turning on the television set can turn off the process that transforms children into people."

11 Yet parents have accepted a television-dominated family life so completely that they cannot see how the medium is involved in whatever problems they might be having. A first-grade teacher reports:

12 "I have one child in the group who's an only child. I wanted to find out more about her family life because this little girl was quite isolated from the group, didn't make friends, so I talked to her mother. Well, they don't have time to do anything in the evening, the mother said. The parents come home after picking up the child at the baby-sitter's. Then the mother fixes dinner while the child watches TV. Then they have dinner and the child goes to bed. I said to this mother, 'Well, couldn't she help you fix dinner? That would be a nice time for the two of you to talk,' and the mother said, 'Oh, but I'd hate to have her miss "Zoom." It's such a good program!' "

13 Even when families make efforts to control television, too often its very presence counterbalances the positive features of family life. A writer and mother of two boys aged 3 and 7 described her family's television schedule in an article in *The New York Times:*

> We were in the midst of a full-scale War. Every day was a new battle and every program was a major skirmish. We agreed it was a bad scene all around and were ready to enter diplomatic negotiations. . . . In principle we have agreed on 2½ hours of TV a day, "Sesame Street," "Electric Company" (with dinner gobbled up in between) and two half-hour shows between 7 and 8:30 which enables the grown-ups to eat in peace and prevents the two boys from destroying one another. Their pre-bed-time choice is dreadful, because, as Josh recently admitted, "There's nothing much on I really like." So . . . it's "What's My Line" or "To Tell the Truth." . . . Clearly there is a need for first-rate children's shows at this time. . . .

14 Consider the "family life" described here: Presumably the father comes home from work during the "Sesame Street"—"Electric Company" stint. The children are either watching television, gobbling their

[10] **Urie Bronfenbrenner:** professor of psychology and human development at Cornell University

dinner, or both. While the parents eat their dinner in peaceful privacy, the children watch another hour of television. Then there is only a half-hour left before bedtime, just enough time for baths, getting pajamas on, brushing teeth, and so on. The children's evening is regimented with an almost military precision. They watch their favorite programs, and when there is "nothing much on I really like," they watch whatever else is on—because *watching* is the important thing. Their mother does not see anything amiss with watching programs just for the sake of watching; she only wishes there were some first-rate children's shows on at those times.

15 Without conjuring up memories of the Victorian era with family games and long, leisurely meals, and large families, the question arises: isn't there a better family life available than this dismal, mechanized arrangement of children watching television for however long is allowed them, evening after evening?

16 Of course, families today still do *special* things together at times: go camping in the summer, go to the zoo on a nice Sunday, take various trips and expeditions. But their *ordinary* daily life together is diminished—that sitting around at the dinner table, that spontaneous taking up of an activity, those little games invented by children on the spur of the moment when there is nothing else to do, the scribbling, the chatting, and even the quarreling, all the things that form the fabric of a family, that define a childhood. Instead, the children have their regular schedule of television programs and bedtime, and the parents have their peaceful dinner together.

17 The author of the article in the *Times* notes that "keeping a family sane means mediating between the needs of both children and adults." But surely the needs of adults are being better met than the needs of the children, who are effectively shunted away and rendered untroublesome, while their parents enjoy a life as undemanding as that of any childless couple. In reality, it is those very demands that young children make upon a family that lead to growth, and it is the way parents accede to those demands that builds the relationships upon which the future of the family depends. If the family does not accumulate its backlog of shared experiences, shared *everyday* experiences that occur and recur and change and develop, then it is not likely to survive as anything other than a caretaking institution.

Family Rituals

18 Ritual is defined by sociologists as "that part of family life that the family likes about itself, is proud of and wants formally to continue." Another text notes that "the development of a ritual by a family is an index of the common interest of its members in the family as a group."

19 What has happened to family rituals, those regular, dependable,

recurrent happenings that gave members of a family a feeling of *belonging* to a home rather than living in it merely for the sake of convenience, those experiences that act as the adhesive of family unity far more than any material advantages?

20 Mealtime rituals, going-to-bed rituals, illness rituals, holiday rituals, how many of these have survived the inroads of the television set?

21 A young woman who grew up near Chicago reminisces about her childhood and gives an idea of the effects of television upon family rituals:

22 "As a child I had millions of relatives around—my parents both come from relatively large families. My father had nine brothers and sisters. And so every holiday there was this great swoop-down of aunts, uncles, and millions of cousins. I just remember how wonderful it used to be. These thousands of cousins would come and everyone would play and ultimately, after dinner, all the women would be in the front of the house, drinking coffee and talking, all the men would be in the back of the house, drinking and smoking, and all the kids would be all over the place, playing hide and seek. Christmas time was particularly nice because everyone always brought all their toys and games. Our house had a couple of rooms with go-through closets, so there were always kids running in a great circle route. I remember it was just wonderful.

23 "And then all of a sudden one year I remember becoming suddenly aware of how different everything had become. The kids were no longer playing Monopoly or Clue or the other games we used to play together. It was because we had a television set which had been turned on for a football game. All of that socializing that had gone on previously had ended. Now everyone was sitting in front of the television set, on a holiday, at a family party! I remember being stunned by how awful that was. Somehow the television had become more attractive."

24 As families have come to spend more and more of their time together engaged in the single activity of television watching, those rituals and pastimes that once gave family life its special quality have become more and more uncommon. Not since prehistoric times when cave families hunted, gathered, ate, and slept, with little time remaining to accumulate a culture of any significance, have families been reduced to such a sameness.

Real People

25 It is not only the activities that a family might engage in together that are diminished by the powerful presence of television in the home. The relationships of the family members to each other are also affected, in both obvious and subtle ways. The hours that the young child spends in a one-way relationship with television people, an involvement that allows for no communication or interaction, surely affect his relationships with real-life people.

26 Studies show the importance of eye-to-eye contact, for instance, in real-life relationships, and indicate that the nature of a person's eye-contact patterns, whether he looks another squarely in the eye or looks to the side or shifts his gaze from side to side, may play a significant role in his success or failure in human relationships. But no eye contact is possible in the child-television relationship, although in certain children's programs people purport to speak directly to the child and the camera fosters this illusion by focusing directly upon the person being filmed. (Mr. Rogers is an example, telling the child "I like you, you're special," etc.) How might such a distortion of real-life relationships affect a child's development of trust, of openness, of an ability to relate well to other *real* people?

27 Bruno Bettelheim° writes:

> Children who have been taught, or conditioned, to listen passively most of the day to the warm verbal communications coming from the TV screen, to the deep emotional appeal of the so-called TV personality, are often unable to respond to real persons because they arouse so much less feeling than the skilled actor. Worse, they lose the ability to learn from reality because life experiences are much more complicated than the ones they see on the screen. . . .

28 A teacher makes a similar observation about her personal viewing experiences:

29 "I have trouble mobilizing myself and dealing with real people after watching a few hours of television. It's just hard to make that transition from watching television to a real relationship. I suppose it's because there was no effort necessary while I was watching, and dealing with real people always requires a bit of effort. Imagine, then, how much harder it might be to do the same thing for a small child, particularly one who watches a lot of television every day."

30 But more obviously damaging to family relationships is the elimination of opportunities to talk, and perhaps more important, to argue, to air grievances, between parents and children and brothers and sisters. Families frequently use television to avoid confronting their problems, problems that will not go away if they are ignored but will only fester and become less easily resolvable as time goes on.

31 A mother reports:

32 "I find myself, with three children, wanting to turn on the TV set when they're fighting. I really have to struggle not to do it because I feel that's telling them this is the solution to the quarrel—but it's so tempting that I often do it."

33 A family therapist discusses the use of television as an avoidance mechanism:

---

27 **Bruno Bettelheim:** German-American psychoanalyst; the quotation is from his book *The Informed Heart* (1960).

34 "In a family I know the father comes home from work and turns on the television set. The children come and watch with him and the wife serves them their meal in front of the set. He then goes and takes a shower, or works on the car or something. She then goes and has her own dinner in front of the television set. It's a symptom of a deeper-rooted problem, sure. But it would help them all to get rid of the set. It would be far easier to work on what the symptom really means without the television. The television simply encourages a double avoidance of each other. They'd find out more quickly what was going on if they weren't able to hide behind the TV. Things wouldn't necessarily be better, of course, but they wouldn't be anesthetized."

35 The decreased opportunities for simple conversation between parents and children in the television-centered home may help explain an observation made by an emergency room nurse at a Boston hospital. She reports that parents just seem to sit there these days when they come in with a sick or seriously injured child, although talking to the child would distract and comfort him. "They don't seem to know *how* to talk to their own children at any length," the nurse observes. Similarly, a television critic writes in *The New York Times:* "I had just a day ago taken my son to the emergency ward of a hospital for stitches above his left eye, and the occasion seemed no more real to me than Maalot or 54th Street, south-central Los Angeles. There was distance and numbness and an inability to turn off the total institution. I didn't behave at all; I just watched. . . ."

36 A number of research studies substantiate the assumption that television interferes with family activities and the formation of family relationships. One survey shows that 78 percent of the respondents indicated no conversation taking place during viewing except at specified times such as commercials. The study notes: "The television atmosphere in most households is one of quiet absorption on the part of family members who are present. The nature of the family social life during a program could be described as 'parallel' rather than interactive, and the set does seem to dominate family life when it is on." Thirty-six percent of the respondents in another study indicated that television viewing was the only family activity participated in during the week.

37 In a summary of research findings on television's effect on family interactions, James Gabardino° states: "The early findings suggest that television had a disruptive effect upon interaction and thus presumably human development. . . . It is not unreasonable to ask: 'Is the fact that the average American family during the 1950's came to include two parents, two children and a television set somehow related to the psychosocial characteristics of the young adults of the 1970's?' "

---

[37] **James Gabardino:** author of an essay entitled "A Note on the Effects of Television Viewing" (1975)

Undermining the Family

38 In its effect on family relationships, in its facilitation of parental withdrawal from an active role in the socialization of their children, and in its replacement of family rituals and special events, television has played an important role in the disintegration of the American family. But of course it has not been the only contributing factor, perhaps not even the most important one. The steadily rising divorce rate, the increase in the number of working mothers, the decline of the extended family, the breakdown of neighborhoods and communities, the growing isolation of the nuclear family—all have seriously affected the family.

39 As Urie Bronfenbrenner suggests, the sources of family breakdown do not come from the family itself, but from the circumstances in which the family finds itself and the way of life imposed upon it by those circumstances. "When those circumstances and the way of life they generate undermine relationships of trust and emotional security between family members, when they make it difficult for parents to care for, educate and enjoy their children, when there is no support or recognition from the outside world for one's role as a parent and when time spent with one's family means frustration of career, personal fulfillment and peace of mind, then the development of the child is adversely affected," he writes.

40 But while the roots of alienation go deep into the fabric of American social history, television's presence in the home fertilizes them, encourages their wild and unchecked growth. Perhaps it is true that America's commitment to the television experience masks a spiritual vacuum, an empty and barren way of life, a desert of materialism. But it is television's dominant role in the family that anesthetizes the family into accepting its unhappy state and prevents it from struggling to better its condition, to improve its relationships, and to regain some of the richness it once possessed.

41 Others have noted the role of mass media in perpetuating an unsatisfactory *status quo.* Leisure-time activity, writes Irving Howe,° "must provide relief from work monotony without making the return to work too unbearable; it must provide amusement without insight and pleasure without disturbance—as distinct from art which gives pleasure through disturbance. Mass culture is thus oriented towards a central aspect of industrial society: the depersonalization of the individual." Similarly, Jacques Ellul° rejects the idea that television is a legitimate means of educating the citizen: "Education . . . takes place only incidentally. The clouding of his consciousness is paramount. . . ."

---

41 **Irving Howe:** American literary and social critic; the quotation is from a 1948 essay, "Notes on Mass Culture."

Jacques Ellul: French social critic; the quotation comes from his book *The Technological Society* (1964).

42 And so the American family muddles on, dimly aware that something is amiss but distracted from an understanding of its plight by an endless stream of television images. As family ties grow weaker and vaguer, as children's lives become more separate from their parents', as parents' educational role in their children's lives is taken over by television and schools, family life becomes increasingly more unsatisfying for both parents and children. All that seems to be left is Love, an abstraction that family members *know* is necessary but find great difficulty giving each other because the traditional opportunities for expressing love within the family have been reduced or destroyed.

43 For contemporary parents, love toward each other has increasingly come to mean successful sexual relations, as witnessed by the proliferation of sex manuals and sex therapists. The opportunities for manifesting other forms of love through mutual support, understanding, nurturing, even, to use an unpopular word, *serving* each other, are less and less available as mothers and fathers seek their independent destinies outside the family.

44 As for love of children, this love is increasingly expressed through supplying material comforts, amusements, and educational opportunities. Parents show their love for their children by sending them to good schools and camps, by providing them with good food and good doctors, by buying them toys, books, games, and a television set of their very own. Parents will even go further and express their love by attending PTA meetings to improve their children's schools, or by joining groups that are acting to improve the quality of their children's television programs.

45 But this is love at a remove, and is rarely understood by children. The more direct forms of parental love require time and patience, steady, dependable, ungrudgingly given time actually spent *with* a child, reading to him, comforting him, playing, joking, and working with him. But even if a parent were eager and willing to demonstrate that sort of direct love to his children today, the opportunities are diminished. What with school and Little League and piano lessons and, of course, the inevitable television programs, a day seems to offer just enough time for a good-night kiss.

STUDY QUESTIONS

1. Although we have added a title to this selection, the title is the one that Winn chose for her whole book, *The Plug-In Drug.* In what senses is television, as characterized by Winn, a drug? What does the title imply about Winn's solution to the problems caused by television watching?

2. In the selection as a whole, what is the function of the first seven paragraphs?
3. Why doesn't Winn advocate higher standards of TV programming?
4. What kinds of evidence does Winn put forward in support of her thesis, or main idea? Do you find some kinds of evidence weightier than others? (Note: nineteen footnotes have been dropped from Winn's text; lack of documentation is therefore not a fair criticism.) Be prepared to cite specifics.
5. Through much of this selection, Winn leaves the impression that TV is *the* crucial factor in warping Americans' personalities and destroying their families. (See, for example, the end of paragraph 8.) In paragraph 38, however, we begin to get a more complex and moderate view. What *is* Winn's considered opinion about the influence of TV? Would her credibility have been improved if she had revealed that view much earlier?
6. In contemporary American society as Winn perceives it, why is *serving* "an unpopular word" (paragraph 43)? Do you agree that it *is* unpopular?

Vladimir Bukovsky

Vladimir Bukovsky, Russian author and political dissenter, spent many years in Soviet prisons, forced-labor camps, and psychiatric asylums before being exiled to the West for life in 1976. "Life Behind Bars" is drawn from *To Build a Castle: My Life as a Dissenter,* translated by Michael Scammell (1977).

LIFE BEHIND BARS*

1 In Siberia I once heard of a method for hunting bears. Somewhere near the bear's usual track you place some bait in a pine tree, usually a piece of carrion. Then you suspend a good, solid, heavy block of wood from the nearest suitable stout branch, blocking the bear's path to the bait but swinging freely at the end of its rope. Sniffing the bait, bruin shins up the trunk and comes face to face with the block of wood. Being what he is, he doesn't even attempt to go around the block, but simply

*Title chosen by editor

shoves it aside and crawls on. The block of wood swings away and comes back, thumping the bear in the ribs. Bruin loses his temper and gives the block a harder shove, and naturally the block comes back harder as well, and so on, harder and harder. Eventually the block of wood knocks him unconscious and out of the tree. This is an approximate description of my relations with the powers that be: the longer the stretch they gave me, the more I tried to do when I was let out; and the more I did, the longer the next stretch they gave me. However, times were changing and my possibilities were growing, and it was difficult to say which of us was the bear and which the wooden block, and how it would all end. I, at any rate, had no thought of retreating.

2 It followed from this that I had planned out not only the next five months but my whole life: ten months in the camp, five years in internal exile, and then, at best, a year of the fever called freedom, and then ten more years of jail and five more in exile. By that time I would be fifty-seven. All right, time for one more turn of the wheel and back in prison in time to die. This was why I hadn't been looking forward to my release, hadn't been counting the days and months. I reminded myself of that genie in the bottle in the *Arabian Nights,* who spent the first five million years vowing to make a rich man of the person who let him out, and the second five million vowing to murder the person who let him out. Let me say that I understood the genie's feelings.

3 There was, however, another reason why I felt obliged to plan out my prison time in advance and see that I spent every minute studying, and that was prison life itself.

4 Anyone who didn't discipline himself, who didn't concentrate his attention on some steady object of study, was in danger of losing his mind, or at the very least of losing control of himself. When subjected to such total isolation and absence of daylight, given the monotony and the constant cold and constant hunger of prison life, a man tended to fall into a kind of half-conscious trance. For hours and maybe even days on end he would sit there, gazing with unseeing eyes at a photograph of his wife and children, or leafing through the pages of a book, taking in and remembering nothing, or else he would suddenly start an endless, senseless altercation with one of his neighbors over some totally trivial issue, bogging down repeatedly in the same arguments, not bothering to listen to what his opponent was saying, and in fact not answering his objections at all. He would find it absolutely impossible to concentrate on anything definite or follow the thread of an argument.

5 Strange things happened to time. On the one hand, it seemed to pass with preternatural speed, beggaring belief. The entire daily routine, with its ordinary, monotonously repetitive events—reveille, breakfast, exercise, dinner, supper, lights-out, reveille, breakfast—fused into a sort of yellowish-brown blur, leaving behind nothing memorable, nothing for the mind to cling to. And lying down at night, a man would be at

a loss to remember what he had been doing all day, what he had eaten for breakfast and what for dinner. Worse still, the days would become indistinguishable from one another and be completely erased from your memory, so that when you woke one day, as if someone had jogged you, you would realize: Christ, it's bath day again! That meant that seven or sometimes even ten days had flown by. And so you lived with the sensation that you were getting a bath every day. On the other hand, this same time could crawl with agonizing slowness: it would seem as if a whole year must have gone by, but no, it was still the same old month, and no end was in sight.

6 Then again, a man could go into paroxysms of rage if something interrupted his monotonous routine. One day, for example, at the start of a new month, they would suddenly take you out for exercise not after breakfast but after dinner instead. What difference, you might ask, would such a little thing make? But this was enough to drive men into frenzies. Or you had a row with one of the guards, or were called out by the instructor and lost your cool with him—and now you couldn't read and couldn't sleep and couldn't think of anything else. The book swam before your eyes, you couldn't keep your mind on anything, and you would be trembling all over. So what? you might say. Nothing new about any of this. How many of these arguments and quarrels, how many rows with the guards had you had in your time? Too many to count. Still, for days and nights afterward you would continue to relive it all in your mind—what he said, what you said, what you might have said but didn't because you couldn't think quickly enough. And how you might have found a particular way of getting under his skin or stopping him dead in his tracks or finding answers that were more cutting and convincing. Like a scratched phonograph record this dialogue would go around and around in your head, and there was no way of stopping it. Or else you would get a picture postcard from home and sit there staring at it like an idiot, the bright colors so exotic and enticing that you couldn't tear your eyes away.

7 I can't say that prison hunger was particularly agonizing—it wasn't a biting hunger but, rather, a prolonged process of chronic undernourishment. You very quickly stopped feeling it badly and were left with a kind of gnawing pain, like a quietly throbbing toothache. You even lost awareness that it was hunger, and only after several months did you notice it hurt to sit on a wooden bench, and at night, no matter which way you turned, something hard seemed to be pressing into you or against you—you would get up several times in the night and shake the mattress, toss and turn from side to side, and still it hurt. Only then did you realize that your bones were sticking out. But by then you didn't care anymore. Nevertheless, you didn't get out of your bunk too quickly in the mornings, otherwise your head would spin.

8 The most unpleasant thing of all was the sensation of having lost your personality. It was as if your soul, with all its intricacies, convolutions, hidden nooks and crannies, had been pressed by a giant flatiron, so that it was now as smooth and flat as a starched dickey. Jail makes you anonymous. As a result, every man strives to stand out from the crowd, to stress his individuality, to appear better and superior to the rest. There used to be constant fights in the criminals' cells, constant struggles for leadership, culminating even in murder. Among the political prisoners, of course, there was none of that, but after four or five months of sitting in the same cell with the same people, you got to know them so well that you came to detest them, and they you. At any moment of the day you knew what they were going to do next, what they were thinking, what question they were about to ask you. And it usually ended up with nobody saying anything to anybody, because they already knew all there was to know. You wondered at the paucity of man's resources, if after six months we have nothing left to say to each other.

9 It was particularly irritating when one of your cell mates had an unconscious tic—of sniffing his nose, say, or tapping his foot. After a couple of months you couldn't bear it any longer and were ready to kill him. Yet if you were separated and put in different cells, or if you did a spell in the box, and met again after some time apart, you were like bosom pals—you smothered one another with questions, stories, bits of news, reminiscences, and celebrated for a whole week. There are cases, of course, of total psychological incompatibility, when men can't bear to live two days in the same cell with one another yet are destined to spend years. In general it is possible to divide mankind into two categories—those you could share a cell with and those you couldn't. But then *your* opinion is never asked. You are obliged to be extraordinarily tolerant of your cell mates and to suppress your own habits and peculiarities: you have to adapt yourself to everybody and get along with everybody, otherwise life becomes unbearable.

10 Now multiply all these burdens by years and years, square them, add all the years you've served in other camps and investigation prisons, and you will understand why it is essential to fill every spare minute of your time with constant activity—best of all with studying some complex subject that demands enormous concentration. From the unremitting electric light, your eyelids start to itch and grow inflamed. You read the same phrase dozens and dozens of times and still you can't grasp it. With a superhuman effort you master a page, but no sooner have you turned it than you've forgotten it again. Go back. Read it twenty, thirty times. Don't allow yourself a cigarette until you've finished the chapter, don't allow yourself to think of anything else, don't dream, don't get distracted, don't even allow yourself to go to the toilet—nothing in the world is more important than to finish what you have set yourself for that day. And if, by the next day, you've forgotten

it all, go back and read it again. And if you've finished a whole book, you can allow yourself the luxury of a day off—but only one, because after the first day your memory starts to slacken again, your attention wanders, and you slowly start to go under, like a drowning man—down, down, until there's a roaring in your ears and you see spots before your eyes, and it's touch and go whether you will ever come up again.

11 This is particularly noticeable when you are alone in the punishment cell, in the box. There, you get no paper, no pencil, and no books. They don't take you out for exercise or to the bathhouse; you get fed only every other day; the only window is blocked; and the one electric light bulb is set in a niche right at the top of the wall, where it meets the ceiling, so that its feeble light barely illuminates the ceiling. A ledge jutting out from the wall is your table, another your chair—ten minutes is as long as you can sit on it. At night they issue you a bare wooden duckboard° for a bed; blankets or warm clothes are forbidden. In the corner there is usually a latrine bucket, or else simply a hole in the floor that stinks to high heaven all day. In short, it's a concrete box. Smoking is forbidden. The place is indescribably filthy. Dried gobs of bloody saliva adorn the walls from the TB sufferers who have been incarcerated here before you. And right here is where you start to go under, to slip down to the very bottom, into the ooze and the slime. The words they have for it in jail express it exactly—you "go down" to the box, and you "come up" again.

12 You spend your first two or three days down there groping around the entire cell—maybe somebody has managed to smuggle some tobacco in and has left a bit behind, or has tucked away a fag end somewhere. You poke into every little hollow and crack. Day and night still mean something to you. You spend most of the day walking up and down, and at night you try to sleep. But the cold and hunger and boredom wear you down. You can doze off for only ten to fifteen minutes at a time before leaping up again and running in place for three-quarters of an hour to get yourself warm. Then you doze off for fifteen minutes again, huddled either on your duckboard (at night) or on the concrete floor (by day), with one knee drawn up under you and your back to the wall, until it's time to jump up again and start running.

13 Gradually you lose all sense of reality. Your body stiffens, your movements become mechanical, and the more time passes the more you turn into some sort of inanimate object. Three times a day they bring you a drink of hot water, and that water affords you indescribable pleasure, melting your insides, as it were, and bringing you temporarily to life. For about twenty minutes or so, an exquisite ache permeates your entire being. Twice a day, before you use the latrine, they give you

---

[11] **duckboard:** a board laid over mud to form a walkway

a scrap of old newspaper and you read it greedily, devouring every word, several times over. In your mind's eye you run over every book you have ever read, every person you have ever met, every song you have ever heard. You begin doing additions and multiplications in your head. You remember snatches of tunes and conversations. Time comes to a halt. You fall into a stupor, starting up and running about the cell for a while, then lapsing into a daze again, but it doesn't help the time to pass. Gradually the patches on the walls start to weave themselves into faces, as if the entire cell were adorned with the portraits of prisoners who have been here before you—it is a picture gallery of all your predecessors.

14 You can spend hours making them out, questioning them, arguing with them, quarreling, and making up again. But after a while they don't help to pass the time either. You know everything there is to know about them, as if you've been cell mates for half a lifetime. Some of them irritate you, while others are still bearable. There are some that need to be cut short right at the beginning, otherwise you can't get rid of them. They will bore you to tears with miserable, stupid stories about their miserable, stupid lives. They will spin yarns and invent things about themselves if they detect that you're not listening to them. They are disgustingly fidgety and servile. Others stay silent and glower at you —with them you have to keep a sharp eye open: the moment you drop off they'll swipe your rations. There are also friendly, sociable lads, usually the younger ones—with them it's possible to swap a joke. They are easygoing, never downhearted, and will do anything just to keep you company. They are usually in for hooliganism, gang rape, or a gang robbery. The corner place, over the latrine bucket, belongs to a veteran crook who knows all the ropes. Before you know where you are, he is scheming, setting groups at one another, and all of them at you. He whispers in the corners with them, exchanges meaningful glances. Underlining his own importance and authority and addressing no one in particular, he tells tall stories about the old days, reminiscing about transit prisons, labor camps, murdered prisoners. He is clearly out to start a fight, to set it up the way he wants it. He knows who should get what and who not. There is no way of avoiding a serious confrontation with him, and the sooner you get it over with the better, before he forms his little gang and consolidates his authority. But then all this too recedes, disappears, and leaves you alone with eternity, alone in the abyss.

15 It is hard to understand where you yourself end and infinity begins. Your body is no longer you, your thoughts are no longer yours, they come and go of their own accord, independently of your wishes. But do you have any wishes? I am absolutely convinced that death is not a cosmic void, not a blissful zero. No, that would be too comforting, too simple. Death must be an agonizing repetition, an unbearable sameness. And that is why you fall prey to a monotonous, obsessive state

somewhere between a waking dream and meditating in your sleep. This agonizing sense of emptiness festers in your consciousness like an open wound, and it is a long long time before the scar tissue forms in your soul. Nothing at all remains in your memory from this period—it is a total blank.

STUDY QUESTIONS

1. As an excerpt from a chapter, this selection cannot be regarded as a complete essay. Nevertheless, Bukovsky's opening fable of the hunted bear serves as an indirect introduction to his situation and his personality. In what way did that story prepare you for what follows? In what way is it *not* an "essayistic" introduction? (That is, how does it raise expectations that are not fulfilled?)
2. As a political prisoner who had set his conscience against the state, Bukovsky was entitled to feel superior to the common criminals serving time for "hooliganism, gang rape, or a gang robbery" (paragraph 14). Why do you suppose he places so little emphasis on this distinction between types of prisoners? Would his account of prison life have been more, or less, convincing if he had represented himself as rallying his fellow dissidents, politically educating the common criminals, and defying the authority of his jailers?
3. If all references to *political* imprisonment had been omitted, do you think you still could have guessed that Bukovsky was not a common criminal? If so, be prepared to say why.
4. Why does Bukovsky include only one sentence in paragraph 3?
5. Which personal pronouns (*I, you,* etc.) does Bukovsky favor in telling his story, and what is the rhetorical effect of that choice?
6. Do you believe Bukovsky when he declares himself "absolutely convinced" (paragraph 15) that death "must be an agonizing repetition"? What is he trying to communicate to us at this point?

Ada Louise Huxtable

Ada Louise Huxtable is an architectural historian and critic. A member of the editorial board of the *New York Times,* she has written several books, including *Kicked a Building Lately?* (1976), from which "Houston" is taken.

HOUSTON

1 This is a car's-eye view of Houston—but is there any other? It is a short report on a fast trip to the city that has supplanted Los Angeles in current intellectual mythology as the city of the future. You'd better believe. Houston is the place that scholars flock to for the purpose of seeing what modern civilization has wrought. Correctly perceived and publicized as freeway city, mobile city, space city, strip city, and speculator city, it is being dissected by architects and urban historians as a case study in new forms and functions. It even requires a new definition of urbanity. Houston is *the* city of the second half of the twentieth century.

2 But what strikes the visitor accustomed to cities shaped by rivers, mountains, and distinguishing topography, by local identity and historical and cultural conditioning, is that this is instant city, and it is nowhere city.

3 Houston is totally without the normal rationales of geography and evolutionary social growth that have traditionally created urban centers and culture. From the time that the Allen brothers came here from New York in 1836 and bought the featureless land at the junction of two bayous (they could not get the site they really wanted), this city has been an act of real estate, rather than an act of God or man. Houston has been willed on the flat, uniform prairie not by some planned ideal, but by the expediency of land investment economics, first, and later by oil and petrochemical prosperity.

4 This is not meant to be an unfavorable judgment. It is simply an effort to convey the extraordinary character of this city—to suggest its unique importance, interest, and impact. Its affluence and eccentricities have been popularly celebrated. It is known to be devoutly conservative, passionately devoted to free enterprise and non-governmental interference. It is famous, or notorious, for the fact that, alone among the country's major cities, it has no zoning—no regulations on what anyone builds, anywhere—and the debate rages over whether this makes it better or worse than other cities. (It's a draw, with pluses and minuses that have a lot to do with special local conditions.)

5 Now the fifth largest city in the country, Houston has had its most

phenomenal expansion since the Second World War. At last count, it covered over 500 square miles and had a population of 1.4 million, with a half million more in surrounding Harris County. A thousand new people move in every week. This record-setting growth has leapfrogged over open country without natural boundaries, without land use restrictions, moving on before anything is finished, for a kind of development as open-ended as the prairie. It has jumped across smaller, fully incorporated cities within the vast city limits. The municipality can legally annex 10 percent of its urban area in outlying land or communities every year, and the land grab has been continuous and relentless.

6 Houston is a study in paradoxes. There are pines and palm trees, skyscrapers and sprawl; Tudor townhouses stop abruptly as cows and prairie take over. It deals in incredible extremes of wealth and culture. In spite of its size, one can find no real center, no focus. "Downtown" boasts a concentration of suave towers, but they are already challenged by other, newer commercial centers of increasing magnitude that form equally important nodes on the freeway network that ties everything together. Nor are these new office and shopping complexes located to serve existing communities in the conventional sense. They are created in a vacuum, and people come by automobile, driving right into their parking garages. They rise from expressway ribbons and seas of cars.

7 Houston is all process and no plan. Gertrude Stein° said of Oakland that there was no there, there. One might say of Houston that one never gets there. It feels as if one is always on the way, always arriving, always looking for the place where everything comes together. And yet as a city, a twentieth-century city, it works remarkably well. If one excepts horrendous morning and evening traffic jams as all of Houston moves to and from home and work, it is a lesson in how a mobile society functions, the values it endorses, and what kind of world it makes.

8 Houston is different from the time one rises in the morning to have the dark suddenly dispelled by a crimson aureole on a horizon that seems to stretch full circle, and a sun that appears to rise below eye level. (New Yorkers are accustomed to seeing only fractured bits and pieces of sky.) From a hotel of sophisticated excellence that might be Claridge's°-on-the-prairie, furnished with an owner-oilman's private collection of redundant boiserie and Sevres,° one drives past fountains of detergent blue.

9 Due north on Main Street is "downtown," a roughly 20-block cluster of commercial towers begun in the 1920s and thirties and dou-

---

7 **Gertrude Stein:** (1874–1946) American author, raised chiefly in Oakland, California, but later a long-time expatriate in Paris

8 **Claridge's:** fashionable London hotel

boiserie, Sevres: respectively, sculptured paneling, esp. that of French architecture in the eighteenth century; (usually *Sèvres*) fine porcelain made in this suburb of Paris

bled in size and numbers in the 1960s and seventies, sleek symbols of prosperity and power. They are paradigms of the corporate style. The names they bear are Tenneco, Shell Plaza, Pennzoil Place, Humble, and Houston Natural Gas, and their architects have national reputations.

10 In another paradox, in this country of open spaces, the towers are increasingly connected by tunnels underground. Houston's environment is strikingly "internalized" because of the area's extremes of heat and humidity. It is the indoors one seeks for large parts of the year, and that fact has profoundly affected how the city builds and lives.

11 The enclosed shopping center is Houston's equivalent of the traditional town plaza—a clear trend across the country. The Post Oak Galleria, a $20-million product of Houston developer Gerald Hines and architects Hellmuth, Obata and Kassabaum, with Neuhaus and Taylor, is characteristically large and opulent. A 420,000-square-foot, 600-foot long, three-level, covered shopping mall, it is part of a 33-acre commercial, office, and hotel complex off the West Loop Freeway, at the city's western edge.

12 The Galleria is the place to see and be seen: it is meeting place, promenade, and social center. It also offers restaurants, baubles from Tiffany and Nieman-Marcus, a galaxy of specialty shops equivalent to Madison Avenue, and an ice-skating rink comparable to Rockefeller Center's, all under a chandelier-hung glass roof. One can look up from the ice-skating to see joggers circling the oblong glass dome. The Galleria is now slated for an expansion larger than the original.

13 These enterprises do not require outdoor settings; they are magnets that can be placed anywhere. In fact, one seeks orientation by the freeways and their man-made landmarks (Southwest Freeway and Sharpstown, West Loop and Post Oak Tower) rather than by reference to organic patterns of growth. Climate, endless open topography, speculator economics and spectator consumerism, and, of course, the car have determined Houston's free-wheeling, vacuum-packed life and environment.

14 For spectator sports, one goes to the Astrodome to the southwest, which has created its own environment—the Astrodomain [sic] of assiduously cultivated amusements and motels. Popular and commercial culture are well served in Houston. There is also high, or middle, culture, for which the "brutalist" forms of the Alley Theater by New York architect Ulrich Franzen, and the neutral packaging of Jones Hall for the performing arts, by the Houston firm of Caudill, Rowlett, Scott, have been created. They stand in the shadow of the downtown oil industry giants that have provided their funding.

15 Farther south on Main are the Fine Arts Museum, with its handsome extension by Mies van der Rohe, and the Contemporary Arts Association building, a sharp-edged, metal trapezoid by Gunnar Birkets. They cling together among odd vacant lots in a state of decaying or becoming, next to a psychoanalytic center.

16 Because the city has no zoning, these surreal juxtapositions prevail. A hamburger stand closes the formal vista of Philip Johnson's delicate, Miesian arcade at St. Thomas University. Transitional areas, such as Westheimer, not only mirror the city's untrammeled development in ten-year sections, but are freely altered as old houses are turned into new shops and restaurants, unhampered by zoning taboos. (Conventionally zoned cities simply rezone their deteriorating older residential neighborhoods to save their tax base and facilitate the same economic destiny. The process just takes a little longer.)

17 Houston's web of freeways is the consummate example of the twentieth-century phenomenon known as the commercial strip. The route of passage attracts sales, services, and schlock in continuous road-oriented structures—gas stations, drive-ins, and displays meant to catch the eye and fancy at 60 miles an hour. There are fixed and mobile signs, and signs larger than buildings ("buildingboards," according to students of the Pop° environment). Style, extracted as symbols, becomes a kind of sign in itself, evoking images from Rapunzel° to Monticello. There are miles of fluttering metallic pennants (used cars), a giant lobster with six shooters, cowboy hat, and scarf (seafood), a turning, life-size plaster bull (American International Charolais Association), and a revolving neon piano. The strip is full of intuitive wit, invention, and crass, but also real creativity—a breathtaking affront to normal sensibility that is never a bore.

18 Directly behind the freeways, one short turn takes the driver from the strip into pine and live oak-alleyed streets of comfortable and elegant residential communities (including the elite and affluent River Oaks). They have maintained their environmental purity by deed restrictions passed on from one generation of buyers to another.

19 Beyond these enclaves, anything goes. Residential development is a spin-the-wheel happening that hops, skips, and jumps outward, each project seemingly dropped from the sky—but always on the freeway. The southwest section, which was prairie before the 1950s, is now the American Dream incarnate. There is a continuing rivalry of you-name-it styles that favor French and Anglo-Saxon labels and details. If you live in Westminster, authentic-looking London street signs on high iron fences frame views of the flat Texas plains. You know you're home when you get to La Cour du Roi° or Robin Hood Dell.

20 Because Houston is an urban invention, this kind of highly salable make-believe supplies instant history and architecture; it is an anchor to time and place where neither is defined. All of those values that

---

17 **Pop:** referring to pop art, a movement of the 1950s and '60s that drew artistic attention to ordinary objects such as flags, soup cans, and comic strips

Rapunzel: fairy-tale maiden imprisoned in a tower

19 **La Cour du Roi:** (Fr.) the court of the king

accrue throughout centuries of civilization—identity, intimacy, scale, complexity, style—are simply created out of whole cloth, or whole prairie, with unabashed commercial eclecticism. How else to establish a sense of place or community, to indicate differences where none exist?

21 Houston is a continuous series of such cultural shocks. Its private patronage, on which the city depends for its public actions, has a cosmic range. There is the superb, *echt*°-Houston eccentricity of Judge Roy Hofheinz's personal quarters in the Astrodome, done in a kind of Astrobaroque of throne chairs, gold phones, and temple dogs, with a pick-a-religion, fake stone chapel (good for bullfighters or politicians who want to meditate), shooting gallery, and presidential suite, tucked into the periphery of the stadium, complete with views of the Astros and Oilers. At the other end of the esthetic scale there is the Rothko° Chapel, where the blood-dark paintings of the artist's pre-suicide days have been brought together by Dominique de Menil—a place of overwhelming, icy death. One welcomes the Texas sunshine.

22 Houston is not totally without planned features. It has large and handsome parks and the landscaped corridor of the Buffalo Bayou that are the result of philanthropic forethought. There are universities and a vast medical center.

23 But no one seems to feel the need for the public vision that older cities have of a hierarchy of places and buildings, an organized concept of function and form. Houston has a downtown singularly without amenities. The fact that money and population are flowing there from the rest of the country is considered cause for celebration, not for concern with the city's quality. This city bets on a different and brutal kind of distinction—of power, motion, and sheer energy. Its values are material fulfillment, mobility, and mass entertainment. Its returns are measured on its commercial investments. These contemporary ideals have little to do with the deeper or subtler aspects of the mind or spirit, or even with the more complex, human pleasure potential of a hedonistic culture.

24 When we build a new city, such as Houston, it is quite natural that we build in this image, using all of our hardware to serve its uses and desires. We create new values and new dimensions in time and space. The expanded, mobile city deals in distance and discontinuity; it "explodes" community. It substitutes fantasy for history. Houston is devoted to moon shots, not moon-viewing. The result is a significant, instructive, and disquieting city form.

25 What Houston possesses to an exceptional degree is an extraordinary, unlimited vitality. One wishes that it had a larger conceptual reach, that social and cultural and human patterns were as well under-

---

[21] **echt:** (Ger.) real, genuine

Rothko: Mark Rothko (1903–1970), American expressionist painter

stood as dollar dynamism. But this kind of vitality is the distinguishing mark of a great city in any age. And Houston today is the American present and future. It is an exciting and disturbing place.

STUDY QUESTIONS

1. What tone or mood do you perceive in Huxtable's opening sentence? Has she made an effective beginning?
2. Think of some adjectives or phrases that might help you to characterize Huxtable's style, or total manner of writing. Isolate several of her sentences that strike you as distinctive, not because of what they are saying, but because they "sound like Huxtable."
3. Huxtable writes both as a student of architecture and as a social critic. What connections does she draw between financial realities on one side and styles of building on the other? What does Houston's architecture tell us about the city's relation to the past?
4. A resident of Houston might complain that Huxtable, in writing of "nowhere city" (paragraph 2), looks down upon this "act of real estate" (paragraph 3). Would you be able to defend Huxtable, wholly or partially, against that charge? If so, which passages would you cite?
5. In what ways does Huxtable reveal that her standards of judgment, whether or not they favor Houston, were formed elsewhere?
6. In paragraph 18, after discussing Houston as an unzoned city, Huxtable refers to certain alleys that have "maintained their environmental purity by deed restrictions." Is this a contradiction? What does it tell us about Houston?
7. A writer who is trying to understand and appreciate a strange phenomenon may nevertheless want to express her own, more traditional, values and preferences. Does Huxtable do this? If so, where?
8. If this is indeed an essay exploring a cause-and-effect relation, what do you see as the principal cause and effect?

Roger Angell

A frequent contributor to *The New Yorker,* Roger Angell has published books of fiction and sports commentary. "The Cool Bubble," written in 1966, was first collected in *The Summer Game* (1972).

THE COOL BUBBLE

1 With two out in the top of the first inning on the afternoon of May 23, 1965, Jimmy Wynn, the center fielder of the Houston Astros, moved under a fly ball just struck by Jim Ray Hart, of the visiting San Francisco Giants. Looking upward, Wynn pounded his glove confidently, then anxiously, and then froze in horror. The ball had vanished into a pure Monet° cloud of overhead beams, newly painted off-white skylights, and diffused Texas sunlight, and now it suddenly rematerialized a good distance behind Wynn and plumped to earth like a thrombosed pigeon. Three runs scored, the Giants eventually won, 5–2, and the next day a squad of workmen ascended the skies and, with paint guns, made the final severance between Houston baseball and the outdoors. Up to the moment of Hart's fly, it might have been assumed that the summer sport played last year in Houston's gigantic new air-conditioned Astrodome, which is the world's first indoor ballpark, was merely baseball under glass—the same old game, now happily sheltered from the voracious mosquitoes and dismaying swelter of the Texas Gulf Coast. However, the unexpected local discovery that sunshine had become inimical to the national pastime (in preseason practices and exhibition games, before the initial coat of paint was slapped on the skylights, a few players had begun wearing their batting helmets in the outfield) only completed what actually was a radical break with baseball's past and hastened further changes. Through the rest of last season, the grass in the crepuscular° dome yellowed and withered, was painted green in the infield, and finally had to be replaced with new sodding, which fared no better. When ballplayers reconvened in the Astrodome this spring, they stepped out onto an infield made of new green plastic carpeting called Astro Turf.

2 It was not just the prospect of witnessing weatherless baseball played on Chemstrand grass under an acrylic-painted Lucite sky that induced me to travel to Houston last month to see the Astros open their first 1966 home stand. There was also the fact that the Astros' first

---

1 **Monet:** Claude Monet (1840–1926), French impressionist painter
crepuscular: dim, resembling twilight

indoor season had been a rousing success, in spite of their customary ninth-place finish. Houston jumped from a 1964 home attendance of 725,773, smallest in the National League, to a gate of 2,151,470, barely second to that of the World Champion Dodgers, and more than six hundred thousand higher than the best American League home draw. Since half of the majors' twenty teams have been born or have moved to new cities in the past twelve years, all in panting search of new audiences, these figures were of remarkable interest; Houston seemed on its way to becoming the capital of Baseball's Age of Alteration.

3 So it was that I found myself, early in the evening of April 18, sitting in a cushioned deep-purple loge seat in left field of the Harris County Domed Stadium (as the Astrodome is formally named) and listening to the Jeff Davis High School band's pregame rendition of "The Good Old Summertime." The only good and old object in view at the time was Robin Roberts, the erstwhile ace of the Phillies and Orioles and now the Astros' senior mound statesman, who was warming up near the right-field stands preparatory to taking on the Dodgers. He toiled earnestly, though surrounded by distractions. A group of female scholars from Tyler Junior College assembled along the foul lines and did some high kicks in unison, wearing cowboy hats and peach satin body stockings. The groundkeepers smoothing the base paths were dressed in fake bright orange space suits and fake white plastic space helmets. Each level of the stands was painted a different color—royal blue, gold, purple, black, tangerine, and crimson—and I had the momentary sensation that I was sinking slowly through the blackberry-brandy layer of a pousse-café.° The Astro Turf infield was green, but more the shade of a billiard table than a lawn. Only the outfield grass (which will be replaced with Astro Turf later this year) was reassuring; it looked like any Westchester back yard after a five-year drought. The lacy overhead pattern of beams and cloudy panes arching up from the brilliant circle of field lights made a soft and surprising sky above me. Leaning back in my theater seat, I measured its height by eye and saw that it was far above the reach of any fly ball, and then I wondered why someone hadn't placed an altitude mark at the apex of the roof, to match the "340," "390," and "406" signs along the outfield wall and thus supply us with baseball's latest statistic.

4 The elegant stands slowly filled, the ceremonials slipped by (the National League president with a plaque, Dinah Shore with the anthem, a county judge with the first ball), and baseball was allowed to begin. It turned out to be the same old game, the same game as ever. I could tell, because there was Robin Roberts out on the mound fiddling with

[3] **pousse-café:** (Fr.) a glass of various liqueurs arranged in layers

his right pants leg between pitches. There, too, were the Dodgers, the champions, instantly ripping off singles, bunting, scurrying for the extra base, taking charge of the game from the very beginning, just as they did in the World Series last fall. Only the fact that Maury Wills was thrown out stealing second kept them down to two runs in the first inning and sustained the hopes of the locals. I presumed that the Houston fans were hopeful, but it was hard to be certain. It was a thinnish turnout for an opening game—just over twenty-five thousand—and the spectators near me, who were remarkably well dressed, also appeared to be unaccustomed to indoor shouting. It developed, however, that they were merely waiting for directions. With two out in the home half of the first, Jimmy Wynn drew a base on balls, and the center screen of the Astrodome's huge, three-panel electronic scoreboard above the outfield pavilion seats burst forth with a noisy, animated depiction of a bugle bugling, followed by the lettered command "CHARGE!" *"Charge!"* responded the crowd with one voice. The fans near me were still laughing over this display of *a capella* ferocity when Joe Morgan flied out and the tiny rally came to a close.

5 Several scoreboards in big-league parks are now wired for bugle calls and CHARGE! injunctions (the device was born, I believe, in Los Angeles), but comic cavalry attacks are only the beginning of the Houston scoreboard's repertoire. The thing is four hundred and seventy-four feet long and cost two million dollars, and there is room on its various partitions for simultaneous presentation of the game's lineups and scoring, out-of-town baseball results, messages of welcome to fan groups, plugs for Astro souvenirs, and gigantic animated commercials. These last flash on between innings—routine cartoon plugs for potato chips, gasoline, an airline, and so forth, accompanied by sound effects but without a spoken message. This is the only mercy, for the giant set is impossible not to look at, and there is no "off" switch. Actually, there was plenty to watch and enjoy on the field in that first game, in which Roberts, in search of his two-hundred-and-eighty-second major-league win, was throwing a potpourri of soft junk and being outpitched by a twenty-one-year-old Dodger rookie named Don Sutton, who has been in organized baseball for exactly one year, but the scoreboard and its busy screen seemed anxious to improve on the baseball. In the second inning, second baseman Morgan and third baseman Bob Aspromonte came up with successive brilliant stops for the Astros, to rob Jim Lefebvre and Lou Johnson of base hits; there were shouts and applause in the stands, but the scoreboard commanded "OLÉ!" and was obeyed. By the middle innings, I found that I was giving the game only half my attention, along with everyone else. I kept lifting my eyes to that immense, waiting presence above the players. In the eighth, with the Astros behind, 5–1, Sonny Jackson led off the home half with a nifty bunt, and when Morgan singled him along, some fans began a hopeful,

rhythmic clapping, instantly surpassed by the appearance on the screen of a giant female silhouette dancing the Frug,° and then the words "GO-GO." The Astros went-went for two runs, but the Dodgers added another of their own and won the game, 6–3. As I walked down the broad ramps of the Astrodome and, oddly, stepped outdoors, I heard a good many Texans around me still talking about something that had taken place way back in the second inning, when Chuck Harrison had doubled off the left-field wall, for the Astros' first hit. The man in charge of the scoreboard evidently thought the ball had gone into the stands, for he pressed the button touching off the board's home-run celebration display—an immense, multicolor, forty-five-second extravaganza depicting an exploding ballpark, shooting cowboys, ricocheting bullets, a snorting steer with flags on his horns, a mounted cowboy with lariat, and a fusillade of skyrockets. This time, when it was all over Harrison was still standing on second, and the screen boffed the crowd with its next message, "OOPS." A minute or two later, catcher John Bateman also doubled, and the home team scored, but no one in the postgame crowd seemed to remember that. The board had been the big hit of the evening.

6 Baseball, of course, is not the only main event at the Domed Stadium. In the past year, it has put on such disparate attractions as Judy Garland, the Ringling Brothers circus, a rodeo, a boat show, a polo match, the home football games of the University of Houston, a bloodless bullfight, and a Billy Graham crusade. Some of these bombed and some did excellent business, but what emerged most startlingly was the fact that the Astrodome itself is its own best attraction. In the first year, close to four hundred and ninety thousand visitors paid a dollar apiece just to walk around inside the place. Most of these were out-of-towners, but in Houston itself the Astrodome seems to rank second only to the nearby Manned Spacecraft Center as a source of self-congratulation. Certainly there is far more conversational enthusiasm about the building than about the sport it was built to house; a local sportswriter told me he had never heard *anyone* say, "I'm an Astro fan." During my stay, I found that when I forced myself to look at the Astrodome as a work of art, my admiration for the improbable cool bubble grew with each visit. The exterior is especially pleasing—a broad, white-screened shell of such excellent proportions that you doubt its true dimensions until you stand at its base. The Astrodome is the world's biggest indoor arena, but its ramps are gentle, its portals and aisles brilliantly marked, and its various levels so stacked and tilted that immensity is reduced and made undiscouraging. There are almost no bad seats in the house, and the

---

[5] **Frug:** a dance, derived from the twist, popular in the 1960s

floors are so antiseptically clean that one hesitates before parting with a peanut shell or a cigarette butt.

7 Ballplayers like the Astrodome, too. Descending to the playing field during batting practices (I tried to pull up a blade of Astro-Turf to chew on while standing behind the batting cage, but the stuff is pluckproof), I talked to various Dodgers and Astros and found them unanimous in the view that the lighting is now excellent, the prefab infield very fast but perhaps not as fast as Dodger Stadium's brickyard, but the chilled, windless air profoundly unconducive to the long ball. Last year, only fifty-seven homers were struck in Houston, which is only a third of the total in most parks. Wes Parker, the young Dodger first baseman, said, "It's a park for singles hitters. Hit the ball on the ground, *ffft,* and it'll likely go through. Good for our kind of team. I'll tell you, though, I just discovered something funny about this fake grass. Watch bunts on it. Watch what happens to them." I studied the next dozen-odd bunts laid down in practice, and each time, the spinning ball, catching the nap of the AstroTurf, suddenly veered off toward first base, like a marble dropped on the floor in a housing development. Later, after practice, I went out and walked around on the new surface, which has the consistency of an immense doormat. I dug down with my fingers and found the spine of one of the hidden foul-line-to-foul-line zippers that hold the new infield together; I had the sudden feeling that if I unzipped it, I might uncover the world's first plastic worm.

8 The worst seats for baseball in the Astrodome are the most expensive—the narrow topmost ring of "Sky Boxes," which are sold on a season-long basis in blocks of twenty-four or thirty seats. Such an investment in the national pastime costs a minimum of $14,784 per season, and entitles the boxholder to approximately the same view of the ballplayers as he might have of a herd of prize cattle seen from a private plane. There are other perquisites, though, including membership in the Skydome Club, a private snuggery in the Astrodome that offers Lucite womb chairs, a picture-window view of downtown Houston, and an Oriental restaurant equipped with kimono-clad Japanese waitresses and electric *hibachi* stoves. (Buyers of single season tickets have to make do with membership at the Astrodome Club, a capacious Turkey-red lounge and restaurant, with beaded curtains, swinging saloon doors, and the longest bar in Texas.) Each Sky Box is connected to an individual small apartment containing a living room, bathroom, refrigerator, and closed-circuit TV set. These roomettes are heavily decorated in Texas provincial, motel Tudor, and other "themes," and I can only say I found them immensely glum—sad, soft caves for indoor sportsmen. The institution is popular, however; women who are invited to a Sky Box dinner party and game can sometimes find their names in the society columns the next day, and a Texas businessman standing behind the Sky Box seats, with his foot on a railing, a glass of bourbon in his hand, and a ball game in progress far below, is sometimes in the

mood for a little wheeling and dealing with the other good old boys he finds up there at the top level of the biggest new arena in the world.

9 Studying millionaires is Houston's favorite year-round entertainment, and Judge Roy Hofheinz, the Kublai Khan° of the Domed Stadium, is the most entertaining millionaire in town. He has been, variously, a campaign manager for Lyndon Johnson, a boy-wonder jurist, mayor of Houston, a real-estate developer, and a promoter and owner of radio and television stations. Hofheinz is not one of the big rich, like John W. Mecom, who seems to have succeeded the late Jesse Jones as Houston's financial vizier, but he talks more and gets into more fights than any other moneyman in sight. Hofheinz's fallings-out are epochal. Among others, he has squabbled with Jesse Jones; with K.S. (Bud) Adams, Jr., the owner of the American Football League's Houston Oilers (the Oilers do not play their home games in the Astrodome); and with R.E. (Bob) Smith, his former senior partner in Houston Sports Association, Inc., the company that owns the Astros and rents the stadium from Harris County for an annual payment of three-quarters of a million dollars. This last blowup, a year ago, ended with the Judge buying up most of Smith's interest, and he now owns 86 per cent of the Astros. Hofheinz's experience in baseball is minimal, and most of the club's field operations rested in the hands of general manager Paul Richards, a former manager of the Orioles and a widely admired baseball thinker. Experienced Hofheinz-watchers predicted that there would be amity in the organization until the day Hofheinz decided he had surpassed Richards in baseball wisdom—a day that apparently arrived last December, when Hofheinz abruptly fired Richards (whose contract had five years to run), along with farm director Eddie Robinson and manager Luman Harris. The new team manager is Grady Hatton, and the Astros are now a pure Hofheinz fief.

10 Houston looks on Hofheinz with a mixture of awe, amusement, and anxiety. There is the undeniable fact that the prodigious idea of a domed year-round stadium was entirely the Judge's, and without his plans for the new miracle park Houston almost certainly would not have been granted a franchise in the league expansion of 1962. It was also Hofheinz's energy and promotional optimism that got the necessary bond issues approved and launched, and his hand is recognizable in every corridor and catwalk of the finished marvel. Any remaining Houston doubts about the Judge's genius are now centered on the awesome financial weight that is being balanced on top of the dome, and on the recent population implosion of top executives at the Houston Sports Association. The precise break-even point of Astroperations has not been made public, but the stadium's financial overhead is known to be

---

[9] **Kublai Khan:** (1216–1294) founder of the Mongol dynasty in China

Texas-sized. The electric bill alone, covering lights and air-conditioning, comes to thirty thousand dollars a month. The best estimates of the amount of business required to keep the Domed Stadium afloat come down to about a hundred and twenty-five days of active operation at an average attendance of twenty thousand. This means that the Astros must continue to draw handsomely during their eighty dates at home, and that numerous additional attractions will have to be encouraged. No one in Houston doubts the Judge's energy and imagination, but Harris County voted in an investment of some thirty-one million dollars toward the success of the Astrodome—a sum that adds a certain sense of zesty involvement to each taxpayer's daily Hofheinz-watch.

11 I visited the Judge one afternoon in his famous Astrodome office—a two-story business pad of such comically voluptuous decor and sybaritic furnishings that I was half convinced it had been designed by, say, John Lennon. My awed gaze took in hanging Moorish lamps and back-lit onyx wall panels in His Honor's sanctum, a pair of giant Oriental lions guarding the black marble and rosewood judicatorial desk, a golden telephone awaiting the Hofheinzian ear, and, at the far end of the boardroom, a suspended baldachin° above the elevated red-and-gilt magisterial throne. It would have been irreverent to talk baseball in these surroundings, but luckily the Judge received me in his box on an upper floor, which offered an expansive vista of the lofty, gently breathing dome and a distant view of some Astros working out in the batting cage. Hofheinz is a tall, thick-waisted man with lank hair, heavy black-rimmed spectacles, and small hands, in which he constantly rotates a giant cigar. We sat in gold plush swivel chairs overlooking the field and drank coffee out of gold cups, while the Judge talked about the long, tedious process of building a pennant contender from scratch. I asked about the Houston audience's devotion to baseball, observing that I had seen very few local patrons keeping score during the game, and Hofheinz said, "This park keeps 'em interested enough so they don't *have* to keep busy with a pencil and scorecard. Why, in most other parks you got nothing to do but watch the game, keep score, and sit on a hard wooden seat. This place was built to keep the fans happy. They've got our good seats, fine restaurants, and our scoreboard to look at, and they don't have to make a personal sacrifice to like baseball." He tapped the ash from his heater into a gold ashtray shaped like a fielder's glove, and went on. "We have removed baseball from the rough-and-tumble era, I don't believe in the old red-necked sports concept, and we are disproving it here. We're in the business of sports entertainment. Baseball isn't a game to which your individuals come alone just to watch the game. They come for social enjoyment. They like to entertain and *be* enter-

[11] **baldachin:** an ornamental canopy

tained at the ballpark. Our fans are more like the ones they have out in California. We don't have any of those rowdies or semi-delinquents who follow the Mets."

12 I started to put in a small word for rowdies, but Hofheinz continued. "We have by far a higher percentage of fans in the upper economic brackets than you'll find in any other park," he said, "but we *also* have the best seats and service at the dollar-fifty level. You're competing for attention in sports entertainment, and you've got to create new kinds of fans. We make a big effort to bring out the ladies. There are plenty of mothers and grandmothers who have just learned about the double play from some Little Leaguer, and now for the first time here's a ballpark where you would *want* to bring them and let them develop into real fans. And once they've seen what it's like here, they won't feel so bad about letting their husbands and boys go off to the ball game any old time they want."

13 For the remainder of my stay, I tried to concentrate on Houston baseball, instead of its setting, and I saw the Astros split a pair of lively games with the Dodgers. The first was one of those baseball rarities, a complete turnabout, in which the Astros, after giving up ten hits and five runs in the first four innings, suddenly bounced back with batches of runs of their own while entirely bottling up their tormentors, and won going away, 8–5. John Bateman's fourth-inning homer set off the scoreboard's steers and rockets for their first sanctioned gala of the year, and in the fifth the home side, assisted by some absent-minded Dodger fielding, batted around and drove Don Drysdale from the mound. This was perhaps less of a feat than it sounds, for Drysdale was far from sharp after his long, much-publicized dual holdout with Sandy Koufax, but it was popular; there is nothing like the public shaming of a hundred-thousand-dollar-a-year man to tone up a crowd. The Astros got some first-class pitching from a tough workmanlike reliever named Mike Cuellar, who struck out nine Dodgers with his down-breaking screwball. The next night, the Astros almost pulled out another, but they were up against Claude Osteen, the least publicized and perhaps the best No. 3 pitcher in the league, who fanned Jim Gentile with the tying run aboard in the ninth, and they lost a 3–2 squeaker.

14 The Astros are a curiosity, for they are a team without a star, present or past, unless one counts such mini-celebrities as Jimmy Wynn or Larry Dierker. Invented, along with the Mets, in the league expansion of 1962, they have consistently displayed a shabby competence that has kept them above New York in the standings every year, and has probably cost them much of the rich affection and attention generated by the Mets' anti-heroes.

15 There is no real doubt, however, that the Astros are on the way and will someday break into the tough, embattled territory of the National League's first division, but a healthy franchise, particularly in new

baseball territory, also requires the building of a sizable body of young, resilient, and truly knowledgeable fans. No one knows much about the loyalties and passions of the Houston baseball audience, in spite of those enormous attendance figures of last season, for it is impossible to guess how many of the two million ticket-buyers came to see the Astros and how many to see the Astrodome. During the Dodger games, I kept moving about in the stands and changing neighbors, but I could not penetrate the placid bonhomie of those small, citified, early-season crowds or convince myself that we were watching a sporting event. There was applause at the appropriate moments, but not much tonsil-straining, and the scattered booing was mostly directed at the ball and strike calls of the home-plate umpire, which is bush.° No one booed an Astro player. No one got into a fight; a fight at the Astrodome would be as shocking as fisticuffs in the College of Cardinals. And always, as before, the applause and attention of the fans around me would be interrupted, redirected, and eventually muffled by the giant scoreboard and its central screen. It commanded "CHARGE" and "GO-GO" for every Astro base-runner, it saluted a homer by the Dodgers' Wes Parker with the word "TILT," and when it broke in on a lively dispute at third base, the spectators forgot about the real thing and sat back in their armchairs to watch a cartoon umpire argue with a cartoon manager.

16 Toward the end of the last game, my irritation took me out to the pavilion seats in center field (Astropatrons, untouched by the sun, do not sit in bleachers), and here I found the first unscattered group of recognizable fans in Houston. It was a shirt-sleeved, short-sleeved crowd, Negro and white, full of young people. There were some big families, complete with sleeping babies, and a blond teen-age girl next to me wore a patch on the arm of her sweater that said "Future Homemaker of America." Some of the men wore straw cowboy hats, some were in city coconut straws. Shortly after I arrived, Dave Nicholson led off the Astro sixth with a triple off Osteen that almost landed in our laps, and at once the entire pavilion crowd was on its feet, shouting and cheering. The scoreboard, I remembered later, was behind us, but we didn't seem to need it. And then in the top of the seventh, when Houston pitcher Bob Bruce was in heavy trouble, first baseman Chuck Harrison speared a hopper° by Maury Wills and then hesitated a moment over his play. I jumped up and yelled, "Home! Throw home!," and it came to me suddenly that I had company: a hundred fans near me were screaming the same advice. Harrison got our message and threw to Bateman, who tagged out Nate Oliver at the plate, and we all sat down, grinning at one another.

---

[15] **bush:** bush league, lacking class

[16] **speared a hopper:** caught a high-bouncing ground ball

17 Baseball is an extraordinarily subtle and complex game, and the greatest subtlety of all may well be the nature of its appeal to the man in the stands. The expensive Houston experiment does not truly affect the players or much alter the sport played down on the field, but I think it does violence to baseball—and, incidentally, threatens its own success—through a total misunderstanding of the game's old mystery. I do not agree with Judge Hofheinz that a ballpark is a notable center for socializing or propriety, or that many spectators will continue to find refreshment in returning to a giant living room—complete with manmade weather, wall-to-wall carpeting, clean floors, and unrelenting TV show—that so totally, so drearily, resembles the one he has just left. But these complaints are incidental. What matters, what appalls, in Houston is the attempt being made there to alter the quality of baseball's time. Baseball's clock ticks inwardly and silently, and a man absorbed in a ball game is caught in a slow, green place of removal and concentration and in a tension that is screwed up slowly and ever more tightly with each pitcher's windup and with the almost imperceptible forward lean and little half-step with which the fielders accompany each pitch. Whatever the pace of the particular baseball game we are watching, whatever its outcome, it holds us in its own continuum and mercifully releases us from our own. Any persistent effort to destroy this unique phenomenon, to "use up" baseball's time with planned distractions, will in fact transform the sport into another mere entertainment and thus hasten its descent to the status of a boring and stylized curiosity.

18 It seems to me that the Houston impresarios are trying to build a following by the distraction and entire control of their audience's attention—aiming at a sort of wraparound, programmed environment, of the kind currently under excited discussion by new thinkers of the electronic age. I do not wish them luck with this vulgar venture, and I hope that in the end they may remember that baseball has always had a capacity to create its own lifelong friends—sometimes even outdoors. One Houston lady told me that she had been a fan for more than thirty years, beginning when she was a schoolgirl and the Houston Buffs were a Cardinal farm. "I remember a lot of players from back then," she said. "I saw them all before they went up to the majors and became famous. Howie Pollett and Danny Murtaugh were my *gods.* And I remember something else. Buff Stadium back in the old days used to be right next to a bakery—Fehr's Bakery, that's what it was called! I'll never forget sitting in the stands in the afternoon and watching the games, and the sweet smell of fresh bread in the air all around."

STUDY QUESTIONS

1. How does Angell convince us that he is in a position to write authoritatively about baseball? That is, in what ways does he show himself to have more knowledge than the typical fan?
2. What values does Angell openly or implicitly associate with baseball?
3. What is Angell's chief feeling about the Astrodome scoreboard?
4. In Angell's survey of the Astrodome, what is the significance of his visit to the pavilion area (paragraph 16)?
5. What is the thesis, or main idea, of this essay, and where if anywhere is it stated?
6. In what sense does this essay deserve to be classified as an instance of cause-and-effect presentation? Could it also be seen as an argument? If so, what do you think Angell is arguing *for?*
7. Think of "The Cool Bubble" as falling into three parts, with breaks before paragraphs 6 and 13. How would you characterize the emphasis of each part?
8. Angell's essay concludes by recounting an anecdote told him by "a Houston lady." What is the point of that story, and how does it provide a fitting conclusion?
9. What does Angell's language tell us about his general view of the world? Choose several examples of distinctive-looking expressions and be prepared to discuss them in this context.

COMPARING AND CONTRASTING

Larry Woiwode

The novelist and poet Larry Woiwode is the author of several books, including the novels *What I'm Going to Do, I Think* and *Beyond the Bedroom Wall: A Family Album.* "Guns" first appeared in *Esquire* in 1975.

GUNS

1 Once in the middle of a Wisconsin winter I shot a deer, my only one, while my wife and daughter watched. It had been hit by a delivery truck along a country road a few miles from where we lived and one of its rear legs was torn off at the hock; a shattered shin and hoof lay steaming in the red-beaded snow. The driver of the truck and I stood and watched as it tried to leap a fence, kicked a while at the top wire it was entangled in, flailing the area with fresh ropes of blood, and then went hobbling across a pasture toward a wooded hill. Placid cows followed it with a curious awe. "Do you have a rifle with you?" the driver asked. "No, not with me. At home." He looked once more at the deer, then got in his truck and drove off.

2 I went back to our Jeep where my wife and daughter were waiting, pale and withdrawn, and told them what I was about to do, and suggested that they'd better stay at home. No, they wanted to be with me, they said; they wanted to watch. My daughter was three and a half at the time. I got my rifle, a .22, a foolishly puny weapon to use on a deer but the only one I had, and we came back and saw that the deer was lying in some low brush near the base of the hill; no need to trail its blatant spoor. When I got about a hundred yards off, marveling at how it could have made it so far in its condition through snow that came over my boot tops, the deer tried to push itself up with its front legs, then collapsed. I aimed at the center of its skull, thinking, *This will be the*

quickest, and heard the bullet ricochet off and go singing through the woods.

3 The deer was on its feet, shaking its head as though stung, and I fired again at the same spot, quickly, and apparently missed. It was now moving at its fastest hobble up the hill, broadside to me, and I took my time to sight a heart shot. Before the report even registered in my mind, the deer went down in an explosion of snow and lay struggling there, spouting blood from its stump and a chest wound. I was shaking by now. Deer are color-blind as far as science can say, and as I went toward its quieting body to deliver the coup de grace, I realized I was being seen in black and white, and then the deer's eye seemed to home in on me, and I was struck with the understanding that I was its vision of approaching death. And then I seemed to enter its realm through its eye and saw the countryside and myself in shades of white and grey. *But I see the deer in color,* I thought.

4 A few yards away, I aimed at its head once more, and there was the crack of a shot, the next-to-last round left in the magazine. The deer's head came up, and I could see its eye clearly now, dark, placid, filled with an appeal, it seemed, and then felt the surge of black and white surround and subsume me again. The second shot, or one of them, had pierced its neck; a grey-blue tongue hung out over its jaw; urine was trickling from below its tail; a doe. I held the rifle barrel inches from its forehead, conscious of my wife's and daughter's eyes on me from behind, and as I fired off the final and fatal shot, felt myself drawn by them back into my multicolored, many-faceted world again.

5 I don't remember my first gun, the heritage is so ingrained in me, but know I've used a variety of them to kill birds, reptiles, mammals, amphibians, plant life, insects (bees and butterflies with a shotgun), fish that came too close to shore—never a human being, I'm quick to interject, although the accumulated carnage I've put away with bullets since boyhood is probably enough to add up to a couple of cows, not counting the deer; and have fired, at other targets living and fairly inert, an old ten gauge with double hammers that left a welt on my shoulder that lasted a week, a Mauser, a twelve-gauge sawed-off shotgun, an M-16, at least a dozen variations on the .22—pump, bolt action, lever action, target pistols, special scopes and sights and stocks —a .410 over-and-under, a zip gun that blew up and scattered shrapnel that's still imbedded in my arm, an Italian carbine, a Luger, and, among others, a fancily engraved, single-trigger, double-barreled twenty gauge at snowballs thrown from behind my shoulder out over a bluff; and on that same bluff on the first day of this year, after some wine and prodding, I found myself at the jittering rim of stutters from a paratrooper's lightweight machine gun with a collapsible, geometrically reinforced metal stock, watched the spout of its trajectory of tangible tracers go off across the night toward the already-set sun, and

realized that this was perhaps the hundredth weapon I'd had performing in my hands.

6 I was raised in North Dakota, near the edge of the West, during the turbulence and then the aftermath of the Second World War, which our country ended in such an unequivocal way there was a sense of vindication about our long-standing fetish for guns, not to say pride in it, too. "Bang! Bang! You're dead," returns to me from that time without the least speck of friction or reflection. When we weren't playing War, or Cowboys and Indians, or Cops and Robbers, we were reading War Comics (from which you could order for less than a dollar little cardboard chests of plastic weaponry and soldiers to stage your own debacles), or Westerns, or listening to *The Lone Ranger* and *Richard Diamond, Private Detective* and other radio shows—all of which openly glorified guns, and the more powerful the better.

7 My fantasies, when I was frustrated, angry, or depressed, were rife with firearms of the most lethal sort, flying shot, endless rounds of shattering ammunition; the enemy bodies blown away and left in bloody tableaux. And any gun was an engineered instrument—much more far-ranging and accurate than bows and arrows or slingshots—that detached you from your destructiveness or crime or sometimes even from being a source of death.

8 I've only owned three firearms in my life as an adult. Two I brought back to the shops within a week after I'd bought them, realizing I was trying to reach out in some archaic way, and the limits to my maturity and imagination that that implied, plus the bother to my daughter of their powing sounds; and the third, the .22, after trembling over it a few years and using it to shoot holes in the floor to enact a between-the-legs suicide, I gave away. To my younger brother. Who was initiated into the buck-fever fraternity in the forests of northern Wisconsin when he was an adolescent by a seasoned local who said to him, "If you see anything moving out there tomorrow, boy, *shoot* it. You can check out later what it is. Nobody gives a shit up here." And on a hunting trip years later, an acquaintance from the village my brother lived in then, a lawyer, was shot in the head with a deer rifle, but somehow survived. And even went back to practicing law. It was thought to be an accident at first, what with all the bullets embroidering the air that day, and then rumor had it that another member of the party hunting on adjoining land, an old friend of the lawyer's, had found out a week before the season that the lawyer had been having his wife for a while. The two men were polite enough to one another in the village after that, my brother said, but not such good friends, of course. Just balanced, justice-balanced males.

9 For months and seasons after I'd shot the crippled doe, every time we passed the field in our Jeep, my daughter would say, "Here's where Daddy shooted the deer." In exactly that manner, using the tone and

detachment of a storyteller or tourist guide. And I'd glance into the rearview mirror and see her in her car seat, studying the hill with troubled and sympathetic eyes. One day I stopped. "Does it bother you so much that I shot it?" I asked. There was no answer, and then I saw that she was nodding her head, her gaze still fixed on the hill.

10 "Well, if I wouldn't have, it could have suffered a long time. You saw how badly hurt it was. It couldn't have lived that way. I didn't like doing it, either, but it was best for the deer. When I told the game warden about it, he even thanked me and said, 'Leave it for the foxes and crows.' They have to eat, too, you know, and maybe the deer made the winter easier for them." And I thought, Oh, what a self-justifying fool and ass and pig you are. Why didn't you leave her at home? Why didn't you go to the farmer whose land the deer was on, which would have been as quick or quicker than going back for the .22—a man who would have had a deer rifle, or at least a shotgun with rifled slugs, and would have put the deer away with dispatch in one shot and might have even salvaged the hide and venison? And who could say it wouldn't have lived, the way some animals do after tearing or chewing off a limb caught in a trap? Who was to presume it wouldn't have preferred to die a slow death in the brush, looking out over the pasture, as the crimson stain widening in the snow drew away and dimmed its colorless world until all went black? Why not admit that I was a common backcountry American and, like most men of my mold, had used an arsenal of firearms to kill and was as excited about putting away a deer as moved by compassion for its suffering? Then again, given my daughter's understanding and the person I am, perhaps she sensed this, and more.

11 I once choked a chicken to death. It was my only barefaced, not to say barehanded, confrontation with death and the killer in me and happened on my grandparents' farm. I couldn't have been more than nine or ten and no firearms were included or necessary. I was on my knees and the chicken fluttered its outstretched wings with the last of the outraged protest. I gripped, beyond release, above its swollen crop, its beak gaping, translucent eyelids sliding up and down. An old molting specimen. A hen, most likely; a worse loss, because of eggs, than a capon or cock. My grandfather, who was widely traveled and world-wise, in his eighties then, and had just started using a cane from earlier times, came tapping at that moment around the corner of the chicken coop and saw what I was doing and started gagging at the hideousness of it, did a quick assisted spin away and never again, hours later nor for the rest of his life, for that matter, ever mentioned the homicidal incident to me. Keeping his silence, he seemed to understand; and yet whenever I'm invaded by the incident, the point of it seems to be his turning away from me.

12 My wife once said she felt I wanted to kill her. A common enough feeling among long-married couples, I'm sure, and not restricted to

either sex (I know, for instance, that there were times when she wanted to kill me), but perhaps with firsthand experience infusing the feeling, it became too much to endure. I now live in New York City, where the clock keeps moving toward my suitcase, alone, and she and my daughter in the Midwest. The city has changed in the seven years since the three of us lived here together. There are more frivolous and not-so-frivolous wares—silk kerchiefs, necklaces and rings, roach clips, rolling papers, socks, a display of Florida coral across a convertible top, books of every kind—being sold in the streets than anybody can remember seeing in recent years. People openly saying that soon it will be like the Thirties once were, with us *all* in the streets selling our apples, or whatever, or engaged in a tacit and friendly sort of gangsterism to survive. Outside my window, a spindly deciduous species has a sign strung on supporting posts on either side of it, in careful hand-lettering, that reads, THIS TREE GIVES OXYGEN. GIVE IT LOVE. More dogs in the streets and parks than they'd remembered, and more canine offal sending up its open-ended odor; at least half the population giving up cigarette smoking, at last, for good, they say, and many actually are. The mazed feeling of most everywhere now of being in the midst of a slowly forging and forgiving reciprocity. An air of bravura about most everybody in maintaining one's best face, with a few changes of costumish clothing to reflect it, perhaps, no matter what might yet evolve. A unisex barbershop or boutique on nearly every other block, it seems.

13 Sometimes I think this is where I really belong. Then a man is gunned down in a neighborhood bar I used to drop into and the next day a mob leader assassinated, supposedly by members of his own mob. *Perhaps this is where I'm most at home,* I equivocate again and have an image of myself in a Stetson traveling down a crosstown street at a fast-paced and pigeon-toed shamble toward the setting sun (setting this far east, but not over my wife and daughter yet), my eyes cast down and shoulders forward, hands deep in my empty Levi pockets, a suspect closet-faggot-cowboy occasionally whistled at by queens.°

14 I won't (and can't) refute my heritage, but I doubt that I'll use a firearm again, or, if I do, only in the direst sort of emergency. Which I say to protect my flanks. The bloody, gun-filled fantasies seldom return now, and when they do they're reversed: I'm the one being shot, or shot at, or think I am.

---

[13] **queens:** effeminate homosexuals

STUDY QUESTIONS

1. What expectations did you experience on seeing Woiwode's title? Did the essay match those expectations? What risks does a writer run, and what possible advantages does he or she stand to gain, in choosing a title that gives so little indication of the essay's actual emphasis?
2. Why does Woiwode begin (paragraphs 1–4) with the episode of his killing the wounded deer? Suppose, as a contrast, he had begun by telling us that the values he had held in his boyhood have been called into question by a changed climate of opinion. How would his relation to his readers have been affected by that change in rhetorical strategy?
3. In paragraph 3 Woiwode says that, as he was about to finish off the wounded deer, he saw himself as the deer must have been seeing *him*. Reread that paragraph and then ask yourself how it connects with other parts of the essay, including its first and last sentences.
4. How would you characterize Woiwode's total attitude toward guns? (If your answer is a simple one, reread the essay.)
5. What is the importance of Woiwode's daughter in the thematic development of this essay? You will find pertinent information in paragraphs 1, 8–10, and 12–13.
6. Why does Woiwode go back to the episode of his strangling the chicken (paragraph 11)? What light does that episode throw on his assessment of himself?
7. Reread the complex and unanticipated paragraph 12. What would you say is its function in the total strategy of Woiwode's essay? How does it change our way of thinking about the author who has handled so many guns?
8. In paragraph 13 Woiwode tells us about a fantasy of himself that he sometimes entertains ("myself in a Stetson . . ."). Look carefully at that paragraph and think about the relation of Woiwode's fantasy to everything we have been told about him. Does the fantasy come as a shock? In what sense does it belong in an essay entitled "Guns"?
9. If you were asked to choose between the following attempts to characterize Woiwode's main theme, which one would you pick, and why? (a) gun control; (b) country values versus city values; (c) changing social norms; (d) self-hatred. What case could be made for each of the options you have ruled out?
10. If this is indeed an essay of comparison and contrast, it is one in which the two terms are brought together rather late, and with very little drawing of explicit conclusions. What *is* the main difference that Woiwode invites us to see, and how has he convinced us that it matters?

Daniel J. Boorstin

Daniel J. Boorstin, currently Librarian of Congress and professor of history at the University of Chicago, has also been director of the Smithsonian Institution's National Museum of History and Technology. His books include the prizewinning trilogy *The Americans* and *The Image; Or, What Happened to the American Dream* (1962), from which the present selection is excerpted.

THE PSEUDO-EVENT*

ADMIRING FRIEND:
"My, that's a beautiful baby you have there!"
MOTHER:
"Oh, that's nothing—you should see his photograph!"

1 The simplest of our extravagant expectations concerns the amount of novelty in the world. There was a time when the reader of an unexciting newspaper would remark, "How dull is the world today!" Nowadays he says, "What a dull newspaper!" When the first American newspaper, Benjamin Harris' *Publick Occurrences Both Forreign and Domestick,* appeared in Boston on September 25, 1690, it promised to furnish news regularly once a month. But, the editor explained, it might appear oftener "if any Glut of Occurrences happen." The responsibility for making news was entirely God's—or the Devil's. The newsman's task was only to give "an Account of such considerable things as have arrived unto our Notice."

2 Although the theology behind this way of looking at events soon dissolved, this view of the news lasted longer. "The skilled and faithful journalist," James Parton observed in 1866, "recording with exactness and power the thing that has come to pass, is Providence addressing men." The story is told of a Southern Baptist clergyman before the Civil War who used to say, when a newspaper was brought in the room, "Be kind enough to let me have it a few minutes, till I see how the Supreme Being is governing the world." Charles A. Dana, one of the great American editors of the nineteenth century, once defended his extensive reporting of crime in the New York *Sun* by saying, "I have always felt that whatever the Divine Providence permitted to occur I was not too proud to report."

3 Of course, this is now a very old-fashioned way of thinking. Our

---

*Title chosen by editor

current point of view is better expressed in the definition by Arthur MacEwen, whom William Randolph Hearst made his first editor of the San Francisco *Examiner:* "News is anything that makes a reader say, 'Gee whiz!' " Or, put more soberly, "News is whatever a good editor chooses to print."

4 We need not be theologians to see that we have shifted responsibility for making the world interesting from God to the newspaperman. We used to believe there were only so many "events" in the world. If there were not many intriguing or startling occurrences, it was no fault of the reporter. He could not be expected to report what did not exist.

5 Within the last hundred years, however, and especially in the twentieth century, all this has changed. We expect the papers to be full of news. If there is no news visible to the naked eye, or to the average citizen, we still expect it to be there for the enterprising newsman. The successful reporter is one who can find a story, even if there is no earthquake or assassination or civil war. If he cannot find a story, then he must make one—by the questions he asks of public figures, by the surprising human interest he unfolds from some commonplace event, or by "the news behind the news." If all this fails, then he must give us a "think piece"—an embroidering of well-known facts, or a speculation about startling things to come.

6 This change in our attitude toward "news" is not merely a basic fact about the history of American newspapers. It is a symptom of a revolutionary change in our attitude toward what happens in the world, how much of it is new, and surprising, and important. Toward how life can be enlivened, toward our power and the power of those who inform and educate and guide us, to provide synthetic happenings to make up for the lack of spontaneous events. Demanding more than the world can give us, we require that something be fabricated to make up for the world's deficiency. This is only one example of our demand for illusions.

7 Many historical forces help explain how we have come to our present immoderate hopes. But there can be no doubt about what we now expect, nor that it is immoderate. Every American knows the anticipation with which he picks up his morning newspaper at breakfast or opens his evening paper before dinner, or listens to the newscasts every hour on the hour as he drives across country, or watches his favorite commentator on television interpret the events of the day. Many enterprising Americans are now at work to help us satisfy these expectations. Many might be put out of work if we should suddenly moderate our expectations. But it is we who keep them in business and demand that they fill our consciousness with novelties, that they play God for us.

8 The new kind of synthetic novelty which has flooded our experience I will call "pseudo-events." The common prefix "pseudo" comes from the Greek word meaning false, or intended to deceive. Before I recall the historical forces which have made these pseudo-events possi-

ble, have increased the supply of them and the demand for them, I will give a commonplace example.

9 The owners of a hotel, in an illustration offered by Edward L. Bernays in his pioneer *Crystallizing Public Opinion* (1923), consult a public relations counsel. They ask how to increase their hotel's prestige and so improve their business. In less sophisticated times, the answer might have been to hire a new chef, to improve the plumbing, to paint the rooms, or to install a crystal chandelier in the lobby. The public relations counsel's technique is more indirect. He proposes that the management stage a celebration of the hotel's thirtieth anniversary. A committee is formed, including a prominent banker, a leading society matron, a well-known lawyer, an influential preacher, and an "event" is planned (say a banquet) to call attention to the distinguished service the hotel has been rendering the community. The celebration is held, photographs are taken, the occasion is widely reported, and the object is accomplished. Now this occasion is a pseudo-event, and will illustrate all the essential features of pseudo-events.

10 This celebration, we can see at the outset, is somewhat—but not entirely—misleading. Presumably the public relations counsel would not have been able to form his committee of prominent citizens if the hotel had not actually been rendering service to the community. On the other hand, if the hotel's services had been all that important, instigation by public relations counsel might not have been necessary. Once the celebration has been held, the celebration itself becomes evidence that the hotel really is a distinguished institution. The occasion actually gives the hotel the prestige to which it is pretending.

11 It is obvious, too, that the value of such a celebration to the owners depends on its being photographed and reported in newspapers, magazines, newsreels, on radio, and over television. It is the report that gives the event its force in the minds of potential customers. The power to make a reportable event is thus the power to make experience. One is reminded of Napoleon's apocryphal reply to his general, who objected that circumstances were unfavorable to a proposed campaign: "Bah, I make circumstances!" The modern public relations counsel—and he is, of course, only one of many twentieth-century creators of pseudo-events—has come close to fulfilling Napoleon's idle boast. "The counsel on public relations," Mr. Bernays explains, "not only knows what news value is, but knowing it, he is in a position to *make news happen.* He is a creator of events."

12 The intriguing feature of the modern situation, however, comes precisely from the fact that the modern news makers are not God. The news they make happen, the events they create, are somehow not quite real. There remains a tantalizing difference between man-made and God-made events.

13 A pseudo-event, then, is a happening that possesses the following characteristics:

14 (1) It is not spontaneous, but comes about because someone has planned, planted, or incited it. Typically, it is not a train wreck or an earthquake, but an interview.

15 (2) It is planted primarily (not always exclusively) for the immediate purpose of being reported or reproduced. Therefore, its occurrence is arranged for the convenience of the reporting or reproducing media. Its success is measured by how widely it is reported. Time relations in it are commonly fictitious or factitious; the announcement is given out in advance "for future release" and written as if the event had occurred in the past. The question, "Is it real?" is less important than, "Is it newsworthy?"

16 (3) Its relation to the underlying reality of the situation is ambiguous. Its interest arises largely from this very ambiguity. Concerning a pseudo-event the question, "What does it mean?" has a new dimension. While the news interest in a train wreck is in *what* happened and in the real consequences, the interest in an interview is always, in a sense, in *whether* it really happened and in what might have been the motives. Did the statement really mean what it said? Without some of this ambiguity a pseudo-event cannot be very interesting.

17 (4) Usually it is intended to be a self-fulfilling prophecy. The hotel's thirtieth-anniversary celebration, by saying that the hotel is a distinguished institution, actually makes it one.

18 A perfect example of how pseudo-events can dominate is the recent popularity of the quiz show format. Its original appeal came less from the fact that such shows were tests of intelligence (or of dissimulation) than from the fact that the situations were elaborately contrived —with isolation booths, armed bank guards, and all the rest—and they purported to inform the public.

19 The application of the quiz show format to the so-called "Great Debates" between Presidential candidates in the election of 1960 is only another example. These four campaign programs, pompously and self-righteously advertised by the broadcasting networks, were remarkably successful in reducing great national issues to trivial dimensions. With appropriate vulgarity, they might have been called the $400,000 Question (Prize: a $100,000-a-year job for four years). They were a clinical example of the pseudo-event, of how it is made, why it appeals, and of its consequences for democracy in America.

20 In origin the Great Debates were confusedly collaborative between politicians and news makers. Public interest centered around the pseudo-event itself: the lighting, make-up, ground rules, whether notes would be allowed, etc. Far more interest was shown in the performance than in what was said. The pseudo-events spawned in turn by the Great

Debates were numberless. People who had seen the shows read about them the more avidly, and listened eagerly for interpretations by news commentators. Representatives of both parties made "statements" on the probable effects of the debates. Numerous interviews and discussion programs were broadcast exploring their meaning. Opinion polls kept us informed on the nuances of our own and other people's reactions. Topics of speculation multiplied. Even the question whether there should be a fifth debate became for a while a lively "issue."

21 The drama of the situation was mostly specious, or at least had an extremely ambiguous relevance to the main (but forgotten) issue: which participant was better qualified for the Presidency. Of course, a man's ability, while standing under klieg lights, without notes, to answer in two and a half minutes a question kept secret until that moment, had only the most dubious relevance—if any at all—to his real qualifications to make deliberate Presidential decisions on long-standing public questions after being instructed by a corps of advisers. The great Presidents in our history (with the possible exception of F.D.R.) would have done miserably; but our most notorious demagogues would have shone. A number of exciting pseudo-events were created—for example, the Quemoy-Matsu issue.° But that, too, was a good example of a pseudo-event: it was created to be reported, it concerned a then-quiescent problem, and it put into the most factitious and trivial terms the great and real issue of our relation to Communist China.

22 The television medium shapes this new kind of political quiz-show spectacular in many crucial ways. Theodore H. White has proven this with copious detail in his *The Making of the President: 1960* (1961). All the circumstances of this particular competition for votes were far more novel than the old word "debate" and the comparisons with the Lincoln-Douglas Debates suggested. Kennedy's great strength in the critical first debate, according to White, was that he was in fact not "debating" at all, but was seizing the opportunity to address the whole nation; while Nixon stuck close to the issues raised by his opponent, rebutting them one by one. Nixon, moreover, suffered a handicap that was serious only on television: he has a light, naturally transparent skin. On an ordinary camera that takes pictures by optical projection, this skin photographs well. But a television camera projects electronically, by an "image-orthicon tube" which has an x-ray effect. This camera penetrates Nixon's transparent skin and brings out (even just after a shave) the tiniest hair growing in the follicles beneath the surface. For the decisive first program Nixon wore a make-up called "Lazy Shave" which was ineffective under these conditions. He there-

---

[21] **Quemoy-Matsu issue:** Candidates Nixon and Kennedy debated whether these two islands near the Chinese mainland should be defended as territory of the Nationalist Chinese regime centered in Taiwan.

fore looked haggard and heavy-bearded by contrast to Kennedy, who looked pert and clean-cut.

23 This greatest opportunity in American history to educate the voters by debating the large issues of the campaign failed. The main reason, as White points out, was the compulsions of the medium. "The nature of both TV and radio is that they abhor silence and 'dead time.' All TV and radio discussion programs are compelled to snap question and answer back and forth as if the contestants were adversaries in an intellectual tennis match. Although every experienced newspaperman and inquirer knows that the most thoughtful and responsive answers to any difficult question come after long pause, and that the longer the pause the more illuminating the thought that follows it, nonetheless the electronic media cannot bear to suffer a pause of more than five seconds; a pause of thirty seconds of dead time on air seems interminable. Thus, snapping their two-and-a-half-minute answers back and forth, both candidates could only react for the cameras and the people, they could not think." Whenever either candidate found himself touching a thought too large for two-minute exploration, he quickly retreated. Finally the television-watching voter was left to judge, not on issues explored by thoughtful men, but on the relative capacity of the two candidates to perform under television stress.

24 Pseudo-events thus lead to emphasis on pseudo-qualifications. Again the self-fulfilling prophecy. If we test Presidential candidates by their talents on TV quiz performances, we will, of course, choose presidents for precisely these qualifications. In a democracy, reality tends to conform to the pseudo-event. Nature imitates art.

25 We are frustrated by our very efforts publicly to unmask the pseudo-event. Whenever we describe the lighting, the make-up, the studio setting, the rehearsals, etc., we simply arouse more interest. One newsman's interpretation makes us more eager to hear another's. One commentator's speculation that the debates may have little significance makes us curious to hear whether another commentator disagrees.

26 Pseudo-events do, of course, increase our illusion of grasp on the world, what some have called the American illusion of omnipotence. Perhaps, we come to think, the world's problems can really be settled by "statements," by "Summit" meetings, by a competition of "prestige," by overshadowing images, and by political quiz shows.

27 Once we have tasted the charm of pseudo-events, we are tempted to believe they are the only important events. Our progress poisons the sources of our experience. And the poison tastes so sweet that it spoils our appetite for plain fact. Our seeming ability to satisfy our exaggerated expectations makes us forget that they are exaggerated.

STUDY QUESTIONS

1. What is the effect of Boorstin's epigraph (quotation preceding his first paragraph)? How does the epigraph serve to govern our response to paragraphs 1 and 2?
2. What, in Boorstin's view, is the essential difference between the older and more recent conceptions of news? Do you think it would be possible for us to restore the older conception? What obstacles would such a project face?
3. Why does Boorstin give his example of the hotel's anniversary celebration (paragraphs 9–11) *before* listing the features of a typical pseudo-event?
4. What is a self-fulfilling prophecy (paragraph 17), and how is the "self-fulfilling" component essential to a pseudo-event?
5. Why does Boorstin enclose the name *Great Debates* (paragraph 19) in quotation marks? Relate your answer to the discussion of those debates in following paragraphs.
6. At the end of paragraph 19, Boorstin uses the "Great Debates" as an illustration of the "consequences for democracy in America" implied by pseudo-events. What do those consequences appear to be? Do you agree with Boorstin's assessment?

Enrique Hank Lopez

Enrique Hank Lopez is a lawyer who now lives in New York. He is a coeditor of *Dialogos,* a Mexican literary journal. "Back to Bachimba" first appeared in *Horizon* in 1967.

BACK TO BACHIMBA

1 I am a *pocho* from Bachimba, a rather small Mexican village in the state of Chihuahua, where my father fought with the army of Pancho Villa.° He was, in fact, the only private in Villa's army.

2 *Pocho* is ordinarily a derogatory term in Mexico (to define it succinctly, a *pocho* is a Mexican slob who has pretensions of being a

[1] **Pancho Villa:** Francisco Villa (1877–1923), Mexican outlaw and revolutionary who fought against both the Mexican government's troops, or *federales* (paragraph 3), and an American expeditionary force led by General John J. Pershing (paragraph 17)

gringo sonofabitch), but I use it in a very special sense. To me that word has come to mean "uprooted Mexican," and that's what I have been all my life. Though my entire upbringing and education took place in the United States, I have never felt completely American; and when I am in Mexico, I sometimes feel like a displaced gringo with a curiously Mexican name—Enrique Preciliano Lopez y Martinez de Sepulveda de Sapien (. . . de Quien-sabe-quien°). One might conclude that I'm either a schizo-cultural Mexican or a cultured schizoid American.

3 In any event, the schizo-ing began a long time ago, when my father and many of Pancho Villa's troops fled across the border to escape the oncoming *federales* who eventually defeated Villa. My mother and I, traveling across the hot desert plains in a buckboard wagon, joined my father in El Paso, Texas, a few days after his hurried departure. With more and more Villistas swarming into El Paso every day, it was quickly apparent that jobs would be exceedingly scarce and insecure; so my parents packed our few belongings and we took the first available bus to Denver. My father had hoped to move to Chicago because the name sounded so Mexican, but my mother's meager savings were hardly enough to buy tickets for Colorado.

4 There we moved into a ghetto of Spanish-speaking residents who chose to call themselves Spanish-Americans and resented the sudden migration of their brethren from Mexico, whom they sneeringly called *surumatos* (slang for "southerners"). These so-called Spanish-Americans claimed direct descent from the original conquistadores° of Spain. They also insisted that they had *never* been Mexicans, since their region of New Spain (later annexed to the United States) was never a part of Mexico. But what they claimed most vociferously—and erroneously—was an absence of Indian ancestry. It made no difference that any objective observer could see by merely looking at them the results of considerable fraternization between the conquering Spaniards and the Comanche and Navaho women who crossed their paths. Still, these *manitos,*° as they were snidely labeled by the *surumatos,* stubbornly refused to be identified with Mexico, and would actually fight anyone who called them Mexican. So intense was this intergroup rivalry that the bitterest "race riots" I have ever witnessed—and engaged in—were between the look-alike, talk-alike *surumatos* and *manitos* who lived near Denver's Curtis Park. In retrospect the harsh conflicts between us were all the more silly and self-defeating when one recalls

---

[2] **de Quien-sabe-quien:** (Span.) of who-knows-who; i.e., descended from still further unidentified ancestors

[4] **conquistadores:** (Span.) conquerors; specifically, the sixteenth-century Spanish conquerors of Mexico and Peru

manitos: (Span.) "little hands"

that we were all lumped together as "spiks" and "greasers" by the Anglo-Saxon community.

5 Predictably enough, we *surumatos* began huddling together in a subneighborhood within the larger ghetto, and it was there that I became painfully aware that my father had been the only private in Pancho Villa's army. Most of my friends were the sons of captains, colonels, majors, and even generals, though a few fathers were admittedly mere sergeants and corporals. My father alone had been a lowly private in that famous Division del Norte. Naturally I developed a most painful complex, which led me to all sorts of compensatory fibs. During one brief spell I fancied my father as a member of the dreaded *los dorados,* the "golden ones," who were Villa's favorite henchmen. (Later I was to learn that my father's cousin, Martin Lopez, was a genuine and quite notorious *dorado.*) But all my inventions were quickly un-invented by my very own father, who seemed to take a perverse delight in being Pancho's only private.

6 No doubt my chagrin was accentuated by the fact that Pancho Villa's exploits were a constant topic of conversation in our household. My entire childhood seems to be shadowed by his presence. At our dinner table, almost every night, we would listen to endlessly repeated accounts of this battle, that stratagem, or some great act of Robin Hood kindness by *el centauro del norte.*° I remember how angry my parents were when they saw Wallace Beery in *Viva Villa!* "Garbage by stupid gringos" they called it. They were particularly offended by the sweaty, unshaven sloppiness of Beery's portrayal. "Pancho Villa was clean and orderly, no matter how much he chased after women. This man's a dirty swine."

7 As if to deepen our sense of *Villismo,*° my parents also taught us "Adelita" and *"Se llevaron el cañon para Bachimba"* ("They took the cannons to Bachimba"), the two most famous songs of the Mexican revolution. Some twenty years later (during my stint at Harvard Law School), while strolling along the Charles River, I would find myself softly singing *"Se llevaron el cañon para Bachimba, para Bachimba, para Bachimba"* over and over again. That's all I could remember of that poignant rebel song. Though I had been born there, I had always regarded "Bachimba" as a fictitious, made-up, Lewis Carroll° kind of word. So that eight years ago, when I first returned to Mexico, I was literally stunned when I came to a crossroad south of Chihuahua and saw an old road marker: "Bachimba 18 km." Then it really exists—I shouted inwardly—Bachimba is a real town! Swinging onto the narrow, poorly paved road, I gunned the motor and sped toward the

---

6 **el centauro del Norte:** (Span.) the centaur (man-horse) of the north

7 **Villismo:** devotion to Pancho Villa

Lewis Carroll: Charles Dodgson (1832–1898), British mathematician and author of *Alice in Wonderland*

town I'd been singing about since infancy. It turned out to be a quiet, dusty village with a bleak worn-down plaza that was surrounded by nondescript buildings of uncertain vintage.

8 Aside from the songs about Bachimba and Adelita and all the folk tales about Villa's guerrilla fighters, my early years were strongly influenced by our neighborhood celebrations of Mexico's two most important patriotic events: Mexican Independence Day on September 16, and the anniversary of the battle of Puebla° on May 5. On those two dates Mexicans all over the world are likely to become extremely chauvinistic. In Denver we would stage annual parades that included three or four floats skimpily decorated with crepe-paper streamers, a small band, several adults in threadbare battle dress, and hundreds of kids marching in wild disorder. It was during one of these parades—I was ten years old then—that I was seized with acute appendicitis and had to be rushed to a hospital. The doctor subsequently told my mother that I had made a long, impassioned speech about the early revolutionist Miguel Hidalgo° while the anesthetic was taking hold, and she explained with pardonable pride that it was the speech I was to make at Turner Hall that evening. Mine was one of the twenty-three *discursos*° scheduled on the postparade program, a copy of which my mother still retains. My only regret was missing the annual *discurso* of Don Miguel Gomez, my godfather, a deep-throated orator who would always climax his speech by falling to his knees and dramatically kissing the floor, almost weeping as he loudly proclaimed: "*Ay, Mexico! Beso tu tierra, tu mero corazón*" ("Ah, Mexico! I kiss your sacred soil, the very heart of you"). He gave the same oration for seventeen years, word for word and gesture for gesture, and it never failed to bring tears to his eyes. But not once did he return to Chihuahua, even for a brief visit.

9 My personal Mexican-ness eventually produced serious problems for me. Upon entering grade school I learned English rapidly and rather well, always ranking either first or second in my class; yet the hard core of me remained stubbornly Mexican. This chauvinism may have been a reaction to the constant racial prejudice we encountered on all sides. The neighborhood cops were always running us off the streets and calling us "dirty greasers," and most of our teachers frankly regarded us as totally inferior. I still remember the galling disdain of my sixth-grade teacher, whose constant mimicking of our heavily accented speech drove me to a desperate study of *Webster's Dictionary* in the hope of acquiring a vocabulary larger than hers. Sadly enough, I succeeded

---

[8] **battle of Puebla:** famous victory of Mexican over French forces, 1862
Miguel Hidalgo: (1753–1811) Mexican priest, patriot, and revolutionist
discursos: speeches

only too well, and for the next few years I spoke the most ridiculous high-flown rhetoric in the Denver public schools. One of my favorite words was "indubitably," and it must have driven everyone mad. I finally got rid of my accent by constantly reciting "Peter Piper picked a peck of pickled peppers" with little round pebbles in my mouth. Somewhere I had read about Demosthenes.°

10 During this phase of my childhood the cultural tug of war known as "Americanization" almost pulled me apart. There were moments when I would identify completely with the gringo world (what could have been more American than my earnest high-voiced portrayal of George Washington, however ridiculous the cotton wig my mother had fashioned for me?); then quite suddenly I would feel so acutely Mexican that I would stammer over the simplest English phrase. I was so ready to take offense at the slightest slur against Mexicans that I would imagine prejudice where none existed. But on other occasions, in full confidence of my belonging, I would venture forth into social areas that I should have realized were clearly forbidden to little *chicanos* from Curtis Park. The inevitable rebuffs would leave me floundering in self-pity; it was small comfort to know that other minority groups suffered even worse rebuffs than we did.

11 The only non-Mexican boy on our street was a Negro named Leroy Logan, who was probably my closest childhood friend. Leroy was the best athlete, the best whistler, the best liar, the best horseshoe player, the best marble shooter, the best mumblety-pegger, and the best shoplifter in our neighborhood. He was also my "partner," and I thus entitled myself to a fifty-fifty share of all his large triumphs and petty thefts. Because he considered "Mexican" a derogatory word bordering on obscenity, Leroy would pronounce it "Mesican" so as to soften its harshness. But once in a while, when he'd get angry with me, he would call me a "lousy Mesican greasy spik" with the most extraordinarily effective hissing one can imagine. And I'm embarrassed to admit that I would retaliate by calling him "alligator bait." As a matter of fact, just after I had returned from the hospital, he came to visit me, and I thoughtlessly greeted him with a flippant "Hi, alligator ba———" I never finished the phrase because Leroy whacked me on the stomach with a Ping-pong paddle and rushed out of my house with great, sobbing anger.

12 Weeks later, when we had re-established a rather cool rapport, I tried to make up for my stupid insult by helping him steal cabbages from the vegetable trucks that rumbled through our neighborhood on their way to the produce markets. They would come down Larimer

---

[9] **Demosthenes:** (384–322 B.C.) Athenian orator and statesman who overcame a speech defect by speaking with pebbles in his mouth

Street in the early dawn, and Leroy and I would sneak up behind them at the 27th Street stop sign, where they were forced to pause for cross traffic. Then Leroy, with a hooked pole he had invented, would stab the top cabbages and roll them off the truck. I would be waiting below to catch them with an open gunny sack. Our system was fabulously successful for a while, and we found a ready market for the stolen goods; but one morning, as I started to unfurl my sack, a fairly large cabbage conked me on the head. Screaming with pain, I lunged at Leroy and tried to bite him. He, laughing all the while—it was obviously a funny scene—glided out of my reach, and finally ran into a nearby alley. We never engaged in commercial affairs thereafter.

13 Still and all, I remember him with great affection and a touch of sadness. I say sadness because eventually Leroy was to suffer the misery of being an outsider in an already outside ghetto. As he grew older, it was apparent that he longed to be a Mexican, that he felt terribly dark and alone. "Sometimes," he would tell me, "I feel like my damn skin's too tight, like I'm gonna bust out of it." One cold February night I found him in the coal shed behind Pacheco's store, desperately scraping his forearm with sandpaper, the hurt tears streaming down his face. "I got to get this off, man. I can't stand all this blackness." We stood there quietly staring at the floor for a long, anguished moment, both of us miserable beyond word or gesture. Finally he drew a deep breath, blew his nose loudly, and mumbled half audibly, "Man, you sure lucky to be a Mesican."

14 Not long after this incident Leroy moved out of Denver to live with relatives in Georgia. When I saw him off at the bus station, he grabbed my shoulder and whispered huskily, "You gonna miss me, man. You watch what I tellya." "Indubitably," I said. "Aw, man, cut that stuff. You the most fancy-pants Mesican I know." Those were his last words to me, and they caused a considerable dent in my ego. Not enough, however, to diminish my penchant for fancy language. The dictionary continued to be my comic book well into high school.

15 Speaking of language, I am reminded of a most peculiar circumstance: almost every Mexican-American lawyer that I've ever met speaks English with a noticeable Spanish accent, this despite the fact that they have all been born, reared, and educated exclusively in America. Of the forty-eight lawyers I have in mind, only three of us are free of any accent. Needless to say our "cultural drag" has been weighty and persistent. And one must presume that our ethnic hyphens shall be with us for many years to come.

16 My own Mexican-ness, after years of decline at Harvard University, suddenly burst forth again when I returned to Chihuahua and stumbled on the town of Bachimba. I had long conversations with an uncle I'd never met before, my father's younger brother, Ramon. It was Tio Ramon who chilled my spine with eyewitness stories about Pancho Villa's legendary *dorados,* one of whom was Martin Lopez. "He was

your second cousin. The bravest young buck in Villa's army. And he became a *dorado* when he was scarcely seventeen years old because he dared to defy Pancho Villa himself. As your papa may have told you, Villa had a bad habit of burying treasure up in the mountains and also burying the man he took with him to dig the hole for it. Well, one day he chose Martin Lopez to go with him. Deep in the mountains they went, near Parral. And when they got to a suitably lonely place, Pancho Villa told him to dig a hole with pick and shovel. Then, when Martin had dug down to his waist, Villa leveled a gun at the boy. "Say your prayers, *muchacho.*° You shall stay here with the gold—forever." But Martin had come prepared. In his large right boot he had a gun, and when he rose from his bent position, he was pointing that gun at Villa. They stood there, both ready to fire, for several seconds, and finally Don Pancho started to laugh in that wonderful way of his. "*Bravo, bravo, muchacho!* You've got more guts than a man. Get out of that hole, boy. I need you for my *dorados.*"

17 Tio Ramon's eyes were wet with pride. "But what is more important, he died with great valor. Two years later, after he had terrorized the *federales* and Pershing's gringo soldiers, he was finally wounded and captured here in Bachimba. It was a bad wound in his leg, finally turning to gangrene. Then one Sunday morning they hauled Martin Lopez and three other prisoners to the plaza. One by one they executed the three lesser prisoners against that wall. I was up on the church tower watching it all. Finally it was your uncle's turn. They dragged him off the buckboard wagon and handed him his crutches. Slowly, painfully, he hobbled to the wall and stood there. Very straight he stood. 'Do you have any last words?' said the captain of the firing squad. With great pride Martin tossed his crutches aside and stood very tall on his one good leg. 'Give me, you yellow bastards, give me a gun—and I'll show you who is the man among . . .' Eight bullets crashed into his chest and face, and I never heard that final word. That was your second cousin. You would have been proud to know him."

18 As I listened to Tio Ramon's soft nostalgic voice that evening, there in the sputtering light of the kerosene lamp on his back patio, I felt as intensely Mexican as I shall ever feel.

19 But not for long. Within six weeks I was destined to feel *less* Mexican than I had ever felt. The scene of my trauma was the Centro Mexicano de Escritores,° where the finest young writers of Mexico met regularly to discuss works in progress and to engage in erudite literary and philosophical discussions. Week after week I sat among them, dumb struck by my inadequacy in Spanish and my total ignorance of

---

16 **muchacho:** (Span.) boy

19 **Centro Mexicano de Escritores:** Mexican Writers' Center

their whole frame of reference. How could I have possibly imagined that I was Mexican? Those conversations were a dense tangle of local and private allusions, and the few threads I could grasp only magnified my ignorance. The novelist Juan Rulfo was then reading the initial drafts of his *Pedro Páramo,* later to be acclaimed the best avant-garde fiction in Mexican literature. Now that I have soaked myself in the *ambiance* of Mexico, Rulfo's novel intrigues me beyond measure; but when he first read it at the Centro, he might just as well have been reading "Jabberwocky"° in Swahili for all I understood of it. And because all of the other Mexican writers knew and greatly appreciated *Páramo,* I could only assume that I was really "too gringo" to comprehend it. For this reason, I, a person with no great talent for reticence, never opened my mouth at the Centro. In fact, I was so shell-shocked by those sessions that I even found it difficult to converse with my housekeeper about such simple matters as dirty laundry or the loose doorknob in the bathroom.

20 Can any of us really go home again? I, for one, am convinced that I have no true home, that I must reconcile myself to a schizo-cultural limbo, with a mere hyphen to provide some slight cohesion between my split selves. This inevitable splitting is a plague and a pleasure. Some mornings as I glide down the Paseo de la Reforma,° perhaps the most beautiful boulevard in the world, I am suddenly angered by the *machismo,* or aggressive maleness, of Mexican drivers who crowd and bully their screeching machines through dense traffic. What terrible insecurity, what awful dread of emasculation, produces such assertive bully-boy conduct behind a steering wheel? Whatever the reasons, there is a part of me that can never accept this much-celebrated *machismo.* Nor can I accept the exaggerated nationalism one so frequently encounters in the press, on movie screens, over the radio, in daily conversations—that shrill barrage of slogans proclaiming that "there is only one Mexico."

21 Recently, when I expressed these views to an old friend, he smiled quite knowingly: "Let's face it, Hank, you're not really a Mexican—despite that long, comical name of yours. You're an American through and through." But that, of course, is a minority view and almost totally devoid of realism. One could just as well say that Martin Luther King is not a Negro, that he's merely an American. But the plain truth is that neither I nor Martin Luther King can escape the fact that we are a Mexican and a Negro whose roots are so deeply planted in the United States that we have grown those strong little hyphens that make us Mexican-American and Negro-American. This assertion may not please some idealists who would prefer to blind themselves to our obvious

[19] **"Jabberwocky":** a nonsense poem in *Through the Looking Glass,* by Lewis Carroll (paragraph 7)
[20] **Paseo de la Reforma:** central boulevard in Mexico City

ethnic and racial differences, who are unwittingly patronizing when they insist that we are all alike and indistinguishable. But the politicians, undoubtedly the most pragmatic creatures in America, are completely aware that ethnic groups *do* exist and that they seem to huddle together, bitch together, and sometimes vote together.

22 When all is said and done, we hyphenated Americans are here to stay, bubbling happily or unhappily in the great nonmelting pot. Much has been gained and will be gained from the multiethnic aspects of the United States, and there is no useful purpose in attempting to wish it away or to homogenize it out of existence. In spite of the race riots in Watts° and ethnic unrest elsewhere, there would appear to be a kind of modus vivendi developing on almost every level of American life.

23 And if there are those of us who may never feel completely at home, we can always make that brief visit to Bachimba.

STUDY QUESTIONS

1. What expectations did you feel in reading Lopez's title? Were those expectations fulfilled? Could it be said that Lopez's title sets up the first of many surprises?
2. What is the effect of Lopez's first two paragraphs? Consider especially the language Lopez uses about his background. Is the author displaying a low estimation of himself, or is he preparing to show us that his relation to his background is out of the ordinary? What clues to Lopez's individuality do you find in these paragraphs?
3. Which ethnic rivalries seem to be of more significance to Lopez, those between Mexican-Americans and others or those among groups of Mexican-Americans? Why?
4. What perspective does Lopez take toward his childhood self? In treating his early years, what is he revealing about his present view of things?
5. What is Lopez's point in observing that Mexican-American lawyers tend to speak English with "a noticeable Spanish accent" (paragraph 15)? How does that remark bear on his own situation?
6. One of Lopez's early traits, he tells us, was "a penchant for fancy language" (paragraph 14). Judging from this essay, what do you suppose is Lopez's adult relation to language? Be ready to cite instances that support your impressions.
7. What is the role in this essay of the black child Leroy Logan (paragraphs 11–14)? What insight into racial prejudice does Lopez convey in telling of his friendship with Leroy?

---

22 **Watts:** chiefly black ghetto in Los Angeles

8. What is the effect of Lopez's second-hand story about the career and death of his second cousin Martin Lopez (paragraphs 16–18)? How would the essay have been significantly different in effect if it had ended with the telling of that story?

Paul Fussell

Paul Fussell, professor of English at Rutgers University, is the author of several books, including *The Great War and Modern Memory.* The present essay was first published in 1979.

THE STATIONARY TOURIST

1 To start, two bits of data. When you entered Manhattan by the Lincoln Tunnel twenty years ago you saw from the high west bank of the Hudson a vision that lifted your heart and in some measure redeemed the potholes and noise and lunacy and violence of the city. You saw the magic row of transatlantic liners nuzzling the island, their classy, frivolous red and black and white and green uttering their critique of the utility beige-gray of the buildings. In the row might be the *Queen Mary* or the *Queen Elizabeth* or the *Mauretania,* the *United States* or the *America* or the *Independence,* the *Rafaello* or the *Michelangelo* or the *Liberté.* These were the last attendants of the age of travel, soon to fall victim to the jet plane and the cost of oil and the cost of skilled labor.

2 A second bit of data, this one rather nasty. An official of the Guyanese government was recently heard to say that Jonestown° might be turned into a profitable tourist attraction, "on the order of Auschwitz or Dachau."° The disappearance of the ships from the Hudson, like the remark from Guyana, helps define the advanced phase of the age of tourism.

3 The rudimentary phase began more than a century ago, in England, because England was the first country to undergo industrialization and urbanization. The tediums of industrial work made "vacations" necessary, while the unwholesomeness of England's great soot-caked

---

2 **Guyanese, Jonestown:** The Rev. Jim Jones, founder of the People's Temple, ordered a mass suicide of his followers in 1978 after members of the cult had murdered the investigating Congressman Leo Ryan. Their settlement of Jonestown was located in the small South American nation of Guyana.

Auschwitz, Dachau: sites of Nazi extermination camps in World War II

cities made any place abroad, by flagrant contrast, appear almost mystically salubrious, especially in an age of rampant tuberculosis. Contributing to the rise of tourism in the nineteenth century was the bourgeois vogue of romantic primitivism. From James "Ossian" Macpherson in the late eighteenth century to D. H. Lawrence in the early twentieth, intellectuals and others discovered special virtue in primitive peoples and places. Tourism is egalitarian or it is nothing, and its egalitarianism is another index of its origins in the nineteenth century. It is difficult to be a snob and a tourist at the same time, whether in the National Park campsites of America or Hitler's Strength-through-Joy cruises or the current Clubs Méditerranées, where nudity and pop-beads replace clothes and cash. By going primitive one becomes "equal." Wearing a lava-lava° and sporting a "Polynesian" flower behind the ear, one plays out even in 1979 a fantasy devised well over a century ago, a fantasy implying that if simple is good, sincere is even better.

4 It was not always thus. Before tourism there was travel, and before travel there was exploration. Each is roughly assignable to its own age in modern history: exploration belongs to the Renaissance, travel to the bourgeois age, tourism to our proletarian moment. There is an obvious blurring at the edges. What we recognize as tourism in its contemporary form was making inroads on travel as early as the mid-nineteenth century, when Thomas Cook got the bright idea of shipping sightseeing groups to the Continent, and though the Renaissance is over, there are still a few explorers. Tarzan's British father, Lord Greystoke, was exploring Africa in the twentieth century while tourists were being herded around the Place de l'Opéra.

5 And the terms *exploration, travel,* and *tourism* are slippery. In 1855 what we would call exploration is often called travel, as in *The Art of Travel,* by Francis Galton. His title seems to promise advice about securing deck chairs in favorable locations and hints about tipping on shipboard, but his subtitle makes his intention clear: *Shifts and Contrivances Available in Wild Countries.* Galton's advice to "travelers" is very different from the matter in a Baedeker.° Indeed, his book is virtually a survival manual, with instructions on blacksmithing, making your own black powder, descending cliffs with ropes, and defending a camp against natives: "Of all European inventions, nothing so impresses and terrifies savages as fireworks, especially rockets. . . . A rocket, judiciously sent up, is very likely to frighten off an intended attack and save bloodshed." On the other hand, the word *travel* in modern usage is equally misleading, as in phrases like *travel agency* and *the travel industry,* where what the words are disguising is *tourist agency*

³ **lava-lava:** skirt worn by both sexes in Polynesia

⁵ **Baedeker:** the informal name of many guidebooks, meant to do away with the need for guided tours, issued by the German publisher Karl Baedeker (1801–1859)

and *the tourist industry,* the idea of a *travel industry* constituting a palpable contradiction in terms if we understand what real travel once was.

6 It's been said that explorers are to the ordinary traveler what the saint is to the average church congregation. The athletic, paramilitary activity of exploration ends in knighthoods for Sir Francis Drake and Sir Aurel Stein and Sir Edmund Hillary.° No traveler, and certainly no tourist, is ever knighted for his performances, although the strains he may undergo can be as memorable as the explorer's. All three make journeys, but the explorer seeks the undiscovered, the traveler that which has been discovered by the mind working in history, the tourist that which has been discovered by entrepreneurship and prepared for him by the arts of publicity. The genuine traveler is, or used to be, in the middle between the two extremes. If the explorer moves toward the risks of the formless and the unknown, the tourist moves toward the security of pure cliché. It is between these two poles that the traveler mediates, retaining all he can of the excitement of the unpredictable attaching to exploration and fusing that with the pleasure of "knowing where one is" belonging to tourism.

7 But travel is work. Etymologically a traveler is one who suffers *travail,* a word deriving in its turn from Latin *tripalium,* a torture instrument consisting of three stakes designed to rack the body. Before the development of tourism, travel was conceived to be like study, and its fruits were considered to be the adornment of the mind and the formation of the judgment. The traveler was a student of what he sought, and he was assisted by aids like the thirty-four volumes of the Medieval Town Series, now, significantly, out of print.

8 One by-product of real travel was something that has virtually disappeared, the travel book, a record of an inquiry and a report of the effect of the inquiry on the mind and imagination of the traveler. The travel books of D. H. Lawrence are an example, and they date from the last days of genuine travel. His Italian journeys, says Anthony Burgess, "by post-bus or cold late train or on foot are in that great laborious tradition which produced genuine travel books." And Paul Theroux, whose *Great Railway Bazaar* is one of the few *travel* books to emerge from our age of tourism, observes that "travel writing is a funny thing" because "the worst trips make the best reading, which is why Graham Greene's *The Lawless Roads* and Kinglake's *Eothen* are so superb." On the other hand, easy, passive travel results in books that offer "little more than chatting," or, like former British Prime Minister Edward Heath's *Travels,* "smug boasting." "Let the tourist be cush-

---

[6] **Sir Francis Drake, Sir Aurel Stein, Sir Edmund Hillary:** respectively, a British sailor and adventurer (1540–1596) who sailed around the world in 1577–1580; a Hungarian-English archaeologist and geographer (1862–1943), famous for his explorations of Central Asia; and a New Zealand explorer and mountain climber, leader of the first conquest of Mt. Everest

ioned against misadventure," says Lawrence Durrell; "your true traveler will not feel that he has had his money's worth unless he brings back a few scars." Although I have been both traveler and tourist, it was as a traveler, not a tourist, that I once watched my wallet and passport slither down a Turkish toilet at Bodrum,° and it was the arm of a traveler that reached deep, deep into that cloaca to retrieve them. If exploration promised adventures, travel was travel because it held out high hopes of misadventures.

9 From the outset, mass tourism attracted the class-contempt of killjoys who conceived themselves independent travelers and thus superior by reason of intellect, education, curiosity, and spirit. In the mid-nineteenth century Charles Lever laments in *Blackwood's Magazine:*

> *It seems that some enterprizing and unscrupulous man* [he means Thomas Cook] *has devised the project of conducting some forty or fifty persons . . . from London to Naples and back for a fixed sum. He contracts to carry them, feed them, and amuse them. . . . When I first read the scheme . . . I caught at the hope that the speculation would break down. I imagined that the characteristic independence of Englishmen would revolt against a plan that reduces the traveler to the level of his trunk and obliterates every trace and trait of the individual. I was all wrong. As I write, the cities of Italy are deluged with droves of these creatures.*

Lever's word *droves* suggests sheep or cattle and reminds us how traditional in antitourist fulminations animal images are (cf. *herded,* above). "Of all noxious animals," Francis Kilvert wrote in the 1870s, "the most noxious is the tourist." And if not animals, insects. The Americans descending on Amalfi° in the 1920s, according to Osbert Sitwell, resemble "a swarm of very noisy transatlantic locusts," and the tourists at Levanto° in the 1930s, according to his sister Edith, are "the most awful people with legs like flies who come in to lunch in bathing costume—flies, centipedes." We may wonder who these loathsome creatures are, where they come from, what they think they're doing, and what happens to us all when for several weeks each year we go about resembling them.

10 I am assuming that travel is now impossible and that tourism is all we have left. Travel implies variety of means and independence of arrangements. The disappearance not just of the transatlantic lovelies but of virtually all passenger ships except cruise vessels (tourism with a vengeance), and the increasing difficulty of booking hotel space in advance if one is not on a tour, measure the plight of those who aspire still to travel in the old sense. Last spring I planned a trip to the Orient and the South Pacific, hoping that in places so remote and, I dreamed,

---

[8] **Bodrum:** (usually *Budrum*) Turkish city known in ancient times as Halicarnassus

[9] **Amalfi:** town southeast of Naples in southern Italy

Levanto: seaside town in northwest Italy

backward, something like travel might still just be possible. I saw myself lolling at the rail unshaven in a dirty white linen suit as the crummy little ship approached Bora Bora or Fiji in a damp heat that made one wonder whether death by yaws° or dengue fever° might be an attractive alternative. Too late for such daydreams. I found that just as I was inquiring, passenger ship travel in the Pacific disappeared—in April, 1978, to be precise. That month the ships of both the Matson and the Pacific Far East Lines were laid up for good, done in by the extortions of the oil-producing nations. In the same month even a small, Chinese-owned "steam navigation company" running a regular service between Hong Kong and Singapore put away its toys. Formerly it had been possible to call at the isolated island of Betio and Tarawa Atoll° to pay respects to the ghosts of the United States and Japanese Marines, and an enterprising couple had built a small inn there. Now access to Betio and Tarawa is by air only, and the plane flies on alternate Thursdays, which means you have to stay there two weeks if you go at all. No one will go there now. I did not go there but to the big places with big hotels and big airports served by big planes. I came to know what Frederic Harrison meant when he said, "We go abroad, but we travel no longer." Only he wrote this in 1887. I suppose it's all a matter of degree. Perhaps the closest one could approach an experience of travel today would be to drive in an old automobile with doubtful tires through Romania or Afghanistan without hotel reservations and somehow to get by on terrible French.

11 One who has hotel reservations and speaks no French is a tourist. Anthropologists are fond of defining him, although in their earnestness they tend to miss his essence. Thus Valene L. Smith in *Hosts and Guests: The Anthropology of Tourism:* "A tourist is a temporarily leisured person who voluntarily visits a place away from home for the purpose of experiencing a change." But that pretty well defines a traveler, too. What distinguishes the tourist is the motives, few of which are ever openly revealed: to raise social status at home and to allay social anxiety; to realize fantasies of erotic freedom; and most important, to derive secret pleasure from posing momentarily as a member of a social class superior to one's own, to play the role of a "shopper" and spender whose life becomes significant and exciting only when one is exercising power by choosing what to buy. Cant as the tourist may of the Taj Mahal and Mt. Etna at sunset, his real target is the immense Ocean Terminal at Hong Kong, with its miles of identical horrible camera and tape-recorder shops. The fact that the tourist is best

---

[10] **yaws:** tropical disease that causes raspberrylike skin eruptions
dengue fever: infectious, eruptive tropical fever causing severe pain in joints and muscles
Betio, Tarawa Atoll: scenes of fierce battles between Japanese and American forces in World War II

defined as a fantasist equipped temporarily with unaccustomed power is better known to the tourist industry than to anthropology.

12 For tourist fantasies to bloom satisfactorily, certain conditions must be established. First, the tourist's mind must be entirely emptied so that a sort of hypnotism can occur. Unremitting Muzak is a help here, and it is carefully provided in hotels, restaurants, elevators, tour buses, cable cars, planes, and excursion boats. The tourist is assumed to know nothing, a tradition upheld by the American magazine *Travel* (note the bogus title), which is careful to specify that London is in England and Venice in Italy. If the tourist is granted a little awareness, it is always of the most retrograde kind, like the Thirties belief, which he is assumed to hold, that "transportation," its varieties and promise, is itself an appropriate subject of high regard. (Think of the 1939 New York World's Fair, or the Thirties murals in the Chrysler Building, where variety, celerity, and novelty in means of transport are thought inherently interesting: "Getting There Is Half the Fun.") A current day-tour out of Tokyo honors this convention. The ostensible object is to convey a group of tourists to a spot where they can wonder at the grandeurs of natural scenery. In pursuit of this end, they are first placed in a "streamlined" train whose speed of 130 miles per hour is frequently called to their attention. They are then transferred to an air-conditioned "coach" that whisks them to a boat, whence, after a ten-minute ride, they are ushered into a funicular to ascend a spooky gorge, after which, back to the bus, et cetera. The whole day's exercise is presented as a marvel of contrivance in which the sheer variety of the conveyances supplies a large part of the attraction. Hydrofoils are popular for similar reasons, certainly not for their efficiency. Of the four I've been on in the past few years, two have broken down spectacularly, one in Manila Bay almost sinking after encountering a submerged log at sophomoric high speed.

13 Tourist fantasies fructify best when tourists are set down not in places but in pseudoplaces, passing through subordinate pseudoplaces, like airports, on the way. Real places are odd and call for interpretation. They are the venue of the traveler. Pseudoplaces entice by their familiarity and call for instant recognition: "We have arrived." One striking post-World War II phenomenon has been the transformation of numerous former small countries into pseudoplaces or tourist commonwealths, whose function is simply to entice tourists and sell them things. This has happened remarkably fast. As recently as 1930 Alec Waugh could report that Martinique had no tourists because there was no accommodation for them. Now, Martinique would seem to be about nothing but tourists, like Haiti, the Dominican Republic, Barbados, Bermuda, Hong Kong, Fiji, and the Greek Islands.

14 The tourist is readied for his ultimate encounter with placelessness by passing first through the uniform airport. Only forty years ago the

world's airports exhibited distinctive characteristics betokening differences in national character and style. Being in one was not precisely like being in another. In Graham Greene's novel of 1935, *England Made Me,* the character Fred Hall, we are told,

> *knew the airports of Europe as well as he had once known the stations on the Brighton line—shabby Le Bourget; the great scarlet rectangle of the Tempelhof as one came in from London in the dark . . . ; the white sand blowing up round the shed at Tallinn; Riga, where the Berlin to Leningrad plane came down and bright pink mineral waters were sold in a tin-roofed shed.*

That sort of variety would be unthinkable now, when, as Bernard Bergonzi says, airport design has become a "ubiquitous international idiom."

15 Moving through the airport—or, increasingly, being moved, on a literal endless belt—the tourist arrives at his next nonplace, the airplane interior. The vapid non-allusive cheerfulness of its décor betrays its design and manufacture as Southern Californian. Evelyn Waugh, one of the heroes of the last age of travel, the Twenties and Thirties, was among the first to notice

> *the curious fact that airplanes have added nothing to our enjoyment of height. The human eye still receives the most intense images when the observer's feet are planted on the ground or on a building. The airplane belittles all it discloses.*

The calculated isolation from the actual that is tourism ("We fly you above the weather") is reflected as well in the design of the last of the serious passenger liners, the *QE II.* Here the designers carefully eliminated the promenade deck, formerly the place where you were vouchsafed some proximity to the ocean. Now, as John Malcolm Brinnin has said, "Travelers who love the sea, delight in studying its moods, and like to walk in the sight and smell of it, were left with almost no place to go." Except to the bars and fruit machines, doubtless the intention. As the ship has been obliged to compete in the illusion of placelessness with the airport and the jet, its interior design has given over its former ambitions of alluding to such identifiable places as country estates with fireplaces and libraries, urban tea-dance parlors, and elegant conservatories full of palms, ferns, and wicker, and instead has embraced the universal placeless style, eschewing organic materials like wood and real fabric in favor of spray-painted metal and dun plastic. I don't want to sound too gloomy, but there's a relation here between other "replacements" characterizing contemporary life: the replacement of coffee cream by ivory-colored powder, for example, or of silk and wool by nylon, or glass by Lucite, eloquence by jargon, fish by fish sticks, merit by publicity, motoring by driving, travel by tourism. A corollary of that last replacement is that ships have been replaced by cruise ships, small movable pseudoplaces making an endless transit between larger fixed pseudoplaces. But even a cruise ship is preferable to a plane. It is healthier because you can exercise on it, and it is more romantic because you can copulate on it.

16 Safe and efficient uniform international jet service began in earnest around 1957. That's an interesting moment in the history of human passivity. It's the approximate moment when radio narrative and drama, requiring the audience to do some of the work by supplying the missing visual dimension with its own imagination, found themselves replaced by television, which now does it all for the "viewer"—or fixed tourist, if you will. Supplying the missing dimension is exactly what real travel used to require, and it used to assume a large body of people willing to travail to earn illumination.

17 But ironically the tourist is not without his own kinds of travails, which the industry never prepares him for and which make tourism always something less than the ecstasy proposed. The sense that he is being swindled and patronized, or that important intelligence is being withheld from him, must trouble even the dimmest at one time or another. In addition to the incomprehensible but clearly crucial airport loudspeaker harangues, the tourist is faced by constant rhetorical and contractual challenges. He meets one the moment he accepts the standard airline baggage check and reads, "This is not the Luggage Ticket (Baggage Check) as described in Article 4 of the Warsaw Convention or the Warsaw Convention as amended by the Hague Protocol 1955." The question arises, If this baggage check is not that one, what is it? If it is not that Luggage Ticket (Baggage Check), how do you get the real one? And what does the real one say when you finally get it? Does it say, "This *is* the Luggage Ticket (Baggage Check) as described in . . . . On no account accept any substitute"? Or, "Persons accepting substitutes for the Luggage Ticket (Baggage Check) as described in Article 4 . . . will legally and morally have no recourse when their baggage is diverted (lost), and in addition will be liable to severe penalties, including immediate involuntary repatriation at their own expense"?

18 Another cause of tourist travail is touts. The word *tout,* designating a man hounding a tourist to patronize a certain hotel or shop, dates approximately from Cook's first organized excursion to the Paris Exposition of 1855. Some tourist brochures will gingerly hint at such hazards as sharks, fetid water, and appalling food, but I've never seen one that prepared the tourist for the far greater threat of the tout.

19 Tour guides are touts by nature, required to lead tourists to shops where purchases result in commissions. In Kyoto° recently a scholarly guide to the religious monuments, full of dignity and years, had to undergo the humiliation of finally conducting his group of tourists to

---

[19] **Kyoto:** historic Japanese city famed for its temples

a low ceramics shop. He nearly wept. Tour guides are also by nature café touts: "Let's rest here a moment. I know you're tired. You can sit down and order coffee, beer, or soft drinks." And souvenir-shop touts: "This place has the best fly-whisks (postcards, scarabs,° amber, coral, camera film, turquoise, pocket calculators) in town, and because you are with me you will not be cheated." All kinds of tourists are fair game for touts, but Americans seem their favorite targets, not just because of their careless ways with money and their instinctive generosity but also because of their non-European innocence about the viler dimensions of human nature and their desire to be liked, their impulse to say "Good morning" back instead of "Go away." It's a rare American who, asked, "Where you from, Sir?" will venture "Screw you" instead of "Boise."

20 Touts make contemporary tourism a hell of importunity, and many of my memories of tourist trips reduce to memories of particular touts. There was the money-changing tout at Luxor° so assiduous that I dared not leave the hotel for several days; and the gang of guide-touts outside Olaffson's Hotel, Port-au-Prince,° who could be dealt with only by hiring one to fend off the others. There was the nice, friendly waiter at the best hotel in Colombo, Sri Lanka, whose kindly inquiries about one's plans cloaked his intention to make one lease his brother's car. There was the amiable student of English in Shiraz° whose touching efforts at verbal self-improvement brought him gradually to the essential matter, the solicitation of a large gift. There was the sympathetic acquaintance in Srinagar° whose free boat-ride ended at his canal-side carpet outlet. There was the civilized assistant manager of the Hotel Peninsula, Hong Kong, an establishment so pretentious that it picks up its clients at the airport in Rolls-Royces, who, after being repulsed at the desk, finally came up to my room to tout the hotel's tours. There were the well-got-up young men of Manila who struck up conversations, innocently expressing interest in your children and place of residence, and then gradually, and in their view subtly, began to beg. Rejected there, they then touted for shops. They then turned pimps, and, that failing, whores. The Philippines is a notable tout venue, like Turkey, Iran, Mexico, Egypt, and India. All are in the grip of a developing capitalism, halfway between the primitive and the overripe. In London there are no touts: it's easier there to make a living without the constant fear of humiliating rebuff. On the

[19] **scarabs:** gems cut to resemble beetles

[20] **Luxor:** town in Upper Egypt; site of ancient Thebes

Port-au-Prince: capital of Haiti

Shiraz: city in southwest Iran

Srinagar: capital city of Kashmir

other hand, there are none in Papua New Guinea° either. It is not yet sufficiently "developed," which means it doesn't yet have a sense of a richer outside world that can be tapped. In the same way, your real native of a truly primitive place doesn't steal from tourists. Not out of primitive virtue but out of ignorance: unlike a resident of, say, Naples, he doesn't know what incredible riches repose in travelers' luggage and handbags.

21 As I have said, it is hard to be a snob and a tourist at the same time. A way to combine both roles is to become an antitourist. Despite the suffering he undergoes, the antitourist is not to be confused with the traveler, for his motives are less those of inquiry than of self-protection. Dean MacCannell, author of the anthropological study *The Tourist,* remembers a resident of an island like Nantucket who remonstrated when, arriving, MacCannell offered to start the car before the ferry docked. "Only tourists do that," he was told. Abroad, the techniques practiced by antitourists anxious to assert their difference from all those tourists are more shifty. All involve attempts to merge into the surroundings, like speaking the language, even badly. Some dissimulations are merely mechanical, like a man's shifting his wedding ring from the left to the right hand. A useful trick is ostentatiously not carrying a camera. If asked about this deficiency by a camera-carrying tourist, one scores points by saying, "I never carry a camera. If I photograph things, I find I don't really see them." Another device is staying in the most unlikely hotels, although this is risky, like the correlative technique of eschewing taxis in favor of local public transportation (the more complicated and confusing the better), which may end with the antitourist stranded miles out of town, cold and alone on the last tram of the night. Another risky technique is programmatically consuming the local food, no matter how nasty, and affecting to relish sheep's eyes, fried cicadas, and shellfish taken locally—that is, from the sewagey little lagoon. Dressing with attention to local coloration used to be harder before jeans became the international costume of the pseudo-leisured. But jeans are hard for those around sixty to get away with, and the antitourist must be careful to prevent betrayal by jackets, trousers, shoes, and even socks and neckties (if still worn) differing subtly from the local norms.

22 Sedulously avoiding the standard sights is probably the best method of disguising your touristhood. In London one avoids Westminster Abbey and heads instead for the Earl of Burlington's eighteenth-century villa at Chiswick. In Venice one must walk by circuitous smelly back passages far out of one's way to avoid being seen in the Piazza San Marco. In Athens one disdains the Acropolis in favor of the eminence

---

[20] **Papua New Guinea:** Papua and New Guinea are alternative names for a large island north of Australia

preferred by the locals, the Lycabettus. Each tourist center has its interdicted zone: in Rome you avoid the Spanish Steps and the Fontana di Trevi, in Paris the Deux Magots and the whole Boul' Mich area, in Nice the Promenade des Anglais, in Egypt Giza with its excessively popular pyramids and sphinx, in Hawaii Waikiki. Avoiding Waikiki brings up the question of why one's gone to Hawaii at all, but that's exactly the problem.

23 Driving on the Continent, it's essential to avoid outright giveaways like the French TT license plate. Better to drive a car registered in the country you're touring (the more suave rental agencies know this) if you can't find one from some unlikely place like Bulgaria or Syria. Plates entirely in Arabic are currently much favored by antitourists, and they have the additional advantage of frustrating policemen writing tickets for illegal parking.

24 Perhaps the most popular way for the antitourist to demarcate himself from the tourists, because he can have a drink while doing it, is for him to lounge—cameraless—at a café table and with palpable contempt scrutinize the passing sheep through half-closed lids, making all movements very slowly. Here the costume providing the least danger of exposure is jeans, a thick, dark-colored turtleneck, and longish hair. Any conversational gambits favored by lonely tourists, like "Where are you from?" can be deflected by vagueness. Instead of answering Des Moines or Queens, you say, "I spend a lot of time abroad" or "That's really hard to say." If hard-pressed, you simply mutter *"Je ne parle pas anglais,"*° look at your watch, and split.

25 The antitourist's persuasion that he is really a traveler instead of a tourist is both a symptom and a cause of what the British journalist Alan Brien has designated *tourist angst,*° defined as "a gnawing suspicion that after all . . . you are still a tourist like every other tourist." As a uniquely modern form of self-contempt, *tourist angst* often issues in bizarre emotional behavior, and it is surprising that it has not yet become a classic for psychiatric study. "A student of mine in Paris," writes MacCannell, "a young man from Iran dedicated to the [student] revolution, half stammering, half shouting, said to me, 'Let's face it, we are all tourists!' Then, rising to his feet, his face contorted with . . . self-hatred, he concluded dramatically in a hiss: 'Even *I* am a tourist.' "

26 *Tourist angst* like this is distinctly a class signal. Only the upper elements of the middle classes suffer from it, and in summer especially it is endemic in places like Florence and Mikonos° and Crete. It is rare in pseudoplaces like Disneyland, where people have come just because other people have come. This is to say that the working class finds

---

[24] **"Je ne parle pas anglais":** (Fr.) "I don't speak English"

[25] **angst:** (Ger.) anguish, anxiety

[26] **Mikonos:** mountainous island southeast of Greece in the Aegean Sea

nothing shameful about tourism. It is the middle class that has read and heard just enough to sense that being a tourist is somehow offensive and scorned by an imagined upper class that it hopes to emulate and, if possible, be mistaken for. The irony is that extremes meet: the upper class, unruffled by contempt from any source, happily enrolls in Lindblad Tours or makes its way up the Nile in tight groups being lectured at by a tour guide artfully disguised as an Oxbridge° archeologist. Sometimes the antitourist's rage to escape the appearance of tourism propels him around a mock full-circle, back to a simulacrum of exploration. Hence the popularity of African safaris among the upper middle class. One tourist agency now offers package exploristic expeditions to Everest and the Sahara, and to Sinai by camel caravan, "real expeditions for the serious traveler looking for more than an adventurous vacation." Something of the acute discomfort of exploration and the uncertainty of real travel can be recovered by accepting an invitation to "traverse Spain's Sierra Nevada on horseback ($528.00)."

27 But the antitourist deludes only himself. We are all tourists, and there is no escape. Every year there are more than 200 million of us, and when we are jetted in all directions and lodged in our pseudoplaces, we constitute four times the population of France. The decisions we imagine ourselves making are shaped by the Professor of Tourism at Michigan State University and by the "Travel Administrators" now being trained at the New School and by the International Union of Official Travel Organizations, whose publications indicate what it has in mind for us: *Factors Determining Selection of Sites for Tourism Development,* for example, or *Potential International Supply of Tourism Resources.* Our freedom and mobility diminish at the same time their expansion is loudly proclaimed; while more choices appear to solicit us, fewer actually do. The ships will not come back to the Hudson, and some place in Guyana will doubtless be selected as a site for tourism development. The tourist is locked in, and as MacCannell has pointed out, as a type the tourist is "one of the best models of modern man-in-general."

STUDY QUESTIONS

1. What is the effect of Fussell's opening sentence, and how do you account for that effect? How, when the first two paragraphs are complete, do the "two bits of data" fit together?
2. Fussell's distinctions between exploration, travel, and tourism are

---

[26] **Oxbridge:** a made-up word combining the names of the two great British universities Oxford and Cambridge

clearly central to the point of this essay. What are those distinctions? Why, if exploration is historically the earliest of the three categories, didn't Fussell choose to discuss it first?
3. Why does Fussell bother, in paragraph 5, to challenge two uses of the word *travel?*
4. What role do quotations play in this essay? How do they lend substance to Fussell's main point?
5. Why does Fussell call airports "subordinate pseudoplaces" (paragraph 13)?
6. Fussell laments the extinction of transatlantic liners, but he seems to have little or no respect for what might be considered the next best thing, cruise ships. Why?
7. What, in Fussell's conception, is an antitourist? What is ironical about the antitourist's situation?
8. Despite its generally formal manner, Fussell's essay is also conspicuously *informal* in certain ways. What informal touches do you find, and why do you suppose Fussell has indulged in them?
9. What is Fussell's total attitude toward the world of tourism? How upset, if at all, does he appear to be?

PART III
ARGUING

ARGUING FROM EXPERIENCE

John McMurtry

Having retired as a professional football player in Canada, John McMurtry now teaches at the University of Guelph, Ontario, specializing in social and political philosophy. He is the author of *The Structure of Marx's World-View.* The present essay first appeared in 1971.

KILL 'EM! CRUSH 'EM! EAT 'EM RAW!

1 A few months ago my neck got a hard crick in it. I couldn't turn my head; to look left or right I'd have to turn my whole body. But I'd had cricks in my neck since I started playing grade-school football and hockey, so I just ignored it. Then I began to notice that when I reached for any sort of large book (which I do pretty often as a philosophy teacher at the University of Guelph) I had trouble lifting it with one hand. I was losing the strength in my left arm, and I had such a steady pain in my back I often had to stretch out on the floor of the room I was in to relieve the pressure.

2 A few weeks later I mentioned to my brother, an orthopedic surgeon, that I'd lost the power in my arm since my neck began to hurt. Twenty-four hours later I was in a Toronto hospital not sure whether I might end up with a wasted upper limb. Apparently the steady pounding I had received playing college and professional football in the late Fifties and early Sixties had driven my head into my backbone so that the discs had crumpled together at the neck—"acute herniation"—and had cut the nerves to my left arm like a pinched telephone wire (without nerve stimulation, of course, the muscles atrophy, leaving the arm crippled). So I spent my Christmas holidays in the hospital in heavy traction and much of the next three months with my neck in a brace. Today most of the pain has gone, and I've recovered most of the strength in my arm. But from time to time I still have to don the brace, and surgery remains a possibility.

3 Not much of this will surprise anyone who knows football. It is a sport in which body wreckage is one of the leading conventions. A few days after I went into hospital for that crick in my neck, another brother, an outstanding football player in college, was undergoing spinal surgery in the same hospital two floors above me. In his case it was a lower, more massive herniation, which every now and again buckled him so that he was unable to lift himself off his back for days at a time. By the time he entered the hospital for surgery he had already spent several months in bed. The operation was successful, but, as in all such cases, it will take him a year to recover fully.

4 These aren't isolated experiences. Just about anybody who has ever played football for any length of time, in high school, college or one of the professional leagues, has suffered for it later physically.

5 Indeed, it is arguable that body shattering is the very *point* of football, as killing and maiming are of war. (In the United States, for example, the game results in 15 to 20 deaths a year and about 50,000 major operations on knees alone.) To grasp some of the more conspicuous similarities between football and war, it is instructive to listen to the imperatives most frequently issued to the players by their coaches, teammates and fans. "Hurt 'em!" "Level 'em!" "Kill 'em!" "Take 'em apart!" Or watch for the plays that are most enthusiastically applauded by the fans. Where someone is "smeared," "knocked silly," "creamed," "nailed," "broken in two," or even "crucified." (One of my coaches when I played corner linebacker with the Calgary Stampeders in 1961 elaborated, often very inventively, on this language of destruction: admonishing us to "unjoin" the opponent, "make 'im remember you" and "stomp 'im like a bug.") Just as in hockey, where a fight will bring fans to their feet more often than a skillful play, so in football the mouth waters most of all for the really crippling block or tackle. For the kill. Thus the good teams are "hungry," the best players are "mean," and "casualties" are as much a part of the game as they are of a war.

6 The family resemblance between football and war is, indeed, striking. Their languages are similar: "field general," "long bomb," "blitz," "take a shot," "front line," "pursuit," "good hit," "the draft" and so on. Their principles and practices are alike: mass hysteria, the art of intimidation, absolute command and total obedience, territorial aggression, censorship, inflated insignia and propaganda, blackboard manoeuvres and strategies, drills, uniforms, formations, marching bands and training camps. And the virtues they celebrate are almost identical: hyper-aggressiveness, coolness under fire and suicidal bravery. All this has been implicitly recognized by such jock-loving Americans as media stars General Patton and President Nixon, who have talked about war as a football game. Patton wanted to make his Second World War tank men look like football players. And Nixon, as we know, is fond of comparing attacks on Vietnam to football plays and drawing coachly diagrams on a blackboard for TV war fans.

7 One difference between war and football, though, is that there is little or no protest against football. Perhaps the most extraordinary thing about the game is that the systematic infliction of injuries excites in people not concern, as would be the case if they were sustained at, say, a rock festival, but a collective rejoicing and euphoria. Players and fans alike revel in the spectacle of a combatant felled into semiconsciousness, "blindsided," "closelined" or "decapitated." I can remember, in fact, being chided by a coach in pro ball for not "getting my hat" injuriously into a player who was already lying helpless on the ground. (On another occasion, after the Stampeders had traded the celebrated Joe Kapp to BC, we were playing the Lions in Vancouver and Kapp was forced on one play to run with the ball. He was coming "down the chute," his bad knee wobbling uncertainly, so I simply dropped on him like a blanket. After I returned to the bench I was reproved for not exploiting the opportunity to unhinge his bad knee.)

8 After every game, of course, the papers are full of reports on the day's injuries, a sort of post-battle "body count," and the respective teams go to work with doctors and trainers, tape, whirlpool baths, cortisone and morphine to patch and deaden the wounds before the next game. Then the whole drama is reenacted—injured athletes held together by adhesive, braces and drugs—and the days following it are filled with even more feverish activity to put on the show yet again at the end of the next week. (I remember being so taped up in college that I earned the nickname "mummy.") The team that survives this merry-go-round spectacle of skilled masochism with the fewest incapacitating injuries usually wins. It is a sort of victory by ordeal: "We hurt them more than they hurt us."

9 My own initiation into this brutal circus was typical. I loved the game from the moment I could run with a ball. Played shoeless on a green open field with no one keeping score and in a spirit of reckless abandon and laughter, it's a very different sport. Almost no one gets hurt and it's rugged, open and exciting (it still is for me). But then, like everything else, it starts to be regulated and institutionalized by adult authorities. And the fun is over.

10 So it was as I began the long march through organized football. Now there was a coach and elders to make it clear by their behavior that beating other people was the only thing to celebrate and that trying to shake someone up every play was the only thing to be really proud of. Now there were severe rule enforcers, audiences, formally recorded victors and losers, and heavy equipment to permit crippling bodily moves and collisions (according to one American survey, more than 80% of all football injuries occur to fully equipped players). And now there was the official "given" that the only way to keep playing was to wear suffocating armor, to play to defeat, to follow orders silently and to renounce spontaneity for joyless drill. The game had been, in short,

ruined. But because I loved to play and play skillfully, I stayed. And progressively and inexorably, as I moved through high school, college and pro leagues, my body was dismantled. Piece by piece.

11 I started off with torn ligaments in my knee at 13. Then, as the organization and the competition increased, the injuries came faster and harder. Broken nose (three times), broken jaw (fractured in the first half and dismissed as a "bad wisdom tooth," so I played with it for the rest of the game), ripped knee ligaments again. Torn ligaments in one ankle and a fracture in the other (which I remember feeling relieved about because it meant I could honorably stop drill-blocking a 270-pound defensive end). Repeated rib fractures and cartilage tears (usually carried, again, through the remainder of the game). More dislocations of the left shoulder than I can remember (the last one I played with because, as the Calgary Stampeder doctor said, it "couldn't be damaged any more"). Occasional broken or dislocated fingers and toes. Chronically hurt lower back (I still can't lift with it or change a tire without worrying about folding). Separated right shoulder (as with many other injuries, like badly bruised hips and legs, needled with morphine for the games). And so on. The last pro game I played—against Winnipeg Blue Bombers in the Western finals in 1961—I had a recently dislocated left shoulder, a more recently wrenched right shoulder and a chronic pain centre in one leg. I was so tied up with soreness I couldn't drive my car to the airport. But it never occurred to me or anyone else that I miss a play as a corner linebacker.

12 By the end of my football career, I had learned that physical injury—giving it and taking it—is the real currency of the sport. And that in the final analysis the "winner" is the man who can hit to kill even if only half his limbs are working. In brief, a warrior game with a warrior ethos into which (like almost everyone else I played with) my original boyish enthusiasm had been relentlessly taunted and conditioned.

13 In thinking back on how all this happened, though, I can pick out no villains. As with the social system as a whole, the game has a life of its own. Everyone grows up inside it, accepts it and fulfills its dictates as obediently as helots.° Far from ever questioning the principles of the activity, people simply concentrate on executing these principles more aggressively than anybody around them. The result is a group of people who, as the leagues become of a higher and higher class, are progressively insensitive to the possibility that things could be otherwise. Thus, in football, anyone who might question the wisdom or enjoyment of putting on heavy equipment on a hot day and running full speed at someone else with the intention of knocking him senseless would be

---

[13] **helots:** slaves, serfs

regarded simply as not really a devoted athlete and probably "chicken." The choice is made straightforward. Either you, too, do your very utmost to efficiently smash and be smashed, or you admit incompetence or cowardice and quit. Since neither of these admissions is very pleasant, people generally keep any doubts they have to themselves and carry on.

14 Of course, it would be a mistake to suppose that there is more blind acceptance of brutal practices in organized football than elsewhere. On the contrary, a recent Harvard study has approvingly argued that football's characteristics of "impersonal acceptance of inflicted injury," an overriding "organization goal," the "ability to turn oneself on and off" and being, above all, "out to win" are of "inestimable value" to big corporations. Clearly, our sort of football is no sicker than the rest of our society. Even its organized destruction of physical well-being is not anomalous. A very large part of our wealth, work and time is, after all, spent in systematically destroying and harming human life. Manufacturing, selling and using weapons that tear opponents to pieces. Making ever bigger and faster predator-named cars with which to kill and injure one another by the million every year. And devoting our very lives to outgunning one another for power in an ever more destructive rat race. Yet all these practices are accepted without question by most people, even zealously defended and honored. Competitive, organized injuring is integral to our way of life, and football is simply one of the more intelligible mirrors of the whole process: a sort of colorful morality play showing us how exciting and rewarding it is to Smash Thy Neighbor.

15 Now it is fashionable to rationalize our collaboration in all this by arguing that, well, man *likes* to fight and injure his fellows and such games as football should be encouraged to discharge this original-sin urge into less harmful channels than, say, war. Public-show football, this line goes, plays the same sort of cathartic role as Aristotle said stage tragedy does: without real blood (or not much), it releases players and audience from unhealthy feelings stored up inside them.

16 As an ex-player in this seasonal coast-to-coast drama, I see little to recommend such a view. What organized football did to me was make me *suppress* my natural urges and re-express them in an alienating, vicious form. Spontaneous desires for free bodily exuberance and fraternization with competitors were shamed and forced under ("If it ain't hurtin' it ain't helpin' ") and in their place were demanded armored mechanical moves and cool hatred of all opposition. Endless authoritarian drill and dressing-room harangues (ever wonder why competing teams can't prepare for a game in the same dressing room?) were the kinds of mechanisms employed to reconstruct joyful energies into mean and alien shapes. I am quite certain that everyone else around me was being similarly forced into this heavily equipped military precision and

angry antagonism, because there was always a mutinous attitude about full-dress practices, and everybody (the pros included) had to concentrate incredibly hard for days to whip themselves into just one hour's hostility a week against another club. The players never speak of these things, of course, because everyone is so anxious to appear tough.

17 The claim that men like seriously to battle one another to some sort of finish is a myth. It only endures because it wears one of the oldest and most propagandized of masks—the romantic combatant. I sometimes wonder whether the violence all around us doesn't depend for its survival on the existence and preservation of this tough-guy disguise.

18 As for the effect of organized football on the spectator, the fan is not released from supposed feelings of violent aggression by watching his athletic heroes perform it so much as encouraged in the view that people-smashing is an admirable mode of self-expression. The most savage attackers, after all, are, by general agreement, the most efficient and worthy players of all (the biggest applause I ever received as a football player occurred when I ran over people or slammed them so hard they couldn't get up). Such circumstances can hardly be said to lessen the spectators' martial tendencies. Indeed it seems likely that the whole show just further develops and titillates the North American addiction for violent self-assertion. Perhaps it is for this reason that Trudeau became a national hero when he imposed the "big play," the War Measures Act, to smash the other team, the FLQ° and its supporters, at the height of the football season. Perhaps, as well, it helps explain why the greater the zeal of U.S. political leaders as football fans (Johnson, Nixon, Agnew), the more enthusiastic the commitment to hard-line politics. At any rate there seems to be a strong correlation between people who relish tough football and people who relish intimidating and beating the hell out of commies, hippies, protest marchers and other opposition groups.

19 Watching well-advertised strong men knock other people around, make them hurt, is in the end like other tastes. It does not weaken with feeding and variation in form. It grows.

20 I got out of football in 1962. I had asked to be traded after Calgary had offered me a $25-a-week-plus-commissions off-season job as a clothing-store salesman. ("Dear Mr. Finks:" I wrote. [Jim Finks was then the Stampeders' general manager.] "Somehow I do not think the dialectical subtleties of Hegel, Marx and Plato would be suitably oriented amidst the environmental stimuli of jockey shorts and herringbone suits. I hope you make a profitable sale or trade of my contract to the

---

[18] **Trudeau, FLQ:** Canadian Prime Minister Pierre Elliot Trudeau, who, in struggling to keep the French-speaking province of Quebec within the Canadian state, opposed the activists of the Front for the Liberation of Quebec

East.") So the Stampeders traded me to Montreal. In a preseason inter-squad game with the Alouettes I ripped the cartilages in my ribs on the hardest block I'd ever thrown. I had trouble breathing and I had to shuffle-walk with my torso on a tilt. The doctor in the local hospital said three weeks rest, the coach said scrimmage in two days. Three days later I was back home reading philosophy.

STUDY QUESTIONS

1. How does McMurtry keep us mindful that he is now a professor of philosophy? Why is that identification important to his relationship with us as his readers?
2. In paragraph 5 McMurtry proposes that "body shattering" may be "the very *point* of football," and in paragraph 8 he refers to the "skilled masochism" (or pleasure in enduring pain) of the sport. Are these ideas sustained by evidence? Would McMurtry's case have been stronger or weaker without them?
3. How does McMurtry's experience as a professional football player lend authority to his argument? Be prepared to cite instances.
4. Whom does McMurtry blame for football violence, and why?
5. In the total strategy of McMurtry's essay, what functions are performed by paragraphs 15–19?
6. Defenders of organized football often argue that the second-hand violence involved in being a fan helps to prevent more dangerous and direct outbreaks of aggression in daily life. What would McMurtry say about that argument? Do you agree or disagree with his apparent position?
7. What is the effect of the stories McMurtry tells about himself in his closing paragraph?
8. What is the thesis of McMurtry's argument, and where (if anywhere) is it stated?
9. Under what other categories besides "Arguing from Experience" might this essay have been included?

George Orwell

The British essayist and novelist George Orwell (1903–1950), author of the classics *Homage to Catalonia, Animal Farm,* and *1984,* has been called "the conscience of his generation." "Shooting an Elephant," written in 1936, deals with the period when Orwell, as a member of the Indian Imperial Police, was undergoing experiences that were turning him permanently against the whole idea of one country's colonial domination of another.

SHOOTING AN ELEPHANT

1 In Moulmein, in lower Burma, I was hated by large numbers of people—the only time in my life that I have been important enough for this to happen to me. I was sub-divisional police officer of the town, and in an aimless, petty kind of way anti-European feeling was very bitter. No one had the guts to raise a riot, but if a European woman went through the bazaars alone somebody would probably spit betel juice over her dress. As a police officer I was an obvious target and was baited whenever it seemed safe to do so. When a nimble Burman tripped me up on the football field and the referee (another Burman) looked the other way, the crowd yelled with hideous laughter. This happened more than once. In the end the sneering yellow faces of young men that met me everywhere, the insults hooted after me when I was at a safe distance, got badly on my nerves. The young Buddhist priests were the worst of all. There were several thousands of them in the town and none of them seemed to have anything to do except stand on street corners and jeer at Europeans.

2 All this was perplexing and upsetting. For at that time I had already made up my mind that imperialism was an evil thing and the sooner I chucked up my job and got out of it the better. Theoretically—and secretly, of course—I was all for the Burmese and all against their oppressors, the British. As for the job I was doing, I hated it more bitterly than I can perhaps make clear. In a job like that you see the dirty work of Empire at close quarters. The wretched prisoners huddling in the stinking cages of the lock-ups, the grey, cowed faces of the long-term convicts, the scarred buttocks of the men who had been flogged with bamboos—all these oppressed me with an intolerable sense of guilt. But I could get nothing into perspective. I was young and ill-educated and I had had to think out my problems in the utter silence that is imposed on every Englishman in the East. I did not even know that the British Empire is dying, still less did I know that it is a great deal better than the younger empires that are going to supplant it. All

I knew was that I was stuck between my hatred of the empire I served and my rage against the evil-spirited little beasts who tried to make my job impossible. With one part of my mind I thought of the British Raj° as an unbreakable tyranny, as something clamped down, *in saecula saeculorum,*° upon the will of prostrate peoples: with another part I thought that the greatest joy in the world would be to drive a bayonet into a Buddhist priest's guts. Feelings like these are the normal by-products of imperialism; ask any Anglo-Indian official, if you can catch him off duty.

3 One day something happened which in a roundabout way was enlightening. It was a tiny incident in itself, but it gave me a better glimpse than I had had before of the real nature of imperialism—the real motives for which despotic governments act. Early one morning the sub-inspector at a police station the other end of the town rang me up on the 'phone and said that an elephant was ravaging the bazaar. Would I please come and do something about it? I did not know what I could do, but I wanted to see what was happening and I got on to a pony and started out. I took my rifle, an old .44 Winchester and much too small to kill an elephant, but I thought the noise might be useful *in terrorem.*° Various Burmans stopped me on the way and told me about the elephant's doings. It was not, of course, a wild elephant, but a tame one which had gone "must."° It had been chained up, as tame elephants always are when their attack of "must" is due, but on the previous night it had broken its chain and escaped. Its mahout,° the only person who could manage it when it was in that state, had set out in pursuit, but had taken the wrong direction and was now twelve hours' journey away, and in the morning the elephant had suddenly reappeared in the town. The Burmese population had no weapons and were quite helpless against it. It had already destroyed somebody's bamboo hut, killed a cow and raided some fruit-stalls and devoured the stock; also it had met the municipal rubbish van and, when the driver jumped out and took to his heels, had turned the van over and inflicted violences upon it.

4 The Burmese sub-inspector and some Indian constables were waiting for me in the quarter where the elephant had been seen. It was a very poor quarter, a labyrinth of squalid bamboo huts, thatched with palm-leaf, winding all over a steep hillside. I remember that it was a cloudy, stuffy morning at the beginning of the rains. We began questioning the people as to where the elephant had gone and, as usual, failed to get any definite information. That is invariably the case in the

---

[2] **Raj:** the British administration of colonial India (including Burma)
in saecula saeculorum: (Lat.) for ever and ever

[3] **in terrorem:** (Lat.) in terror; for the purpose of causing fright
"must": sexual arousal, "heat"
mahout: (Hindi) the keeper or driver of an elephant

East; a story always sounds clear enough at a distance, but the nearer you get to the scene of events the vaguer it becomes. Some of the people said that the elephant had gone in one direction, some said that he had gone in another, some professed not even to have heard of any elephant. I had almost made up my mind that the whole story was a pack of lies, when we heard yells a little distance away. There was a loud, scandalized cry of "Go away, child! Go away this instant!" and an old woman with a switch in her hand came round the corner of a hut, violently shooing away a crowd of naked children. Some more women followed, clicking their tongues and exclaiming; evidently there was something that the children ought not to have seen. I rounded the hut and saw a man's dead body sprawling in the mud. He was an Indian, a black Dravidian° coolie, almost naked, and he could not have been dead many minutes. The people said that the elephant had come suddenly upon him round the corner of the hut, caught him with its trunk, put its foot on his back and ground him into the earth. This was the rainy season and the ground was soft, and his face had scored a trench a foot deep and a couple of yards long. He was lying on his belly with arms crucified and head sharply twisted to one side. His face was coated with mud, the eyes wide open, the teeth bared and grinning with an expression of unendurable agony. (Never tell me, by the way, that the dead look peaceful. Most of the corpses I have seen looked devilish.) The friction of the great beast's foot had stripped the skin from his back as neatly as one skins a rabbit. As soon as I saw the dead man I sent an orderly to a friend's house nearby to borrow an elephant rifle. I had already sent back the pony, not wanting it to go mad with fright and throw me if it smelt the elephant.

5 The orderly came back in a few minutes with a rifle and five cartridges, and meanwhile some Burmans had arrived and told us that the elephant was in the paddy fields below, only a few hundred yards away. As I started forward practically the whole population of the quarter flocked out of the houses and followed me. They had seen the rifle and were all shouting excitedly that I was going to shoot the elephant. They had not shown much interest in the elephant when he was merely ravaging their homes, but it was different now that he was going to be shot. It was a bit of fun to them, as it would be to an English crowd; besides they wanted the meat. It made me vaguely uneasy. I had no intention of shooting the elephant—I had merely sent for the rifle to defend myself if necessary—and it is always unnerving to have a crowd following you. I marched down the hill, looking and feeling a fool, with the rifle over my shoulder and an ever-growing army of people jostling at my heels. At the bottom, when you got away from

[4] **Dravidian:** member of an Australoid race inhabiting much of southern India and parts of Ceylon

the huts, there was a metalled road and beyond that a miry waste of paddy fields a thousand yards across, not yet ploughed but soggy from the first rains and dotted with coarse grass. The elephant was standing eight yards from the road, his left side towards us. He took not the slightest notice of the crowd's approach. He was tearing up bunches of grass, beating them against his knees to clean them and stuffing them into his mouth.

6 I had halted on the road. As soon as I saw the elephant I knew with perfect certainty that I ought not to shoot him. It is a serious matter to shoot a working elephant—it is comparable to destroying a huge and costly piece of machinery—and obviously one ought not to do it if it can possibly be avoided. And at that distance, peacefully eating, the elephant looked no more dangerous than a cow. I thought then and I think now that his attack of "must" was already passing off; in which case he would merely wander harmlessly about until the mahout came back and caught him. Moreover, I did not in the least want to shoot him. I decided that I would watch him for a little while to make sure that he did not turn savage again, and then go home.

7 But at that moment I glanced round at the crowd that had followed me. It was an immense crowd, two thousand at the least and growing every minute. It blocked the road for a long distance on either side. I looked at the sea of yellow faces above the garish clothes—faces all happy and excited over this bit of fun, all certain that the elephant was going to be shot. They were watching me as they would watch a conjurer about to perform a trick. They did not like me, but with the magical rifle in my hands I was momentarily worth watching. And suddenly I realized that I should have to shoot the elephant after all. The people expected it of me and I had got to do it; I could feel their two thousand wills pressing me forward, irresistibly. And it was at this moment, as I stood there with the rifle in my hands, that I first grasped the hollowness, the futility of the white man's dominion in the East. Here was I, the white man with his gun, standing in front of the unarmed native crowd—seemingly the leading actor of the piece; but in reality I was only an absurd puppet pushed to and fro by the will of those yellow faces behind. I perceived in this moment that when the white man turns tyrant it is his own freedom that he destroys. He becomes a sort of hollow, posing dummy, the conventionalized figure of a sahib.° For it is the condition of his rule that he shall spend his life in trying to impress the "natives," and so in every crisis he has got to do what the "natives" expect of him. He wears a mask, and his face grows to fit it. I had got to shoot the elephant. I had committed myself

---

[7] **sahib:** (Hindi) master, especially as used toward Europeans

to doing it when I sent for the rifle. A sahib has got to act like a sahib; he has got to appear resolute, to know his own mind and do definite things. To come all that way, rifle in hand, with two thousand people marching at my heels, and then to trail feebly away, having done nothing—no, that was impossible. The crowd would laugh at me. And my whole life, every white man's life in the East, was one long struggle not to be laughed at.

8 But I did not want to shoot the elephant. I watched him beating his bunch of grass against his knees, with that preoccupied grandmotherly air that elephants have. It seemed to me that it would be murder to shoot him. At that age I was not squeamish about killing animals, but I had never shot an elephant and never wanted to. (Somehow it always seems worse to kill a *large* animal.) Besides, there was the beast's owner to be considered. Alive, the elephant was worth at least a hundred pounds; dead, he would only be worth the value of his tusks, five pounds, possibly. But I had got to act quickly. I turned to some experienced-looking Burmans who had been there when we arrived, and asked them how the elephant had been behaving. They all said the same thing: he took no notice of you if you left him alone, but he might charge if you went too close to him.

9 It was perfectly clear to me what I ought to do. I ought to walk up to within, say, twenty-five yards of the elephant and test his behavior. If he charged, I could shoot; if he took no notice of me, it would be safe to leave him until the mahout came back. But also I knew that I was going to do no such thing. I was a poor shot with a rifle and the ground was soft mud into which one would sink at every step. If the elephant charged and I missed him, I should have about as much chance as a toad under a steam-roller. But even then I was not thinking particularly of my own skin, only of the watchful yellow faces behind. For at that moment, with the crowd watching me, I was not afraid in the ordinary sense, as I would have been if I had been alone. A white man mustn't be frightened in front of "natives"; and so, in general, he isn't frightened. The sole thought in my mind was that if anything went wrong those two thousand Burmans would see me pursued, caught, trampled on and reduced to a grinning corpse like that Indian up the hill. And if that happened it was quite probable that some of them would laugh. That would never do. There was only one alternative. I shoved the cartridges into the magazine and lay down on the road to get a better aim.

10 The crowd grew very still, and a deep, low, happy sigh, as of people who see the theatre curtain go up at last, breathed from innumerable throats. They were going to have their bit of fun after all. The rifle was a beautiful German thing with cross-hair sights. I did not then know that in shooting an elephant one would shoot to cut an imaginary bar running from ear-hole to ear-hole. I ought, therefore, as the ele-

phant was sideways on, to have aimed straight at his ear-hole; actually I aimed several inches in front of this, thinking the brain would be further forward.

11 When I pulled the trigger I did not hear the bang or feel the kick —one never does when a shot goes home—but I heard the devilish roar of glee that went up from the crowd. In that instant, in too short a time, one would have thought, even for the bullet to get there, a mysterious, terrible change had come over the elephant. He neither stirred nor fell, but every line of his body had altered. He looked suddenly stricken, shrunken, immensely old, as though the frightful impact of the bullet had paralysed him without knocking him down. At last, after what seemed a long time—it might have been five seconds, I dare say—he sagged flabbily to his knees. His mouth slobbered. An enormous senility seemed to have settled upon him. One could have imagined him thousands of years old. I fired again into the same spot. At the second shot he did not collapse but climbed with desperate slowness to his feet and stood weakly upright, with legs sagging and head drooping. I fired a third time. That was the shot that did for him. You could see the agony of it jolt his whole body and knock the last remnant of strength from his legs. But in falling he seemed for a moment to rise, for as his hind legs collapsed beneath him he seemed to tower upward like a huge rock toppling, his trunk reaching skywards like a tree. He trumpeted, for the first and only time. And then down he came, his belly towards me, with a crash that seemed to shake the ground even where I lay.

12 I got up. The Burmans were already racing past me across the mud. It was obvious that the elephant would never rise again, but he was not dead. He was breathing very rhythmically with long rattling gasps, his great mound of a side painfully rising and falling. His mouth was wide open—I could see far down into caverns of pale pink throat. I waited a long time for him to die, but his breathing did not weaken. Finally I fired my two remaining shots into the spot where I thought his heart must be. The thick blood welled out of him like red velvet, but still he did not die. His body did not even jerk when the shots hit him, the tortured breathing continued without a pause. He was dying, very slowly and in great agony, but in some world remote from me where not even a bullet could damage him further. I felt that I had got to put an end to that dreadful noise. It seemed dreadful to see the great beast lying there, powerless to move and yet powerless to die, and not even to be able to finish him. I sent back for my small rifle and poured shot after shot into his heart and down his throat. They seemed to make no impression. The tortured gasps continued as steadily as the ticking of a clock.

13 In the end I could not stand it any longer and went away. I heard later that it took him half an hour to die. Burmans were bringing

dahs° and baskets even before I left, and I was told they had stripped his body almost to the bones by the afternoon.

14 Afterwards, of course, there were endless discussions about the shooting of the elephant. The owner was furious, but he was only an Indian and could do nothing. Besides, legally I had done the right thing, for a mad elephant has to be killed, like a mad dog, if its owner fails to control it. Among the Europeans opinion was divided. The older men said I was right, the younger men said it was a damn shame to shoot an elephant for killing a coolie, because an elephant was worth more than any damn Coringhee coolie. And afterwards I was very glad that the coolie had been killed; it put me legally in the right and it gave me a sufficient pretext for shooting the elephant. I often wondered whether any of the others grasped that I had done it solely to avoid looking a fool.

STUDY QUESTIONS

1. What impression of Orwell do we get from his opening paragraph? Is that impression altered later? Why do you think Orwell began in this manner?
2. Why is it important for Orwell to include his vivid description of "the dirty work of Empire" (paragraph 2)?
3. A writer who once served as a colonial policeman, and who is now utterly opposed to colonialism, might be expected to tell us how he came to understand and sympathize with the "native" culture on its own terms. Does Orwell do so? What view of the Burmese does he appear to take? Would the point of his essay have come across more, or less, effectively if he had projected a different attitude toward the "natives"?
4. In his second paragraph, Orwell reveals that at the time of this incident he had already "made up [his] mind that imperialism was an evil thing." What effect does this information have on our interpretation of the story that Orwell proceeds to tell? Does it strengthen or weaken the intended effect of his essay?
5. Why does Orwell tell us in paragraph 3 that the story he is about to tell was "enlightening," but then refrain for some time from telling us what was enlightening about it? Where does the point become explicit? And in what ways does his story exemplify that point?
6. What tone and level of diction do you find Orwell characteris-

---

[13] **dahs:** large heavy knives

tically using in this essay? Be prepared to cite examples. Can you relate the tone and level of Orwell's language to his general attitude toward his subject matter?

7. In paragraph 7 Orwell tells us about his thoughts as he realized that he would have to shoot the elephant. Is it likely that Orwell arrived at all of those reflections on the spot? If not, which ones probably came later? As an essayist, what justification would Orwell have for "reading back" a subsequent idea into a dramatic situation?
8. Orwell is extremely vivid, first in describing the squashed corpse of the coolie (paragraph 4), and then in describing the death agonies of the elephant (paragraphs 11–12). Is this merely "hard-boiled prose" for its own sake, or is the vividness necessary to Orwell's purpose? Be ready to support your answer.
9. Carefully study Orwell's concluding paragraph, and be prepared to discuss any "shocking" effects you find in it. Has Orwell undermined his essay with this rather daring paragraph, or has he given further emphasis to his argument?
10. As he became more famous in years subsequent to the writing of "Shooting an Elephant," Orwell was often praised for his ability to look beyond the interests of parties and factions and to take a universally human point of view. What signs of that ability do you detect in this essay?
11. Under what other headings besides "Arguing from Experience" could this essay have been included?

Joseph Epstein

Joseph Epstein teaches at Northwestern University and edits *The American Scholar.* He is the author of *Divorced in America* and a book of essays, *Familiar Territory: Observations on American Life* (1979), including the present selection.

RUNNING AND OTHER VICES

1 Whenever I see someone jogging by, body glistening with sweat, face contorted with pain, I think of a fellow with whom I went to high school, one Taxicab Rabinowitz by name. Rabinowitz earned his vehicular sobriquet, as W. C. Fields might have put it, from traveling almost exclusively by cab. I did not know him well, but on those occasions when I did see the Cab, as intimates called him, he inevitably appeared

to be either emerging from or entering into yet another taxicab. Taxicab Rabinowitz was one of those boys who go directly from early childhood to middle age without ever stopping at youth. I imagine he began shaving around the age of nine. He wore pointed-toed shoes with alligator trim. He was wide in the flanks, soft in the middle; the omnipresent cigarette on his lip—a Pall Mall, unfiltered, if memory serves—was as much a part of his physiognomy as his well-pomaded hair. Taxicab Rabinowitz was of course unthinkable in a gym suit or athletic togs of any kind, with the exception of a checkered suit to be worn at the track. He was, with his cabs and cigarettes and puffy body, the very antithesis of all that is implied by the phrase "in shape."

2 "In shape?" I can easily hear Rabinowitz asking. "In shape for what?" That is not a bad question, to which I shall return presently, but first I want to say that the reason I think of Taxicab Rabinowitz whenever I see a jogger is that he, the Cab, is the last man in the world I can imagine jogging. Miami Beach, Las Vegas, Palm Springs, whichever pleasure spa Taxicab Rabinowitz now inhabits, he is surely not running around it but is much more likely to be seated—most probably in the back of a cab, from where he must long ago have concluded that cab meters, not human beings, are for running.

3 If Taxicab Rabinowitz is the last man in the world I can imagine taking up a regular regimen of running, then I am the next-to-the-last man. I am, if only in the physical realm, too virtuous as it is. Here is my dismal record: I drink, but scarcely ever to excess. I weigh exactly what the weight charts inform me I ought to weigh (the result of avoiding too frequent indulgence in fattening foods, every one of which I love). I play racquetball, usually twice a week. My cholesterol count is where it ought to be, my blood pressure is normal. I have recently quit smoking cigarettes, a habit of more than twenty years' standing. I both retire and rise early. Quite sickening, is it not? Also a bit worrisome. Enjoying such good health has of late caused me to think myself a perfect potential victim for being run over by a school bus. ("He was in his prime, Emily, never sick a day in his life.") But to enter upon a running regimen is more virtuous than even I care to be.

4 No mistake, it is the virtuousness of runners that appalls—the notion that their running makes them a select breed, an elite of sorts, whose elitism, though anchored in physical activity, goes well beyond the physical. Early last year the *Wall Street Journal* ran an article about people in cars harassing joggers and runners along roadsides: honking at them, spitting at them, nudging them with front bumpers, in some instances running them off the road. The motive, the joggers and runners assumed, was envy of their superior health. Ah, how readily the scene sets itself in the mind! A jogging couple, resplendent in polyester warm-up suits, blond brows aglow with a fine coat of perspiration; then up drives a long Lincoln, one of those gas guzzlers that got us into the energy crisis to begin with; the fat, beetle-browed driver behind the

wheel shifts a cigar stub in his jaw, slips the Lincoln out of Cruisomatic, and, muttering obscenities, aims his car toward the jogging couple—who embody good health, sensible economy, and (let's face it) everything America could, and indeed ought to, be.

5 Implicit in this scene, too, is the notion that joggers and runners are an endangered species of sorts, though few things could be further from the truth. For twenty-six-mile marathon races in Boston, New York, and Chicago, runners turn out by the thousands; soon the mark of a bush-league town will be that it does not have a marathon. Yet marathon runners are but a minuscule portion of people who run noncompetitively: those who run before work in the early morning or after work in the early evening, the weekend runners, and those who run whenever they can. They have become part of the landscape, these joggers and runners, sometimes the first thing one sees out the window in the morning. One sees them chugging alongside the Potomac in Washington, up and down every street and footpath in Eugene, Oregon, at sunup in Manhattan, in middle western parks. Chicago has already had a jogging rapist whose victims have been women jogging in forest preserves. A commonly cited figure for the American running population is twenty-five million.

6 This surging pedestrianism seems to disregard strict social confines. Running/jogging is not something done chiefly by the upper middle class, nor is it preponderantly suburban. The young go in for it in great numbers, of course, but the middle-aged are padding along with them, and even the quite old are huffing not far behind. Running is unisex at all but the competitive levels, and as many (perhaps more) women as men seem to be swept up by it. Motives for running seem as varied as the backgrounds of runners; among them are wanting to lose weight, gain muscle tone, take fresh air and exercise, feel achievement, extend and test physical capacity. More arcane motives for running, if they were not present to begin with, have since been supplied. Running "highs" are now spoken of. In some of the books about running, not simply exercise but "ecstasy" is held to lie just down the path. In short, the oily fingers of the consciousness movement have taken hold. "Sweat reaches places nothing else reaches," says Dr. George Sheehan, one of the gurus of running. "Sweat cleanses you."

7 And the purveyors of running gear, one ought quickly to add, pick you even cleaner. Among the advantages of running, one might suppose, is that it would seem to require so little in the way of equipment; shoes, shorts, a road—doesn't that about cover it? Not quite. No sooner had the fad of running begun in earnest than abreast of it trotted up the publishers, manufacturers, merchandisers. These running dogs of capitalism are even now running all the way to the bank. They founded magazines, such as *Runner's World* and *The Runner,* that seek to proselytize even as they preach to the converted. Books in plenty continue to appear: practical manuals like *Guidelines to Successful Jogging, Aerobics for*

Women, Computerized Running Training Programs; books holding out hope and promise such as *The Joy of Running* and *Run for Your Life;* biographies of long-distance runners; and books of philosophic purport such as *Running and Being: The Total Experience* (this last by Dr. Sheehan, who has become something of a J. P. Sartre° in an athletic supporter).

8 Riffling through the pages of the new magazines devoted to running, one could conclude from the advertisements that there are more kinds of running shoes now on the market in America than there are feet. But this is not to speak of such auxiliary items as special arch supports, heel protectors, insoles; nor of fog-repellents for glasses, or skin lube to prevent chafing under the arms, or runner's mittens; nor of warm-up suits, singlets, socks, and shorts (one manufacturer sells shorts that he advertises as "almost like running nude"). Then there are metric conversion scales, chronographs and stopwatches, wallets that attach to running shoes, pouches to fit on the back of shorts. One of my favorite items is a "jogging stick," comparable to a military swagger stick, to be carried along while running and to be used, apparently, for beating off dogs, muggers, perhaps smokers.

9 Ours is an age of health, and the runner is surely our most fanatical seeker after health, a Hassid at the altar of Hygeia.° Various explanations have been adduced for the excessive concern with health in our day. The novelist Mary Gordon, for example, feels that it has to do with politics taking a turn inward. Unable to control the external world of events, she explains, we seek to control the internal world of our bodies. "If we can't stop Seabrook,"° writes Miss Gordon, "maybe we can lengthen our Achilles tendons." There may well be something to this. Others seem to feel that a political profile can be discerned among running folk; as I write, a comedy revue in the Middle West carries the title *Great Jogging Liberals.* But I think something rather more fundamental is entailed. I think it is, at bottom, the fear of death that keeps joggers and runners jogging and running. This seems to me a reasonable enough fear, and one we all share. The only difference between joggers and runners and the rest of us, when it comes to the fear of death, is that they are doing something about it: they are running from it.

10 Our own age of health has a historical precedent in the early and middle Victorian age in England. The setting for the nineteenth-century concern with health seems to have been rampant sickness and arbitrary death. In a recent book, *The Healthy Body and Victorian Culture* (Harvard

---

[7] **J. P. Sartre:** Jean-Paul Sartre (1905–1980), French novelist, playwright, and philosopher. His advocacy of existentialism connects him (with comic remoteness) to the *Being* of Dr. Sheehan's title.

[9] **Hassid, Hygeia:** respectively, a mystically joyous Jewish zealot (usually spelled *Hasid*); the Greek goddess of health

Seabrook: a proposed nuclear power plant in New Hampshire, the site of many demonstrations by antinuclear activists

University Press), Bruce Haley notes: "Nothing occupies a nation's mind with the subject of health like a general contagion." England in the 1830s and 1840s, according to Professor Haley, was lashed by three tidal waves of contagious diseases: "the first, from 1831 to 1833, included two influenza epidemics and the initial appearance of cholera; the second, from 1836 to 1842, encompassed major epidemics of influenza, typhus, smallpox, and scarlet fever; in the third, from 1846 to 1849, there were occurrences of typhus, typhoid, and cholera." As a result of such devastations, the English became health-minded, and the body became a thing to be cultivated as sedulously as the mind—perhaps even more so. In England this was the time of the rise of many sports, among them mountaineering, cycling, lawn tennis, rugby, rowing, badminton, and roller skating. This was the time of the installation of games into the regular life of public schools. (The Battle of Waterloo won on the playing fields of Eton and all that—which, according to Professor Haley's researches, the Duke of Wellington never in fact said.) This was, finally, the time of the rise of what was known as muscular Christianity.°

11 The analogy between the Victorian setting and our own is not altogether tidy, but it does have some things to recommend it. We currently live under no fear of contagion, but every one of us has had to shiver at the black prospects of cancer or heart disease. Much of our concern with diet in recent years is about these grim prospects. We must not choke up the arteries with fat, or send the blood pressure rocketing, or breathe the bad air, or swallow anything on Dr. Nader's Index of Prohibited Foods. ("Whoso speaks on Health," wrote the Victorian G. H. Lewes, "is sure of a large audience"—which might serve as a gloss on Ralph Nader's career.) Like the Victorian age, too, our own has seen an efflorescence of sport, and not alone spectator sport. Over the past decade alone, participants in tennis, skiing, backpacking, racquetball, and jogging and running have all grown hugely in number. In part this growth has had to do with an increase in leisure and a fairly steady level of affluence—what is nowadays considered an acceptable pair of ski boots runs to around $250—but in even greater part it has had to do with our slightly terrified concern about not getting proper exercise, being healthy, staying in shape. If the Victorians went in for muscular Christianity, we, in our more secular age, appear ready to settle for simple muscularity.

12 The late Robert Hutchins, when chancellor of the University of Chicago, used to say that whenever he felt like exercising he would lie down till the feeling passed, which inevitably it did quite soon. Hutchins also said that if you have to watch the meter, don't take a cab.

---

10 **muscular Christianity:** an outlook championed by the British novelist and clergyman Charles Kingsley (1819–1875), whereby Christian faith and robust health were recommended together

(These two apothegms ought to qualify him as Taxicab Rabinowitz's man for all seasons.) But Hutchins's advice had certain limitations. Tall and slender, absolutely princely in carriage, Robert Hutchins was one of those fortunate creatures who came by his physical elegance naturally. (He probably also had most of his cab fares paid by other people or by expense account.) Hutchins was, it will be remembered, the man who dropped football from the University of Chicago; implicit in his decision was the idea that the life of the mind need have no further traffic with the life of the body—once the majoritarian view among intellectuals and academics. Hutchins believed and they believed, along with Montaigne, that it was sufficient to maintain "the soul and reason in good trim."

13 In an extraordinary reversal, it now often appears that the best way to maintain the soul and reason in trim is first to have the heart and legs and lungs in trim. This, too, is not altogether new. Professor Haley quotes a character in a Charles Kingsley novel of 1871: "Believe me, it may be a very materialist view of things: but fact is fact—the *corpus sanum* is father to the *mens sana.*"[13] Most regular runners would seem to hold to this notion. Attend, for example, to James F. Fixx, author of *The Complete Book of Running,* arguing *against* the idea of running as a religion:

> It's easy enough to see how running got confused with religion. Running can, it's true, make you imagine yourself a better person than you are. Yesterday, I ran for an hour through a seaside park near my home in Connecticut. The last of the leaves were tumbling in the wind. I ran past three imperturbable skunks, a raccoon, a family of squirrels busily laying in a winter's supplies. A pheasant noisily took to the air at the sound of running shoes on gravel. By the time I got home, I felt refreshed and beatified. I know of no human activity, except perhaps sex, that can do so much in so brief a time, and do it so wonderfully.

14 Mr. Fixx is a temperate, no doubt altogether reasonable man. He does not talk about being in touch with the spirit while running; he does not confuse sweat with salvation. Neither does he equate modern-day runners with a persecuted religious sect, as I have heard another running maven, a man named Joel Henning, do. Yet when I read a passage like Mr. Fixx's above, why do I wish its author, not exactly ill, but a plague of life's little inconveniences? As he runs through his seaside park, I hope that he will one day perturb those three skunks sufficiently for them to loose their most noxious perfume upon him; that the raccoon will take a small bite out of his, Mr. Fixx's, running shoe; that the pheasant who now noisily takes to the air at the sound of Mr. Fixx's foot on gravel will instead smile at the sound of the same foot squishing in pheasant droppings.

---

[13] **corpus sanum, mens sana:** (Lat.) healthy body, healthy mind. Epstein is reversing the terms of a Roman truism, "a healthy mind within a healthy body."

15 Quite a little animus I seem to have built up here. Whence does this animus derive? From, I suspect, Mr. Fixx's and other runners' avowed self-satisfaction, from their not altogether suppressed smugness. Note, for example, the nudging reference to sexual activity in Mr. Fixx's last sentence. He is saying that his running is splendid, no question about it, but that his sex is even better. This leads one to think that a jackpot awaits the author of a guidebook to be entitled *Sex While Running.*

16 If my animus is strong, it is not solitary. More than one person has remarked upon the great boringness of running as a conversational subject. The vanity of the long-distance runner has become notorious. Tom Wolfe, among his series of monthly drawings in *Harper's,* has a particularly devastating drawing of a grotesquely misshapen middle-aged couple running through a Marin-County-like suburb.° The drawing is entitled "The Joggers' Prayer," and the prayer reads:

> Almighty God, as we sail with pure aerobic grace and striped orthotic feet past the blind portals of our fellow citizens, past their chuckroast lives and their necrotic cardiovascular systems and rusting hips and slipped discs and desiccated lungs, past their implacable inertia and inability to persevere and rise above the fully pensioned world they live in and to push themselves to the limits of their capacity and achieve the White Moment of slipping through The Wall, borne aloft on one's Third Wind, past their Cruisomatic cars and upholstered lawn mowers and their gummy-sweet children already at work like little fat factories producing arterial plaque, the more quickly to join their parents in their joyless bucket-seat landau ride toward the grave—help us, dear Lord, we beseech Thee, as we sail past this cold-lard desolation, to be big about it.

17 The smugness of runners, their vanity, may be inherent in the very activity of running itself. Runners chalk up achievement daily, or at least on each day that they run. They have had the body out for a tune-up, a cleaning, an overhaul, whereas the rest of us haven't. Their situation is akin to that of the woman whose car is just out of the car wash or the man who has just had a shoeshine. How grubby, at such moments, everyone else's cars and shoes look! A pity, really. One would think people would have enough self-respect not to let their personal possessions get so run down. A man named Joe Henderson, a consulting editor to *Runner's World,* remarks in that magazine about not missing his daily run in nearly four years: "That's what I'm proudest of: There's something in the way I run that keeps me eager and healthy." Implicit in that sentence is the thought, "And you, Pudge, your *not* running is doubtless what keeps you logy and sickly." Reading the writings of

---

16 **Marin County:** affluent suburban area north of San Francisco, noted for devotion to leisure activities and self-improvement

runners, listening to them talk, one is reminded of Proust° describing Albertine on her first appearance at the beach at Balbec, leading her little band of friends who all had "that mastery over their limbs which comes from perfect bodily condition and a sincere contempt for the rest of humanity."

18 The contempt of joggers and runners for the rest of humanity is often quite sincere, but I am not sure that it is deserved. Apart from competitive long-distance runners, who tend to be a self-enclosed and solitary lot in a lonely and grueling sport, most joggers and runners are not, at least in my experience and observation, among the best athletes. This may have to do with the fact that running has never been rated very high by serious athletes, other than as a means to an end. Often it has been used by coaches and trainers as a salubrious punishment for such misdeeds as reporting in overweight at the beginning of a season, missing a practice, fouling up in one way or another. Few athletes who have known the pleasure of sport at a fairly high level can content themselves with running as a source of satisfaction in and of itself. Serious athletes understand the need to be in shape, but in shape for something quite palpable: the game that they play. Joggers and runners are people who are content merely to be in shape for its own sake.

19 The pleasure of jogging and running is rather like that of wearing a fur coat in Texas in August: the true joy comes in being able to take the damn thing off. And because the runner or jogger regards running and jogging as its own end, an element of puritanical fanaticism easily insinuates itself. Thus a writer on the subject named Tom Osler, who does "not wish to be numbered with those who make claims of special life-extending benefits from it [running]," turns out to have run once for twenty-four hours straight, covering a distance of 114 miles (not, surely, everybody's idea of a day well spent). Thus *Runner's World* informs female readers that it is quite all right to run pregnant, right up to the day of delivery. There are people who are now beginning to run up mountains. Soon, doubtless, races will be held in which the contestants will wear lead in their shoes, or carry snow tires in their arms, or strap their accountants on their backs. If it feels good to remove a fur coat in Texas in August, how much better it will feel to remove a fur coat, leather leggings, and a tank helmet in Yucatan.

20 Committed joggers and runners would dispute all this. As for the argument that others use running as a means to an end while for them it is an end in itself, this they wouldn't concede at all. Running is not merely getting in shape per se; it is, many runners would reply, getting in shape for life. "Since I started running regularly, my outlook is better,

---

[17] **Proust:** Marcel Proust (1871–1922), French author of the monumental novel *Remembrance of Things Past*

my confidence greater, my self-regard higher"—such is the kind of testimonial one finds in the letters columns of the running magazines. Besides, what is the matter with getting in shape per se? Is not good health one of those things worth pursuing as an end in itself?

21 It is, up to a point. The point is when the concern with good health becomes unseemly—almost, one is tempted to say, unhealthy. The most cheering thing about good health is that it allows one not to think about one's health. Think too closely about it, dwell on it too long, and, lo, it will depart. Has there ever been a less robust crowd than the customers (and usually the clerks) in health food stores—with their sallow skins, dull eyes, bony carcasses, the human equivalent of horses ready to be shipped off to the glue factory? Joggers and runners, though they look rather better, are similarly preoccupied, even obsessed, with their bodies. "I eat bread sparingly," writes Tom Osler. "In the summer, I consume large quantities of fruit juices. . . . I do not use salt at the table or at the stove. I do not use sugar, because it seems to make my skin break out in acne." In an article titled "Running Through Pregnancy" in *Runner's World,* we learn that runners "have little trouble with irregularity. Some even experience a frequency increase in bowel movements." In the pages of the same magazine Joe Henderson reports that he thinks of a running high "as the way we're supposed to feel when not constipated." If one did not know what was being talked about—running—one might feel like an eavesdropper listening in on conversations in a nursing home for the elderly.

22 As it turns out, many joggers and runners do seem to require a certain amount of nursing, and the precise benefits of jogging and running are very much in the flux of controversy. As nearly as I can make out, internists appear to think jogging/running quite a good thing for circulation, respiration, general metabolism. Orthopedists, bone and joint men, appear to deplore it, citing its potential for injury: shin splints, stone bruises, tendonitis of the knee or ankle, spinal troubles. All physicians agree that great care must be taken, especially if one is past forty years old, when too strenuous a running program can be dangerous. To die from a heart attack while jogging seems neither a glorious nor a philosophical death. The French used to speak of dying as "stumbling into eternity," which seems to me far preferable to running toward the same destination.

23 While runners come from a diversity of backgrounds, there is much to unite them. An article in *The Runner* puts it thus: "The enemy lines are drawn. Divergent lifestyles foster a see-saw phenomenon. One side must be put down for the other to go up: smoker versus non-smoker, vegetarian versus meat-eater, runner versus non-runner." If ever two groups were opposed, surely these two groups are runners and smokers. Running is one of the few things that cannot be done while smoking, and smoking is one of the chief things runners despise. The same article in *The Runner* notes that "a lot of runners are extremely

obnoxious about that [smoking]. They're pompous. They're rude. They go and take a cigarette out of someone's hand."

24 Yet why, pressed to a hasty generalization, do I tend to prefer the company of smokers over that of runners? The most obvious reason is that smokers are not always talking about their smoking and their bad health in the way runners, when not on crutches, tend to talk about their running and good health. Smokers as a group tend therefore to be rather less boring than runners. But the reasons, I think, go deeper.

25 Although Robert Coles° has not yet written a book about them, smokers are today something of a persecuted minority in the United States. A friend who works in a large corporation reports to me that at least one department head there refuses to hire smokers because other people in the department stridently complain about the smoke. States and municipalities have of late held referendums—and some have put laws upon the books—outlawing smoking in public places. We may one day be headed for a new Volstead Act° prohibiting smoking. Smokers meanwhile have come to take on the hesitant manners of the persecuted. "Do you mind if I smoke?" once the most perfunctory of questions, is perfunctory no longer. "Damn right I mind, buddy!" can come shooting back in response.

26 "The exquisite vice," as Oscar Wilde called smoking cigarettes, has become the nasty habit. Where once the cigarette was an accoutrement of elegance—think of André Malraux,° Humphrey Bogart, Franklin Delano Roosevelt, all of whom could almost be said to have worn cigarettes, and worn them very well—the cigarette has now become a mark of enslavement to a shameful habit. "God gave us tobacco to quiet our passions and soothe our grief," says a character in Balzac. But no longer. Nowadays it is said that around 80 percent of all smokers would like to be able to quit.

27 That roughly 100,000 of the 390,000 annual deaths owed to cancer can be linked to smoking, that smoking is a great stimulus to heart attack, that it reduces sexual appetite in men, that some 37,000,000 people will shorten their lives because of smoking—none of this would most smokers dispute. As I believed it as a smoker, so do they believe it. The fact is that smoking has nothing to do with belief, or with rationality. But quitting smoking is one of the world's great small nuisances—"Quitting smoking is easy," said Mark Twain, a cigar smoker, "I have done it a thousand times"—so difficult in its way that comparing

[25] **Robert Coles:** Harvard psychologist whose multivolume work *Children of Crisis* deals with several poverty-stricken American minorities

Volstead Act: 1919 act of Congress implementing the Eighteenth Amendment to the Constitution, forbidding the sale of alcoholic beverages

[26] **André Malraux:** (1901–1976) French novelist, archaeologist, art critic, and statesman

nicotine addiction with that of alcohol and heroin, while farfetched, is not altogether crazy. Having finally succeeded in stopping smoking after many abortive attempts, I now find that I have exchanged one habit for another, and today spend half my waking hours with a hard candy or lozenge in my mouth. I may be one of the first men in history to die of tooth decay.

28 Yet smoking, and struggling to quit smoking, does give one a keen sense of human imperfectibility. My attempts to quit smoking—so small and mean a thing, as I keep telling myself, to ask of so large and generous an intelligence—long ago killed off the last remaining vestiges of utopianism in me. I do not mean to imply that smoking makes anyone more intelligent. Given all that is known about smoking, it is a supremely unintelligent thing to do. Toward the end of my struggle I found myself smoking less and despising myself more. But this most pertinacious and exasperating habit teaches a healthy regard for human limitation.

29 Runners, on the other hand, are full of thoughts of human possibility. If one runs seven miles in the spring, perhaps by autumn one can do ten miles. The pages of the running magazines revel in the mention of runners in their seventies and eighties. I have read about a new magazine calling itself *Nutrition Health Review,* which (according to an ad in the magazine *Mother Jones*) asks, "Can You Live to Be 100?" The question is rhetorical, and the answer is that, watching what you eat and imbibe, you can indeed. But why stop at 100? Why not 120, or 150, or 200?

30 "What!" Frederick the Great° is supposed to have said to a general who informed him of his troops' refusal to go into battle. "Do they expect to live forever?" Runners, like all truly self-absorbed perfectibilitarians, do seem to expect to live forever. Perhaps they do not expect to run forever—only up to the age of (say) ninety, at which point many could be got to agree to taper off. "I grow old . . . I grow old . . . I shall wear the bottoms of my trousers rolled," says J. Alfred Prufrock.° But were he a runner, he would doubtless add: "But, look, above my rolled-up trousers I wear the two-toned singlet of tricot from Sport International, which prevents chafing and whose mesh bottom prevents it from clinging, thus helping me keep dry. While below I wear the Wildcat running shoe, from Autry Industries, Inc., whose thick heel and ankle padding helps protect my Achilles tendons." Our new Prufrock shall no longer walk but now run upon the beach / no longer hear the mermaids singing, each to each / but only the pounding of blood in his ears / drowning out thoughts of death and other legitimate fears.

---

30 **Frederick the Great:** (1712–1786) King of Prussia from 1740 to 1786

J. Alfred Prufrock: the timid, self-doubting "hero" of "The Love Song of J. Alfred Prufrock," by the American poet T. S. Eliot (1888–1964)

STUDY QUESTIONS

1. What does Epstein's title lead us to expect about the tone of his essay? Is our expectation met?
2. Among the "other vices" promised in his title, Epstein dwells on only one, smoking. Look through the essay for references to smoking, and ask yourself what thematic use Epstein has made of this "other vice."
3. Why does Epstein begin by describing his old friend Taxicab Rabinowitz? What is the effect of that portrait on our response to the rest of the essay?
4. As in any humorous essay, Epstein's comic effects depend on highly controlled uses of language. He relies, for example, on puns (plays on words) such as the characterization of the purveyors of running accessories as "running dogs of capitalism" (paragraph 7). What further puns can you spot in Epstein's essay? Can you find other instances of language that has been chosen for its comic possibilities?
5. What advantage does Epstein gain by his frequent use of quotations? What does the range of those quotations—the variety of sources from which Epstein draws—tell us about his attitudes and experience?
6. Study paragraph 8 as an instance of Epstein's general effort to control his readers' response to the vogue of jogging. What rhetorical devices can you identify there? Are they successful, in your opinion?
7. Why, when Epstein's primary area of interest is contemporary America, does he devote paragraphs 10 and 11 to a discussion of Victorian England?
8. Epstein rarely discusses his own character and tastes, yet he allows us to make inferences about them throughout the essay. What self-portrait does he draw, and how does he convey it?
9. Despite its many comic touches, this essay has a serious point to make, and Epstein clearly subscribes to certain values that considerably matter to him. What *is* the point, and what do you take Epstein's values to be?

James Baldwin

James Baldwin has been recognized as an outstanding American novelist and essayist since the 1950s. Raised in New York City, he has spent much of his adult life abroad, chiefly in France. The essay below, now often cited as a classic, appeared in his first collection, *Notes of a Native Son* (1955).

STRANGER IN THE VILLAGE

1 From all available evidence no black man had ever set foot in this tiny Swiss village before I came. I was told before arriving that I would probably be a "sight" for the village; I took this to mean that people of my complexion were rarely seen in Switzerland, and also that city people are always something of a "sight" outside of the city. It did not occur to me—possibly because I am an American—that there could be people anywhere who had never seen a Negro.

2 It is a fact that cannot be explained on the basis of the inaccessibility of the village. The village is very high, but it is only four hours from Milan and three hours from Lausanne. It is true that it is virtually unknown. Few people making plans for a holiday would elect to come here. On the other hand, the villagers are able, presumably, to come and go as they please—which they do: to another town at the foot of the mountain, with a population of approximately five thousand, the nearest place to see a movie or go to the bank. In the village there is no movie house, no bank, no library, no theater; very few radios, one jeep, one station wagon; and, at the moment, one typewriter, mine, an invention which the woman next door to me here had never seen. There are about six hundred people living here, all Catholic—I conclude this from the fact that the Catholic church is open all year round, whereas the Protestant chapel, set off on a hill a little removed from the village, is open only in the summertime when the tourists arrive. There are four or five hotels, all closed now, and four or five *bistros,* of which, however, only two do any business during the winter. These two do not do a great deal, for life in the village seems to end around nine or ten o'clock. There are a few stores, butcher, baker, *épicerie,*° a hardware store, and a money-changer—who cannot change travelers' checks, but must send them down to the bank, an operation which takes two or three days. There is something called the *Ballet Haus,* closed in the winter and used for God knows what, certainly not ballet, during the summer. There seems to be

---

[2] **épicerie:** (Fr.) grocery store

only one schoolhouse in the village, and this for the quite young children; I suppose this to mean that their older brothers and sisters at some point descend from these mountains in order to complete their education—possibly, again, to the town just below. The landscape is absolutely forbidding, mountains towering on all four sides, ice and snow as far as the eye can reach. In this white wilderness, men and women and children move all day, carrying washing, wood, buckets of milk or water, sometimes skiing on Sunday afternoons. All week long boys and young men are to be seen shoveling snow off the rooftops, or dragging wood down from the forest in sleds.

3 The village's only real attraction, which explains the tourist season, is the hot spring water. A disquietingly high proportion of these tourists are cripples, or semicripples, who come year after year—from other parts of Switzerland, usually—to take the waters. This lends the village, at the height of the season, a rather terrifying air of sanctity, as though it were a lesser Lourdes.° There is often something beautiful, there is always something awful, in the spectacle of a person who has lost one of his faculties, a faculty he never questioned until it was gone, and who struggles to recover it. Yet people remain people, on crutches or indeed on deathbeds; and wherever I passed, the first summer I was here, among the native villagers or among the lame, a wind passed with me—of astonishment, curiosity, amusement, and outrage. That first summer I stayed two weeks and never intended to return. But I did return in the winter, to work; the village offers, obviously, no distractions whatever and has the further advantage of being extremely cheap. Now it is winter again, a year later, and I am here again. Everyone in the village knows my name, though they scarcely ever use it, knows that I come from America—though this, apparently, they will never really believe: black men come from Africa—and everyone knows that I am the friend of the son of a woman who was born here, and that I am staying in their chalet. But I remain as much a stranger today as I was the first day I arrived, and the children shout *Neger! Neger!* as I walk along the streets.

4 It must be admitted that in the beginning I was far too shocked to have any real reaction. In so far as I reacted at all, I reacted by trying to be pleasant—it being a great part of the American Negro's education (long before he goes to school) that he must make people "like" him. This smile-and-the-world-smiles-with-you routine worked about as well in this situation as it had in the situation for which it was designed, which is to say that it did not work at all. No one, after all, can be liked whose human weight and complexity cannot be, or has not been, admitted. My smile was simply another unheard-of phenomenon which al-

---

[3] **Lourdes:** town in southern France to which Catholics make pilgrimages, often in the hope of miraculous cures

lowed them to see my teeth—they did not, really, see my smile and I began to think that, should I take to snarling, no one would notice any difference. All of the physical characteristics of the Negro which had caused me, in America, a very different and almost forgotten pain were nothing less than miraculous—or infernal—in the eyes of the village people. Some thought my hair was the color of tar, that it had the texture of wire, or the texture of cotton. It was jocularly suggested that I might let it all grow long and make myself a winter coat. If I sat in the sun for more than five minutes some daring creature was certain to come along and gingerly put his fingers on my hair, as though he were afraid of an electric shock, or put his hand on my hand, astonished that the color did not rub off. In all of this, in which it must be conceded there was the charm of genuine wonder and in which there was certainly no element of intentional unkindness, there was yet no suggestion that I was human: I was simply a living wonder.

5 I knew that they did not mean to be unkind, and I know it now; it is necessary, nevertheless, for me to repeat this to myself each time that I walk out of the chalet. The children who shout *Neger!* have no way of knowing the echoes this sound raises in me. They are brimming with good humor and the more daring swell with pride when I stop to speak with them. Just the same, there are days when I cannot pause and smile, when I have no heart to play with them; when, indeed, I mutter sourly to myself, exactly as I muttered on the streets of a city these children have never seen, when I was no bigger than these children are now: *Your* mother *was a nigger.* Joyce° is right about history being a nightmare—but it may be the nightmare from which no one *can* awaken. People are trapped in history and history is trapped in them.

6 There is a custom in the village—I am told it is repeated in many villages—of "buying" African natives for the purpose of converting them to Christianity. There stands in the church all year round a small box with a slot for money, decorated with a black figurine, and into this box the villagers drop their francs. During the *carnaval* which precedes Lent, two village children have their faces blackened—out of which bloodless darkness their blue eyes shine like ice—and fantastic horsehair wigs are placed on their blond heads; thus disguised, they solicit among the villagers for money for the missionaries in Africa. Between the box in the church and the blackened children, the village "bought" last year six or eight African natives. This was reported to me with pride by the wife of one of the *bistro* owners and I was careful to express astonishment and pleasure at the solicitude shown by the village for the souls of black folk. The *bistro* owner's wife beamed with a pleasure far more genuine than my own and seemed to feel that I might

5 **Joyce:** James Joyce (1882–1941), Irish novelist; the statement Baldwin paraphrases is found in *A Portrait of the Artist as a Young Man* (1916).

now breathe more easily concerning the souls of at least six of my kinsmen.

7 I tried not to think of these so lately baptized kinsmen, of the price paid for them, or the peculiar price they themselves would pay, and said nothing about my father, who having taken his own conversion too literally never, at bottom, forgave the white world (which he described as heathen) for having saddled him with a Christ in whom, to judge at least from their treatment of him, they themselves no longer believed. I thought of white men arriving for the first time in an African village, strangers there, as I am a stranger here, and tried to imagine the astounded populace touching their hair and marveling at the color of their skin. But there is a great difference between being the first white man to be seen by Africans and being the first black man to be seen by whites. The white man takes the astonishment as tribute, for he arrives to conquer and to convert the natives, whose inferiority in relation to himself is not even to be questioned; whereas I, without a thought of conquest, find myself among a people whose culture controls me, has even, in a sense, created me, people who have cost me more in anguish and rage than they will ever know, who yet do not even know of my existence. The astonishment with which I might have greeted them, should they have stumbled into my African village a few hundred years ago, might have rejoiced their hearts. But the astonishment with which they greet me today can only poison mine.

8 And this is so despite everything I may do to feel differently, despite my friendly conversations with the *bistro* owner's wife, despite their three-year-old son who has at last become my friend, despite the *saluts* and *bonsoirs*° which I exchange with people as I walk, despite the fact that I know that no individual can be taken to task for what history is doing, or has done. I say that the culture of these people controls me —but they can scarcely be held responsible for European culture. America comes out of Europe, but these people have never seen America, nor have most of them seen more of Europe than the hamlet at the foot of their mountain. Yet they move with an authority which I shall never have; and they regard me, quite rightly, not only as a stranger in their village but as a suspect latecomer, bearing no credentials, to everything they have—however unconsciously—inherited.

9 For this village, even were it incomparably more remote and incredibly more primitive, is the West, the West onto which I have been so strangely grafted. These people cannot be, from the point of view of power, strangers anywhere in the world; they have made the modern world, in effect, even if they do not know it. The most illiterate among them is related, in a way that I am not, to Dante, Shakespeare, Mi-

[8] **saluts and bonsoirs:** (Fr.) greetings and good evenings

chelangelo, Aeschylus, Da Vinci, Rembrandt, and Racine; the cathedral at Chartres says something to them which it cannot say to me, as indeed would New York's Empire State Building, should anyone here ever see it. Out of their hymns and dances come Beethoven and Bach. Go back a few centuries and they are in their full glory—but I am in Africa, watching the conquerors arrive.

10 The rage of the disesteemed is personally fruitless, but it is also absolutely inevitable; this rage, so generally discounted, so little understood even among the people whose daily bread it is, is one of the things that makes history. Rage can only with difficulty, and never entirely, be brought under the domination of the intelligence and is therefore not susceptible to any arguments whatever. This is a fact which ordinary representatives of the *Herrenvolk,*° having never felt this rage and being unable to imagine it, quite fail to understand. Also, rage cannot be hidden, it can only be dissembled. This dissembling deludes the thoughtless, and strengthens rage and adds, to rage, contempt. There are, no doubt, as many ways of coping with the resulting complex of tensions as there are black men in the world, but no black man can hope ever to be entirely liberated from this internal warfare—rage, dissembling, and contempt having inevitably accompanied his first realization of the power of white men. What is crucial here is that, since white men represent in the black man's world so heavy a weight, white men have for black men a reality which is far from being reciprocal; and hence all black men have toward all white men an attitude which is designed, really, either to rob the white man of the jewel of his naïveté, or else to make it cost him dear.

11 The black man insists, by whatever means he finds at his disposal, that the white man cease to regard him as an exotic rarity and recognize him as a human being. This is a very charged and difficult moment, for there is a great deal of will power involved in the white man's naïveté. Most people are not naturally reflective any more than they are naturally malicious, and the white man prefers to keep the black man at a certain human remove because it is easier for him thus to preserve his simplicity and avoid being called to account for crimes committed by his forefathers, or his neighbors. He is inescapably aware, nevertheless, that he is in a better position in the world than black men are, nor can he quite put to death the suspicion that he is hated by black men therefore. He does not wish to be hated, neither does he wish to change places, and at this point in his uneasiness he can scarcely avoid having recourse to those legends which white men have created about black men, the most usual effect of which is that the white man finds himself enmeshed, so to speak, in his own language which describes hell, as well

---

[10] **Herrenvolk:** (Ger.) people of status

as the attributes which lead one to hell, as being as black as night.

12 Every legend, moreover, contains its residuum of truth, and the root function of language is to control the universe by describing it. It is of quite considerable significance that black men remain, in the imagination, and in overwhelming numbers in fact, beyond the disciplines of salvation; and this despite the fact that the West has been "buying" African natives for centuries. There is, I should hazard, an instantaneous necessity to be divorced from this so visibly unsaved stranger, in whose heart, moreover, one cannot guess what dreams of vengeance are being nourished; and, at the same time, there are few things on earth more attractive than the idea of the unspeakable liberty which is allowed the unredeemed. When, beneath the black mask, a human being begins to make himself felt one cannot escape a certain awful wonder as to what kind of human being it is. What one's imagination makes of other people is dictated, of course, by the laws of one's own personality and it is one of the ironies of black-white relations that, by means of what the white man imagines the black man to be, the black man is enabled to know who the white man is.

13 I have said, for example, that I am as much a stranger in this village today as I was the first summer I arrived, but this is not quite true. The villagers wonder less about the texture of my hair than they did then, and wonder rather more about me. And the fact that their wonder now exists on another level is reflected in their attitudes and in their eyes. There are the children who make those delightful, hilarious, sometimes astonishingly grave overtures of friendship in the unpredictable fashion of children; other children, having been taught that the devil is a black man, scream in genuine anguish as I approach. Some of the older women never pass without a friendly greeting, never pass, indeed, if it seems that they will be able to engage me in conversation; other women look down or look away or rather contemptuously smirk. Some of the men drink with me and suggest that I learn how to ski—partly, I gather, because they cannot imagine what I would look like on skis—and want to know if I am married, and ask questions about my *métier.*° But some of the men have accused *le sale nègre*°—behind my back—of stealing wood and there is already in the eyes of some of them that peculiar, intent, paranoiac malevolence which one sometimes surprises in the eyes of American white men when, out walking with their Sunday girl, they see a Negro male approach.

14 There is a dreadful abyss between the streets of this village and the streets of the city in which I was born, between the children who shout *Neger!* today and those who shouted *Nigger!* yesterday—the abyss is experience, the American experience. The syllable hurled behind me

---

13 **métier:** (Fr.) profession
le sale nègre: (Fr.) the dirty Negro

today expresses, above all, wonder: I am a stranger here. But I am not a stranger in America and the same syllable riding on the American air expresses the war my presence has occasioned in the American soul.

15 For this village brings home to me this fact: that there was a day, and not really a very distant day, when Americans were scarcely Americans at all but discontented Europeans, facing a great unconquered continent and strolling, say, into a marketplace and seeing black men for the first time. The shock this spectacle afforded is suggested, surely, by the promptness with which they decided that these black men were not really men but cattle. It is true that the necessity on the part of the settlers of the New World of reconciling their moral assumptions with the fact—and the necessity—of slavery enhanced immensely the charm of this idea, and it is also true that this idea expresses, with a truly American bluntness, the attitude which to varying extents all masters have had toward all slaves.

16 But between all former slaves and slave-owners and the drama which begins for Americans over three hundred years ago at Jamestown, there are at least two differences to be observed. The American Negro slave could not suppose, for one thing, as slaves in past epochs had supposed and often done, that he would ever be able to wrest the power from his master's hands. This was a supposition which the modern era, which was to bring about such vast changes in the aims and dimensions of power, put to death; it only begins, in unprecedented fashion, and with dreadful implications, to be resurrected today. But even had this supposition persisted with undiminished force, the American Negro slave could not have used it to lend his condition dignity, for the reason that this supposition rests on another: that the slave in exile yet remains related to his past, has some means—if only in memory—of revering and sustaining the forms of his former life, is able, in short, to maintain his identity.

17 This was not the case with the American Negro slave. He is unique among the black men of the world in that his past was taken from him, almost literally, at one blow. One wonders what on earth the first slave found to say to the first dark child he bore. I am told that there are Haitians able to trace their ancestry back to African kings, but any American Negro wishing to go back so far will find his journey through time abruptly arrested by the signature on the bill of sale which served as the entrance paper for his ancestor. At the time—to say nothing of the circumstances—of the enslavement of the captive black man who was to become the American Negro, there was not the remotest possibility that he would ever take power from his master's hands. There was no reason to suppose that his situation would ever change, nor was there, shortly, anything to indicate that his situation had ever been different. It was his necessity, in the words of

E. Franklin Frazier,° to find a "motive for living under American culture or die." The identity of the American Negro comes out of this extreme situation, and the evolution of this identity was a source of the most intolerable anxiety in the minds and the lives of his masters.

18 For the history of the American Negro is unique also in this: that the question of his humanity, and of his rights therefore as a human being, became a burning one for several generations of Americans, so burning a question that it ultimately became one of those used to divide the nation. It is out of this argument that the venom of the epithet *Nigger!* is derived. It is an argument which Europe has never had, and hence Europe quite sincerely fails to understand how or why the argument arose in the first place, why its effects are so frequently disastrous and always so unpredictable, why it refuses until today to be entirely settled. Europe's black possessions remained—and do remain—in Europe's colonies, at which remove they represented no threat whatever to European identity. If they posed any problem at all for the European conscience, it was a problem which remained comfortingly abstract: in effect, the black man, *as a man,* did not exist for Europe. But in America, even as a slave, he was an inescapable part of the general social fabric and no American could escape having an attitude toward him. Americans attempt until today to make an abstraction of the Negro, but the very nature of these abstractions reveals the tremendous effects the presence of the Negro has had on the American character.

19 When one considers the history of the Negro in America it is of the greatest importance to recognize that the moral beliefs of a person, or a people, are never really as tenuous as life—which is not moral—very often causes them to appear; these create for them a frame of reference and a necessary hope, the hope being that when life has done its worst they will be enabled to rise above themselves and to triumph over life. Life would scarcely be bearable if this hope did not exist. Again, even when the worst has been said, to betray a belief is not by any means to have put oneself beyond its power; the betrayal of a belief is not the same thing as ceasing to believe. If this were not so there would be no moral standards in the world at all. Yet one must also recognize that morality is based on ideas and that all ideas are dangerous—dangerous because ideas can only lead to action and where the action leads no man can say. And dangerous in this respect: that confronted with the impossibility of remaining faithful to one's beliefs, and the equal impossibility of becoming free of them, one can be driven to the most inhuman excesses. The ideas on which American beliefs are based are not, though Americans often seem to think so, ideas which origi-

---

[17] **E. Franklin Frazier:** (1894–1962) Howard University sociologist

nated in America. They came out of Europe. And the establishment of democracy on the American continent was scarcely as radical a break with the past as was the necessity, which Americans faced, of broadening this concept to include black men.

20 This was, literally, a hard necessity. It was impossible, for one thing, for Americans to abandon their beliefs, not only because these beliefs alone seemed able to justify the sacrifices they had endured and the blood that they had spilled, but also because these beliefs afforded them their only bulwark against a moral chaos as absolute as the physical chaos of the continent it was their destiny to conquer. But in the situation in which Americans found themselves, these beliefs threatened an idea which, whether or not one likes to think so, is the very warp and woof of the heritage of the West, the idea of white supremacy.

21 Americans have made themselves notorious by the shrillness and the brutality with which they have insisted on this idea, but they did not invent it; and it has escaped the world's notice that those very excesses of which Americans have been guilty imply a certain, unprecedented uneasiness over the idea's life and power, if not, indeed, the idea's validity. The idea of white supremacy rests simply on the fact that white men are the creators of civilization (the present civilization, which is the only one that matters; all previous civilizations are simply "contributions" to our own) and are therefore civilization's guardians and defenders. Thus it was impossible for Americans to accept the black man as one of themselves, for to do so was to jeopardize their status as white men. But not so to accept him was to deny his human reality, his human weight and complexity, and the strain of denying the overwhelmingly undeniable forced Americans into rationalizations so fantastic that they approached the pathological.

22 At the root of the American Negro problem is the necessity of the American white man to find a way of living with the Negro in order to be able to live with himself. And the history of this problem can be reduced to the means used by Americans—lynch law and law, segregation and legal acceptance, terrorization and concession—either to come to terms with this necessity, or to find a way around it, or (most usually) to find a way of doing both these things at once. The resulting spectacle, at once foolish and dreadful, led someone to make the quite accurate observation that "the Negro-in-America is a form of insanity which overtakes white men."

23 In this long battle, a battle by no means finished, the unforeseeable effects of which will be felt by many future generations, the white man's motive was the protection of his identity; the black man was motivated by the need to establish an identity. And despite the terrorization which the Negro in America endured and endures sporadically until today, despite the cruel and totally inescapable ambivalence of his status in his country, the battle for his identity has long ago been won. He is not a visitor to the West, but a citizen there, an American; as

American as the Americans who despise him, the Americans who fear him, the Americans who love him—the Americans who became less than themselves, or rose to be greater than themselves by virtue of the fact that the challenge he represented was inescapable. He is perhaps the only black man in the world whose relationship to white men is more terrible, more subtle, and more meaningful than the relationship of bitter possessed to uncertain possessor. His survival depended, and his development depends, on his ability to turn his peculiar status in the Western world to his own advantage and, it may be, to the very great advantage of that world. It remains for him to fashion out of his experience that which will give him sustenance, and a voice.

24 The cathedral at Chartres, I have said, says something to the people of this village which it cannot say to me; but it is important to understand that this cathedral says something to me which it cannot say to them. Perhaps they are struck by the power of the spires, the glory of the windows; but they have known God, after all, longer than I have known him, and in a different way, and I am terrified by the slippery bottomless well to be found in the crypt, down which heretics were hurled to death, and by the obscene, inescapable gargoyles jutting out of the stone and seeming to say that God and the devil can never be divorced. I doubt that the villagers think of the devil when they face a cathedral because they have never been identified with the devil. But I must accept the status which myth, if nothing else, gives me in the West before I can hope to change the myth.

25 Yet, if the American Negro has arrived at his identity by virtue of the absoluteness of his estrangement from his past, American white men still nourish the illusion that there is some means of recovering the European innocence, of returning to a state in which black men do not exist. This is one of the greatest errors Americans can make. The identity they fought so hard to protect has, by virtue of that battle, undergone a change: Americans are as unlike any other white people in the world as it is possible to be. I do not think, for example, that it is too much to suggest that the American vision of the world—which allows so little reality, generally speaking, for any of the darker forces in human life, which tends until today to paint moral issues in glaring black and white—owes a great deal to the battle waged by Americans to maintain between themselves and black men a human separation which could not be bridged. It is only now beginning to be borne in on us—very faintly, it must be admitted, very slowly, and very much against our will—that this vision of the world is dangerously inaccurate, and perfectly useless. For it protects our moral high-mindedness at the terrible expense of weakening our grasp of reality. People who shut their eyes to reality simply invite their own destruction, and anyone who insists on remaining in a state of innocence long after that innocence is dead turns himself into a monster.

26 The time has come to realize that the interracial drama acted out on the American continent has not only created a new black man, it has created a new white man, too. No road whatever will lead Americans back to the simplicity of this European village where white men still have the luxury of looking on me as a stranger. I am not, really, a stranger any longer for any American alive. One of the things that distinguishes Americans from other people is that no other people has ever been so deeply involved in the lives of black men, and vice versa. This fact faced, with all its implications, it can be seen that the history of the American Negro problem is not merely shameful, it is also something of an achievement. For even when the worst has been said, it must also be added that the perpetual challenge posed by this problem was always, somehow, perpetually met. It is precisely this black-white experience which may prove of indispensable value to us in the world we face today. This world is white no longer, and it will never be white again.

STUDY QUESTIONS

1. What kinds of readers, in your opinion, constitute Baldwin's intended audience? How can you tell?
2. From what level of diction (high, medium, or low) would you say that Baldwin characteristically draws his language? And does his sentence structure tend to be relatively simple or relatively complex? Find examples of both diction and sentence structure that illustrate your answers. What resultant tone has Baldwin created, and why?
3. What rhetorical advantage does Baldwin gain by beginning his essay with an extensive discussion of the Swiss village and its inhabitants? To arrive at an answer, think of the likely effect Baldwin would have created by beginning with generalizations about the racial hypocrisy of white America and the whole Western world.
4. What does Baldwin mean by the last sentence in paragraph 5, "People are trapped in history and history is trapped in them"? In what way is that statement central to Baldwin's theme?
5. Why does Baldwin devote a paragraph (6) to the village practice of "buying" African natives?
6. Why, in Baldwin's view, is there "a great difference between being the first white man to be seen by Africans and being the first black man to be seen by whites" (paragraph 7)?
7. In what respects, according to Baldwin, was American slavery different from any previous slavery, and what have been the long-term consequences of those differences?

8. How does Baldwin make such adjectives as *naïve, simple,* and *innocent* more damaging than *malicious* in characterizing the racial attitudes of whites?
9. What is meant by the observation, which Baldwin quotes at the end of paragraph 22, that "the Negro-in-America is a form of insanity which overtakes white men"?
10. What do you take to be the thesis, or main idea, of "Stranger in the Village"? Where (if anywhere) is it stated?
11. How does the Swiss villagers' unawareness of Baldwin's human identity become useful to his larger argument?
12. This essay about black-white relations was written in 1953, a year before the Supreme Court's ruling on school desegregation and still longer before the intense civil-rights struggles of the 1960s. In what respects do you find Baldwin's argument "dated"? Does it contain "timeless" elements as well?

ESTABLISHING A PRINCIPLE

James Fallows

James Fallows, Washington editor of *The Atlantic,* has written several controversial and widely discussed articles, including "The Passionless Presidency," "The Musclebound Superpower," and "The Tests and the 'Brightest.' " The essay below first appeared in April 1980, not long after President Carter, in the wake of the Soviet invasion of Afghanistan, asked Congress to reinstitute draft registration.

THE DRAFT: WHY THE COUNTRY NEEDS IT

I am more than angry. I did not give birth to my one and only son to have him snatched away from me 18 years later. My child has been loved and cared for and taught right from wrong and will not *be fed into any egomaniac's war machine.*

Our 18- to 25-year-olds have not brought this world to its present sorry state. Men over the age of 35, down through the centuries, have brought us here, and we women have been in silent accord.

Well, this is one woman, one mother, who says no. *I did not go through the magnificent agony of childbirth to have that glorious young life snuffed out.*

Until the presidents, premiers, supreme rulers, politburos, senators and congressmen of the world are ready to physically, as opposed to verbally, lead the world into combat, they can bloody well forget my child.

Unite mothers! *Don't throw your sons and daughters away. Sometime, somewhere, women have just got to say no.*

No. No. No. No. No. Never my child.

—Louise M. Saylor

(Letter published in the Washington *Post,* January 28, 1980.)

1 Nor my child, Mrs. Saylor. Nor either of my mother's sons when, ten years ago, both were classified I-A. But *whose,* then? As our statesmen talk again of resisting aggression and demonstrating our will—as they talk, that is, of sending someone's sons (or daughters) to bear arms

overseas—the only fair and decent answer to that question lies in a return to the draft.

2 I am speaking here not of the health of the military but of the character of the society the military defends. The circumstances in which that society will choose to go to war, the way its wars will be fought, and its success in absorbing the consequent suffering depend on its answer to the question Whose sons will go?

3 History rarely offers itself in lessons clear enough to be deciphered at a time when their message still applies. But of all the hackneyed "lessons" of Vietnam, one still applies with no reservations: that we wound ourselves gravely if we flinch from honest answers about who will serve. During the five or six years of the heaviest draft calls for Vietnam, there was the starkest class division in American military service since the days of purchased draft deferments in the Civil War. Good intentions lay at the root of many of these inequities. The college-student deferment, the various "hardship" exemptions, Robert McNamara's° plan to give "disadvantaged" youngsters a chance to better themselves in the military, even General Hershey's° intelligence test to determine who could remain in school—all were designed to allot American talent in the most productive way. The intent was to distinguish those who could best serve the nation with their minds from those who should offer their stout hearts and strong backs. The effect was to place the poor and the black in the trenches (and later in the coffins and the rehabilitation wards), and their "betters" in colleges or elsewhere far from the sounds of war. I speak as one who took full advantage of the college-student deferment and later exploited the loopholes in the physical qualification standards that, for college students armed with a doctor's letter and advice from the campus draft counseling center, could so easily be parlayed into the "unfit for service" designation known as a I-Y. Ask anyone who went to college in those days how many of his classmates saw combat in Vietnam. Of my 1200 classmates at Harvard, I know of only two, one of them a veteran who joined the class late. The records show another fifty-five in the reserves, the state-side Army, or military service of some other kind. There may be more; the alumni lists are not complete. See how this compares with the Memorial Roll from a public high school in a big city or a West Virginia hill town.

4 For all the talk about conflict between "young" and "old" that the war caused, the lasting breach was among the young. In the protest marches on the Pentagon and the Capitol, students felt either scorn for or estrangement from the young soldiers who stood guard. What must

---

[3] **Robert McNamara:** Secretary of Defense under Presidents Johnson and Kennedy

General Hershey: General Lewis B. Hershey (1893–1977), for many years head of the U.S. Selective Service System

the soldiers have felt about these, their privileged contemporaries, who taunted them so? To those who opposed the war, the ones who served were, first, animals and killers; then "suckers" who were trapped by the system, deserving pity but no respect; and finally invisible men. Their courage, discipline, and sacrifice counted for less than their collective taint for being associated with a losing war. A returned veteran might win limited redemption if he publicly recanted, like a lapsed Communist fingering his former associates before the HUAC.° Otherwise, he was expected to keep his experiences to himself. Most veterans knew the honor they had earned, even as they knew better than anyone else the horror of the war. They came to resent being made to suppress those feelings by students who chose not to join them and who, having escaped the war without pain, now prefer to put the whole episode in the past. Perhaps no one traversed that era without pain, but pain of the psychic variety left arms, legs, life intact and did not impede progress in one's career. For people of my generation—I speak in the narrow sense of males between the ages of twenty-eight and thirty-six or thirty-seven—this wound will never fully heal. If you doubt that, sit two thirty-two-year-olds down together, one who served in Vietnam and one who did not, and ask them to talk about those years.

5 At least there was theoretical consistency between what the students of those days recommended for others and what they did themselves. Their point was that no one should go to war, starting with them. It should also be said that their objection to the war, at least in my view, was important and right. And while they—we—may have proven more effective and determined in acts of individual salvation than in anything else, they at least paid lip service to the idea of the "categorical imperative," that they should not expect others to bear a burden they considered unacceptable for themselves.

6 I hear little of that tone in the reaction to President Carter's muted call for resumption of draft registration. Within a week of his request in the State of the Union address, I spent time at two small colleges. At both, the sequence of questions was the same. Why is our defense so weak? When will we show the Russians our strength? *Isn't it terrible about the draft?*

7 Senator Kennedy, who so often decried the unfairness of the draft during Vietnam, won cheers from his college audience for his opposition to draft registration, in the same speech in which he suggested beefing up our military presence in the Persian Gulf. Kennedy did go on to argue that we should not shed blood for oil, which is more than most anti-draft groups have done to date. It would have been reassuring to hear

[4] **HUAC:** House Committee on Un-American Affairs, noted in the 1950s for its exposure of alleged Communists

the students say that they oppose registration *because* they oppose a military showdown in the Persian Gulf. Instead many simply say, We don't want to go. I sense that they—perhaps all of us—have come to take for granted a truth so painful that few could bear to face it during Vietnam: that there will be another class of people to do the dirty work. After seven years of the volunteer Army, we have grown accustomed to having suckers on hand.

8 That the volunteer Army is another class can hardly be denied. The Vietnam draft was unfair racially, economically, educationally. By every one of those measures, the volunteer Army is less representative still. Libertarians argue that military service should be a matter of choice, but the plain fact is that service in the volunteer force is too frequently dictated by economics. Army enlisted ranks E1 through E4 —the privates and corporals, the cannon fodder, the ones who will fight and die—are 36 percent black now. By the Army's own projections, they will be 42 percent black in three years. When other "minorities" are taken into account, we will have, for the first time, an army whose fighting members are mainly "non-majority," or, more bluntly, a black and brown army defending a mainly white nation. The military has been an avenue of opportunity for many young blacks. They may well be first-class fighting men. They do not represent the nation.

9 Such a selective bearing of the burden has destructive spiritual effects in a nation based on the democratic creed. But its practical implications can be quite as grave. The effect of a fair, representative draft is to hold the public hostage to the consequences of its decisions, much as children's presence in the public schools focuses parents' attention on the quality of the schools. If citizens are willing to countenance a decision that means that *someone's* child may die, they may contemplate more deeply if there is the possibility that the child will be theirs. Indeed, I would like to extend this principle even further. Young men of nineteen are rightly suspicious of the congressmen and columnists who urge them to the fore. I wish there were a practical way to resurrect the provisions of the amended Selective Service Act of 1940, which raised the draft age to forty-four. Such a gesture might symbolize the desire to offset the historic injustice of the Vietnam draft, as well as suggest the possibility that, when a bellicose columnist recommends dispatching American forces to Pakistan, he might also realize that he could end up as a gunner in a tank.

10 Perhaps the absence of a World War II-scale peril makes such a proposal unrealistic; still, the columnist or congressman should have to contemplate the possibility that his son would be there, in trench or tank. Under the volunteer Army that possibility will not arise, and the lack of such a prospect can affect behavior deeply. Recall how, during Vietnam, protest grew more broad-based and respectable when the

graduate school deferment was eliminated in 1968. For many families in positions of influence, the war was no longer a question of someone else's son. How much earlier would the war have ended had college students been vulnerable from the start?

11 Those newly concerned families were no better and no worse than other people at other times; they were responding to a normal human instinct, of the sort our political system is designed to channel toward constructive ends. It was an instinct that Richard Nixon and Henry Kissinger understood very well, as they deliberately shifted the burden of the war off draftees and finally off Americans, to free their hands to pursue their chosen course. Recall how fast protest ebbed with the coming of the volunteer Army and "Vietnamization"° in the early 1970s. For this reason, the likes of Nixon and Kissinger might regard a return to the draft as a step in the wrong direction, for it would sap the resolve necessary for a strong foreign policy and introduce the weakening element of domestic dissent. At times leaders must take actions that seem heartless and unfair, and that an informed public would probably not approve. Winston Churchill let Coventry° be bombed, because to sound the air-raid sirens and save its citizens would have tipped off the Germans that Britain had broken their code. But in the long run, a nation cannot sustain a policy whose consequences the public is not willing to bear. If it decides not to pay the price to defend itself, it will be defenseless. That is the risk of democracy.

12 What kind of draft? More than anything else, a *fair* one, with as few holes as possible to wriggle through. The 1971 Selective Service Act, passed when the heavy draft calls had already ended, theoretically closed most of the loopholes. But if real trouble should begin, those nine-year-old patches might give way before political pressures unless we concentrate again on the mechanics of an equitable draft. "Fairness" does not mean that everyone need serve. This year 4.3 million people will turn eighteen, 2.2 million women and 2.1 million men. For the last few years, the military has been taking 400,000 people annually into the volunteer Army—or, in raw figures, only one in ten of the total available pool. Using today's mental and physical standards, the military knocks off 30 percent of the manpower pool as unqualified, and it excludes women from combat positions. When these calculations are combined with the diminishing number of young men—only 1.6 million men will turn eighteen in 1993—the military projects that it will need to attract one of every three "qualified and available men" by the end of the 1980s.

---

11 **"Vietnamization":** the Nixon administration's policy of turning over combat duties, insofar as possible, from American to South Vietnamese forces

Coventry: English cathedral city, devastated by German bombing raids early in World War II

13 Read another way, this means that a draft need affect *no more* than one in three—and probably far fewer. To make the draft seem—and be—fair, the pool of potential draftees should be as large as possible, even if only a few will eventually be picked. Those who are "disabled" in the common meaning of that term—the blind, paraplegics—should be excluded, but not the asthmatics and trick-back cases who are perfectly capable of performing non-combat military jobs. The military's physical requirements now assume that nearly all men must theoretically be fit for combat, even though only 14 percent of all male soldiers hold combat jobs. The proportion of draftees destined for combat would probably be higher, since those are the positions now most understrength; if actual fighting should begin it would be higher still. But combat will never represent the preponderance of military positions, and its requirements should not blindly dictate who is eligible for the draft. Instead, everyone without serious handicap should be eligible for selection by lottery—men and women, students and non-students. Once the lottery had determined *who* would serve, assignments based on physical classifications could determine where and how.

14 The question of women's service is the most emotionally troubling aspect of this generally emotional issue, but the progress of domestic politics over the last ten years suggests that the answer is clear. If any sexual distinctions that would deny a woman her place as a construction worker or a telephone pole climber have been forbidden by legislators and courts, what possible distinction can spare women the obligation to perform similar functions in military construction units or the Signal Corps? President Carter recognized this reality in deciding to include women in his initial draft registration order. If women are drafted, they have an iron-clad case for passage of the Equal Rights Amendment. If they are not, their claim for equal treatment elsewhere becomes less compelling. At the same time, it is troubling to think of women in combat, or of mothers being drafted, and a sensible draft law would have to recognize such exceptions.

15 There should be no educational deferments except for students still in high school, and possibly in two other cases. One would be for college students who enroll in ROTC; like their counterparts in the service academies, they would be exchanging four years of protected education for a longer tour of duty as an officer after graduation. The other exception might be for doctors, possessors of a skill the military needs but cannot sensibly produce on its own. If potential doctors wanted to be spared all eligibility for the draft, they could enter a program like the Navy's V-12 during World War II, in which they could take a speeded-up college course and receive a publicly subsidized medical education, after which they would owe several years' service as military doctors. Except in the most far-fetched situations, "hardship" cases should be taken care of by compensation rather than by exemption. If these are permitted, they become an invitation to abuse: who can

forget George Hamilton° pleading hardship as his mother's sole supporting son? Instead, the government should offset hardship with support payments to the needy dependents.

16 One resists the idea of lottery, because it adds to the system the very element of caprice and unfairness it is so important to remove. But since only a fraction of those eligible to serve are actually required, there seems no other equitable way to distribute the burden. With a well-established lottery, every male and female might know at age eighteen whether he or she was near the top of the list and very likely to be called, or near the bottom and almost certainly protected. How far the draft calls went down the list would depend on how many people volunteered and how many more were needed.

17 None of these concerns and prescriptions would matter if the volunteer Army were what it so often seemed in the last few years—a stand-in, a symbol, designed to keep the machinery running and the troops in place, not to be sent into action for any cause less urgent than absolute survival. But now we hear from every quarter that the next decade will be a time of testing, that our will and our strategy and our manpower will be on the line. The nature of this challenge, and the style of our response, are what we should be thinking and talking about now. Our discussions will never be honest, nor our decisions just, as long as we count on "suckers" to do the job.

STUDY QUESTIONS

1. What effect does Fallows produce by supplying the epigraph (quoted passage at the head of the essay) that he has chosen?
2. Which consideration seems more central to Fallows's argument about the draft, the condition of our military forces or the principle of fairness? Why?
3. With respect to American foreign policy, does Fallows strike you more as a "hawk" or as a "dove"? Reconcile your answer with his advocacy of a renewed peacetime draft.
4. If you were to oppose Fallows's position, what considerations would you raise? Do you find that he has anticipated some of them? If so, has he succeeded in neutralizing their force?
5. Is Fallows's case made stronger or weaker by his telling us (paragraph 3) that he avoided military service in the Vietnam period?
6. What, in Fallows's opinion, is the most important difference be-

[15] **George Hamilton:** wealthy Hollywood actor, once romantically linked with a daughter of President Johnson

tween recent opposition to the draft and the opposition that flourished during the Vietnam War?

7. What rhetorical advantages does Fallows gain by reciting the statistics found in paragraph 12?
8. Why is it important, in Fallows's total case, that he propose different rules for the Selective Service System from all previous ones? If his discussion of those rules is indeed important, why does most of it come so late (paragraphs 13–17) in his essay?
9. What is Fallows's main reason for wanting women to be included in the draft? What would a secondary reason be? Has he overlooked any reasons for *not* drafting women?
10. Why does Fallows use the provocative word *suckers* at several points in his essay (paragraphs 4, 7, 17)?

Martin Luther King, Jr.

Martin Luther King, Jr. (1929–1968), founder of the Southern Christian Leadership Conference, was a principal figure in the American civil rights movement of the 1950s and 1960s. In recognition of his contribution to interracial understanding and progress, he received the Nobel Peace Prize in 1964. He was assassinated four years later in Memphis, Tennessee, where he had gone to support a strike of garbage collectors. His numerous books include *Why We Can't Wait* (1964), which contains the present, slightly revised, text of his "Letter from Birmingham Jail." The letter was written in 1963 in answer to a "Public Statement by Eight Alabama Clergymen" protesting demonstrations led by "outsiders" and calling for recourse to "proper channels" instead of confrontation in the streets.

LETTER FROM BIRMINGHAM JAIL

April 16, 1963

My Dear Fellow Clergymen:

1 While confined here in the Birmingham city jail, I came across your recent statement calling my present activities "unwise and untimely." Seldom do I pause to answer criticism of my work and ideas. If I sought to answer all the criticisms that cross my desk, my secretaries would have little time for anything other than such correspondence in the course of the day, and I would have no time for constructive work.

But since I feel that you are men of genuine good will and that your criticisms are sincerely set forth, I want to try to answer your statement in what I hope will be patient and reasonable terms.

2 I think I should indicate why I am here in Birmingham, since you have been influenced by the view which argues against "outsiders coming in." I have the honor of serving as president of the Southern Christian Leadership Conference, an organization operating in every southern state, with headquarters in Atlanta, Georgia. We have some eighty-five affiliated organizations across the South, and one of them is the Alabama Christian Movement for Human Rights. Frequently we share staff, educational and financial resources with our affiliates. Several months ago the affiliate here in Birmingham asked us to be on call to engage in a nonviolent direct-action program if such were deemed necessary. We readily consented, and when the hour came we lived up to our promise. So I, along with several members of my staff, am here because I was invited here. I am here because I have organizational ties here.

3 But more basically, I am in Birmingham because injustice is here. Just as the prophets of the eighth century B.C. left their villages and carried their "thus saith the Lord" far beyond the boundaries of their home towns, and just as the Apostle Paul left his village of Tarsus and carried the gospel of Jesus Christ to the far corners of the Greco-Roman world, so am I compelled to carry the gospel of freedom beyond my own home town. Like Paul, I must constantly respond to the Macedonian° call for aid.

4 Moreover, I am cognizant of the interrelatedness of all communities and states. I cannot sit idly by in Atlanta and not be concerned about what happens in Birmingham. Injustice anywhere is a threat to justice everywhere. We are caught in an inescapable network of mutuality, tied in a single garment of destiny. Whatever affects one directly, affects all indirectly. Never again can we afford to live with the narrow, provincial "outside agitator" idea. Anyone who lives inside the United States can never be considered an outsider anywhere within its bounds.

5 You deplore the demonstrations taking place in Birmingham. But your statement, I am sorry to say, fails to express a similar concern for the conditions that brought about the demonstrations. I am sure that none of you would want to rest content with the superficial kind of social analysis that deals merely with effects and does not grapple with underlying causes. It is unfortunate that demonstrations are taking place in Birmingham, but it is even more unfortunate that the city's white power structure left the Negro community with no alternative.

---

[3] **Macedonian:** pertaining to the Roman province of Macedonia, earlier the Macedonian Empire, including areas of present-day Greece, Yugoslavia, and Bulgaria. The Apostle Paul traveled widely in order to encourage and aid early Christian communities, including those in Macedonia.

6 In any nonviolent campaign there are four basic steps: collection of the facts to determine whether injustices exist; negotiation; self-purification; and direct action. We have gone through all these steps in Birmingham. There can be no gainsaying the fact that racial injustice engulfs this community. Birmingham is probably the most thoroughly segregated city in the United States. Its ugly record of brutality is widely known. Negroes have experienced grossly unjust treatment in the courts. There have been more unsolved bombings of Negro homes and churches in Birmingham than in any other city in the nation. These are the hard, brutal facts of the case. On the basis of these conditions, Negro leaders sought to negotiate with the city fathers. But the latter consistently refused to engage in good-faith negotiation.

7 Then, last September, came the opportunity to talk with leaders of Birmingham's economic community. In the course of the negotiations, certain promises were made by the merchants—for example, to remove the stores' humiliating racial signs. On the basis of these promises, the Reverend Fred Shuttlesworth and the leaders of the Alabama Christian Movement for Human Rights agreed to a moratorium on all demonstrations. As the weeks and months went by, we realized that we were the victims of a broken promise. A few signs, briefly removed, returned; the others remained.

8 As in so many past experiences, our hopes had been blasted, and the shadow of deep disappointment settled upon us. We had no alternative except to prepare for direct action, whereby we would present our very bodies as a means of laying our case before the conscience of the local and the national community. Mindful of the difficulties involved, we decided to undertake a process of self-purification. We began a series of workshops on nonviolence, and we repeatedly asked ourselves: "Are you able to accept blows without retaliating?" "Are you able to endure the ordeal of jail?" We decided to schedule our direct-action program for the Easter season, realizing that except for Christmas, this is the main shopping period of the year. Knowing that a strong economic-withdrawal program would be the by-product of direct action, we felt that this would be the best time to bring pressure to bear on the merchants for the needed change.

9 Then it occurred to us that Birmingham's mayoral election was coming up in March, and we speedily decided to postpone action until after election day. When we discovered that the Commissioner of Public Safety, Eugene "Bull" Connor, had piled up enough votes to be in the run-off, we decided again to postpone action until the day after the run-off so that the demonstrations could not be used to cloud the issues. Like many others, we waited to see Mr. Connor defeated, and to this end we endured postponement after postponement. Having aided in this community need, we felt that our direct-action program could be delayed no longer.

10 You may well ask: "Why direct action? Why sit-ins, marches and

so forth? Isn't negotiation a better path?" You are quite right in calling for negotiation. Indeed, this is the very purpose of direct action. Nonviolent direct action seeks to create such a crisis and foster such a tension that a community which has constantly refused to negotiate is forced to confront the issue. It seeks so to dramatize the issue that it can no longer be ignored. My citing the creation of tension as part of the work of the nonviolent-resister may sound rather shocking. But I must confess that I am not afraid of the word "tension." I have earnestly opposed violent tension, but there is a type of constructive, nonviolent tension which is necessary for growth. Just as Socrates felt that it was necessary to create a tension in the mind so that individuals could rise from the bondage of myths and half-truths to the unfettered realm of creative analysis and objective appraisal, so must we see the need for nonviolent gadflies to create the kind of tension in society that will help men rise from the dark depths of prejudice and racism to the majestic heights of understanding and brotherhood.

11 The purpose of our direct-action program is to create a situation so crisis-packed that it will inevitably open the door to negotiation. I therefore concur with you in your call for negotiation. Too long has our beloved Southland been bogged down in a tragic effort to live in monologue rather than dialogue.

12 One of the basic points in your statement is that the action that I and my associates have taken in Birmingham is untimely. Some have asked: "Why didn't you give the new city administration time to act?" The only answer that I can give to this query is that the new Birmingham administration must be prodded about as much as the outgoing one, before it will act. We are sadly mistaken if we feel that the election of Albert Boutwell as mayor will bring the millennium to Birmingham. While Mr. Boutwell is a much more gentle person than Mr. Connor, they are both segregationists, dedicated to maintenance of the status quo. I have hope that Mr. Boutwell will be reasonable enough to see the futility of massive resistance to desegregation. But he will not see this without pressure from devotees of civil rights. My friends, I must say to you that we have not made a single gain in civil rights without determined legal and nonviolent pressure. Lamentably, it is an historical fact that privileged groups seldom give up their privileges voluntarily. Individuals may see the moral light and voluntarily give up their unjust posture; but, as Reinhold Niebuhr° has reminded us, groups tend to be more immoral than individuals.

13 We know through painful experience that freedom is never voluntarily given by the oppressor; it must be demanded by the oppressed. Frankly, I have yet to engage in a direct-action campaign that was "well timed" in the view of those who have not suffered unduly from the

---

12 **Reinhold Niebuhr:** (1892–1971) American Protestant theologian

disease of segregation. For years now I have heard the word "Wait!" It rings in the ear of every Negro with piercing familiarity. This "Wait" has almost always meant "Never." We must come to see, with one of our distinguished jurists, that "justice too long delayed is justice denied."

14 We have waited for more than 340 years for our constitutional and God-given rights. The nations of Asia and Africa are moving with jetlike speed toward gaining political independence, but we still creep at horse-and-buggy pace toward gaining a cup of coffee at a lunch counter. Perhaps it is easy for those who have never felt the stinging darts of segregation to say, "Wait." But when you have seen vicious mobs lynch your mothers and fathers at will and drown your sisters and brothers at whim; when you have seen hate-filled policemen curse, kick and even kill your black brothers and sisters; when you see the vast majority of your twenty million Negro brothers smothering in an airtight cage of poverty in the midst of an affluent society; when you suddenly find your tongue twisted and your speech stammering as you seek to explain to your six-year-old daughter why she can't go to the public amusement park that has just been advertised on television, and see tears welling up in her eyes when she is told that Funtown is closed to colored children, and see ominous clouds of inferiority beginning to form in her little mental sky, and see her beginning to distort her personality by developing an unconscious bitterness toward white people; when you have to concoct an answer for a five-year-old son who is asking: "Daddy, why do white people treat colored people so mean?"; when you take a cross-country drive and find it necessary to sleep night after night in the uncomfortable corners of your automobile because no motel will accept you; when you are humiliated day in and day out by nagging signs reading "white" and "colored"; when your first name becomes "nigger," your middle name becomes "boy" (however old you are) and your last name becomes "John," and your wife and mother are never given the respected title "Mrs."; when you are harried by day and haunted by night by the fact that you are a Negro, living constantly at tiptoe stance, never quite knowing what to expect next, and are plagued with inner fears and outer resentments; when you are forever fighting a degenerating sense of "nobodiness"—then you will understand why we find it difficult to wait. There comes a time when the cup of endurance runs over, and men are no longer willing to be plunged into the abyss of despair. I hope, sirs, you can understand our legitimate and unavoidable impatience.

15 You express a great deal of anxiety over our willingness to break laws. This is certainly a legitimate concern. Since we so diligently urge people to obey the Supreme Court's decision of 1954 outlawing segregation in the public schools, at first glance it may seem rather paradoxical for us consciously to break laws. One may well ask: "How can you advocate breaking some laws and obeying others?" The answer lies in

the fact that there are two types of laws: just and unjust. I would be the first to advocate obeying just laws. One has not only a legal but a moral responsibility to obey just laws. Conversely, one has a moral responsibility to disobey unjust laws. I would agree with St. Augustine that "an unjust law is no law at all."

16 Now, what is the difference between the two? How does one determine whether a law is just or unjust? A just law is a man-made code that squares with the moral law or the law of God. An unjust law is a code that is out of harmony with the moral law. To put it in the terms of St. Thomas Aquinas: An unjust law is a human law that is not rooted in eternal law and natural law. Any law that uplifts human personality is just. Any law that degrades human personality is unjust. All segregation statutes are unjust because segregation distorts the soul and damages the personality. It gives the segregator a false sense of superiority and the segregated a false sense of inferiority. Segregation, to use the terminology of the Jewish philosopher Martin Buber, substitutes an "I–it" relationship for an "I–thou" relationship and ends up relegating persons to the status of things. Hence segregation is not only politically, economically and sociologically unsound, it is morally wrong and sinful. Paul Tillich° has said that sin is separation. Is not segregation an existential expression of man's tragic separation, his awful estrangement, his terrible sinfulness? Thus it is that I can urge men to obey the 1954 decision of the Supreme Court, for it is morally right; and I can urge them to disobey segregation ordinances, for they are morally wrong.

17 Let us consider a more concrete example of just and unjust laws. An unjust law is a code that a numerical or power majority group compels a minority group to obey but does not make binding on itself. This is *difference* made legal. By the same token, a just law is a code that a majority compels a minority to follow and that it is willing to follow itself. This is *sameness* made legal.

18 Let me give another explanation. A law is unjust if it is inflicted on a minority that, as a result of being denied the right to vote, had no part in enacting or devising the law. Who can say that the legislature of Alabama which set up that state's segregation laws was democratically elected? Throughout Alabama all sorts of devious methods are used to prevent Negroes from becoming registered voters, and there are some counties in which, even though Negroes constitute a majority of the population, not a single Negro is registered. Can any law enacted under such circumstances be considered democratically structured?

19 Sometimes a law is just on its face and unjust in its application. For instance, I have been arrested on a charge of parading without a permit. Now, there is nothing wrong in having an ordinance which

---

16 **Paul Tillich:** (1886–1965) German-American Protestant theologian and philosopher

requires a permit for a parade. But such an ordinance becomes unjust when it is used to maintain segregation and to deny citizens the First-Amendment privilege of peaceful assembly and protest.

20 I hope you are able to see the distinction I am trying to point out. In no sense do I advocate evading or defying the law, as would the rabid segregationist. That would lead to anarchy. One who breaks an unjust law must do so openly, lovingly, and with a willingness to accept the penalty. I submit that an individual who breaks a law that conscience tells him is unjust, and who willingly accepts the penalty of imprisonment in order to arouse the conscience of the community over its injustice, is in reality expressing the highest respect for law.

21 Of course, there is nothing new about this kind of civil disobedience. It was evidenced sublimely in the refusal of Shadrach, Meshach and Abednego to obey the laws of Nebuchadnezzar,° on the ground that a higher moral law was at stake. It was practiced superbly by the early Christians, who were willing to face hungry lions and the excruciating pain of chopping blocks rather than submit to certain unjust laws of the Roman Empire. To a degree, academic freedom is a reality today because Socrates practiced civil disobedience. In our own nation, the Boston Tea Party represented a massive act of civil disobedience.

22 We should never forget that everything Adolf Hitler did in Germany was "legal" and everything the Hungarian freedom fighters° did in Hungary was "illegal." It was "illegal" to aid and comfort a Jew in Hitler's Germany. Even so, I am sure that, had I lived in Germany at the time, I would have aided and comforted my Jewish brothers. If today I lived in a Communist country where certain principles dear to the Christian faith are suppressed, I would openly advocate disobeying that country's antireligious laws.

23 I must make two honest confessions to you, my Christian and Jewish brothers. First, I must confess that over the past few years I have been gravely disappointed with the white moderate. I have almost reached the regrettable conclusion that the Negro's great stumbling block in his stride toward freedom is not the White Citizen's Counciler or the Ku Klux Klanner, but the white moderate, who is more devoted to "order" than to justice; who prefers a negative peace which is the absence of tension to a positive peace which is the presence of justice; who constantly says: "I agree with you in the goal you seek, but I cannot agree with your methods of direct action"; who paternalistically believes he can set the timetable for another man's freedom; who lives by

---

[21] **Shadrach, Meshach, and Abednego, Nebuchadnezzar:** The Old Testament Book of Daniel tells how Nebuchadnezzar, king of Babylon, cast the three named Jewish leaders into a furnace, but released them and praised their God when they emerged unscathed.

[22] **Hungarian freedom fighters:** People who fought unsuccessfully against Soviet troops who crushed the 1956 revolution against the puppet government of Hungary

a mythical concept of time and who constantly advises the Negro to wait for a "more convenient season." Shallow understanding from people of good will is more frustrating than absolute misunderstanding from people of ill will. Lukewarm acceptance is much more bewildering than outright rejection.

24 I had hoped that the white moderate would understand that law and order exist for the purpose of establishing justice and that when they fail in this purpose they become the dangerously structured dams that block the flow of social progress. I had hoped that the white moderate would understand that the present tension in the South is a necessary phase of the transition from an obnoxious negative peace, in which the Negro passively accepted his unjust plight, to a substantive and positive peace, in which all men will respect the dignity and worth of human personality. Actually, we who engage in nonviolent direct action are not the creators of tension. We merely bring to the surface the hidden tension that is already alive. We bring it out in the open, where it can be seen and dealt with. Like a boil that can never be cured so long as it is covered up but must be opened with all its ugliness to the natural medicines of air and light, injustice must be exposed, with all the tension its exposure creates, to the light of human conscience and the air of national opinion before it can be cured.

25 In your statement you assert that our actions, even though peaceful, must be condemned because they precipitate violence. But is this a logical assertion? Isn't this like condemning a robbed man because his possession of money precipitated the evil act of robbery? Isn't this like condemning Socrates because his unswerving commitment to truth and his philosophical inquiries precipitated the act by the misguided populace in which they made him drink hemlock? Isn't this like condemning Jesus because his unique God-consciousness and never-ceasing devotion to God's will precipitated the evil act of crucifixion? We must come to see that, as the federal courts have consistently affirmed, it is wrong to urge an individual to cease his efforts to gain his basic constitutional rights because the quest may precipitate violence. Society must protect the robbed and punish the robber.

26 I had also hoped that the white moderate would reject the myth concerning time in relation to the struggle for freedom. I have just received a letter from a white brother in Texas. He writes: "All Christians know that the colored people will receive equal rights eventually, but it is possible that you are in too great a religious hurry. It has taken Christianity almost two thousand years to accomplish what it has. The teachings of Christ take time to come to earth." Such an attitude stems from a tragic misconception of time, from the strangely irrational notion that there is something in the very flow of time that will inevitably cure all ills. Actually, time itself is neutral; it can be used either destructively or constructively. More and more I feel that the people of ill will have used time much more effectively than have the people of good will. We

will have to repent in this generation not merely for the hateful words and actions of the bad people but for the appalling silence of the good people. Human progress never rolls in on wheels of inevitability; it comes through the tireless efforts of men willing to be co-workers with God, and without this hard work, time itself becomes an ally of the forces of social stagnation. We must use time creatively, in the knowledge that the time is always ripe to do right. Now is the time to make real the promise of democracy and transform our pending national elegy into a creative psalm of brotherhood. Now is the time to lift our national policy from the quicksand of racial injustice to the solid rock of human dignity.

27 You speak of our activity in Birmingham as extreme. At first I was rather disappointed that fellow clergymen would see my nonviolent efforts as those of an extremist. I began thinking about the fact that I stand in the middle of two opposing forces in the Negro community. One is a force of complacency, made up in part of Negroes who, as a result of long years of oppression, are so drained of self-respect and a sense of "somebodiness" that they have adjusted to segregation; and in part of a few middle-class Negroes who, because of a degree of academic and economic security and because in some ways they profit by segregation, have become insensitive to the problems of the masses. The other force is one of bitterness and hatred, and it comes perilously close to advocating violence. It is expressed in the various black nationalist groups that are springing up across the nation, the largest and best-known being Elijah Muhammad's Muslim movement.° Nourished by the Negro's frustration over the continued existence of racial discrimination, this movement is made up of people who have lost faith in America, who have absolutely repudiated Christianity, and who have concluded that the white man is an incorrigible "devil."

28 I have tried to stand between these two forces, saying that we need emulate neither the "do-nothingism" of the complacent nor the hatred and despair of the black nationalist. For there is the more excellent way of love and nonviolent protest. I am grateful to God that, through the influence of the Negro church, the way of nonviolence became an integral part of our struggle.

29 If this philosophy had not emerged, by now many streets of the South would, I am convinced, be flowing with blood. And I am further convinced that if our white brothers dismiss as "rabble-rousers" and "outside agitators" those of us who employ nonviolent direct action, and if they refuse to support our nonviolent efforts, millions of Negroes will, out of frustration and despair, seek solace and security in black-

---

[27] **Elijah Muhammad's Muslim movement:** the Nation of Islam, popularly known as "Black Muslims," an American Islamic sect which, in King's time, identified the white man with the Devil

nationalist ideologies—a development that would inevitably lead to a frightening racial nightmare.

30 Oppressed people cannot remain oppressed forever. The yearning for freedom eventually manifests itself, and that is what has happened to the American Negro. Something within has reminded him of his birthright of freedom, and something without has reminded him that it can be gained. Consciously or unconsciously, he has been caught up by the *Zeitgeist,*° and with his black brothers of Africa and his brown and yellow brothers of Asia, South America and the Caribbean, the United States Negro is moving with a sense of great urgency toward the promised land of racial justice. If one recognizes this vital urge that has engulfed the Negro community, one should readily understand why public demonstrations are taking place. The Negro has many pent-up resentments and latent frustrations, and he must release them. So let him march; let him make prayer pilgrimages to the city hall; let him go on freedom rides—and try to understand why he must do so. If his repressed emotions are not released in nonviolent ways, they will seek expression through violence; this is not a threat but a fact of history. So I have not said to my people: "Get rid of your discontent." Rather, I have tried to say that this normal and healthy discontent can be channeled into the creative outlet of nonviolent direct action. And now this approach is being termed extremist.

31 But though I was initially disappointed at being categorized as an extremist, as I continued to think about the matter I gradually gained a measure of satisfaction from the label. Was not Jesus an extremist for love: "Love your enemies, bless them that curse you, do good to them that hate you, and pray for them which despitefully use you, and persecute you." Was not Amos° an extremist for justice: "Let justice roll down like waters and righteousness like an ever-flowing stream." Was not Paul an extremist for the Christian gospel: "I bear in my body the marks of the Lord Jesus." Was not Martin Luther° an extremist: "Here I stand; I cannot do otherwise, so help me God." And John Bunyan:° "I will stay in jail to the end of my days before I make a butchery of my conscience." And Abraham Lincoln: "This nation cannot survive half slave and half free." And Thomas Jefferson: "We hold these truths to be self-evident, that all men are created equal . . ." So the question is not whether we will be extremists, but what kind of extremists we will be. Will we be extremists for hate or for love? Will we be extremists for

30 **Zeitgeist:** (Ger.) spirit of the age

31 **Amos:** Old Testament prophet

Martin Luther: (1483–1546) German leader of the Protestant Reformation and founder of Lutheranism. The quoted words were spoken in response to a demand that he retract his criticisms of Catholic practices.

John Bunyan: (1628–1688) English preacher and author, twice imprisoned for anti-Catholic activities

the preservation of injustice or for the extension of justice? In that dramatic scene on Calvary's hill three men were crucified. We must never forget that all three were crucified for the same crime—the crime of extremism. Two were extremists for immorality, and thus fell below their environment. The other, Jesus Christ, was an extremist for love, truth and goodness, and thereby rose above his environment. Perhaps the South, the nation and the world are in dire need of creative extremists.

32 I had hoped that the white moderate would see this need. Perhaps I was too optimistic; perhaps I expected too much. I suppose I should have realized that few members of the oppressor race can understand the deep groans and passionate yearnings of the oppressed race, and still fewer have the vision to see that injustice must be rooted out by strong, persistent and determined action. I am thankful, however, that some of our white brothers in the South have grasped the meaning of this social revolution and committed themselves to it. They are still all too few in quantity, but they are big in quality. Some —such as Ralph McGill, Lillian Smith, Harry Golden, James McBride Dabbs, Ann Braden and Sarah Patton Boyle—have written about our struggle in eloquent and prophetic terms. Others have marched with us down nameless streets of the South. They have languished in filthy, roach-infested jails, suffering the abuse and brutality of policemen who view them as "dirty nigger-lovers." Unlike so many of their moderate brothers and sisters, they have recognized the urgency of the moment and sensed the need for powerful "action" antidotes to combat the disease of segregation.

33 Let me take note of my other major disappointment. I have been so greatly disappointed with the white church and its leadership. Of course, there are some notable exceptions. I am not unmindful of the fact that each of you has taken some significant stands on this issue. I commend you, Reverend Stallings, for your Christian stand on this past Sunday, in welcoming Negroes to your worship service on a nonsegregated basis. I commend the Catholic leaders of this state for integrating Spring Hill College several years ago.

34 But despite these notable exceptions, I must honestly reiterate that I have been disappointed with the church. I do not say this as one of those negative critics who can always find something wrong with the church. I say this as a minister of the gospel, who loves the church; who was nurtured in its bosom; who has been sustained by its spiritual blessings and who will remain true to it as long as the cord of life shall lengthen.

35 When I was suddenly catapulted into the leadership of the bus protest in Montgomery, Alabama, a few years ago, I felt we would be supported by the white church. I felt that the white ministers, priests and rabbis of the South would be among our strongest allies. Instead,

some have been outright opponents, refusing to understand the freedom movement and misrepresenting its leaders; all too many others have been more cautious than courageous and have remained silent behind the anesthetizing security of stained-glass windows.

36 In spite of my shattered dreams, I came to Birmingham with the hope that the white religious leadership of this community would see the justice of our cause and, with deep moral concern, would serve as the channel through which our just grievances could reach the power structure. I had hoped that each of you would understand. But again I have been disappointed.

37 I have heard numerous southern religious leaders admonish their worshipers to comply with a desegregation decision because it is the law, but I have longed to hear white ministers declare: "Follow this decree because integration is morally right and because the Negro is your brother." In the midst of blatant injustices inflicted upon the Negro, I have watched white churchmen stand on the sideline and mouth pious irrelevancies and sanctimonious trivialities. In the midst of a mighty struggle to rid our nation of racial and economic injustice, I have heard many ministers say: "Those are social issues, with which the gospel has no real concern." And I have watched many churches commit themselves to a completely otherworldly religion which makes a strange, un-Biblical distinction between body and soul, between the sacred and the secular.

38 I have traveled the length and breadth of Alabama, Mississippi and all the other southern states. On sweltering summer days and crisp autumn mornings I have looked at the South's beautiful churches with their lofty spires pointing heavenward. I have beheld the impressive outlines of her massive religious-education buildings. Over and over I have found myself asking: "What kind of people worship here? Who is their God? Where were their voices when the lips of Governor Barnett° dripped with words of interposition and nullification?° Where were they when Governor Wallace° gave a clarion call for defiance and hatred? Where were their voices of support when bruised and weary Negro men and women decided to rise from the dark dungeons of complacency to the bright hills of creative protest?"

39 Yes, these questions are still in my mind. In deep disappointment I have wept over the laxity of the church. But be assured that my tears have been tears of love. There can be no deep disappointment where

---

[38] **Governor Barnett:** Ross Barnett, segregationist Governor of Mississippi at the time of King's essay

interposition and nullification: a state's assertion that it can oppose and cancel any federal action that it considers to be an encroachment on its sovereignty

Governor Wallace: George Wallace, segregationist Governor of Alabama, later an unsuccessful candidate for President

there is not deep love. Yes, I love the church. How could I do otherwise? I am in the rather unique position of being the son, the grandson and the great-grandson of preachers. Yes, I see the church as the body of Christ. But, oh! How we have blemished and scarred that body through social neglect and through fear of being nonconformists.

40 There was a time when the church was very powerful—in the time when the early Christians rejoiced at being deemed worthy to suffer for what they believed. In those days the church was not merely a thermometer that recorded the ideas and principles of popular opinion; it was a thermostat that transformed the mores of society. Whenever the early Christians entered a town, the people in power became disturbed and immediately sought to convict the Christians for being "disturbers of the peace" and "outside agitators." But the Christians pressed on, in the conviction that they were "a colony of heaven," called to obey God rather than man. Small in number, they were big in commitment. They were too God-intoxicated to be "astronomically intimidated." By their effort and example they brought an end to such ancient evils as infanticide and gladiatorial contests.

41 Things are different now. So often the contemporary church is a weak, ineffectual voice with an uncertain sound. So often it is an archdefender of the status quo. Far from being disturbed by the presence of the church, the power structure of the average community is consoled by the church's silent—and often even vocal—sanction of things as they are.

42 But the judgment of God is upon the church as never before. If today's church does not recapture the sacrificial spirit of the early church, it will lose its authenticity, forfeit the loyalty of millions, and be dismissed as an irrelevant social club with no meaning for the twentieth century. Every day I meet young people whose disappointment with the church has turned into outright disgust.

43 Perhaps I have once again been too optimistic. Is organized religion too inextricably bound to the status quo to save our nation and the world? Perhaps I must turn my faith to the inner spiritual church, the church within the church, as the true *ekklesia*° and the hope of the world. But again I am thankful to God that some noble souls from the ranks of organized religion have broken loose from the paralyzing chains of conformity and joined us as active partners in the struggle for freedom. They have left their secure congregations and walked the streets of Albany, Georgia, with us. They have gone down the highways of the South on tortuous rides for freedom. Yes, they have gone to jail with us. Some have been dismissed from their churches, have lost the support of their bishops and fellow ministers. But they have acted in the faith

---

[43] **ekklesia:** (Gr.) assembly, church

that right defeated is stronger than evil triumphant. Their witness has been the spiritual salt that has preserved the true meaning of the gospel in these troubled times. They have carved a tunnel of hope through the dark mountain of disappointment.

44 I hope the church as a whole will meet the challenge of this decisive hour. But even if the church does not come to the aid of justice, I have no despair about the future. I have no fear about the outcome of our struggle in Birmingham, even if our motives are at present misunderstood. We will reach the goal of freedom in Birmingham and all over the nation, because the goal of America is freedom. Abused and scorned though we may be, our destiny is tied up with America's destiny. Before the pilgrims landed at Plymouth, we were here. Before the pen of Jefferson etched the majestic words of the Declaration of Independence across the pages of history, we were here. For more than two centuries our forebears labored in this country without wages; they made cotton king; they built the homes of their masters while suffering gross injustice and shameful humiliation —and yet out of a bottomless vitality they continued to thrive and develop. If the inexpressible cruelties of slavery could not stop us, the opposition we now face will surely fail. We will win our freedom because the sacred heritage of our nation and the eternal will of God are embodied in our echoing demands.

45 Before closing I feel impelled to mention one other point in your statement that has troubled me profoundly. You warmly commended the Birmingham police force for keeping "order" and "preventing violence." I doubt that you would have so warmly commended the police force if you had seen its dogs sinking their teeth into unarmed, nonviolent Negroes. I doubt that you would so quickly commend the policemen if you were to observe their ugly and inhumane treatment of Negroes here in the city jail; if you were to watch them push and curse old Negro women and young Negro girls; if you were to see them slap and kick old Negro men and young boys; if you were to observe them, as they did on two occasions, refuse to give us food because we wanted to sing our grace together. I cannot join you in your praise of the Birmingham police department.

46 It is true that the police have exercised a degree of discipline in handling the demonstrators. In this sense they have conducted themselves rather "nonviolently" in public. But for what purpose? To preserve the evil system of segregation. Over the past few years I have consistently preached that nonviolence demands that the means we use must be as pure as the ends we seek. I have tried to make clear that it is wrong to use immoral means to attain moral ends. But now I must affirm that it is just as wrong, or perhaps even more so, to use moral means to preserve immoral ends. Perhaps Mr. Connor and his policemen

have been rather nonviolent in public, as was Chief Pritchett in Albany, Georgia, but they have used the moral means of nonviolence to maintain the immoral end of racial injustice. As T. S. Eliot° has said: "The last temptation is the greatest treason: To do the right deed for the wrong reason."

47 I wish you had commended the Negro sit-inners and demonstrators of Birmingham for their sublime courage, their willingness to suffer and their amazing discipline in the midst of great provocation. One day the South will recognize its real heroes. They will be the James Merediths,° with the noble sense of purpose that enables them to face jeering and hostile mobs, and with the agonizing loneliness that characterizes the life of the pioneer. They will be old, oppressed, battered Negro women, symbolized in a seventy-two-year-old woman in Montgomery, Alabama, who rose up with a sense of dignity and with her people decided not to ride segregated buses, and who responded with ungrammatical profundity to one who inquired about her weariness: "My feets is tired, but my soul is at rest." They will be the young high school and college students, the young ministers of the gospel and a host of their elders, courageously and nonviolently sitting in at lunch counters and willingly going to jail for conscience' sake. One day the South will know that when these disinherited children of God sat down at lunch counters, they were in reality standing up for what is best in the American dream and for the most sacred values in our Judaeo-Christian heritage, thereby bringing our nation back to those great wells of democracy which were dug deep by the founding fathers in their formulation of the Constitution and the Declaration of Independence.

48 Never before have I written so long a letter. I'm afraid it is much too long to take your precious time. I can assure you that it would have been much shorter if I had been writing from a comfortable desk, but what else can one do when he is alone in a narrow jail cell, other than write long letters, think long thoughts and pray long prayers?

49 If I have said anything in this letter that overstates the truth and indicates an unreasonable impatience, I beg you to forgive me. If I have said anything that understates the truth and indicates my having a patience that allows me to settle for anything less than brotherhood, I beg God to forgive me.

50 I hope this letter finds you strong in the faith. I also hope that circumstances will soon make it possible for me to meet each of you, not as an integrationist or a civil-rights leader but as a fellow clergyman

---

[46] **T. S. Eliot:** (1888–1964) American poet and convert to Christianity

[47] **James Meredith:** the first black to attend and graduate from the University of Mississippi (1963), despite much harassment

and a Christian brother. Let us all hope that the dark clouds of racial prejudice will soon pass away and the deep fog of misunderstanding will be lifted from our fear-drenched communities, and in some not too distant tomorrow the radiant stars of love and brotherhood will shine over our great nation with all their scintillating beauty.

Yours for the cause of Peace and Brotherhood,

Martin Luther King, Jr.

STUDY QUESTIONS

1. Why does King begin (paragraphs 1 and 2) by stating that he doesn't usually reply to criticism and that he arrived in Birmingham by invitation?
2. Consider the appeals to authority that King makes by invoking famous examples. What strategic purpose is served by that device? And what does the *range* of invoked authorities tell us about King's outlook on the world?
3. Given the situation in which King found himself when he wrote this letter, what is remarkable about his tone? Think of some ways in which that tone is sustained over many pages. How is King's tone related to his political and strategic stance?
4. Find some typical examples of King's figurative language in this essay. What kinds of effects does he create when he lends imaginative coloration to his statements? Do you find his figurative language appropriate or inappropriate to his argumentative purpose?
5. King, himself a preacher, tells us that he comes from a long line of preachers. In addition, clergymen make up the immediate audience of his letter. In what ways does he write *as* a preacher? Do you find him also trying to convince a wider audience?
6. King emphasizes "self-purification" (paragraph 8) as an essential step leading to successful "nonviolent direct action." Why? In what way is this spiritual requirement a practical one as well?
7. What objections to his argument has King foreseen? How does he deal with them?
8. How does King make the abstract term "segregation" vivid to his readers?
9. King dwells at length on the distinction between just and unjust laws (paragraphs 15–20). Why? What does his reasoning on this point tell us about his total outlook? Do you find anything troubling in his position?
10. Why, in discussing civil disobedience, does King place stress on the acceptance of punishment for violations of unjust laws (paragraph 20)?

11. In paragraph 23 King declares that he almost believes "the white moderate" to be a greater menace to racial progress than the outright racist. How does this near-conclusion fit with what he tells us elsewhere about the way progress is achieved?
12. What is King's strategic purpose in introducing the subject of black nationalism (paragraphs 27–29)?
13. One of King's favorite devices is the lengthy sentence which, in many parts, gathers a series of examples and reaches a resounding climax. Find at least one instance of such a sentence, and be prepared to talk about its purpose and effect.

Theodore H. White

Theodore H. White has been a prominent reporter and author since the late 1930s. He is perhaps best known for a series of books *(The Making of the President)* covering the background of presidential campaigns since 1960. The present essay first appeared in *The New York Times Magazine* in November of 1978.

WHY THE JAILING OF FARBER TERRIFIES ME

1 M. A. Farber of *The New York Times* has now been freed from Bergen County's Hackensack° jail. For a total of nearly six weeks he sat in a cell block adjacent to a man who had allegedly murdered his own mother and facing an accused German sodomist awaiting deportation. Farber was there simply for practicing the reporter's calling—charged with both civil and criminal contempt of court for protecting the honor and tradition of that calling.

2 The fact that M. A. Farber is now free pleases me. But the issue raised by his imprisonment will not go away. In fact, his imprisonment terrifies me more and more. For if the Supreme Court does not, in the next few months, rule on this issue, I may follow him to jail. So may any honorable man of our craft. And if our craft is to be made subject to a new jurisprudence that can compel all of us to become official public informers, not only will the press suffer for it—so, too, will the public good.

---

[1] **Hackensack:** city in northeast New Jersey, close to New York City

3 The Law of Unintended Consequences has a dynamic of its own—and the willful refusal of the courts to understand how the American political system and the reporter's craft interlock may some day mark the Farber case as the beginning of a paradigm of Unintended Consequences.

4 To make clear what I see at issue here, I would like first to summarize the summerlong story.

5 In the mid-1960's, 13 people died in a hospital in Oradell, N.J., under strange and unexplained circumstances. The local county investigation found nothing actionable in these deaths and the matter was dropped. Ten years later, acting on a tip, *The New York Times* assigned reporter Farber to investigate the series of incidents again. His stories provoked a new prosecutor to reopen the case and, as a result, a Dr. Mario E. Jascalevich was charged with killing five (later reduced to three) patients by injecting them with curare.° After a 34-week trial, Dr. Jascalevich was found innocent, but before his acquittal, on June 30 of this year, William J. Arnold, the local judge hearing the case, issued a subpoena to reporter Farber (and another to *The New York Times*) ordering him to deliver to the court all the "documents" on which he had based his stories, including "statements, pictures, memoranda, recordings and notes of interviews of witnesses."

6 The subpoena was a sweeping, indiscriminate, vacuum-cleaner order. But I think it was the use of the word "documents" that first upset me—that and the blithe and callous legalese which held that it would not "cause undue hardship to said Myron Farber to be compelled to attend and present" the unspecified documents desired by the court. To believe that it causes no hardship to a reporter to violate his confidences is a monument of ignorance of the reporter's critical role in American public life.

7 A good reporter is a cross between a beggar and a detective, a wheedler and a prosecutor. This is how he collects facts. But the essence of his trade is to know how to sift out of rumor, gossip and hearsay the essential facts and then to arrange those facts so that a story comes out as close to the truth as he can make it.

8 Most of us take notes as we go. Or, if note-taking cramps the person we are talking with, we jot down notes as soon as we can get away and catch breath. We take notes on stenographer's pads, folded copy paper, margins of dinner menus. Sometimes we take notes with ostentatious flourish, either to bully people or to flatter them. Sometimes, after feigning uninterest, we take notes surreptitiously—on a paper napkin under the table, even on toilet paper in the washroom.

9 But these notes can scarcely be called "documents." A large part of what goes into our notes is nonsense—or worse, misinformation.

[5] **curare:** a plant-derived poison which attacks the motor nerves

People use us to plant lies, float allegations, bring others into suspicion or contempt. The most vivid of our notes are often records of indiscretion, indignation, hysteria or malice—in no legal sense "evidence." And I should hate to see men condemned, exonerated or betrayed by the jumble of notes I have piled up in 40 years of reporting.

10 Recently I have had the experience of trying to weave some of my old reporter's notes into a book. I found in those notes so many falsehoods, so many wild conversations, so many confidences of people who trusted me, that I am appalled by how much harm could be squeezed out of them by a smart lawyer, a smart politician, a smart propagandist.

11 I have some wartime notes of a conversation in 1942 with Gen. Douglas MacArthur. In them he excoriated George Marshall and Franklin Roosevelt with such bitterness that, had his remarks been uttered by a second lieutenant, the lieutenant would forthwith have been court-martialed. MacArthur relied on a personal trust in me to let himself spout without being quoted. It was at a low point in his career; nor did he really mean what he said, because there is no reflection of his charges in his own memoirs years later.

12 I have notes, tantamount to an invitation to blackmail, of a conversation in 1960 with a friend of Lyndon Johnson who offered to get me pictures of Jack and Bobby Kennedy in drag at a gay party in Las Vegas if I would promise to publish them. The notes are explicit, but the story was a lie and to print it would have been unconscionable because I believed then and believe now that Lyndon Johnson had nothing to do with the spreading of so false a rumor.

13 My notes contain, however, other, far more important materials and recollections which demonstrate, I hope, a reporter's higher function—to bring to public attention matters of common concern which should be thrust on the agenda of government for official action. I once wrote a story about a famine in the Chinese province of Honan in which millions of people died. The story was printed in *Time* magazine and its publication saved countless lives. But not until now, writing this piece, have I told anyone that I came across the matter because friends in the United States Embassy in Chungking° wanted someone to explore the story in the field. The embassy had received letters from American missionaries in the famine-struck area telling of a desolation and corruption concealed by censorship from the whole world. One of the young diplomats at the embassy called me in, simply put a batch of letters on the table between us, let me read—and said nothing. It was essential to conceal his name, for he was the key "leak." The "leak" was his way of appealing to American conscience beyond the bureaucratic channels of the State Department. Had I exposed him, he would probably have been purged at the time—in 1943—or later by

[13] **Chungking:** city in southwest China on the Yangtze River

John Foster Dulles or Joe McCarthy° when they were blinding the State Department by cleansing it of alleged "Reds."

14 The word "leak" has a derogatory connotation. But some day, perhaps, some school of journalism will give a special course in "leaks" to young officials and aspiring journalists alike, awarding the process called "leaking" the dignity and importance it deserves.

15 We all live in a world increasingly thicketed with bureaucracies. They spread like giant fungoids; no one, not even Congress or the President, understands completely what goes on within these fungal monsters; and among them the medical and hospital bureaucracies come closest to baffling understanding. Without an inside leak, penetration of these thickets is almost impossible. Doctors, nurses, hospital administrators all too frequently cover up for each other. But in their charge lie the weakest and most helpless of our citizens—the ill, the old, the poor, the sad of spirit. Someone must patrol the custodians who are supposed to care for them.

16 In the Oradell hospital case, only a leak could have alerted such a patrol. That leak turned out to be a woman who in 1975 called *The New York Times*'s attention to the fact that helpless people had died, no one knew how, at Riverdell Hospital. The *Times* assigned the story to Farber, who pursued the story with devotion and diligence for four months, springing other leaks as he went. The *Times* then called the situation to public attention by printing a story on its front page, naming no names but placing the matter on the agenda for official investigation.

17 We reporters have to get our information where we can—usually by eyeball observation or legwork; sometimes from libraries and scholars; more often by coaxing politicians, officials and cops to talk; and sometimes by trading information with people in power, offering them our legwork in return for their confidences and superior investigative resources. *We* are responsible for what *we* write; they are responsible for official actions at law. We bring matters to attention; they must decide whether to act. And absolutely essential to the entire process is the reporter's code of honor: Once you pledge that you will protect an informant, the pledge is as binding as the Hippocratic oath on doctors, or the pledge of privacy given to witnesses by grand juries. Even among gangsters, "squealing" is considered a disgrace.

18 Much more, however, than a reporter's honor or disgrace is at stake here. The Farber case is touched with history, which the courts do not seem to understand. For if Farber had been compelled by imprisonment to name his sources, to hand over his notes, all of which are only hearsay evidence, then the unintended consequence of his punishment

---

13 **John Foster Dulles, Joe McCarthy:** respectively, U. S. Secretary of State (1888–1959) under President Eisenhower; "Communist-hunting" Senator from Wisconsin (1909–1957) during the fifties.

could have reshaped—and may still reshape—American political history.

19 For longer than anyone can remember, it has been accepted in American politics that a reporter's protection of his sources could not be violated. No law said so; no ruling said so; it was simply taken for granted. All politicians, from Presidents down, have accepted such shelter. One cannot, for example, write American history from the turn of this century on without writing of what the great "muckrakers" accomplished. There would have been no urban thrust behind the Progressive movement° had not Lincoln Steffens reported in his *The Shame of the Cities* on big-city corruption—and protected his sources. People might have eaten filth and offal for another generation had not Upton Sinclair relied on thinly disguised reporter's privilege in *The Jungle.* Without Ida Tarbell's reporting of the strangulating oil trusts, they might have persisted in full vigor for another generation; and she could not have pursued her investigations had she not been able in clear conscience to protect her sources from reprisal.

20 The protection of sources by reporters has been so long accepted that it is almost superfluous to repeat the reasons for it here—except that the bureaucratic clotting of our lives today makes this privilege ever more essential. More and more, individuals must live in corporate groups, public or private, in a "lock-up" of hierarchies where the whistle-blower, the protester or the just plain conscience-smitten is increasingly subject to dismissal or vengeance—whether in the United States Navy or the Teamsters Union, at I.B.M. in Armonk, N.Y., or in a hospital for the infirm and aged.

21 Often there is no possible way safely to call attention to wrongdoing unless the protester is assured of his anonymity. There would have been no exposure of the My Lai massacre° had it not been for the ability of a brave reporter to persuade a handful of men in the United States Army to tell the truth. The civil-rights movement of the 1960's would have been stalled for years had there been no reporters to tell its story and defy local courts which sought to intimidate them. The revelations of Watergate might never have come about had not two reporters discovered a source, or several sources, whom they protected under the name of "Deep Throat." Had the jurisprudence that threw Farber into prison prevailed in 1974, the attorneys of Messrs. Mitchell, Haldeman and Ehrlichman could have demanded that Mr. Woodward and Mr. Bernstein give up their notes and so reveal the identity/identities of "Deep Throat"—or go to jail.

---

19 **the Progressive movement:** early twentieth-century U.S. reform movement, favoring regulation of big business, female suffrage, child labor laws, and increased popular control over politics

21 **My Lai massacre:** the murder of several hundred South Vietnamese civilians by American troops, led by Lt. William Calley, on March 16, 1968

22 In short, the conduct of American public affairs has for a century or more rested on the right of the American press and its reporters to tell their stories within traditional privileges and with traditional restraints. Now the courts, in a new departure, seem bent on erasing a protection built into the very functioning of the American system. And, since the Constitution is being invoked, we should go on to the Constitutional issues debated in the Farber case, which is presented as a clash between the First and the Sixth Amendments.

23 Neither the First nor the Sixth Amendment actually declares what the debaters have attempted to persuade us they say. The First Amendment says most briefly, "Congress shall make no law . . . abridging the freedom of speech, or of the press. . . ." Around that curt phrase volumes of law have grown up; under its shelter television, publishing, cinema, pornography, polemic and poetry have all flourished; within its protection the American public has become better informed than any other. All reporters and editors have considered that this phrase guarantees the protection of sources, because such protection is essential to the news-gathering procedures of a free press.

24 The Sixth Amendment has been similarly enlarged from its sparse phrases. It has been expanded in common talk to a Constitutional guarantee of "fair trial." Yet the phrase "fair trial" nowhere occurs in the Sixth Amendment. What is promised is simply "speedy and public trial"; the right of the accused to be confronted by the witnesses against him; and that the accused shall have "compulsory process for obtaining witnesses in his favor."° So far in the Farber case, the judges of the bench—from Hackensack, N.J., to the Supreme Court in Washington—seem bent on enlarging this last phrase to an entirely new dimension, compelling newsmen not simply to bear witness themselves but to finger other names which may help a shrewd criminal lawyer discover further witnesses to clear his client. Thus any reporter, by this stretch of interpretation, can become an agent of the court in any criminal process of law.

25 Like all great issues, the Farber case is wrapped in a tangled husk of immediate circumstances that make it immensely difficult for a man of conscience to judge.

26 First is the circumstance that Dr. Jascalevich was being tried for murder. New Jersey has no death penalty, but he could have been imprisoned for life; natural sympathy leads everyone to lean toward the man on trial rather than the abstract concept of press privilege. Every decent person rejoices that the innocent has now been cleared and goes free.

27 There is, next, the circumstance that M. A. Farber has a contract

---

24 **compulsory process . . .:** a right to compel testimony from people who may know something that could help to acquit the defendant

with a publisher to write a book about the Oradell affair—and may, indeed, make money from the book. I, as a reporter who makes his living writing books, do not find this at all dishonorable. But neither Farber nor *The New York Times* concealed the fact that Farber was writing a book. It was a matter of court record as early as May, six weeks before Farber was violently excoriated in open court by a Federal judge, Frederick Lacey, for sacrificing his responsibility on "an altar of greed"; and the actual manuscript was turned over to the court after much fuss before Farber was carted off to jail for a second time in October.

28 And underneath all comes the final circumstance: the insistence of the court on making Farber an agent of the law in defense of the accused—an insistence proven unnecessary, finally, by the jury's verdict.

29 The press has been accused of much in the past 10 years, and much of the accusation smarts because it is true. Some of us have tried to penetrate grand juries, which we should not have done. Some of us have tried to provoke incidents to make good film or good copy, which we should not have done. Some of us have become swollen with our power and have earned fully the opprobrium implied in the term "arrogance of the press."

30 But none of us claim that reporters are above the law. Most of the press would agree that no law protects or should protect a reporter from being called to bear witness in open court. A reporter, like any other citizen who has witnessed an act of violence, a riot or a crime of any kind, must testify to what he saw. Any reporter who steals or burglarizes a document should stand trial for the crime. Nor should any privilege protect a reporter from the laws for libel or the penalties for defamation, if proved. But Farber has broken no law, nor has he refused as a citizen to give testimony. When called to the witness stand by a defense subpoena, he responded for five days to every question—except those demanding that he divulge confidential sources or produce confidential notes.

31 The full power of the court and its compulsions have always been available to the defense to seek out its own witnesses and force them to testify publicly—and in this case such power was used successfully. But the New Jersey court insisted that Farber fully expose his journalist's sources or go to jail for his refusal. Whereupon the Supreme Court refused to accept for judgment this case where the First and Sixth Amendments apparently clash—and, by its silence, not only remanded Farber to jail but expanded the arbitrary power of lower judiciaries everywhere in the Union in an unprecedented manner. So it becomes central to the Farber story to examine to whom this new grant of power is being made—and its consequences. It becomes central to face the fact that the phrase "tyranny of the judiciary" is as unpleasant a truth as "arrogance of the press"—and possibly more dangerous.

32 Every observer of American politics recognizes that, since the early 1950's, the power of the courts has increased enormously. But every

veteran reporter knows that not all judges are spiritual descendants of Holmes, Brandeis and Warren.° All too many judges, wrapped in the black robes of court, are graduate politicians, neither scholars nor Solons;° and, as one descends the hierarchy from the Federal to state to local levels, one finds more and more of them are hacks. Appointments to the bench, in New Jersey as elsewhere, are born of politics; they are influenced by ethnic and racial groups, by labor and business interests, by political clubhouse connections, snobberies of bar associations and law schools—occasionally even by the Mafia. To extend to all these men, through the precedent of the Farber case, the same right to squeeze information, confidences and hearsay out of reporters converts the Sixth Amendment into an instrument of judicial extortion.

33 Judges, like reporters, executives and politicians, suffer from an institutional appetite for more power; they are as sensitive, too, to the judgment of their peers; and thus, by the conjunction of these pressures, they can reduce high justice to tragedy. The great decision, *Brown* v. *Board of Education,* which wiped out all legal grounds for racial segregation in American schools in 1954, was a stark and beautiful act of American high justice. But in the 20 years since, it has been completely wrenched about. Stretching that decision year by year, a scattering of judicial tyrants across the country have destroyed communities, eviscerated cities and succeeded in dividing children and communities by race and color more effectively than ever before. The men of the Bergen County courts and their consenting but silent fellows of the bench may be of perfect faith in believing that the implications of the Sixth Amendment override those of the First. But they may someday find themselves as appalled by the consequences of the Farber decision as the authors of the Dred Scott decision° were by the consequences of theirs.

34 All American life is veined by a web of interlocking privileges, privileges exempting some groups from taxation, privileges protecting other groups from discrimination, privileges excusing yet other groups from regulation. Among the most important of all are the exemptions traditionally granted certain people ever since the Revolution from the majesty, pursuit and cruelty of what passes for justice. No wife, it is held, can be forced to testify against her husband; no cleric against one who confesses to him; no doctor or psychiatrist against his patient. None of these privileges are written into the Constitution any more than

---

32 **Holmes, Brandeis, and Warren:** Oliver Wendell Holmes (1841–1935), Louis Dembitz Brandeis (1856–1941), and Earl Warren (1891–1974), distinguished liberal justices of the U.S. Supreme Court

Solons: wise lawgivers, named after the ancient Athenian statesman Solon

33 **Dred Scott decision:** U.S. Supreme Court decision in 1857, holding that slaves were not to be considered citizens under the Constitution

a reporter's privilege to protect his informants from reprisal is. But they are part of the American way of life.

35 Over the past decade the courts have been closing in on the press—ruling in the 1972 Branzburg decision that a reporter must testify to hearsay within the privacy of a grand jury; ruling in the recent *Stanford Daily* decision that a newspaper is always open to unannounced search and seizure of its records and files, whether it is a party to an action at law or merely a possible source of information. But now, under the precedent of the Farber case if the Supreme Court allows it to stand, no one is safe. Certainly not the small-town newspaper for whom a $5,000-a-day fine could mean disaster unless it yields up all its confidences at the behest of the local judge; probably not the psychiatrist, the priest or the doctor, all those who have enjoyed for so long the unquestioned privilege of confidence and have had that privilege upheld by the courts; and possibly not even the lawyer. Under the Farber ruling, even a Mafioso lawyer or a corrupt official has the right to compel a newspaper or reporter to trace the trail of his reporting from name to name before a black-robed man called "judge" who will then decide whom to expose and whom to protect.

36 In due time, the Supreme Court must decide whether to hear the appeal of *The New York Times* from the punishment imposed on it by local magistrates in New Jersey for refusing to open its files to government. I await the decision with trepidation, not because I fear for *The New York Times*—which does as well financially as it does editorially, thank you—but because I am afraid for myself. If the Farber decision stands, I should at once go back to my files and start burning up my old notes. The denial of reporter's privilege could reach into my home whenever any politician styled "judge" decided to invade my home. And I am equally—indeed, more—afraid for the many innocent people who could be hurt if I were forced to make public all the nonsense and privacies I have learned from or about them. The First Amendment, in final analysis, was not devised to protect any reporter or publisher from the law or to give us special entitlements. The First Amendment is listed as the First to protect the people—because only an informed citizenry makes our kind of republic possible.

STUDY QUESTIONS

1. What doubting questions, if any, crossed your mind when you first read White's title? How has he dealt with the likelihood that such questions would arise?
2. What is the *main* reason, according to White, that reporters should not be forced to reveal confidential sources? What other

reasons does he cite? Why, in your judgment, do they have secondary importance in White's argument?

3. Suppose you wanted to argue against White's position. What considerations would you want to take up? Has White himself anticipated some of them? If so, where?
4. What do you suppose White means by the "Law of Unintended Consequences" (paragraph 3)?
5. Why is it important to White to challenge the use of the word *documents* in the Farber subpoena (paragraph 6)?
6. Why does White choose to tell us about the particular reportorial experiences that he recounts in paragraphs 11–13? Is he merely name-dropping, or is this an important element of his argument?
7. Why does White try to change our attitude toward the word *leak* (paragraph 14)?
8. How is White's argument affected by his conception of recent social changes within the United States?
9. Why, for White and others, is the Farber case complicated by the fact that Farber had a contract for a book? How does White handle this complication? Are you satisfied with his response?
10. Why, in paragraph 29, does White mention some wrongdoing of which reporters have been guilty?
11. What is the basis of White's belief that the Constitution favors his argument about the protection of reporters' sources? If you were to take a contrary view, what reasons could you give?
12. Why is it important for White to attack our usual image of judges? Do you think his attack succeeds?
13. White clearly admires "muckraking" journalists who defy the powerful and alert the public to hidden scandals. Judging from this essay, do you think that White himself is such a journalist? Why, or why not?

Sissela Bok

Sissela Bok, born in Sweden and raised in Switzerland, France, and the United States, teaches ethics and decision-making in medicine in the Harvard–MIT Division of Health Sciences and Technology. The present selection is an excerpt from her widely noted book, *Lying: Moral Choice in Public and Private Life* (1978).

DECEPTIVE SOCIAL SCIENCE RESEARCH*

1 In Stanley Milgram's° obedience experiments, first performed at Yale in 1963, subjects were ostensibly recruited to take part in a study of memory. They were then duped into believing they were to be "teachers" in an experiment in which they would administer painful electric shocks of increasing strength to "learners" whenever the latter made mistakes. The so-called learners were actually actors who grunted, screamed, begged to be released from the experiment. As the subject-teachers administered what they thought was ever stronger punishment, they were observed to see whether they continued or protested, and what their reactions were. A large fraction of them were induced to give the highest range of shock, even when the pseudo-learners cried out that they feared a heart attack.

2 The responses of one subject are described as follows:

> 3 He began the experiment calmly, but became increasingly tense as the experiment proceeded. After administering the 150-volt shock, he began to address the experimenter in agitated tones:
>
> 4 (150 volts delivered.) "You want me to keep going?" (165 volts delivered.) "That guy is hollering in there. There's a lot of them here. He's liable to have a heart condition. You want me to go on?"
>
> 5 (180 volts delivered.) "He can't stand it! I'm not going to kill that man in there! You hear him hollering? He's hollering. He can't stand it. What if something happens to him? I'm not going to get that man sick in there. He's hollering in there. You know what I mean? I mean I refuse to take responsibility. He's getting hurt in there. He's in there hollering. Too many left here. Geez, if he gets them wrong. There's too many of them left. I mean who is going to take responsibility if anything happens to that gentleman?"
>
> 6 (The experimenter accepts responsibility.) "All right." (195 volts delivered.) "You see he's hollering. Hear that? Gee, I don't know." (The experi-

---

*Title chosen by editor

1 **Stanley Milgram:** Yale psychologist and author of the controversial book *Obedience to Authority* (1974), which describes and defends the experiments to which Bok objects

menter says: "The experiment requires that you go on.") "I know it does, sir, but I mean—huh—he don't know what he's in for. He's up to 195 volts."

(210 volts delivered.)

(225 volts delivered.)

9 (240 volts delivered.) "Aw, no! You mean I've got to keep going up with the scale? No, sir, I'm not going to kill that man! I'm not going to give him 450 volts!" (The experimenter says: "The experiment requires that you go on.") "I know it does, but that man is hollering in there, sir."

10 Despite his numerous, agitated objections, which were constant accompaniments to his actions, the subject unfailingly obeyed the experimenter, proceeding to the highest shock level on the generator. He displayed a curious dissociation between word and action. Although at the verbal level he had resolved not to go on, his actions were fully in accord with the experimenter's commands. This subject did not want to shock the victim, and he found it an extremely disagreeable task, but he was unable to invent a response that would free him from E's° authority.

11 The results were quite unexpected. Even the investigators themselves had had no idea that such a high proportion of the subjects could be talked into causing what seemed to be great pain to their fellow human beings. Sixty-two percent of the subjects turned out to obey the experimenter's commands completely.

12 But along with the shock came a profound sense of unease. Human beings had been duped into revealing sides of themselves they would never voluntarily have exhibited. They had been used, manipulated, without consent. Was this a legitimate way to experiment? And could the worth of the results somehow be "balanced" against the discomfort they had felt, the knowledge about themselves they had gained?

13 At first, these questions were debated mostly among psychologists. But, in 1974, when Milgram's book on the subject reached the general public, the debate spread. Up to that time, deceptive research in the social sciences had not been urgently questioned. In medicine, on the other hand, such deception had been found to have a long and sometimes tragic history. As a result, it is now carefully regulated in all biomedical research. Subjects can take part in a study only after their consent has been obtained; and if the study employs deception, as when placebos are used, the subjects must have consented to it in advance. The question arose: Should such a rule not apply to *all* research with human beings?

14 In principle, the Federal regulations do apply to all research so long as there is risk for human subjects. In practice, however, behavioral research is treated very differently—witness the recently revised *Ethical Standards of Psychologists,* adopted in January 1977. These standards

---

[10] **E's:** the experimenter's

merely suggest that investigators obtain informed consent, but make explicit exceptions for those studies which "necessitate concealment or deception":

> 15 d. Openness and honesty are essential characteristics of the relationship between investigator and research participant. When the methodological requirements of a study necessitate concealment or deception, the investigator is required to insure as soon as possible the participant's understanding of the reasons for this action and of a sufficient justification for the procedures employed.
>
> 16 g. The ethical investigator protects participants from physical and mental discomfort, harm, and danger. If a risk of such consequences exists, the investigator is required to inform the participant of that fact, secure consent before proceeding, and take all possible measures to minimize distress. A research procedure must not be used if it is likely to cause serious or lasting harm to a participant.

17 The rudimentary nature of these requirements is striking. When investigators can persuade themselves that deception is for a good purpose and presents no harm, they can proceed with secrecy, disguises, and lies. The choice is up to them, not their dupes. So is the determination of what might harm or cause discomfort.

18 One reason why the Ethical Standards are so permissive is that genuine informed consent might interfere with many studies, for a great deal of research in the social sciences is, by its very nature, deceptive, especially in sociology and social psychology. A situation is in some way contrived; human responses are then observed and measured. If the subjects do not know what is being tested, or even, sometimes, that a test is going on, their responses will be more spontaneous.

19 Beginning with a few isolated deceptive studies early in this century, a veritable flood of such research is now pouring forth from universities, market research organizations, private scholarly groups, and governments. Its results are published in hundreds of journals around the world and taught to thousands of students. If sufficiently striking, these results are then publicized in the press and on television.

20 In one such inquiry, male undergraduates were falsely led to believe that they had been sexually aroused by photographs of men, and their responses to such information studied. In another, subjects were surreptitiously given LSD. In still others, persons who responded to questionnaires on sensitive issues, expressly stated to be anonymous, were traced through invisible codes on the envelopes. In many studies, the subjects are never approached for even a spurious consent to a deceptive study; social scientists may infiltrate groups such as Alcoholics Anonymous or religious or political organizations; they may train children to accost passers-by and make believe they are lost; or they may stage some accident or assault complete with victim, fake blood, and debris, to measure "helping" behavior among bystanders.

21 What excuses are offered for this interference with the subjects' freedom of informed choice? Investigators appeal to two principles: producing benefits and avoiding harm. First, they hope that the research will produce important benefits: not only the general benefit of advancing human knowledge, but more specific social advantages, such as improved teaching techniques or the reduction of violence. The knowledge leading to their goals can often, they argue, be most conclusively demonstrated by means of deceptive experimentation. Thus one investigator explains that:

> A plausible cover story not only masks the experimenter's intention, it can also provide a setting which has great impact on the subject.

22 According to the second claim, since many experiments are utterly harmless, it is a waste of time and energy to impose upon them the kind of requirements which biomedical experiments might well require. This harmlessness is attested in two ways. First, the review committee to which experiments are often submitted does have the right to reject harmful experiments. If an experiment is not rejected, it cannot carry much of a risk for subjects. And second, investigators often accept the burden of explaining the deception to subjects after the experiment is over and justifying their questionable actions. This explanation, often referred to as "debriefing," is believed to prevent abuse and to wipe out any lingering discomforts and anxieties. Why then, ask investigators, in the light of such guarantees, should people want the right to refuse an experiment certain to do them no lasting harm? And is it not unethical *not* to do such harmless experiments which might uncover knowledge we urgently need to have?

A. Alternatives

23 If the public could debate these issues, the very first question would be: Given the fact that any deceptive practice harms not only those lied to, but also liars and trust more generally, what alternatives to deceptive studies are there in the first place? This question is a troublesome one for social science investigators. Unlike the case of a crisis where a lie may be the last resort, experimentation itself can hardly be called a last resort, and deceptive experimentation even less. One alternative to seeking knowledge through lies to subjects is to forego the knowledge sought altogether; another is to seek it nonexperimentally, through studying records and other data; a third alternative is to pursue the knowledge experimentally, but through an honest research design.

24 If these alternatives were publicly discussed, I doubt that the debate would result in a blanket approval of all deceptive studies thought harmless by investigators. Each study would have to be separately evaluated from the point of view of available alternatives. Such a process, if seriously undertaken, would eliminate a great many of

these studies. First to go would be those which seek no new knowledge in the first place, but merely train students in repeating the deceptive models of the past. For training is clearly as effective through honest as through dishonest research designs.

25 Second, those studies which could achieve the desired knowledge by honest means should be required to do so. This might require a greater expenditure of ingenuity and perhaps greater facility in working with records and with statistics. The search for alternatives may well require more training and more imagination than the leap to deceptive techniques.

26 Finally, those studies which can go ahead, even though subjects are asked in advance for their consent to the deceptive experiment, could be given priority over those where no such consent could be sought without invalidating the study.

27 To make such distinctions would require a real change of direction among investigators and experimentation committees. For manipulation has by now become a way of life, to the point where alternatives are not often considered. Every textbook recounts the well-known successes of past deceptive studies. They are repeated and emulated by each incoming generation of social scientists the world over. And committees set up to oversee experimentation often do not (unlike their counterparts overseeing biomedical research) require informed consent by subjects before deceptive studies can be undertaken.

28 But such changes raise a difficult problem. What about research of very likely benefit to society, where alternative models cannot possibly achieve the information a deceptive study might bring—a study, perhaps, designed to learn more about what makes adults abuse children? How might it stand up to the test of public justification? It is hard to imagine that persons might voluntarily reveal the character traits that they can be tricked into revealing in such studies. And it can at least be argued that we still have insufficient experimental documentation of these characteristics.

B. Harm and Benefit

29 In order to answer this question, we have to consider carefully the harmlessness claimed for such studies. Most are now agreed, as the Ethical Standards make clear, that studies producing lasting damage to subjects ought not to be undertaken for the purposes of gaining knowledge in the social sciences: that studies such as the experiments where military personnel were unknowingly given LSD should never have gone forward. Studies such as Milgram's experiment on obedience, therefore, must claim to produce no such lasting harm. And any momentary stress or discomfort must be believed either to vanish by itself or to be removable by the "debriefing" process after the study is over. How would these two claims stand up in the light of public discussion

by groups which include potential subjects of these deceptive experiments?

30 The response of potential subjects would doubtless be that they might well be willing to participate in some such experiments but not in others, and that, moreover, some of them might not want to participate in any. They would probably agree, therefore, that each should judge personally the harmlessness of what is planned for him. What seems painless to one may deeply injure another. What leaves unbearable marks of intrusion on personal privacy in one life will not affect another. To be made to act cruelly, or to be misinformed as to personal sexual responses, will hurt the vulnerable while others escape unharmed.

C. Debriefing

31 But is there not added safety in the "debriefing" process? Can any residual stress or anxiety or sense of invaded privacy not be removed once the study is over? There are two parts to the claims of efficacy for debriefing: an honest description of the study once it is over, and psychological support given by the investigator to allow the subject to cope with the stress or the knowledge gained. Both require scrutiny from the perspective of those who are to receive the benefits of the "debriefing" —the experimental dupes.

32 The first claim for the process of "debriefing" is a very interesting one from the point of view of veracity. Where there has been an experimental inroad on veracity, the claim seems to be that the harm brought by a lie is "erased" by truthful information, much as an antidote for poison wipes out its effects. So long as the harm from the lie does not remain long with the dupe, it will then have had no effect. As Bacon said:

> [. . .] it is not the lie that passeth through the mind but the lie that sinketh in and settleth in it, that doth the hurt. . . .

33 Truthfulness after the fact, then, is held to remove any residual harm the lie may have done, especially if it is conveyed without delay. Some investigators hold that this aspect of debriefing works especially well if they disclose their own discomfort at having lied, and explain why they feel, nevertheless, that the lies are justified. Subjects may respond with disappointment at being so easily duped and at having placed trust in a "cover story." But if the debriefing succeeds, investigators hope to have counteracted the disappointment and enlisted the subject as an ally in the experiment, to the point of promising not to tell *other* subjects about the deception they will encounter.

34 Unfortunately, debriefing does not always succeed. The disappointment may remain; the anxiety or loss of privacy may not be overcome. The experiment may reveal something to subjects about themselves that no debriefing will erase. Subjects may become even more

suspicious after the explanation, and thus less useful for further studies. And they may suffer from the discovery that someone in a position of a model and authority figure resorted to such devious tactics.

35 Some investigators argue that this is reason enough *not* to debrief subjects, except where the harm done can truly be alleviated. For others, the second claim connected with debriefing assumes even greater importance: that even if the antidote of truthfulness does not in itself work, even if it does not wipe out anxiety and guilt and a sense of having been exposed, the psychologist-investigator can. The Ethical Standards state that it is the responsibility of the investigator to "assure that there are no damaging consequences for the participant."

36 Can the subjects be sure that their reactions to stress, anxiety, unpleasant and perhaps degrading discoveries about themselves will be so easy to erase or learn to live with? Do they have the requisite confidence in the ability of psychologists to restore the human spirit after injuries? And even if some are gifted with such an ability, are all? Each of us has a very different sense of privacy lost, of personal space invaded, of knowledge gained that is hard to cope with. These are not always easy to erase or to overcome. To assume the contrary belies the complexity of human responses; it demands greater faith in the restorative skills of investigators than experience warrants.

37 Subjects need, then, to be able to judge for themselves whether an experiment is risky for them and whether they have confidence in debriefing. The judgment of the investigator does not suffice. Such caution on the part of the public would stem neither from a hostility to research nor from a desire to limit academic freedom—two concerns often suspected by scientists to underlie the new turn toward protecting the rights of human subjects of experimentation. Rather, the caution is directed solely to the question of risks from the experiment; for academic freedom has never been construed to be freedom to place others at risk without their consent.

38 But this caution has limits. It cannot be stretched to mean that each and every study should have to go through the same consent procedures. For many studies in the social sciences are totally harmless even by the most exacting standards. Measurements, observations, and nonintrusive experiments can surely often proceed without the slightest risk. Take observations of what pedestrians do when an investigator's stooge jaywalks or talks to himself on street corners; or notes taken on how a crowd welcomes a returning war hero. It would be cumbersome for all and a bit mad to require strict consent to these. How, then, are they best separated out?

Review Committees

39 There is no need for new federal regulations, already proliferated beyond all reason. Rather, the standards already in use for biomedical

research should govern behavioral research as well. These standards require informed consent from subjects in any research that adds "physical, psychological, sociological, or other" risk to their lives. The professions themselves and the many institutional review committees already in existence are, in principle, best qualified to weigh such risks to human subjects. Their mandate is, after all, precisely to set standards and to screen projects: to screen away both those studies too dangerous to carry out, even if subjects could be found to consent to them, and those studies so trivial that no consent is needed.

40 In practice, however, committees do not always serve this function well for social science research. Many studies, and often the shoddiest in design, least competent in execution, never even come before these committees. Those that do are not now screened to require consent by subjects whenever there is a question of risk to subjects—witness the many controversial studies that *have* been passed by committees. This failure to see the risks for subjects is made more inevitable by the fact that so few committees have representation by laymen and potential subjects in the first place.

41 Committee structure and procedure must be reformed, therefore, before the public interest can be said to be safeguarded. Laymen and potential subjects must be represented. Most important, committees must use adequate criteria of what constitutes risk to the subjects of experimentation. They must make it clear that consent requires informing subjects of all that is relevant to their decision, including the purpose of the study and the fact that deception may enter into it. The committees should look sharply, too, whenever risk is possible, for even marginal efforts at coercing the consent of subjects. This may happen when students are required to participate in studies in order to take courses or receive degrees. Among the risks taken seriously must be psychological ones: the damage which some may experience from having revealed themselves unknowingly, from having their privacy invaded, or from discovering something about themselves that will be painful to live with.

42 Learning about people's private, even intimate, behavior and emotions without their consent is very much like surreptitiously listening in on their telephone conversations or looking through their keyholes. Such acts are no less intrusive for being done in the interests of research. The same barriers ought to protect us from these forms of invasion of privacy.

43 If psychological risks are taken into account, deceptive studies such as the obedience research by Milgram could go forward only with subject consent. If consent is refused, this should be taken as an indication that the study ought not to have been done without consent in the first place. (In fact, it would be useful to list a number of deceptive studies merely as examples in a questionnaire, to see which would be more, and which less, acceptable to potential subjects.) If the study

cannot be performed after informed consent because the surprise element is gone, two alternatives remain: to devise a marginally deceptive study so *harmless* to subjects that no consent is needed; or to ask a group of subjects for consent to a number of studies, detailing the risks, but asking consent to secrecy as to when any one would be likely to be in question. The review committee would then have to deliberate to see whether such a procedure provides sufficient protection.

Questions of Professional Responsibility

44 The greatest harm from deceptive experimentation may be that to the investigators themselves, to the students trained in their professions, and to the professions as such. Subjects, after all, may come into contact with deceptive experiments only briefly; but investigators plan the studies, execute them, explain them over and over again to subjects being debriefed, and teach students how to carry them out. The danger of spreading deceptive practices here is twofold. Individually, lies can become a way of life, manipulation habitual. And professionally, deceit can become more commonplace, with growing ranks of participants having fewer and fewer compunctions.

45 For the investigators themselves, the practices may be disagreeable at first; if forced to participate they may become inured to doing what they ordinarily would resist and thus lose a degree of moral sensitivity. Many begin as students and find it difficult to refuse to participate in giving a "cover story" or in the infiltration of a group, especially when they see their professors playing such roles. Neither in classrooms nor in textbooks are they encouraged to make distinctions of an ethical nature. The textbooks occasionally point to the presence of a problem with deception, only to add that research nevertheless requires it. But important distinctions of a moral nature are not made: distinctions between harm to dupes and harm to liars, between an accidental lie and a planned, repeated one, between lies and other deceptions, between routine practices and emergencies, between different excuses or different degrees of justification.

46 This absence of ethical analysis of a questionable research technique in common use leads to a larger question. Is there a place, in universities, for the teaching of deceptive research? Ought academic disciplines to include such techniques? Do other disciplines not exclude them? While every field has its share of duplicity, most do not *teach* it. The teaching function itself, then, has to be questioned where these techniques are concerned. We have to ask: What does it do to students to be placed in situations where professors teach them to deceive, where their grades and professional advancement may depend on their adaptability and ingenuity in working with deceptive techniques?

47 The accumulated effects on individual students must affect the professions themselves. And where the professions become known for

such research, yet another problem arises—each deceptive study comes to contribute to a breakdown in trust. Few activities show such a spread as those of deceptive research. Academic uses have given rise to innumerable commercial uses. Psychologists know that public resistance to participating in research is growing. Pollsters are received with suspicion, often hostility; questionnaires remain unanswered; students—up to now the most easily available group of subjects—are increasingly sophisticated about research processes, to the point where there is real doubt about the validity of the research where their naïveté is assumed. One commentator on the vast deceptive practices in the name of social science holds that:

> These tricks simply strengthen the growing conviction that you can't trust people you don't know. If a mugger doesn't hit you, a credit checker doesn't spy on you, or a salesman doesn't take you to the cleaners, a social scientist will dupe you.

48 It is in the interest of social scientists themselves, then, to protect their standing and the accuracy of their results by taking a stand against the resort to deception without consent and to other underhanded methods, even when no direct harm to subjects can be discerned; to refrain from teaching such methods; and to probe, with students and colleagues, the moral aspects of research.

STUDY QUESTIONS

1. What tone would you say that Bok takes in this piece of argumentation? Be prepared to cite examples. In what way is that tone appropriate or inappropriate to her evident purpose?
2. What, in Bok's view, is the present state of ethical regulation in the field of social-science research? Why does she feel dissatisfied with that degree of discipline?
3. Why does Bok open her discussion by dwelling at length on Stanley Milgram's obedience experiments? Think first about the usefulness of beginning with any single example and then of this example as opposed to others.
4. If you had to make a case in favor of Milgram's procedures, what considerations would you emphasize? Do you think Bok has adequately countered them?
5. Bok asserts that "any deceptive practice harms not only those lied to, but also liars and trust more generally" (paragraph 23). Where does she attempt to establish the truth of that statement? Has she succeeded to your satisfaction?
6. Is Bok saying that no deceptive social-science experimentation should be allowed? Be ready to show which part of her text establishes your answer.

7. What is meant by *debriefing,* and why is it an important concept for Bok to address?
8. On what grounds does Bok prefer peer review committees to government regulation? In her view, how and why should such committees have different membership than they do now?
9. One of Bok's chief rhetorical devices is the asking of a timely question. Locate several such questions and be prepared to discuss their purpose and effect.

QUESTIONING RECEIVED OPINION

Rachel Carson

Rachel Carson (1907–1964) worked for many years as a naturalist with the U.S. Fish and Wildlife Service before achieving fame as the author of a book about oceans, *The Sea Around Us.* "The Obligation to Endure" is taken from her most controversial and influential book, *Silent Spring* (1962), which awakened the American public to the dangers of pesticides and led eventually to the banning of DDT.

THE OBLIGATION TO ENDURE

1 The history of life on earth has been a history of interaction between living things and their surroundings. To a large extent, the physical form and the habits of the earth's vegetation and its animal life have been molded by the environment. Considering the whole span of earthly time, the opposite effect, in which life actually modifies its surroundings, has been relatively slight. Only within the moment of time represented by the present century has one species—man—acquired significant power to alter the nature of his world.

2 During the past quarter century this power has not only increased to one of disturbing magnitude but it has changed in character. The most alarming of all man's assaults upon the environment is the contamination of air, earth, rivers, and sea with dangerous and even lethal materials. This pollution is for the most part irrecoverable; the chain of evil it initiates not only in the world that must support life but in living tissues is for the most part irreversible. In this now universal contamination of the environment, chemicals are the sinister and little-recognized partners of radiation in changing the very nature of the world—the very nature of its life. Strontium 90, released through nuclear explosions into the air, comes to earth in rain or drifts down as fallout, lodges in soil, enters into the grass or corn or wheat grown there, and in time takes up

its abode in the bones of a human being, there to remain until his death. Similarly, chemicals sprayed on croplands or forests or gardens lie long in soil, entering into living organisms, passing from one to another in a chain of poisoning and death. Or they pass mysteriously by underground streams until they emerge and, through the alchemy of air and sunlight, combine into new forms that kill vegetation, sicken cattle, and work unknown harm on those who drink from once pure wells. As Albert Schweitzer° has said, "Man can hardly even recognize the devils of his own creation."

3 It took hundreds of millions of years to produce the life that now inhabits the earth—eons of time in which that developing and evolving and diversifying life reached a state of adjustment and balance with its surroundings. The environment, rigorously shaping and directing the life it supported, contained elements that were hostile as well as supporting. Certain rocks gave out dangerous radiation; even within the light of the sun, from which all life draws its energy, there were short-wave radiations with power to injure. Given time—time not in years but in millennia—life adjusts, and a balance has been reached. For time is the essential ingredient; but in the modern world there is no time.

4 The rapidity of change and the speed with which new situations are created follow the impetuous and heedless pace of man rather than the deliberate pace of nature. Radiation is no longer merely the background radiation of rocks, the bombardment of cosmic rays, the ultraviolet of the sun that have existed before there was any life on earth; radiation is now the unnatural creation of man's tampering with the atom. The chemicals to which life is asked to make its adjustment are no longer merely the calcium and silica and copper and all the rest of the minerals washed out of the rocks and carried in rivers to the sea; they are the synthetic creations of man's inventive mind, brewed in his laboratories, and having no counterparts in nature.

5 To adjust to these chemicals would require time on the scale that is nature's; it would require not merely the years of a man's life but the life of generations. And even this, were it by some miracle possible, would be futile, for the new chemicals come from our laboratories in an endless stream; almost five hundred annually find their way into actual use in the United States alone. The figure is staggering and its implications are not easily grasped—500 new chemicals to which the bodies of men and animals are required somehow to adapt each year, chemicals totally outside the limits of biologic experience.

6 Among them are many that are used in man's war against nature. Since the mid-1940's over 200 basic chemicals have been created for use

---

[2] **Albert Schweitzer:** (1875–1965) humanitarian, musician, mission physician, and Christian philosopher, best known for his medical work in Africa

in killing insects, weeds, rodents, and other organisms described in the modern vernacular as "pests"; and they are sold under several thousand different brand names.

7 These sprays, dusts, and aerosols are now applied almost universally to farms, gardens, forests, and homes—nonselective chemicals that have the power to kill every insect, the "good" and the "bad," to still the song of birds and the leaping of fish in the streams, to coat the leaves with a deadly film, and to linger on in soil—all this though the intended target may be only a few weeds or insects. Can anyone believe it is possible to lay down such a barrage of poisons on the surface of the earth without making it unfit for all life? They should not be called "insecticides," but "biocides."

8 The whole process of spraying seems caught up in an endless spiral. Since DDT was released for civilian use, a process of escalation has been going on in which ever more toxic materials must be found. This has happened because insects, in a triumphant vindication of Darwin's principle of the survival of the fittest, have evolved super races immune to the particular insecticide used, hence a deadlier one has always to be developed—and then a deadlier one than that. It has happened also because, for reasons to be described later, destructive insects often undergo a "flareback," or resurgence, after spraying, in numbers greater than before. Thus the chemical war is never won, and all life is caught in its violent crossfire.

9 Along with the possibility of the extinction of mankind by nuclear war, the central problem of our age has therefore become the contamination of man's total environment with such substances of incredible potential for harm—substances that accumulate in the tissues of plants and animals and even penetrate the germ cells to shatter or alter the very material of heredity upon which the shape of the future depends.

10 Some would-be architects of our future look toward a time when it will be possible to alter the human germ plasm by design. But we may easily be doing so now by inadvertence, for many chemicals, like radiation, bring about gene mutations. It is ironic to think that man might determine his own future by something so seemingly trivial as the choice of an insect spray.

11 All this has been risked—for what? Future historians may well be amazed by our distorted sense of proportion. How could intelligent beings seek to control a few unwanted species by a method that contaminated the entire environment and brought the threat of disease and death even to their own kind? Yet this is precisely what we have done. We have done it, moreover, for reasons that collapse the moment we examine them. We are told that the enormous and expanding use of pesticides is necessary to maintain farm production. Yet is our real problem not one of *overproduction*? Our farms, despite measures to remove acreages from production and to pay farmers *not* to produce, have yielded such a staggering excess of crops that the American taxpayer in

1962 is paying out more than one billion dollars a year as the total carrying cost of the surplus-food storage program. And is the situation helped when one branch of the Agriculture Department tries to reduce production while another states, as it did in 1958, "It is believed generally that reduction of crop acreages under provisions of the Soil Bank° will stimulate interest in use of chemicals to obtain maximum production on the land retained in crops."

12 All this is not to say there is no insect problem and no need of control. I am saying, rather, that control must be geared to realities, not to mythical situations, and that the methods employed must be such that they do not destroy us along with the insects.

13 The problem whose attempted solution has brought such a train of disaster in its wake is an accompaniment of our modern way of life. Long before the age of man, insects inhabited the earth—a group of extraordinarily varied and adaptable beings. Over the course of time since man's advent, a small percentage of the more than half a million species of insects have come into conflict with human welfare in two principal ways: as competitors for the food supply and as carriers of human disease.

14 Disease-carrying insects become important where human beings are crowded together, especially under conditions where sanitation is poor, as in time of natural disaster or war or in situations of extreme poverty and deprivation. Then control of some sort becomes necessary. It is a sobering fact, however, as we shall presently see, that the method of massive chemical control has had only limited success, and also threatens to worsen the very conditions it is intended to curb.

15 Under primitive agricultural conditions the farmer had few insect problems. These arose with the intensification of agriculture—the devotion of immense acreages to a single crop. Such a system set the stage for explosive increases in specific insect populations. Single-crop farming does not take advantage of the principles by which nature works; it is agriculture as an engineer might conceive it to be. Nature has introduced great variety into the landscape, but man has displayed a passion for simplifying it. Thus he undoes the built-in checks and balances by which nature holds the species within bounds. One important natural check is a limit on the amount of suitable habitat for each species. Obviously then, an insect that lives on wheat can build up its population to much higher levels on a farm devoted to wheat than on one in which wheat is intermingled with other crops to which the insect is not adapted.

16 The same thing happens in other situations. A generation or more

---

[11] **Soil Bank:** a federal plan providing cash payments to farmers who cut production of certain surplus crops in favor of soil-enriching ones

ago, the towns of large areas of the United States lined their streets with the noble elm tree. Now the beauty they hopefully created is threatened with complete destruction as disease sweeps through the elms, carried by a beetle that would have only limited chance to build up large populations and to spread from tree to tree if the elms were only occasional trees in a richly diversified planting.

17 Another factor in the modern insect problem is one that must be viewed against a background of geologic and human history: the spreading of thousands of different kinds of organisms from their native homes to invade new territories. This worldwide migration has been studied and graphically described by the British ecologist Charles Elton in his recent book *The Ecology of Invasions.* During the Cretaceous Period, some hundred million years ago, flooding seas cut many land bridges between continents and living things found themselves confined in what Elton calls "colossal separate nature reserves." There, isolated from others of their kind, they developed many new species. When some of the land masses were joined again, about 15 million years ago, these species began to move out into new territories—a movement that is not only still in progress but is now receiving considerable assistance from man.

18 The importation of plants is the primary agent in the modern spread of species, for animals have almost invariably gone along with the plants, quarantine being a comparatively recent and not completely effective innovation. The United States Office of Plant Introduction alone has introduced almost 200,000 species and varieties of plants from all over the world. Nearly half of the 180 or so major insect enemies of plants in the United States are accidental imports from abroad, and most of them have come as hitchhikers on plants.

19 In new territory, out of reach of the restraining hand of the natural enemies that kept down its numbers in its native land, an invading plant or animal is able to become enormously abundant. Thus it is no accident that our most troublesome insects are introduced species.

20 These invasions, both the naturally occurring and those dependent on human assistance, are likely to continue indefinitely. Quarantine and massive chemical campaigns are only extremely expensive ways of buying time. We are faced, according to Dr. Elton, "with a life-and-death need not just to find new technological means of suppressing this plant or that animal"; instead we need the basic knowledge of animal populations and their relations to their surroundings that will "promote an even balance and damp down the explosive power of outbreaks and new invasions."

21 Much of the necessary knowledge is now available but we do not use it. We train ecologists in our universities and even employ them in our governmental agencies but we seldom take their advice. We allow the chemical death rain to fall as though there were no alternative,

whereas in fact there are many, and our ingenuity could soon discover many more if given opportunity.

22 Have we fallen into a mesmerized state that makes us accept as inevitable that which is inferior or detrimental, as though having lost the will or the vision to demand that which is good? Such thinking, in the words of the ecologist Paul Shepard, "idealizes life with only its head out of water, inches above the limits of toleration of the corruption of its own environment . . . Why should we tolerate a diet of weak poisons, a home in insipid surroundings, a circle of acquaintances who are not quite our enemies, the noise of motors with just enough relief to prevent insanity? Who would want to live in a world which is just not quite fatal?"

23 Yet such a world is pressed upon us. The crusade to create a chemically sterile, insect-free world seems to have engendered a fanatic zeal on the part of many specialists and most of the so-called control agencies. On every hand there is evidence that those engaged in spraying operations exercise a ruthless power. "The regulatory entomologists . . . function as prosecutor, judge and jury, tax assessor and collector and sheriff to enforce their own orders," said Connecticut entomologist Neely Turner. The most flagrant abuses go unchecked in both state and federal agencies.

24 It is not my contention that chemical insecticides must never be used. I do contend that we have put poisonous and biologically potent chemicals indiscriminately into the hands of persons largely or wholly ignorant of their potentials for harm. We have subjected enormous numbers of people to contact with these poisons, without their consent and often without their knowledge. If the Bill of Rights contains no guarantee that a citizen shall be secure against lethal poisons distributed either by private individuals or by public officials, it is surely only because our forefathers, despite their considerable wisdom and foresight, could conceive of no such problem.

25 I contend, furthermore, that we have allowed these chemicals to be used with little or no advance investigation of their effect on soil, water, wildlife, and man himself. Future generations are unlikely to condone our lack of prudent concern for the integrity of the natural world that supports all life.

26 There is still very limited awareness of the nature of the threat. This is an era of specialists, each of whom sees his own problem and is unaware of or intolerant of the larger frame into which it fits. It is also an era dominated by industry, in which the right to make a dollar at whatever cost is seldom challenged. When the public protests, confronted with some obvious evidence of damaging results of pesticide applications, it is fed little tranquilizing pills of half truth. We urgently need an end to these false assurances, to the sugar coating of unpalatable

facts. It is the public that is being asked to assume the risks that the insect controllers calculate. The public must decide whether it wishes to continue on the present road, and it can do so only when in full possession of the facts. In the words of Jean Rostand,° "The obligation to endure gives us the right to know."

STUDY QUESTIONS

1. In what ways does Carson ensure that her argument is intelligible not only to fellow biologists but also to her main audience of nonspecialists?
2. What tone does Carson take throughout this essay? How does that tone serve her argumentative purpose?
3. Carson subscribes to the Darwinian view of evolution, whereby organisms are thought to have originated as mutants of other organisms. How is this evolutionary perspective important to her argument?
4. At the end of paragraph 7, Carson urges that certain poisons be called *biocides*. What would be the effect of such a change in terminology?
5. What is Carson's objection (paragraph 15) to the practice of devoting "immense acreages to a single crop"? Would a single-crop farmer be able to defend that practice against Carson's objection?
6. In paragraph 24 Carson alludes to the Bill of Rights, claiming that it fails to mention poisons "only because our forefathers . . . could conceive of no such problem." If you have ready access to the U. S. Constitution (including its amendments) and the Declaration of Independence that preceded it, look to see if Carson's "right" against environmental poisoning *could* be interpreted as a traditionally sanctioned one.
7. What are the main counterarguments that might be raised against Carson's thesis? Has she adequately anticipated them?
8. In the course of her essay, Carson cites several authorities to support her position. What range of expertise is represented by those authorities? Could her case have been made stronger by citation of a wider range of authorities? If your answer is *yes,* be ready to say what kinds of authorities might have proved useful.
9. Where does Carson limit the scope of her claims? What is the effect of such limitation on the strength of her argument?
10. Thanks partly to Carson's own work, public and official attitudes

---

26 **Jean Rostand:** (1894–1977) French author of numerous books on biological topics

toward the environment have changed a good deal since "The Obligation to Endure" was written. In what ways, if any, do you find the essay "dated"? What points, in your view, remain as relevant as ever?

Don B. Kates, Jr.

Don B. Kates, Jr., formerly a civil rights worker and a poverty lawyer for the Office of Economic Opportunity, now teaches constitutional and criminal law at St. Louis University. In addition, he maintains a civil liberties practice in San Francisco. "Against Civil Disarmament" was published in *Harper's* in 1978.

AGAINST CIVIL DISARMAMENT

1 Despite almost 100 years of often bitter debate, federal policy and that of 44 states continues to allow handguns to any sane adult who is without felony convictions. Over the past twenty years, as some of our most progressive citizens have embraced the notion that handgun confiscation would reduce violent crime, the idea of closely restricting handgun possession to police and those with police permits has been stereotyped as "liberal." Yet when the notion of sharply restricting pistol ownership first gained popularity, in the late nineteenth century, it was under distinctly conservative auspices.

2 In 1902, South Carolina banned all pistol purchases, the first and only state ever to do so. (This was nine years before New York began requiring what was then an easily acquired police permit.) Tennessee had already enacted the first ban on "Saturday Night Specials," disarming blacks and the laboring poor while leaving weapons for the Ku Klux Klan and company goons. In 1906, Mississippi enacted the first mandatory registration law for all firearms. In short order, permit requirements were enacted in North Carolina, Missouri, Michigan, and Hawaii. In 1922, a national campaign of conservative business interests for handgun confiscation was endorsed by the (then) archconservative American Bar Association.

3 Liberals at that time were not necessarily opposed in principle to a ban on handguns, but they considered such a move irrelevant and distracting from a more important issue—the prohibition of alcohol. To Jane Addams, William Jennings Bryan, and Eleanor Roosevelt (herself

a pistol carrier), liquor was the cause of violent crime. (Before dismissing this out of hand, remember that homicide studies uniformly find liquor a more prevalent factor than handguns in killings.) Besides, liberals were not likely to support the argument advanced by conservatives for gun confiscation: that certain racial and immigrant groups were so congenitally criminal (and/or politically dangerous) that they could not be trusted with arms. But when liberalism finally embraced handgun confiscation, it was by applying this conservative viewpoint to the entire populace. Now it is all Americans (not just Italians, Jews, or blacks) who must be considered so innately violent and unstable that they cannot be trusted with arms. For, we are told, it is not robbers or burglars who commit most murders, but average citizens killing relatives or friends.

4 It is certainly true that only a little more than 30 percent of murders are committed by robbers, rapists, or burglars, while 45 percent are committed among relatives or between lovers. (The rest are a miscellany of contract killings, drug wars, and "circumstances unknown.") But it is highly misleading to conclude from this that the murderer is, in any sense, an average gun owner. For the most part, murderers are disturbed, aberrant individuals with long records of criminal violence that often include several felony convictions. In terms of endangering his fellow citizen, the irresponsible drinker is far more representative of all drinkers than is the irresponsible handgunner of all handgunners. It is not my intention here to defend the character of the average American handgun owner against, say, that of the average Swiss whose government not only allows, but requires, him to keep a machine gun at home. Rather it is to show how unrealistic it is to think that we could radically decrease homicide by radically reducing the number of civilian firearms. Study after study has shown that even if the *average* gun owner complied with a ban, the one handgun owner out of 3,000 who murders (much less the one in 500 who steals) is not going to give up his guns. Nor would taking guns away from the murderer make much difference in murder rates, since a sociopath with a long history of murderous assault is not too squeamish to kill with a butcher knife, ice pick, razor, or bottle. As for the extraordinary murderers—assassins, terrorists, hit men—proponents of gun bans themselves concede that the law cannot disarm such people any more than it can disarm professional robbers.

5 The repeated appearance of these facts in studies of violent crime has eroded liberal and intellectual support for banning handguns. There is a growing consensus among even the most liberal students of criminal law and criminology that handgun confiscation is just another plausible theory that doesn't work when tried. An article written in 1968 by Mark K. Benenson, longtime American chairman of Amnesty International,[5] concludes that the arguments for gun bans are based upon selective

[5] **Amnesty International:** an organization opposing the imprisonment and mistreatment of political dissenters around the world

misleading statistics, simple-minded non sequiturs, and basic misconceptions about the nature of murder as well as of other violent crimes.

6 A 1971 study at England's Cambridge University confounds one of the most widely believed non sequiturs: "Banning handguns must work, because England does and look at its crime rate!" (It is difficult to see how those who believe this can resist the equally simple-minded pro-gun argument that gun possession deters crime: "Everybody ought to have a machine gun in his house because the Swiss and the Israelis do, and look how low their crime rates are!")

7 The Cambridge report concludes that social and cultural factors (not gun control) account for Britain's low violence rates. It points out that "the use of firearms in crime was very much less" before 1920 when Britain had "no controls of any sort." Corroborating this is the comment of a former head of Scotland Yard that in the mid-1950s there were enough illegal handguns to supply any British criminal who wanted one. But, he continued, the social milieu was such that if a criminal killed anyone, particularly a policeman, his own confederates would turn him in. When this violence-dampening social milieu began to dissipate between 1960 and 1975, the British homicide rate doubled (as did the American rate), while British robbery rates accelerated even faster than those in America. As the report notes, the vaunted handgun ban proved completely ineffective against rising violence in Britain, although the government frantically intensified enforcement and extended controls to long guns as well. Thus, the Cambridge study—the only in-depth study ever done of English gun laws—recommends "abolishing or substantially reducing controls" because their administration involves an immense, unproductive expense and diverts police resources from programs that might reduce violent crime.

8 The latest American study of gun controls was conducted with federal funding at the University of Wisconsin. Advanced computerized techniques allowed a comprehensive analysis of the effect of every form of state handgun restriction, including complete prohibition, on violence in America. Published in 1975, it concludes that "gun-control laws have no individual or collective effect in reducing the rate of violent crime."

9 Many previous studies reaching the same conclusion had been discounted by proponents of a federal ban, who argued that existing state bans cannot be effective because handguns are illegally imported from free-sale states. The Wisconsin study compared rates of handgun ownership with rates of violence in various localities, but it could find *no correlation.* If areas where handgun ownership rates are high have no higher per capita rates of homicide and other violence than areas where such rates are low, the utility of laws designed to lower the rates of handgun ownership seems dubious. Again, the problem is not the "proliferation of handguns" among the law-abiding citizenry, it is the existence of a tiny fraction of irresponsible and criminal own-

ers whom the law cannot possibly disarm of these or other weapons.

10 Far from refuting the Wisconsin study, the sheer unenforceability of handgun bans is the main reason why most experts regard them as not worth thinking about. Even in Britain, a country that, before handguns were banned, had less than 1 percent of the per capita handgun ownership we have, the Cambridge study reports that "fifty years of very strict controls has left a vast pool of illegal weapons."

11 It should be emphasized that liberal defectors from gun confiscation are no more urging people to arm themselves than are those who oppose banning pot or liquor necessarily urging people to indulge in them. They are only saying that national handgun confiscation would bring the federal government into a confrontation with millions of responsible citizens in order to enforce a program that would have no effect upon violence, except the negative one of diverting resources that otherwise might be utilized to some effective purpose. While many criminologists have doubts about the wisdom of citizens trying to defend themselves with handguns, the lack of evidence to justify confiscation requires that this remain a matter of individual choice rather than government fiat.

12 Nor can advocates of gun bans duck the evidence adverse to their position by posing such questions as: Why should people have handguns; what good do they do; why *shouldn't* we ban them? In a free country, the burden is not upon the people to show why they should have freedom of choice. It is upon those who wish to restrict that freedom to show good reason for doing so. And when the freedom is as deeply valued by as many as is handgun ownership, the evidence for infringing upon it must be very strong indeed.

13 If the likely benefits of handgun confiscation have been greatly exaggerated, the financial and constitutional costs have been largely ignored. Consider the various costs of any attempt to enforce confiscation upon a citizenry that believes (whether rightly or not) that they urgently need handguns for self-defense and that the right to keep them is constitutionally guaranteed. Most confiscationists have never gotten beyond the idea that banning handguns will make them magically disappear somehow. Because they loathe handguns and consider them useless, the prohibitionists assume that those who disagree will readily turn in their guns once a national confiscation law is passed. But the leaders of the national handgun prohibition movement have become more realistic. They recognize that defiance will, if anything, exceed the defiance of Prohibition and marijuana laws. After all, not even those who viewed drinking or pot smoking as a blow against tyranny thought, as many gun owners do, that violating the law is necessary to the protection of themselves and their families. Moreover, fear of detection is a lot more likely to keep citizens from constant purchases of liquor or pot than from a single purchase of a handgun, which, properly maintained, will last years.

14 To counter the expected defiance, the leaders of the national confiscation drive propose that handgun ownership be punished by a nonsuspendable mandatory year in prison. The mandatory feature is necessary, for otherwise prosecutors would not prosecute, and judges would not sentence, gun ownership with sufficient severity. The judge of a special Chicago court trying only gun violations recently explained why he generally levied only small fines: The overwhelming majority of the "criminals" who come before him are respectable, decent citizens who illegally carry guns because the police can't protect them and they have no other way of protecting themselves. He does not even impose probation because this would prevent the defendants, whose guns have been confiscated, from buying new ones, which, the judge believes, they need to live and work where they do.

15 These views are shared by judges and prosecutors nationwide; studies find that gun-carrying charges are among the most sympathetically dealt with of all felonies. To understand why, consider a typical case that would have come before this Chicago court if the D.A. had not dropped charges. An intruder raped a woman and threw her out of a fifteenth-floor window. Police arrived too late to arrest him, so they got her roommate for carrying the gun with which she scared him off when he attacked her.

16 Maybe it is not a good idea for this woman to keep a handgun for self-defense. But do we really want to send her to federal prison for doing so? And is a mandatory year in prison reasonable or just for an ordinary citizen who has done nothing more hurtful than keeping a gun to defend herself—when the minimum mandatory sentence for murder is only seven years and most murderers serve little more?

17 Moreover, the kind of nationwide resistance movement that a federal handgun ban would provoke could not be broken by imprisoning a few impecunious black women in Chicago. Only by severely punishing a large number of respectable citizens of every race and social class would resisters eventually be made to fear the law more than the prospect of living without handguns in a violent society. At a very conservative estimate, at least half of our present handgun owners would be expected to defy a federal ban.* To imprison just 1 percent of these 25 million people would require several times as many cells as

---

*I reach this estimate in this fashion: Surveys uniformly find a majority of gun owners support gun registration—in theory. In practice, however, they refuse to register because they believe this will identify their guns for confiscation if and when a national handgun ban eventually passes. In 1968, Chicago police estimated that two-thirds of the city's gun owners had not complied with the new state registration law; statewide noncompliance was estimated at 75 percent. In Cleveland, police estimate that almost 90 percent of handgun owners are in violation of a 1976 registration requirement. My estimate that one out of two handgun owners would defy national confiscation is conservative indeed when between two out of three and nine out of ten of them are already defying registration laws because they believe such laws presage confiscation.

the entire federal prison system now has. The combined federal, state, and local jail systems could barely manage. Of course, so massive an enforcement campaign would also require doubling expenditure for police, prosecutors, courts, and all the other sectors of criminal justice administration. The Wisconsin study closes with the pertinent query: "Are we willing to make sociological and economic investments of such a tremendous nature in a social experiment for which there is no empirical support?"

18 The argument against a federal handgun ban is much like the argument against marijuana bans. It is by no means clear that marijuana is the harmless substance that its proponents claim. But it would take evidence far stronger than we now have to justify the enormous financial, human, institutional, and constitutional costs of continuing to ferret out, try, and imprison even a small percentage of the otherwise law-abiding citizens who insist on having pot. Sophisticated analysis of the criminalization decision takes into account not only the harms alleged to result from public possession of things like pot or guns, but the capacity of the criminal law to reduce those harms and the costs of trying to do so. Unfortunately most of the gun-control debate never gets beyond the abstract merits of guns—a subject on which those who view them with undifferentiated loathing are no more rational than those who love them. The position of all too many gun-banning liberals is indistinguishable from Archie Bunker's views on legalizing pot and homosexuality: "I don't like it and I don't like those who do—so it ought to be illegal."

19 The emotionalism with which many liberals (and conservatives as well) react against the handgun reflects not its reality but its symbolism to people who are largely ignorant of that reality. A 1975 national survey found a direct correlation between support for more stringent controls and the inability to answer simple questions about present federal gun laws. In other words, the less the respondent knew about the subject, the more likely he was to support national confiscation. Liberals advocate severely punishing those who will defy confiscation only because the liberal image of a gun owner is a criminal or right-wing fanatic rather than a poor black woman in Chicago defending herself against a rapist or a murderer. Contrary to this stereotype, most "gun nuts" are peaceful hobbyists whose violence is exclusively of the Walter Mitty° type. Gun owners' views are all too often expressed in right-wing terms (which does nothing for the rationality of the debate) because twenty years of liberal vilification has given them nowhere else to look for support. If only liberals knew it, handgun ownership is disproportionately high among the underprivileged for whom liberals tradition-

19 **Walter Mitty:** the hero of "The Secret Life of Walter Mitty," a story by the American humorist James Thurber (1894–1961) about a henpecked husband who imagines himself in several heroic roles

ally have had most sympathy. As the most recent (1975) national demographic survey reports: "The top subgroups who own a gun *only* for self-defense include blacks (almost half own one for this reason alone), lowest income group, senior citizens." The average liberal has no understanding of why people have guns because he has no idea what it is like to live in a ghetto where police have given up on crime control. Minority and disadvantaged citizens are not about to give up their families' protection because middle-class white liberals living and working in high-security buildings and/or well-policed suburbs tell them it's safer that way.

20 A final cost of national gun confiscation would be the vast accretion of enforcement powers to the police at the expense of individual liberty. The Police Foundation, which ardently endorses confiscation, recently suggested that federal agencies and local police look to how drug laws are enforced as a model of how to enforce firearms laws. Coincidentally, the chief topic of conversation at the 1977 national conference of supporters of federal confiscation was enforcement through house searches of everyone whom sales records indicate may ever have owned a handgun. In fact, indiscriminate search, complemented by electronic surveillance and vast armies of snoopers and informers, is how handgun restrictions are enforced in countries like Holland and Jamaica, and in states like Missouri and Michigan.* Even in England, as the Cambridge report notes, each new Firearms Act has been accompanied by new, unheard-of powers of search and arrest for the police.

21 These, then, are the costs of banning handguns: even attempting an effective ban would involve enormous expenditures (roughly equal to the present cost of enforcing all our other criminal laws combined) to ferret out and jail hundreds of thousands of decent, responsible citizens who believe that they vitally need handguns to protect their families. If this does not terrorize the rest of the responsible handgun owners into compliance, the effort will have to be expanded until millions are jailed and the annual gun-banning budget closely seconds defense spending. And all of this could be accomplished only by abandoning many restraints our Constitution places upon police activity.

22 What would we have to show for all this in terms of crime reduction? Terrorists, hit men, and other hardened criminals who are not deterred by the penalties for murder, robbery, rape, burglary, et cetera are not about to be terrified by the penalties for gun ownership—nor

---

*According to the ACLU, St. Louis police have conducted 25,000 illegal searches in the past few years under the theory that any black man driving a late-model car possesses a handgun.

Michigan court records indicate that almost 70 percent of all firearms charges presented are thrown out because the evidence was obtained through unconstitutional search.

is the more ordinary murderer, the disturbed, aberrant individual who kills out of rage rather than cupidity.

23 What we should have learned from our experience of Prohibition, and England's with gun banning, is that violence can be radically reduced only through long-term fundamental change in the institutions and mores that produce so many violent people in our society. It is much easier to use as scapegoats a commonly vilified group (drinkers or gun owners) and convince ourselves that legislation against them is an easy short-term answer. But violence will never be contained or reduced until we give up the gimmicky programs, the scapegoating, the hypocritical hand-wringing, and frankly ask ourselves whether we are willing to make the painful, disturbing, far-reaching institutional and cultural changes that are necessary.

STUDY QUESTIONS

1. Were you surprised that someone of Kates's background, as described in the headnote to his essay, takes such a strong stand against gun control? What is the connection between that stand and Kates's interest in protecting civil liberties and helping the poor?
2. What rhetorical use does Kates make of standard expectations about "liberal" and "conservative" positions?
3. How does Kates use facts and figures to support his thesis? Be ready to cite some typical examples.
4. Does Kates take due account of objections that might be raised against his argument? Where in the essay do you find such objections being addressed? Can you think of counterarguments that he has failed to consider?
5. In the total strategy of this essay, what do you think is the importance of paragraph 11?
6. Kates offers several reasons for his opposition to gun control. What do you take his *central* reason to be? Why is it more decisive than his other arguments?
7. What tone does Kates adopt throughout his essay? Is his tone suited to the evidence he presents?
8. At several points Kates makes use of analogies, or extended likenesses between two things. *Liquor laws* and *marijuana laws* provide the basis for most of his analogies. What rhetorical use does he make of them?
9. Why does Kates consider it worth emphasizing (paragraphs 14–15) that judges tend to be lenient with people found guilty of illegally possessing firearms?

10. In paragraph 18 Kates refers to the stereotypical television character Archie Bunker. What point is he making, and given the political and social line-up of people for and against gun control, why is it useful to him to mention Archie Bunker?

D. L. Rosenhan

D. L. Rosenhan is a professor of psychology and law at Stanford University and an editor of two textbooks in abnormal psychology. The present article has remained controversial since its first appearance in *Science* magazine in 1973.

ON BEING SANE IN INSANE PLACES

1 If sanity and insanity exist, how shall we know them?

2 The question is neither capricious nor itself insane. However much we may be personally convinced that we can tell the normal from the abnormal, the evidence is simply not compelling. It is commonplace, for example, to read about murder trials wherein eminent psychiatrists for the defense are contradicted by equally eminent psychiatrists for the prosecution on the matter of the defendant's sanity. More generally, there are a great deal of conflicting data on the reliability, utility, and meaning of such terms as "sanity," "insanity," "mental illness," and "schizophrenia" *(1).* Finally, as early as 1934, Benedict suggested that normality and abnormality are not universal *(2).* What is viewed as normal in one culture may be seen as quite aberrant in another. Thus, notions of normality and abnormality may not be quite as accurate as people believe they are.

3 To raise questions regarding normality and abnormality is in no way to question the fact that some behaviors are deviant or odd. Murder is deviant. So, too, are hallucinations. Nor does raising such questions deny the existence of the personal anguish that is often associated with "mental illness." Anxiety and depression exist. Psychological suffering exists. But normality and abnormality, sanity and insanity, and the diagnoses that flow from them may be less substantive than many believe them to be.

4 At its heart, the question of whether the sane can be distinguished from the insane (and whether degrees of insanity can be distinguished from each other) is a simple matter: do the salient characteristics that

lead to diagnoses reside in the patients themselves or in the environments and contexts in which observers find them? From Bleuler, through Kretschmer,[4] through the formulators of the recently revised *Diagnostic and Statistical Manual* of the American Psychiatric Association, the belief has been strong that patients present symptons, that those symptoms can be categorized, and, implicitly, that the sane are distinguishable from the insane. More recently, however, this belief has been questioned. Based in part on theoretical and anthropological considerations, but also on philosophical, legal, and therapeutic ones, the view has grown that psychological categorization of mental illness is useless at best and downright harmful, misleading, and pejorative at worst. Psychiatric diagnoses, in this view, are in the minds of the observers and are not valid summaries of characteristics displayed by the observed *(3–5)*.

5 Gains can be made in deciding which of these is more nearly accurate by getting normal people (that is, people who do not have, and have never suffered, symptoms of serious psychiatric disorders) admitted to psychiatric hospitals and then determining whether they were discovered to be sane and, if so, how. If the sanity of such pseudopatients were always detected, there would be prima facie evidence that a sane individual can be distinguished from the insane context in which he is found. Normality (and presumably abnormality) is distinct enough that it can be recognized wherever it occurs, for it is carried within the person. If, on the other hand, the sanity of the pseudopatients were never discovered, serious difficulties would arise for those who support traditional modes of psychiatric diagnosis. Given that the hospital staff was not incompetent, that the pseudopatient had been behaving as sanely as he had been outside of the hospital, and that it had never been previously suggested that he belonged in a psychiatric hospital, such an unlikely outcome would support the view that psychiatric diagnosis betrays little about the patient but much about the environment in which an observer finds him.

6 This article describes such an experiment. Eight sane people gained secret admission to 12 different hospitals *(6)*. Their diagnostic experiences constitute the data of the first part of this article; the remainder is devoted to a description of their experiences in psychiatric institutions. Too few psychiatrists and psychologists, even those who have worked in such hospitals, know what the experience is like. They rarely talk about it with former patients, perhaps because they distrust information coming from the previously insane. Those who have worked in psychiatric hospitals are likely to have adapted so thoroughly to the

---

[4] **Bleuler, Kretschmer:** Paul Eugen Bleuler (1857–1939), Swiss psychiatrist and pioneer in the diagnosis and treatment of psychoses; Ernst Kretschmer (1888–1964), German psychiatrist who attempted to correlate body types with susceptibility to different mental disorders

settings that they are insensitive to the impact of that experience. And while there have been occasional reports of researchers who submitted themselves to psychiatric hospitalization *(7),* these researchers have commonly remained in the hospitals for short periods of time, often with the knowledge of the hospital staff. It is difficult to know the extent to which they were treated like patients or like research colleagues. Nevertheless, their reports about the inside of the psychiatric hospital have been valuable. This article extends those efforts.

Pseudopatients and Their Settings

7 The eight pseudopatients were a varied group. One was a psychology graduate student in his 20's. The remaining seven were older and "established." Among them were three psychologists, a pediatrician, a psychiatrist, a painter, and a housewife. Three pseudopatients were women, five were men. All of them employed pseudonyms, lest their alleged diagnoses embarrass them later. Those who were in mental health professions alleged another occupation in order to avoid the special attentions that might be accorded by staff, as a matter of courtesy or caution, to ailing colleagues *(8).* With the exception of myself (I was the first pseudopatient and my presence was known to the hospital administrator and chief psychologist and, so far as I can tell, to them alone), the presence of pseudopatients and the nature of the research program was not known to the hospital staffs *(9).*

8 The settings were similarly varied. In order to generalize the findings, admission into a variety of hospitals was sought. The 12 hospitals in the sample were located in five different states on the East and West coasts. Some were old and shabby, some were quite new. Some were research-oriented, others not. Some had good staff-patient ratios, others were quite understaffed. Only one was a strictly private hospital. All of the others were supported by state or federal funds or, in one instance, by university funds.

9 After calling the hospital for an appointment, the pseudopatient arrived at the admissions office complaining that he had been hearing voices. Asked what the voices said, he replied that they were often unclear, but as far as he could tell they said "empty," "hollow," and "thud." The voices were unfamiliar and were of the same sex as the pseudopatient. The choice of these symptoms was occasioned by their apparent similarity to existential symptoms. Such symptoms are alleged to arise from painful concerns about the perceived meaninglessness of one's life. It is as if the hallucinating person were saying, "My life is empty and hollow." The choice of these symptoms was also determined by the *absence* of a single report of existential psychoses in the literature.

10 Beyond alleging the symptoms and falsifying name, vocation, and employment, no further alterations of person, history, or circumstances

were made. The significant events of the pseudopatient's life history were presented as they had actually occurred. Relationships with parents and siblings, with spouse and children, with people at work and in school, consistent with the aforementioned exceptions, were described as they were or had been. Frustrations and upsets were described along with joys and satisfactions. These facts are important to remember. If anything, they strongly biased the subsequent results in favor of detecting sanity, since none of their histories or current behaviors were seriously pathological in any way.

11 Immediately upon admission to the psychiatric ward, the pseudopatient ceased simulating *any* symptoms of abnormality. In some cases, there was a brief period of mild nervousness and anxiety, since none of the pseudopatients really believed that they would be admitted so easily. Indeed, their shared fear was that they would be immediately exposed as frauds and greatly embarrassed. Moreover, many of them had never visited a psychiatric ward; even those who had, nevertheless had some genuine fears about what might happen to them. Their nervousness, then, was quite appropriate to the novelty of the hospital setting, and it abated rapidly.

12 Apart from that short-lived nervousness, the pseudopatient behaved on the ward as he "normally" behaved. The pseudopatient spoke to patients and staff as he might ordinarily. Because there is uncommonly little to do on a psychiatric ward, he attempted to engage others in conversation. When asked by staff how he was feeling, he indicated that he was fine, that he no longer experienced symptoms. He responded to instructions from attendants, to calls for medication (which was not swallowed), and to dining-hall instructions. Beyond such activities as were available to him on the admissions ward, he spent his time writing down his observations about the ward, its patients, and the staff. Initially these notes were written "secretly," but as it soon became clear that no one much cared, they were subsequently written on standard tablets of paper in such public places as the dayroom. No secret was made of these activities.

13 The pseudopatient, very much as a true psychiatric patient, entered a hospital with no foreknowledge of when he would be discharged. Each was told that he would have to get out by his own devices, essentially by convincing the staff that he was sane. The psychological stresses associated with hospitalization were considerable, and all but one of the pseudopatients desired to be discharged almost immediately after being admitted. They were, therefore, motivated not only to behave sanely, but to be paragons of cooperation. That their behavior was in no way disruptive is confirmed by nursing reports, which have been obtained on most of the patients. These reports uniformly indicate that the patients were "friendly," "cooperative," and "exhibited no abnormal indications."

The Normal Are Not Detectably Sane

14 Despite their public "show" of sanity, the pseudopatients were never detected. Admitted, except in one case, with a diagnosis of schizophrenia *(10),* each was discharged with a diagnosis of schizophrenia "in remission." The label "in remission" should in no way be dismissed as a formality, for at no time during any hospitalization had any question been raised about any pseudopatient's simulation. Nor are there any indications in the hospital records that the pseudopatient's status was suspect. Rather, the evidence is strong that, once labeled schizophrenic, the pseudopatient was stuck with that label. If the pseudopatient was to be discharged, he must naturally be "in remission"; but he was not sane, nor, in the institution's view, had he ever been sane.

15 The uniform failure to recognize sanity cannot be attributed to the quality of the hospitals, for, although there were considerable variations among them, several are considered excellent. Nor can it be alleged that there was simply not enough time to observe the pseudopatients. Length of hospitalization ranged from 7 to 52 days, with an average of 19 days. The pseudopatients were not, in fact, carefully observed, but this failure clearly speaks more to traditions within psychiatric hospitals than to lack of opportunity.

16 Finally, it cannot be said that the failure to recognize the pseudopatients' sanity was due to the fact that they were not behaving sanely. While there was clearly some tension present in all of them, their daily visitors could detect no serious behavioral consequences—nor, indeed, could other patients. It was quite common for the patients to "detect" the pseudopatients' sanity. During the first three hospitalizations, when accurate counts were kept, 35 of a total of 118 patients on the admissions ward voiced their suspicions, some vigorously. "You're not crazy. You're a journalist, or a professor [referring to the continual note-taking]. You're checking up on the hospital." While most of the patients were reassured by the pseudopatient's insistence that he had been sick before he came in but was fine now, some continued to believe that the pseudopatient was sane throughout his hospitalization *(11).* The fact that the patients often recognized normality when staff did not raises important questions.

17 Failure to detect sanity during the course of hospitalization may be due to the fact that physicians operate with a strong bias toward what statisticians call the type 2 error *(5).* This is to say that physicians are more inclined to call a healthy person sick (a false positive, type 2) than a sick person healthy (a false negative, type 1). The reasons for this are not hard to find: it is clearly more dangerous to misdiagnose illness than health. Better to err on the side of caution, to suspect illness even among the healthy.

18 But what holds for medicine does not hold equally well for psy-

chiatry. Medical illnesses, while unfortunate, are not commonly pejorative. Psychiatric diagnoses, on the contrary, carry with them personal, legal, and social stigmas *(12).* It was therefore important to see whether the tendency toward diagnosing the sane insane could be reversed. The following experiment was arranged at a research and teaching hospital whose staff had heard these findings but doubted that such an error could occur in their hospital. The staff was informed that at some time during the following 3 months, one or more pseudopatients would attempt to be admitted into the psychiatric hospital. Each staff member was asked to rate each patient who presented himself at admissions or on the ward according to the likelihood that the patient was a pseudopatient. A 10-point scale was used, with a 1 and 2 reflecting high confidence that the patient was a pseudopatient.

19 Judgments were obtained on 193 patients who were admitted for psychiatric treatment. All staff who had had sustained contact with or primary responsibility for the patient—attendants, nurses, psychiatrists, physicians, and psychologists—were asked to make judgments. Forty-one patients were alleged, with high confidence, to be pseudopatients by at least one member of the staff. Twenty-three were considered suspect by at least one psychiatrist. Nineteen were suspected by one psychiatrist *and* one other staff member. Actually, no genuine pseudopatient (at least from my group) presented himself during this period.

20 The experiment is instructive. It indicates that the tendency to designate sane people as insane can be reversed when the stakes (in this case, prestige and diagnostic acumen) are high. But what can be said of the 19 people who were suspected of being "sane" by one psychiatrist and another staff member? Were these people truly "sane," or was it rather the case that in the course of avoiding the type 2 error the staff tended to make more errors of the first sort—calling the crazy "sane"? There is no way of knowing. But one thing is certain: any diagnostic process that lends itself so readily to massive errors of this sort cannot be a very reliable one.

The Stickiness of Psychodiagnostic Labels

21 Beyond the tendency to call the healthy sick—a tendency that accounts better for diagnostic behavior on admission than it does for such behavior after a lengthy period of exposure—the data speak to the massive role of labeling in psychiatric assessment. Having once been labeled schizophrenic, there is nothing the pseudopatient can do to overcome the tag. The tag profoundly colors others' perceptions of him and his behavior.

22 From one viewpoint, these data are hardly surprising, for it has long been known that elements are given meaning by the context in

which they occur. Gestalt psychology° made this point vigorously, and Asch *(13)* demonstrated that there are "central" personality traits (such as "warm" versus "cold") which are so powerful that they markedly color the meaning of other information in forming an impression of a given personality *(14)*. "Insane," "schizophrenic," "manic-depressive," and "crazy" are probably among the most powerful of such central traits. Once a person is designated abnormal, all of his other behaviors and characteristics are colored by that label. Indeed, that label is so powerful that many of the pseudopatients' normal behaviors were overlooked entirely or profoundly misinterpreted. Some examples may clarify this issue.

23 Earlier I indicated that there were no changes in the pseudopatient's personal history and current status beyond those of name, employment, and, where necessary, vocation. Otherwise, a veridical description of personal history and circumstances was offered. Those circumstances were not psychotic. How were they made consonant with the diagnosis of psychosis? Or were those diagnoses modified in such a way as to bring them into accord with the circumstances of the pseudopatient's life, as described by him?

24 As far as I can determine, diagnoses were in no way affected by the relative health of the circumstances of a pseudopatient's life. Rather, the reverse occurred: the perception of his circumstances was shaped entirely by the diagnosis. A clear example of such translation is found in the case of a pseudopatient who had had a close relationship with his mother but was rather remote from his father during his early childhood. During adolescence and beyond, however, his father became a close friend, while his relationship with his mother cooled. His present relationship with his wife was characteristically close and warm. Apart from occasional angry exchanges, friction was minimal. The children had rarely been spanked. Surely there is nothing especially pathological about such a history. Indeed, many readers may see a similar pattern in their own experiences, with no markedly deleterious consequences. Observe, however, how such a history was translated in the psychopathological context, this from the case summary prepared after the patient was discharged.

> 25 This white 39-year-old male . . . manifests a long history of considerable ambivalence in close relationships, which begins in early childhood. A warm relationship with his mother cools during his adolescence. A distant relationship to his father is described as becoming very intense. Affective stability is absent. His attempts to control emotionality with his wife and children are punctuated by angry outbursts and, in the case of the children, spankings. And while he says that he has several good

---

22 **Gestalt psychology:** a school of perception psychology emphasizing whole patterns and configurations as opposed to their component units

friends, one senses considerable ambivalence embedded in those relationships also. . . .

26 The facts of the case were unintentionally distorted by the staff to achieve consistency with a popular theory of the dynamics of a schizophrenic reaction *(15).* Nothing of an ambivalent nature had been described in relations with parents, spouse, or friends. To the extent that ambivalence could be inferred, it was probably not greater than is found in all human relationships. It is true the pseudopatient's relationships with his parents changed over time, but in the ordinary context that would hardly be remarkable—indeed, it might very well be expected. Clearly, the meaning ascribed to his verbalizations (that is, ambivalence, affective instability) was determined by the diagnosis: schizophrenia. An entirely different meaning would have been ascribed if it were known that the man was "normal."

27 All pseudopatients took extensive notes publicly. Under ordinary circumstances, such behavior would have raised questions in the minds of observers, as, in fact, it did among patients. Indeed, it seemed so certain that the notes would elicit suspicion that elaborate precautions were taken to remove them from the ward each day. But the precautions proved needless. The closest any staff member came to questioning these notes occurred when one pseudopatient asked his physician what kind of medication he was receiving and began to write down the response. "You needn't write it," he was told gently. "If you have trouble remembering, just ask me again."

28 If no questions were asked of the pseudopatients, how was their writing interpreted? Nursing records for three patients indicate that the writing was seen as an aspect of their pathological behavior. "Patient engages in writing behavior" was the daily nursing comment on one of the pseudopatients who was never questioned about his writing. Given that the patient is in the hospital, he must be psychologically disturbed. And given that he is disturbed, continuous writing must be a behavioral manifestation of that disturbance, perhaps a subset of the compulsive behaviors that are sometimes correlated with schizophrenia.

29 One tacit characteristic of psychiatric diagnosis is that it locates the sources of aberration within the individual and only rarely within the complex of stimuli that surrounds him. Consequently, behaviors that are stimulated by the environment are commonly misattributed to the patient's disorder. For example, one kindly nurse found a pseudopatient pacing the long hospital corridors. "Nervous, Mr. X?" she asked. "No, bored," he said.

30 The notes kept by pseudopatients are full of patient behaviors that were misinterpreted by well-intentioned staff. Often enough, a patient would go "berserk" because he had, wittingly or unwittingly, been mistreated by, say, an attendant. A nurse coming upon the scene would rarely inquire even cursorily into the environmental stimuli of the pa-

tient's behavior. Rather, she assumed that his upset derived from his pathology, not from his present interactions with other staff members. Occasionally, the staff might assume that the patient's family (especially when they had recently visited) or other patients had stimulated the outburst. But never were the staff found to assume that one of themselves or the structure of the hospital had anything to do with a patient's behavior. One psychiatrist pointed to a group of patients who were sitting outside the cafeteria entrance half an hour before lunchtime. To a group of young residents he indicated that such behavior was characteristic of the oral-acquisitive nature of the syndrome. It seemed not to occur to him that there were very few things to anticipate in a psychiatric hospital besides eating.

31 A psychiatric label has a life and an influence of its own. Once the impression has been formed that the patient is schizophrenic, the expectation is that he will continue to be schizophrenic. When a sufficient amount of time has passed, during which the patient has done nothing bizarre, he is considered to be in remission and available for discharge. But the label endures beyond discharge, with the unconfirmed expectation that he will behave as a schizophrenic again. Such labels, conferred by mental health professionals, are as influential on the patient as they are on his relatives and friends, and it should not surprise anyone that the diagnosis acts on all of them as a self-fulfilling prophecy. Eventually, the patient himself accepts the diagnosis, with all of its surplus meanings and expectations, and behaves accordingly *(5).*

32 The inferences to be made from these matters are quite simple. Much as Zigler and Phillips have demonstrated that there is enormous overlap in the symptoms presented by patients who have been variously diagnosed *(16),* so there is enormous overlap in the behaviors of the sane and the insane. The sane are not "sane" all of the time. We lose our tempers "for no good reason." We are occasionally depressed or anxious, again for no good reason. And we may find it difficult to get along with one or another person—again for no reason that we can specify. Similarly, the insane are not always insane. Indeed, it was the impression of the pseudopatients while living with them that they were sane for long periods of time—that the bizarre behaviors upon which their diagnoses were allegedly predicated constituted only a small fraction of their total behavior. If it makes no sense to label ourselves permanently depressed on the basis of an occasional depression, then it takes better evidence than is presently available to label all patients insane or schizophrenic on the basis of bizarre behaviors or cognitions. It seems more useful, as Mischel *(17)* has pointed out, to limit our discussions to *behaviors,* the stimuli that provoke them, and their correlates.

33 It is not known why powerful impressions of personality traits, such as "crazy" or "insane," arise. Conceivably, when the origins of and stimuli that give rise to a behavior are remote or unknown, or when the behavior strikes us as immutable, trait labels regarding the *behaver* arise.

When, on the other hand, the origins and stimuli are known and available, discourse is limited to the behavior itself. Thus, I may hallucinate because I am sleeping, or I may hallucinate because I have ingested a peculiar drug. These are termed sleep-induced hallucinations, or dreams, and drug-induced hallucinations, respectively. But when the stimuli to my hallucinations are unknown, that is called craziness, or schizophrenia—as if that inference were somehow as illuminating as the others.

The Experience of Psychiatric Hospitalization

34 The term "mental illness" is of recent origin. It was coined by people who were humane in their inclinations and who wanted very much to raise the station of (and the public's sympathies toward) the psychologically disturbed from that of witches and "crazies" to one that was akin to the physically ill. And they were at least partially successful, for the treatment of the mentally ill *has* improved considerably over the years. But while treatment has improved, it is doubtful that people really regard the mentally ill in the same way that they view the physically ill. A broken leg is something one recovers from, but mental illness allegedly endures forever *(18).* A broken leg does not threaten the observer, but a crazy schizophrenic? There is by now a host of evidence that attitudes toward the mentally ill are characterized by fear, hostility, aloofness, suspicion, and dread *(19).* The mentally ill are society's lepers.

35 That such attitudes infect the general population is perhaps not surprising, only upsetting. But that they affect the professionals—attendants, nurses, physicians, psychologists, and social workers—who treat and deal with the mentally ill is more disconcerting, both because such attitudes are self-evidently pernicious and because they are unwitting. Most mental health professionals would insist that they are sympathetic toward the mentally ill, that they are neither avoidant nor hostile. But it is more likely that an exquisite ambivalence characterizes their relations with psychiatric patients, such that their avowed impulses are only part of their entire attitude. Negative attitudes are there too and can easily be detected. Such attitudes should not surprise us. They are the natural offspring of the labels patients wear and the places in which they are found.

36 Consider the structure of the typical psychiatric hospital. Staff and patients are strictly segregated. Staff have their own living space, including their dining facilities, bathrooms, and assembly places. The glassed quarters that contain the professional staff, which the pseudopatients came to call "the cage," sit out on every dayroom. The staff emerge primarily for caretaking purposes—to give medication, to conduct a therapy or group meeting, to instruct or reprimand a patient. Otherwise, staff keep to themselves, almost as if the disorder that afflicts their charges is somehow catching.

37 So much is patient-staff segregation the rule that, for four public

hospitals in which an attempt was made to measure the degree to which staff and patients mingle, it was necessary to use "time out of the staff cage" as the operational measure. While it was not the case that all time spent out of the cage was spent mingling with patients (attendants, for example, would occasionally emerge to watch television in the dayroom), it was the only way in which one could gather reliable data on time for measuring.

38 The average amount of time spent by attendants outside of the cage was 11.3 percent (range, 3 to 52 percent). This figure does not represent only time spent mingling with patients, but also includes time spent on such chores as folding laundry, supervising patients while they shave, directing ward cleanup, and sending patients to off-ward activities. It was the relatively rare attendant who spent time talking with patients or playing games with them. It proved impossible to obtain a "percent mingling time" for nurses, since the amount of time they spent out of the cage was too brief. Rather, we counted instances of emergence from the cage. On the average, daytime nurses emerged from the cage 11.5 times per shift, including instances when they left the ward entirely (range, 4 to 39 times). Late afternoon and night nurses were even less available, emerging on the average 9.4 times per shift (range, 4 to 41 times). Data on early morning nurses, who arrived usually after midnight and departed at 8 A.M., are not available because patients were asleep during most of this period.

39 Physicians, especially psychiatrists, were even less available. They were rarely seen on the wards. Quite commonly, they would be seen only when they arrived and departed, with the remaining time being spent in their offices or in the cage. On the average, physicians emerged on the ward 6.7 times per day (range, 1 to 17 times). It proved difficult to make an accurate estimate in this regard, since physicians often maintained hours that allowed them to come and go at different times.

40 The hierarchical organization of the psychiatric hospital has been commented on before *(20),* but the latent meaning of that kind of organization is worth noting again. Those with the most power have least to do with patients, and those with the least power are most involved with them. Recall, however, that the acquisition of role-appropriate behaviors occurs mainly through the observation of others, with the most powerful having the most influence. Consequently, it is understandable that attendants not only spend more time with patients than do any other members of the staff—that is required by their station in the hierarchy—but also, insofar as they learn from their superiors' behavior, spend as little time with patients as they can. Attendants are seen mainly in the cage, which is where the models, the action, and the power are.

41 I turn now to a different set of studies, these dealing with staff response to patient-initiated contact. It has long been known that the

amount of time a person spends with you can be an index of your significance to him. If he initiates and maintains eye contact, there is reason to believe that he is considering your requests and needs. If he pauses to chat or actually stops and talks, there is added reason to infer that he is individuating you. In four hospitals, the pseudopatient approached the staff member with a request which took the following form: "Pardon me, Mr. [or Dr. or Mrs.] X, could you tell me when I will be eligible for grounds privileges?" (or ". . . when I will be presented at the staff meeting?" or ". . . when I am likely to be discharged?"). While the content of the question varied according to the appropriateness of the target and the pseudopatient's (apparent) current needs the form was always a courteous and relevant request for information. Care was taken never to approach a particular member of the staff more than once a day, lest the staff member become suspicious or irritated. In examining these data, remember that the behavior of the pseudopatients was neither bizarre nor disruptive. One could indeed engage in good conversation with them.

42 The data for these experiments are shown in Table 1, separately for physicians (column 1) and for nurses and attendants (column 2). Minor differences between these four institutions were overwhelmed by the degree to which staff avoided continuing contacts that patients had initiated. By far, their most common response consisted of either a brief response to the question, offered while they were "on the move" and with head averted, or no response at all.

Table 1. Self-initiated contact by pseudopatients with psychiatrists and nurses and attendants, compared to contact with other groups.

				University medical center		
			University campus			
	Psychiatric hospitals		(nonmedical)	Physicians		
Contact	(1) Psychiatrists	(2) Nurses and attendants	(3) Faculty	(4) "Looking for a psychiatrist"	(5) "Looking an for internist"	(6) No additional comment
Responses						
Moves on, head averted (%)	71	88	0	0	0	0
Makes eye contact (%)	23	10	0	11	0	0
Pauses and chats (%)	2	2	0	11	0	10
Stops and talks (%)	4	0.5	100	78	100	90
Mean number of questions answered (out of 6)	*	*	6	3.8	4.8	4.5
Respondents (No.)	13	47	14	18	15	10
Attempts (No.)	185	1283	14	18	15	10

*Not applicable.

43 The encounter frequently took the following bizarre form: (pseudopatient) "Pardon me, Dr. X. Could you tell me when I am eligible for grounds privileges?" (physician) "Good morning, Dave. How are you today?" (Moves off without waiting for a response.)

44 It is instructive to compare these data with data recently obtained at Stanford University. It has been alleged that large and eminent universities are characterized by faculty who are so busy that they have no time for students. For this comparison, a young lady approached individual faculty members who seemed to be walking purposefully to some meeting or teaching engagement and asked them the following six questions.

45 1) "Pardon me, could you direct me to Encina Hall?" (at the medical school: ". . . to the Clinical Research Center?").
2) "Do you know where Fish Annex is?" (there is no Fish Annex at Stanford).
3) "Do you teach here?"
4) "How does one apply for admission to the college?" (at the medical school: ". . . to the medical school?").
5) "Is it difficult to get in?"
6) "Is there financial aid?"

46 Without exception, as can be seen in Table 1 (column 3), all of the questions were answered. No matter how rushed they were, all respondents not only maintained eye contact, but stopped to talk. Indeed, many of the respondents went out of their way to direct or take the questioner to the office she was seeking, to try to locate "Fish Annex," or to discuss with her the possibilities of being admitted to the university.

47 Similar data, also shown in Table 1 (columns 4, 5, and 6), were obtained in the hospital. Here too, the young lady came prepared with six questions. After the first question, however, she remarked to 18 of her respondents (column 4), "I'm looking for a psychiatrist," and to 15 others (column 5), "I'm looking for an internist." Ten other respondents received no inserted comment (column 6). The general degree of cooperative responses is considerably higher for these university groups than it was for pseudopatients in psychiatric hospitals. Even so, differences are apparent within the medical school setting. Once having indicated that she was looking for a psychiatrist, the degree of cooperation elicited was less than when she sought an internist.

Powerlessness and Depersonalization

48 Eye contact and verbal contact reflect concern and individuation; their absence, avoidance and depersonalization. The data I have presented do not do justice to the rich daily encounters that grew up around matters of depersonalization and avoidance. I have records of patients who were beaten by staff for the sin of having initiated verbal contact.

During my own experience, for example, one patient was beaten in the presence of other patients for having approached an attendant and told him, "I like you." Occasionally, punishment meted out to patients for misdemeanors seemed so excessive that it could not be justified by the most radical interpretations of psychiatric canon. Nevertheless, they appeared to go unquestioned. Tempers were often short. A patient who had not heard a call for medication would be roundly excoriated, and the morning attendants would often wake patients with, "Come on, you m—f—s, out of bed!"

49 Neither anecdotal nor "hard" data can convey the overwhelming sense of powerlessness which invades the individual as he is continually exposed to the depersonalization of the psychiatric hospital. It hardly matters *which* psychiatric hospital—the excellent public ones and the very plush private hospital were better than the rural and shabby ones in this regard, but, again, the features that psychiatric hospitals had in common overwhelmed by far their apparent differences.

50 Powerlessness was evident everywhere. The patient is deprived of many of his legal rights by dint of his psychiatric commitment *(21).* He is shorn of credibility by virtue of his psychiatric label. His freedom of movement is restricted. He cannot initiate contact with the staff, but may only respond to such overtures as they make. Personal privacy is minimal. Patient quarters and possessions can be entered and examined by any staff member, for whatever reason. His personal history and anguish is available to any staff member (often including the "grey lady" and "candy striper" volunteer) who chooses to read his folder, regardless of their therapeutic relationship to him. His personal hygiene and waste evacuation are often monitored. The water closets may have no doors.

51 At times, depersonalization reached such proportions that pseudopatients had the sense that they were invisible, or at least unworthy of account. Upon being admitted, I and other pseudopatients took the initial physical examinations in a semipublic room, where staff members went about their own business as if we were not there.

52 On the ward, attendants delivered verbal and occasionally serious physical abuse to patients in the presence of other observing patients, some of whom (the pseudopatients) were writing it all down. Abusive behavior, on the other hand, terminated quite abruptly when other staff members were known to be coming. Staff are credible witnesses. Patients are not.

53 A nurse unbuttoned her uniform to adjust her brassiere in the presence of an entire ward of viewing men. One did not have the sense that she was being seductive. Rather, she didn't notice us. A group of staff persons might point to a patient in the dayroom and discuss him animatedly, as if he were not there.

54 One illuminating instance of depersonalization and invisibility occurred with regard to medications. All told, the pseudopatients were

administered nearly 2100 pills, including Elavil, Stelazine, Compazine, and Thorazine, to name but a few. (That such a variety of medications should have been administered to patients presenting identical symptoms is itself worthy of note.) Only two were swallowed. The rest were either pocketed or deposited in the toilet. The pseudopatients were not alone in this. Although I have no precise records on how many patients rejected their medications, the pseudopatients frequently found the medications of other patients in the toilet before they deposited their own. As long as they were cooperative, their behavior and the pseudopatients' own in this matter, as in other important matters, went unnoticed throughout.

55 Reactions to such depersonalization among pseudopatients were intense. Although they had come to the hospital as participant observers and were fully aware that they did not "belong," they nevertheless found themselves caught up in and fighting the process of depersonalization. Some examples: a graduate student in psychology asked his wife to bring his textbooks to the hospital so he could "catch up on his homework"—this despite the elaborate precautions taken to conceal his professional association. The same student, who had trained for quite some time to get into the hospital, and who had looked forward to the experience, "remembered" some drag races that he had wanted to see on the weekend and insisted that he be discharged by that time. Another pseudopatient attempted a romance with a nurse. Subsequently, he informed the staff that he was applying for admission to graduate school in psychology and was very likely to be admitted, since a graduate professor was one of his regular hospital visitors. The same person began to engage in psychotherapy with other patients—all of this as a way of becoming a person in an impersonal environment.

The Sources of Depersonalization

55 What are the origins of depersonalization? I have already mentioned two. First are attitudes held by all of us toward the mentally ill—including those who treat them—attitudes characterized by fear, distrust, and horrible expectations on the one hand, and benevolent intentions on the other. Our ambivalence leads, in this instance as in others, to avoidance.

57 Second, and not entirely separate, the hierarchical structure of the psychiatric hospital facilitates depersonalization. Those who are at the top have least to do with patients, and their behavior inspires the rest of the staff. Average daily contact with psychiatrists, psychologists, residents, and physicians combined ranged from 3.9 to 25.1 minutes, with an overall mean of 6.8 (six pseudopatients over a total of 129 days of hospitalization). Included in this average are time spent in the admissions interview, ward meetings in the presence of a senior staff member, group and individual psychotherapy contacts, case presentation confer-

ences, and discharge meetings. Clearly, patients do not spend much time in interpersonal contact with doctoral staff. And doctoral staff serve as models for nurses and attendants.

58 There are probably other sources. Psychiatric installations are presently in serious financial straits. Staff shortages are pervasive, staff time at a premium. Something has to give, and that something is patient contact. Yet, while financial stresses are realities, too much can be made of them. I have the impression that the psychological forces that result in depersonalization are much stronger than the fiscal ones and that the addition of more staff would not correspondingly improve patient care in this regard. The incidence of staff meetings and the enormous amount of record-keeping on patients, for example, have not been as substantially reduced as has patient contact. Priorities exist, even during hard times. Patient contact is not a significant priority in the traditional psychiatric hospital, and fiscal pressures do not account for this. Avoidance and depersonalization may.

59 Heavy reliance upon psychotropic medication tacitly contributes to depersonalization by convincing staff that treatment is indeed being conducted and that further patient contact may not be necessary. Even here, however, caution needs to be exercised in understanding the role of psychotropic drugs. If patients were powerful rather than powerless, if they were viewed as interesting individuals rather than diagnostic entities, if they were socially significant rather than social lepers, if their anguish truly and wholly compelled our sympathies and concerns, would we not *seek* contact with them, despite the availability of medications? Perhaps for the pleasure of it all?

The Consequences of Labeling and Depersonalization

60 Whenever the ratio of what is known to what needs to be known approaches zero, we tend to invent "knowledge" and assume that we understand more than we actually do. We seem unable to acknowledge that we simply don't know. The needs for diagnosis and remediation of behavioral and emotional problems are enormous. But rather than acknowledge that we are just embarking on understanding, we continue to label patients "schizophrenic," "manic-depressive," and "insane," as if in those words we had captured the essence of understanding. The facts of the matter are that we have known for a long time that diagnoses are often not useful or reliable, but we have nevertheless continued to use them. We now know that we cannot distinguish insanity from sanity. It is depressing to consider how that information will be used.

61 Not merely depressing, but frightening. How many people, one wonders, are sane but not recognized as such in our psychiatric institutions? How many have been needlessly stripped of their privileges of citizenship, from the right to vote and drive to that of handling their

own accounts? How many have feigned insanity in order to avoid the criminal consequences of their behavior, and, conversely, how many would rather stand trial than live interminably in a psychiatric hospital —but are wrongly thought to be mentally ill? How many have been stigmatized by well-intentioned, but nevertheless erroneous, diagnoses? On the last point, recall again that a "type 2 error" in psychiatric diagnosis does not have the same consequences it does in medical diagnosis. A diagnosis of cancer that has been found to be in error is cause for celebration. But psychiatric diagnoses are rarely found to be in error. The label sticks, a mark of inadequacy forever.

62 Finally, how many patients might be "sane" outside the psychiatric hospital but seem insane in it—not because craziness resides in them, as it were, but because they are responding to a bizarre setting, one that may be unique to institutions which harbor nether people? Goffman *(4)* calls the process of socialization to such institutions "mortification" —an apt metaphor that includes the processes of depersonalization that have been described here. And while it is impossible to know whether the pseudopatients' responses to these processes are characteristic of all inmates—they were, after all, not real patients—it is difficult to believe that these processes of socialization to a psychiatric hospital provide useful attitudes or habits of response for living in the "real world."

Summary and Conclusions

63 It is clear that we cannot distinguish the sane from the insane in psychiatric hospitals. The hospital itself imposes a special environment in which the meanings of behavior can easily be misunderstood. The consequences to patients hospitalized in such an environment—the powerlessness, depersonalization, segregation, mortification, and self-labeling—seem undoubtedly countertherapeutic.

64 I do not, even now, understand this problem well enough to perceive solutions. But two matters seem to have some promise. The first concerns the proliferation of community mental health facilities, of crisis intervention centers, of the human potential movement, and of behavior therapies that, for all of their own problems, tend to avoid psychiatric labels, to focus on specific problems and behaviors, and to retain the individual in a relatively nonpejorative environment. Clearly, to the extent that we refrain from sending the distressed to insane places, our impressions of them are less likely to be distorted. (The risk of distorted perceptions, it seems to me, is always present, since we are much more sensitive to an individual's behaviors and verbalizations than we are to the subtle contextual stimuli that often promote them. At issue here is a matter of magnitude. And, as I have shown, the magnitude of distortion is exceedingly high in the extreme context that is a psychiatric hospital.)

65 The second matter that might prove promising speaks to the need

to increase the sensitivity of mental health workers and researchers to the *Catch 22* position of psychiatric patients. Simply reading materials in this area will be of help to some such workers and researchers. For others, directly experiencing the impact of psychiatric hospitalization will be of enormous use. Clearly, further research into the social psychology of such total institutions will both facilitate treatment and deepen understanding.

66 I and the other pseudopatients in the psychiatric setting had distinctly negative reactions. We do not pretend to describe the subjective experiences of true patients. Theirs may be different from ours, particularly with the passage of time and the necessary process of adaptation to one's environment. But we can and do speak to the relatively more objective indices of treatment within the hospital. It could be a mistake, and a very unfortunate one, to consider that what happened to us derived from malice or stupidity on the part of the staff. Quite the contrary, our overwhelming impression of them was of people who really cared, who were committed and who were uncommonly intelligent. Where they failed, as they sometimes did painfully, it would be more accurate to attribute those failures to the environment in which they, too, found themselves than to personal callousness. Their perceptions and behavior were controlled by the situation, rather than being motivated by a malicious disposition. In a more benign environment, one that was less attached to global diagnosis, their behaviors and judgments might have been more benign and effective.

References and Notes

1. P. Ash, *J. Abnorm. Soc. Psychol.* **44,** 272 (1949); A. T. Beck, *Amer. J. Psychiat.* **119,** 210 (1962); A. T. Boisen, *Psychiatry* **2,** 233 (1938); N. Kreitman, *J. Ment. Sci.* **107,** 876 (1961); N. Kreitman, P. Sainsbury, J. Morrisey, J. Towers, J. Scrivener, *ibid.,* p. 887; H. O. Schmitt and C. P. Fonda, *J. Abnorm. Soc. Psychol.* **52,** 262 (1956); W. Seeman, *J. Nerv. Ment. Dis.* **118,** 541 (1953). For an analysis of these artifacts and summaries of the disputes, see J. Zubin, *Annu. Rev. Psychol.* **18,** 373 (1967); L. Phillips and J. G. Draguns, *ibid.* **22,** 447 (1971).
2. R. Benedict, *J. Gen. Psychol.* **10,** 59 (1934).
3. See in this regard H. Becker, *Outsiders: Studies in the Sociology of Deviance* (Free Press, New York, 1963); B. M. Braginsky, D. D. Braginsky, K. Ring, *Methods of Madness: The Mental Hospital as a Last Resort* (Holt, Rinehart & Winston, New York, 1969); G. M. Crocetti and P. V. Lemkau, *Amer. Sociol. Rev.* **30,** 577 (1965); E. Goffman, *Behavior in Public Places* (Free Press, New York, 1964); R. D. Laing, *The Divided Self: A Study of Sanity and Madness* (Quadrangle, Chicago, 1960); D. L. Phillips, *Amer. Sociol. Rev.* **28,** 963 (1963); T. R. Sarbin, *Psychol. Today* **6,** 18 (1972); E. Schur, *Amer. J. Sociol.* **75,** 309 (1969); T. Szasz, *Law, Liberty and Psychiatry* (Macmillan, New York, 1963); *The Myth of Mental Illness: Foundations of a Theory of Mental Illness* (Hoeber Harper, New York, 1963). For a critique of some of these views, see W. R. Gove, *Amer. Sociol. Rev.* **35,** 873 (1970).
4. E. Goffman, *Asylums* (Doubleday, Garden City, N.Y., 1961).
5. T. J. Scheff, *Being Mentally Ill: A Sociological Theory* (Aldine, Chicago, 1966).

6. Data from a ninth pseudopatient are not incorporated in this report because, although his sanity went undetected, he falsified aspects of his personal history, including his marital status and parental relationships. His experimental behaviors therefore were not identical to those of the other pseudopatients.

7. A. Barry, *Bellevue Is a State of Mind* (Harcourt Brace Jovanovich, New York, 1971); I. Belknap, *Human Problems of a State Mental Hospital* (McGraw-Hill, New York, 1956); W. Caudill, F. C. Redlich, H. R. Gilmore, E. B. Brody, *Amer. J. Orthopsychiat.* **22,** 314 (1952); A. R. Goldman, R. H. Bohr, T. A. Steinberg, *Prof. Psychol.* **1,** 427 (1970); unauthored, *Roche Report* **1** (No. 13), 8 (1971).

8. Beyond the personal difficulties that the pseudopatient is likely to experience in the hospital, there are legal and social ones that, combined, require considerable attention before entry. For example, once admitted to a psychiatric institution, it is difficult, if not impossible, to be discharged on short notice, state law to the contrary notwithstanding. I was not sensitive to these difficulties at the outset of the project, nor to the personal and situational emergencies that can arise, but later a writ of habeas corpus was prepared for each of the entering pseudopatients and an attorney was kept "on call" during every hospitalization. I am grateful to John Kaplan and Robert Bartels for legal advice and assistance in these matters.

9. However distasteful such concealment is, it was a necessary first step to examining these questions. Without concealment, there would have been no way to know how valid these experiences were; nor was there any way of knowing whether whatever detections occurred were a tribute to the diagnostic acumen of the staff or to the hospital's rumor network. Obviously, since my concerns are general ones that cut across individual hospitals and staffs, I have respected their anonymity and have eliminated clues that might lead to their identification.

10. Interestingly, of the 12 admissions, 11 were diagnosed as schizophrenic and one, with the identical symptomatology, as manic-depressive psychosis. This diagnosis has a more favorable prognosis, and it was given by the only private hospital in our sample. On the relations between social class and psychiatric diagnosis, see A. deB. Hollingshead and F. C. Redlich, *Social Class and Mental Illness: A Community Study* (Wiley, New York, 1958).

11. It is possible, of course, that patients have quite broad latitudes in diagnosis and therefore are inclined to call many people sane, even those whose behavior is patently aberrant. However, although we have no hard data on this matter, it was our distinct impression that this was not the case. In many instances, patients not only singled us out for attention, but came to imitate our behaviors and styles.

12. J. Cumming and E. Cumming, *Community Ment. Health* **1,** 135 (1965); A. Farina and K. Ring, *J. Abnorm. Psychol.* **70,** 47 (1965); H. E. Freeman and O. G. Simmons, *The Mental Patient Comes Home* (Wiley, New York, 1963); W. J. Johannsen, *Ment. Hygiene* **53,** 218 (1969); A. S. Linsky, *Soc. Psychiat.* **5,** 166 (1970).

13. S. E. Asch, *J. Abnorm. Soc. Psychol.* **41,** 258 (1946); *Social Psychology* (Prentice-Hall, New York, 1952).

14. See also I. N. Mensh and J. Wishner, *J. Personality* **16,** 188 (1947); J. Wishner, *Psychol. Rev.* **67,** 96 (1960); J. S. Bruner and R. Tagiuri, in *Handbook of Social Psychology,* G. Lindzey, Ed. (Addison-Wesley, Cambridge, Mass., 1954), vol. 2, pp. 634–654; J. S. Bruner, D. Shapiro, R. Tagiuri, in *Person Perception and Interpersonal Behavior,* R. Tagiuri and L. Petrullo, Eds. (Stanford Univ. Press, Stanford, Calif., 1958), pp. 277–288.

15. For an example of a similar self-fulfilling prophecy, in this instance dealing with the "central" trait of intelligence, see R. Rosenthal and L. Jacobson, *Pygmalion in the Classroom* (Holt, Rinehart & Winston, New York, 1968).

16. E. Zigler and L. Phillips, *J. Abnorm. Soc. Psychol.* **63,** 69 (1961). See also R. K. Freudenberg and J. P. Robertson, *A.M.A. Arch. Neurol. Psychiatr.* **76,** 14 (1956).

17. W. Mischel, *Personality and Assessment* (Wiley, New York, 1968).

18. The most recent and unfortunate instance of this tenet is that of Senator Thomas Eagleton.

19. T. R. Sarbin and J. C. Mancuso, *J. Clin. Consult. Psychol.* **35,** 159 (1970); T. R. Sarbin, *ibid.* **31,** 447 (1967); J. C. Nunnally, Jr., *Popular Conceptions of Mental Health* (Holt, Rinehart & Winston, New York, 1961).

20. A. H. Stanton and M. S. Schwartz, *The Mental Hospital: A Study of Institutional Participation in Psychiatric Illness and Treatment* (Basic, New York, 1954).

21. D. B. Wexler and S. E. Scoville, *Ariz. Law Rev.* **13,** 1 (1971).

22. I thank W. Mischel, E. Orne, and M. S. Rosenhan for comments on an earlier draft of this manuscript.

STUDY QUESTIONS

1. For an article appearing in a scientific journal, Rosenhan's essay bears an unusually indefinite and suggestive title. Why do you think he chose that title? Can you find more than one meaning in the phrase *insane places?*
2. As a "pseudopatient" himself, Rosenhan could probably have written a vivid and compelling first-person account of his experiences in mental hospitals. Why do you think he chose not to do so? Think about his main audience and his argumentative purpose.
3. What do you suppose is the intended effect of Rosenhan's one-sentence opening paragraph?
4. In the total strategy of Rosenhan's essay, what function do you think is served by paragraph 3?
5. What was the basis of Rosenhan's decision to gather information through the ruse of planting "pseudopatients" in various mental hospitals? Do you think he could have gotten reliable and significant data in some less devious way?
6. What ethical and/or scientific objections could be raised against Rosenhan's research method? Do you feel that those objections are satisfactorily answered by the results he obtained?
7. Were you surprised to learn that mental patients but not hospital staff members could readily identify the pseudopatients as sane? What important point is illustrated by such a fact?
8. What significance do you attach to the behavior of the pseudopatients that is described in paragraph 55?
9. Why is Rosenhan skeptical about the effectiveness of increasing the ratio of staff members to patients in mental hospitals? What, in his view, is the chief source of "depersonalization" in the handling of patients?
10. What important difference does Rosenhan see between a diagnosis of mental illness and one of physical illness? Why is that difference important?
11. Unlike other authors in this book, Rosenhan uses a standard scientific form for citing references. What do you think are the main advantages and disadvantages of such a form?

Garrett Hardin

For many years Garrett Hardin has been a professor of human ecology at the University of California, Santa Barbara. His provocative books include *Exploring New Ethics for Survival, Mandatory Motherhood,* and *Promethean Ethics.* The essay below can be found in *The Limits of Altruism: An Ecologist's View of Survival* (1977).

ETHICAL IMPLICATIONS OF CARRYING CAPACITY

1 Seldom in human affairs does a massive governmental operation succeed better than its proposers dared dream, but the Marshall Plan° did. The economy of Europe was reconstructed in a shorter time than had been thought possible. Of course the Europeans themselves were primarily responsible; but money from the United States played a crucial role.

2 While this effort was going on, the Luce° journals (principally *Time* and *Life*) and Secretary of State John Foster Dulles were calling for a "new moral offensive"—but no one (not even they) quite knew what they meant. Then a minor worker in the State Department had an idea. His name was Ben Hardy. Why not extend the Marshall Plan to the world? Making no progress in State, he pulled strings and brought his idea to the attention of Harry Truman. The President liked it, and on 20 January 1949 he announced to the world that the United States "would accept the economic and social development of the underdeveloped territories on earth as a binding obligation." Thus was the modern institution of foreign aid born.

3 It really is a new institution. Occasionally in the past Americans had sent food, clothing, or money to a stricken people, as we did to the Armenians in the 1920s; but the operation had always been a strictly temporary affair with most of the funds coming from private sources. The action was always a response to a crisis—military devastation, a volcanic eruption, an earthquake, or the like. What began in 1949 was an attempt to deal not with a crisis but with a crunch—with the chronic poverty that had afflicted two-thirds of the world for centuries. The missionary spirit that brought Christ to the heathen in the nineteenth

---

[1] **Marshall Plan:** the plan proposed by Secretary of State George C. Marshall in 1947, and adopted by the American government, to help European countries rebuild their shattered economies in the wake of World War II

[2] **Luce:** Henry Luce (1898–1967) was the influential publisher of *Time, Life,* and *Fortune* magazines.

century was reborn in the twentieth to bring prosperity to the poor. (Note that Secretary Dulles was a missionary child.)

4 From the first we had to wrestle with the problem of a label to attach to the objects of our charity. *Heathen* and *savages* were all right for the Victorians but not for us; even the accurate term *poor* would, we felt, hurt the feelings of the objects of our attentions. Since most of the rich and well-fed countries had a high degree of industrial development, the application of *post hoc* reasoning° led to the conclusion that *development = prosperity,* so the poor countries were promptly labeled *undeveloped.* But before long everyone caught on to the fact that it was just a polite word for *poor,* so this term had to be abandoned. One face-saving euphemism after another had to be replaced as its "cover" was penetrated. The time-series ran: undeveloped → underdeveloped → developing → catch-up countries → emerging nations → Third World countries—"The Flight of the Euphemisms," we might call this ballet.

5 In the late 1950s W. W. Rostow° proposed a vivid image: the "takeoff point." Each country's economy was like an airplane: all that was necessary to get it flying was to accelerate it ("develop" it) to the point where the economy could *take off* from the ground and then it was on its own. Foreign aid would thenceforth no longer be needed.

6 Alas! With few and arguable exceptions it has not worked out that way. The globalized Marshall Plan has not repeated the brilliant success of its progenitor. In addition to the substantial contributions of other countries, the United States itself spent $80 billion on genuine development aid (leaving out military aid that masqueraded as such). A quarter of a century and $80 billion later things are pretty much as they were —the gap between rich and poor countries is virtually unchanged. Why?

7 To begin with, there are many differences between postwar Europe and the poor world. Europe was faced with the job of *re*building a kind of civilization she had once known and was sure she could build again; but the poor were asked to create something utterly new in their experience. Europe's adult population is more than 98% literate; that of the poor countries is 2–30% literate. The philosophy of European people is Faustian–Promethean°—"can do" and "let's try" are ingrained attitudes; traditionally poor people are essentially fatalistic. Europe's population had for a long time grown at less than one-half percent per year. Poor countries were growing faster than that; in most of them

---

[4] **post hoc reasoning:** the mistaken inference that, because one event followed another, it must have been caused by it

[5] **W. W. Rostow:** American economist whose views on development dominated much planning in the 1960s

[7] **Faustian–Promethean:** Faust and Prometheus were legendary heroes who defied divine prohibitions in order to acquire knowledge forbidden to the human race.

population increase soon approached three percent per year. The Marshall Plan was focused on about 100 million people; foreign aid had to deal with two billion—twenty times as many. The money allotted by the United States was about the same in the two programs—in the neighborhood of $3 billion per year. Even if the theory of the takeoff point is correct, so small an impetus to the ship of state might be only enough to make the crash at the end of the runway worse.

8 Many of us think the development theory of poverty is wrong. The technological image of the takeoff point is too mechanical. The phrase emphasizes speed only—as though poor countries and rich countries differed merely in some quantity measured along a single continuum. But the significant differences are categorical, cultural, fundamental. Psychologically the cultures of industrial and nonindustrial systems are worlds apart; you cannot get from one to the other just by going faster. The glib assumption that we can (and should) "make them just like us," which ruled the religious missionary efforts of the nineteenth century, rules the foreign aid missions of the twentieth.

9 A more fundamental approach to poverty is needed. All problems of fitting cultures to resources must be examined against the concept of the carrying capacity. Let us see first how it applies to other animals. That done we can then see what modifications need to be made in applying it to the human situation.

10 The disaster that develops when carrying capacity is ignored is marvelously clear in the population history of the reindeer on St. Matthew Island. In 1944, 24 females and five males were turned loose on this island in the Bering Sea. Food was abundant, there were no predators, and hunting by man was negligible during the next twenty years. By 1957 the population had swelled to 1,350 reindeer; in the summer of 1963 it reached its peak of over 6,000 and then "crashed" during the winter when food was at its minimum. Three years later there were only 42 animals, all adults and all but one female. The future of the herd was in doubt.

11 A biologist studying the situation closely came to the conclusion that the carrying capacity of the environment was about five deer per square kilometer. That is, if the number never rose higher than this the herd could survive indefinitely—even through hard winters—in good health. In 1957 the island had only four deer per square kilometer, and they were 50 percent heavier than the animals on the mainland. The greater weight was no doubt accounted for by two factors: plenty of food, and lack of selective pressure against the fatter (and slower) animals by predators.

12 By 1963, the year of the crash, there were 18 animals per square kilometer, and the average weight had dropped back to that of the mainland herds. In the process of crashing the island population virtually destroyed all the lichens on which reindeer depend.

13 This story is a highly abnormal one. Population crashes in nature

are rare. Most of the time a population fluctuates within rather narrow limits. Figure 1 can stand as a generalization for most populations most of the time. The population level called P_1 is presumed to be at or near the carrying capacity. When the population rises much above it the excess provokes increased activity by the population-controlling factors —disease, predators, or (more rarely) starvation. The more severe control causes increased mortality, bringing the population back down near P_1, and the cycle starts over again. (If predators are involved they have their cycle too, which is much like that of the prey, but with a time-delay.) The principal difference between different populations is in the gap between P_1 and P_2. In finely adjusted natural systems the gap will be very small. Such stable systems are characteristic of complex tropical rain forests. At the other extreme is the notorious example of the Arctic lemming, which lives in a relatively simple environment. The association of ecological complexity with population stability is thought to be an essential one, though the theory is in an unsatisfactory state.

14 The biological system on the 333 square kilometers of St. Matthew Island was obviously too simple: predators were missing. There was nothing to hold the population at or below the carrying capacity; consequently the reindeer population greatly overshot its proper level, overgrazed the plants and crashed, leaving the environment in shambles. The disaster could have been prevented by plugging suitable predators into the system—wolves, perhaps. More bluntly: by death. All organisms naturally and necessarily reproduce too much for their own good; for life to be sweet it must have death as a countervailing force.

15 Accepting the necessity of death even for wild animals comes hard for many people. The management of deer herds in the United States in the first half of the twentieth century was a disgrace. Because we

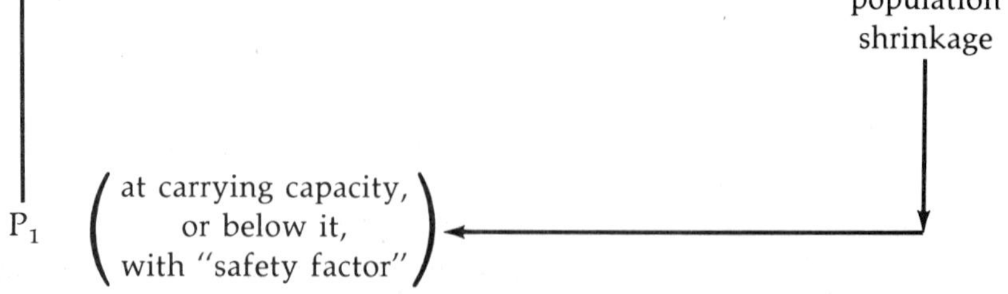

Figure 1. A population cycle with effective but not perfect control by predators. P_2 is greater than P_1. The more perfect the control the smaller the difference between P_2 and P_1.

would not accept and plan for timely deaths we caused many more deaths, which were untimely and more painful. The literature on which we have been raised glorifies the lamb and vilifies the wolf. We eliminated most of the predators in the United States and then wondered why our too-numerous deer showed signs of painful malnutrition. Our compassion for the "innocent" and helpless caused us to pass game laws that prohibited the shooting of does and fawns. Bucks, being males, were apparently not "innocent," though they were hardly any less helpless in front of a high-powered rifle. One buck suffices to fertilize many does, so population growth is affected very little when only bucks are shot.

16 By the late 1930s it was apparent to a few game managers what was wrong. The academic subject of game management was virtually created by Aldo Leopold (1887–1948), who began his life as an enthusiastic wolf hunter but changed his position 180 degrees when he realized that carrying capacity had to be the central concept in game management. It was not easy to reeducate a brainwashed public. A cruel blow to rational management was struck in 1942, when Walt Disney's *Bambi* was released. Many a biologist regards it as the most pornographic film ever put out. Its unqualified glorification of motherhood and babyhood and its vilification of hunters made the task of educating the public to the facts of life very difficult for a while.

17 The year after *Bambi* the state of Wisconsin, desperately trying to reduce its too-large and miserable deer population, authorized an open season on all deer. The resultant killing of 128,000 deer was not enough to solve the overpopulation problem but it was more than enough to evoke a public outcry against the measure. Leopold, as its principal architect, came in for particular attack. One of the arguments of his opponents is worth repeating for the light it throws on population problems.

18 Taking a census of wildlife is difficult, for obvious reasons. Sampling methods of uncertain reliability must be used. Leopold never tried to gloss over the unreliability of the game managers' estimates, because he knew it did not matter. His opponents did not understand that. When Leopold admitted that the estimate of 500,000 deer in Wisconsin before the 1943 deer-kill was a "pure guess" he was pilloried with these words:

> The infamous and bloody 1943 deer slaughter was sponsored by . . . Mr. Aldo Leopold, who admitted in writing that the figures he used were PURE GUESSWORK. . . . Imagine our fine deer herd shot to pieces by a man who rates himself as a Professor and used a GUESS instead of facts?

The point, which the indignant critic did not understand, is that you do not have to count the deer to know if there is overpopulation. You should look at two things: the deer themselves (do they show signs of malnutrition?) and their environment (does it show signs of the degradation that follows from exceeding its carrying capacity?). Neither area nor population size need be known with any degree of accuracy: carrying capacity is the target we must keep our eye on as we look for the signs of exceeding it that are easy to read—once we know what to look for.

19 It took twenty years for the Wisconsin public to get over the shock of the "massacre of '43" and be willing to examine the hunting problem rationally. Similar scenarios have been enacted in other states. The battle for rationality has to be fought state by state, county by county. It is a struggle to get people to see the centrality of the concept of carrying capacity.

20 Our primary concern here is with human populations, but before going on to these there are a few more principles we need to establish using nonhuman animals as exemplars.

21 First, it is ironically all too easy to get public support for measures that are counterproductive. In the dead of winter a report comes in of starving deer in the state parks. (Not so many would be starving, of course, if there were more predators.) Without thinking of the consequences, hunters and Bambi-lovers join hands and respond to the "emergency" in the same way: they pay to have bales of hay taken to the feeding grounds by truck or helicopter. Deer lives are saved, and the next spring the population begins its yearly growth from a higher level. This means that the next "emergency" will be greater and that meeting it with an input from an external food bank will bring the population —and the trouble—to a still higher level. The destructive system is diagrammed in Figure 2. Instead of a $P_1 \rightarrow P_2 \rightarrow P_1$ cycle, we have a $P_1 \rightarrow P_2 \rightarrow P_3 \rightarrow P_4 \ldots$ escalator, because of the inputs of food from outside the system. Or, to change the image, external inputs act like the pawl

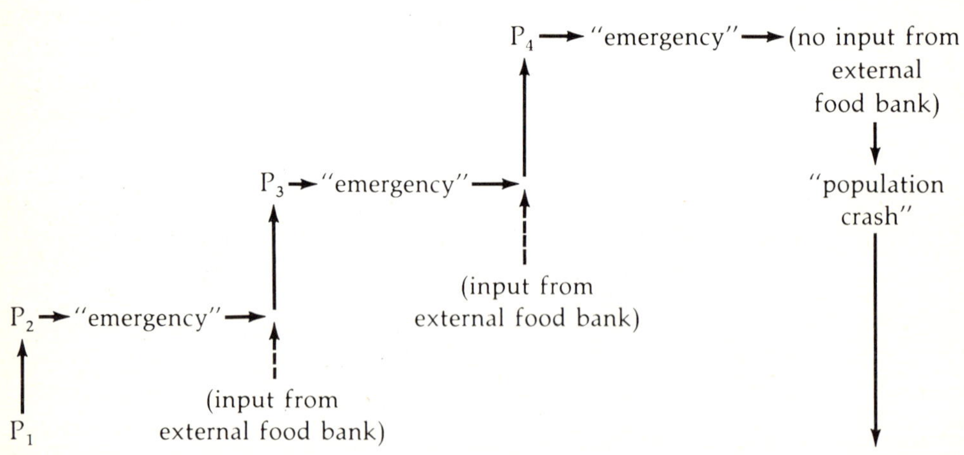

Figure 2. Escalation of emergencies by ill-advised input of food. P_{n+1} is greater than P_n. The input of food from outside the system acts like the pawl of a ratchet, preventing the normal adjustment downward.

of a ratchet,° keeping the population from dropping back to its original level. That might be all right if the world were infinite and if "philanthropic" inputs from outside the system could go on forever at ever higher levels. But they cannot. Some fine day philanthropy dries up, and the overexploited natural system (grass, lichens, or whatever) proves incapable of supporting the artificially large population. The crime of exceeding the carrying capacity is paid for with a population crash.

22 The same short-sighted "humanitarianism" that sponsors winter feeding also leads to killing predators and restricting hunting by human beings. Because hunters speak and vote, their cause is better presented than that of the nonhuman predators. That is a pity because natural predation is better for the well-being of a prey population than are human hunters. Natural predators are natural economists: they try to get their food with the least effort. Healthy prey animals in the prime of adulthood are difficult to catch, so predators focus most of their attention on the young, the old, and the sick. What they leave is a herd in splendid average health—and not growing so rapidly. Human hunters, seeking handsome trophies, pursue a contrary policy. Population control by hunters is consequently qualitatively inferior to that by natural predators. Fortunately, the case for natural predators is now beginning to be heard. Books like Farley Mowat's *Never Cry Wolf* are beginning to free the public mind from the stereotype of the Big Bad Wolf in "Little Red Riding Hood."

23 The struggle for rational game management has shown us that we must take a hard look at the "self-serving" argument. Most of the people who argued for extending the limits of legal hunting were themselves hunters. Opponents immediately denounced their argument as "self-serving": it was said that they wanted to change the rules just so they could shoot more deer.

24 In truth, the argument of the hunters *was* self-serving. The important policy question is this: was it also a good argument? In the interests of the herd, was there a need for killing more animals? Since the answer is yes, we reach an important general conclusion: *An argument that is self-serving may still be true.* The utility of identifying the self-serving character of an argument is that it puts us on the alert for prejudice and error. Any argument that is self-serving should be suspected, but it must not be dismissed out of hand. We must reason together.

25 One additional point needs to be made. If we extend the domain of ethics to include nonhuman animals, what is the ethics of killing deer? Should we follow the absolute rule "Thou shalt not kill"? Not if we have the well-being of the deer population in mind. Whenever the number of animals exceeds the carrying capacity of the environment by ever so little we should kill the excess as promptly as possible, before

---

[21] **pawl of a ratchet:** a pivoted bar that fits into the teeth of a wheel so as to prevent reversal of motion

the stress of the excess degrades the environment and reduces its carrying capacity. As a matter of fact, prudence dictates that we apply control measures well before the carrying capacity is reached.

26 So long as the population is well below the carrying capacity there is no *need* to kill any of the animals. (There may be a *desire* to—on the part of some men—but that is another problem.) In other words, asked if the rule "Thou shalt not kill" is a good one we must answer, "It depends." Once we understand the ethical implications of carrying capacity we abandon ethical absolutism in favor of ethical relativism, or "situation ethics." The morality of an act, as we said before, depends on the state of the system at the time the act is performed.

27 It may be objected that we have merely replaced one absolute proscription ("Thou shalt not kill") by another ("Thou shalt not suffer the carrying capacity to be exceeded"). So we have; but we have not necessarily fallen into the absolutist trap. We recognize that the second directive may also be invalidated under some circumstances. I do not at the moment know what these might be, but an ethical situationist always tries to keep his mind open to the possibility of further changes in the moral directives he perforce has to adopt to give some stability to daily life.

28 Now we come to the human situation. Immediately the reader may bristle at his inference—it is certainly not my implication—that we must kill human beings whenever population exceeds carrying capacity. But, playing the role of both controllers and controlled, we human beings are unwilling to do so. We have good reasons for refusing, the validity of which I accept. *There is no need to kill:* we have better and more humane ways of achieving the same end, namely making population size match the carrying capacity. The question is, what are these better means? And how can we bring ourselves to use them?

29 Before proceeding with the inquiry we need to note one way in which the previous analysis is deficient for the human situation. The diagrams and the argument that accompanied them implicitly assumed that carrying capacity (ignoring fluctuations) is static. For most species most of the time, that is true. That was the assumption Malthus° made when he wrote his *Essay on Population* in 1798. Unfortunately for Malthus's reputation, the carrying capacity of the earth for human beings has grown fantastically since his day. In part, it has increased because new lands have been opened up to human settlement (but this process is almost at an end). Even more important has been the growth of science and technology. Irrigation, fertilization, and new genetic strains

29 **Malthus:** Thomas Robert Malthus (1766–1834), British economist who argued that without intervening catastrophes, the rate of population increase will generally outstrip the means of subsistence.

of plants and animals have greatly increased productivity per hectare. So why worry? Can't this go on forever?

30 Marx's collaborator Friedrich Engels (1820–1895) said it could:

> the productivity of the land can be infinitely increased by the application of capital, labour and science.

This sentiment, expressed in 1844, has been in the mainstream of Communist doctrine down to the present time; it has also been taken up by many non-Communists, e.g., promoters and developers of large commercial enterprises, the more extreme of the technological optimists and even a few of the older economists, now fortunately being displaced. Scientists almost without exception disagree: they live in a world governed by conservation principles, which have been called "impotence principles" by the physicist Edmund Whittaker (1873–1956). In the scientists' view, nothing is created. Matter is changed from one form to another, and every change is paid for by the loss of useful energy ("negative entropy"). To "create" one thing is to have less of something else; and there is always a loss of useful energy. And, as we have become particularly aware in recent years, the creation of useful things is always accompanied by the creation of noxious by-products—"pollution" we call them—which take still more energy to process into less noxious substances.

31 Living is an expensive game, and the greater the density of population the more expensive it becomes. If we want reasonably pure air and pure water the carrying capacity of the earth is much less than it is if we do not care what we breathe and drink. More generally, for the human population, once it numbers in the hundreds of millions, what we call the carrying capacity is inversely related to the material standard of living we choose. He who says "The earth can support still more people" is always right: for, until we reach absolute rock bottom, we can always lower the standard of living another notch and support a larger population. The question is, which do we want: the maximum number of people at the minimum standard of living—or a smaller number at a comfortable, or even gracious, standard of living? We are our own caretakers: the choice is ours.

32 We can choose not to choose, of course. Choosing and implementing the choice may be politically so difficult that we cannot, or will not, control our own future. In that case, humanity's population history will be not too different from that of uncontrolled animal populations: sooner or later there will be a dreadful population crash. If the human population of the world does suffer a general crash the result will be more dreadful than anything ever known for any other animal population. How so?

33 Harrison Brown, I believe, was the first person to appreciate the uniquely vulnerable situation of the most "advanced" of contemporary human societies. In a book published a generation ago this geophysicist

called attention to the significance of the progress of technology for the possibility of repeating this progress after a crash. The single substance copper can illustrate a large class of problems. Long before the invention of writing, men learned how to smelt copper and make tools and weapons from copper and bronze. Suppose our present civilization fell apart, as it might following an all-out nuclear war or a gigantic population crash: could we pick ourselves up and rebuild technological civilization as we know it? We probably could not.

34 Looking only at the copper component of the problem, we should note that preliterate man managed to create the Bronze Age only because of the ready availability of copper ores assaying greater than 20 percent; there was even some native copper from which to make the first copper tools around 8000 B.C. Only the most primitive of means are required to process high-grade ores. But now we are reduced to extracting our copper from ores that assay less than 1 percent, and soon we will have nothing better than 0.1 percent. It takes a very sophisticated technology to deal with low-grade ores, a technology that only a large population of technologically advanced people can muster. So it is for many other materials—special steels, solid-state electronic devices, and highly purified chemicals. Our many technologies form an incredible network of mutual support, mutual dependence. If this network were disrupted by thermonuclear war, which, at the same time, reduced the population to a small fraction of its former size, and then that fraction had to scratch out a living under conditions of severe poverty, it is doubtful if our kind of technology would ever be rebuilt. To do so would require great capital expenditures over several decades. Capital is income deferred. A poor people is understandably reluctant to defer much income. If several decades are required before there is a substantial payoff, the problem of rebuilding technology following the crash becomes a problem of making sacrifices for posterity. That is always a hard thing to do; the poor find it almost impossibly hard.

35 Moreover, what would be the emotional "set" of humanity following "the bomb" or the crash? Is it not conceivable that the survivors might just decide that what we call "civilization" is not worth rebuilding? And who would then say that they were wrong?

36 *No civilization has ever recovered after ruining its environment.* The civilizations of Egypt, of the Tigris-Euphrates valley, of the Indus River, and of Rome were replaced by other civilizations from the outside. If we ruin the whole world, where is the "outside" to renew our civilization? On all counts, it looks as though our civilization, once fallen, will never be replaced by another of comparable quality. If we esteem what we have we must somehow defuse both the nuclear bomb and the population bomb.

37 Population can be controlled only by making hard decisions. There is no fundamental reason why we cannot do it. The question is, who is the *we* that acts? Policy must revolve around this identification.

38 The basic fact of our world is that there are many *wes.* The number shows no signs of diminishing. There are now about three times as many countries in the United Nations as there were when the organization was formed some thirty years ago. Some of them are merely old nations newly admitted, but many are nations newly created by the fission of old ones. No instance of fusion has occurred during this thirty years, but fission continues.

39 Each nation insists on its sovereignty. What does that mean? The sovereignty claimed boils down to this: a nation's spokesmen let us know what they are responsible *for*—but say nothing of what they are responsible *to.* They say they are responsible for the survival and continued multiplication of their people, but they do not acknowledge responsibility to anyone for what that growth does to the rest of the world and to the future. That is true of poor nations and rich nations alike. Talk about "Spaceship Earth" is peppered with loud claims of "rights" coupled with equally vehement disclaimers of Frankelian responsibility.°

40 The fact of national sovereignty, as it exists at present, had better be accepted. But when a nation denies that it has any responsibility to make its population match the carrying capacity of its own land, it would be foolish for other nations to accept responsibility for keeping alive millions of people the procreation of whom they had nothing to do with. Yet that is what spokesmen for the "Third World" (the current euphemism for "poor countries") asserted at the United Nations conference on population in Bucharest in 1974. In effect, what Third World spokesmen said was this: "We in the poor countries have the right to produce as many children as we want to: you in the rich have the responsibility of keeping them alive." Out of that conference, and one on food in Rome later in the same year, came the proposal for setting up a World Food Bank. The operational rules of the proposed "bank" are a blueprint for disaster.

41 In the first place the word *bank* is a misnomer. Two generations ago there were a score of countries that were significant grain exporters by virtue of the fact that they produced an excess. Now there are only five: Argentina, Australia, Canada, France, and the United States. Although food production is increasing nearly everywhere, there is almost no increase in per capita food production except in those five countries, so we must assume that the future will be as bleak as the recent past. That means that the depositors of the bank would always be one group of countries, and the withdrawers another. This arrangement hardly corresponds to the workings of a bank: it is more like a siphon.

42 The proposal, then, amounts to this: that we build world policy

---

[39] **Frankelian responsibility:** the obligation, advocated by American social philosopher Charles Frankel, to weigh the consequences of one's actions for the total affected system

on the ideal Karl Marx stated in 1875, "From each according to his ability, to each according to his needs." But this famous phrase merely defines the system of the commons: people take from a common store whatever they think they need. The end result, if such a policy is continued indefinitely, will be a tragedy. Figure 2 diagrams the scenario: we have only to change "external food bank" to "world food bank." The nature of the ultimate population crash is a suitable subject for nightmares.

43 Predation and disease are the commonest controllers of population in other species. Human beings have no predators now, and disease has almost been conquered. Death is the commonest controlling event for other species; for death, we human beings can substitute non-birth. The technology of contraception, while less perfect than we would like, is quite adequate to the task. Our problem is to use this technology intensively and extensively enough to do the job.

44 If the tragedy of the commons is to be prevented each unit that claims sovereignty—each nation—must accept Frankelian responsibility and adjust its population to match the carrying capacity of its land. That does not mean that any nation need be self-sufficient with respect to all its material needs. No industrialized nation has within its own borders everything it needs—copper, chrome, bauxite, oil, vanadium, etc. But a properly run country will produce surpluses of some things, which it can then trade for what it lacks. Every country can be self-reliant (even though few or none can be totally self-sufficient). When a country has become self-reliant it can be said to be living within the carrying capacity of its land. Thus we see that the concept of carrying capacity in the human realm is significantly different than in the animal.

45 Since population and the standard of living are inversely related to each other, when population increases the material standard of living must fall, if a country is to continue to be self-reliant. Conversely, if a people want to "live higher on the hog" and still be self-reliant, they must find a way to reduce their population. There is no simple connection between the natural wealth of a nation and its per capita income. Some of the poorest nations of the world live in lands of great natural wealth—India, for instance. There are just too many people there; if India had only 75 million people (instead of her 600 million) her population density would be the same as that of the United States and life could be very comfortable.

46 The sight of starving millions in poor countries may move compassionate people to send food for the emergency. But *emergency* is usually a misnomer: it is not a temporary crisis but a permanent crunch (which fluctuates in intensity, of course). The intended effect of sending food is to save lives; the more successfully this goal is met the greater the danger of an unintended side effect—the weakening of the springs of action that might otherwise lead a harassed people to bring population and carrying capacity into balance.

47 For a well-fed citizen of a wealthy nation to point out that a poor country will be better off in the long run without inputs of food from the outside inevitably leads to the charge that the advice is "self-serving." So it may be. But we must go behind that charge and ask: Does withholding food serve the needs of the needy as well *in the long run?*

48 When I was in India in 1970 I was gratified to learn that many educated Indians understand their situation very well. I was fortunate enough to have an hour's conference with a member of the Indian planning commission. He recounted his reaction to the events of 1965–66, when, for two years running, the United States sent ten million tons of grain to make up for a shortfall in Indian agriculture. It has been estimated that this saved the lives of 50 million Indians. With the second year's shipment President Johnson privately told the Indian leaders that they could expect no more. We could help in crises but not in crunches: the Indians had better learn to take care of themselves. My informant told me that he and others in government had been indignant at the time; but faced with necessity they exerted themselves to improve Indian agriculture, and did. The hard line taken by the United States may have been self-serving but it also served the needs of India, the greatest of which is the need to be self-reliant.

49 We will do little good in the international sphere until we recognize that the greatest need of a poor country is not material: call it psychological, moral, spiritual, or what you will. The basic issue is starkly raised in a story of personal heroism that unfolded in South America a few years ago. A plane carrying a Uruguayan rugby team crashed in the remote Andes, leaving most of the passengers alive. After they got a radio receiver working they listened day after day to news of the Chilean air force flying in search of them. Finally came the day when the small group of listeners outside the shattered plane heard that the search had been called off because the Chileans figured they could not possibly be alive. Most of the Uruguayans were inside the hull of the plane and had not heard the news. "What shall we tell the others?" one of the listeners asked.

50 "We mustn't tell them," said Marcelo. "At least let them go on hoping."

51 "No," said Nicolich. "We must tell them. They must know the worst."

52 "I can't, I can't," said Marcelo, still sobbing into his hands.

53 "I'll tell them," said Nicolich, and he turned back toward the entrance to the plane.

54 He climbed through the hole in the wall of suitcases and rugby shirts, crouched at the mouth of the dim tunnel, and looked at the mournful faces which were turned toward him.

55 "Hey, boys," he shouted. "There's some good news! We just heard it on the radio. They've called off the search."

56 Inside the crowded cabin there was silence. As the hopelessness of their predicament enveloped them, they wept.

57 "Why the hell is that good news?" Páez shouted angrily at Nicolich.

58 "Because it means," he said, "that we're going to get out of here on our own."

59 And they did get out. Not all of them. Many died. But if they had not heard the bad news, if they had stayed there waiting, waiting—*all* would have died.

60 This true story, I submit, bears a close resemblance to the moral situation of poor countries. The greatest gift we can give them is the knowledge that they are on their own.

61 For corroborative evidence, consider the contrasting cases of China and India. Fifty years ago these countries were equally overpopulated, equally miserable, and their futures looked equally bleak. During this period, particularly during the past twenty-five years, we have given massive aid to India. (So have other rich nations.) Because of a political falling-out we have given nothing to Maoist China (neither have any other nations, except the USSR, briefly). Today China is immensely better off, both physically and psychologically. She has not solved her population problem, but she is much closer than India to doing so. Millions of people died during China's time of troubles; but she had the great advantage of receiving no help from us. She was on her own, and she knew it. India, by contrast, was handicapped by our "help."

62 *Help*—what a dangerous word that is! It is not the name for an act; it is the name for an interpretation of an act. When the people in power in the United States sent soldiers and arms into Vietnam in the early 1960s, they genuinely thought they were helping the Vietnamese. When we of the industrial world built a dam on the Zambezi River in Africa and created Lake Kariba we called it "help," though it displaced 57,000 people from their ancestral farms and increased the extent of infection by schistosome worms.° When we sent pesticides—a loaded word, like "help"—to the cotton farmers of the Cañete Valley in Peru we called it "help," though the resultant destruction of the predators of the insect pests created a boomerang effect that nearly wiped out cotton growing in the valley. And whenever amiable people fly hay into over-populated deer country they too say they are "helping."

63 The word we are looking for is *intervention;* this is a neutral, descriptive word that leaves open the question of interpreting it. Feeding deer on winter-feeding grounds is intervention in the lives of the deer; it may help them, it may harm them. Killing predators is intervention. Building a dam is intervention; so also is sending people supplies of DDT, medicines, food, bombers, napalm, military advisers, agricultural experts, miracle grains, and Hollywood movies. There is no law of nature that says that every well-intentioned act of intervention deserves the name of "help." In fact, experience indicates that the contrary is closer to the

---

62 **schistosome worms:** elongated worms that cause a grave parasitic disease, schistosomiasis

truth. The effects of intervention must never be assumed: they remain to be proved.

64 We are lucky (and so are the recipients of our attentions) when our interventions are no worse than harmless. When our government buys the grain of American farmers and ships it to a starving and over-populated country it certainly helps our farmers, our railroads, our grain elevator operators, and our shipowners to grow rich. It even helps a few bureaucrats to keep their jobs. But does it help the people of the nation in which we intervene? Does it help them not only today, but tomorrow and the day after? That remains to be proved.

65 Of course, leaving a country to its own devices does not insure that it will solve its problems. When political changes are called for—and to some extent they invariably are—it is hard to know what measures or events will facilitate the needed changes. But we should know by now that people on the outside are unlikely to be able to bring about a needed political change. About the only thing outside meddling can do is interfere with internal progress.

66 In every country, rich or poor, there is a great variety of opinion and talent. It is a mistake to say, as many do, that "poor countries demand this" or "poor countries demand that." A country is not an organism: it has no voice. People have voices: different people, different voices. The shrill and demanding voices heard in Budapest and Rome were only some of the voices of the Third World: they were the voices of self-selected spokesmen. If we meet their demands and set up a commons in food from which their countries can draw at will we will weaken the urge toward self-reliance; we will reward misguided prophets. But if we ignore these prophets they will lose in political power and other voices will be heard in their countries. Some of them may have answers that will do some good. A course of apparent non-action on our part may be the best way to encourage constructive action inside needy countries.

67 Population control—home-grown population control—is the greatest need. We may be able to help by offering rewards to countries that make progress in population control. If we adopt this policy we must be very clear in our own minds about this important matter: we must concern ourselves only with the end to be achieved and not with the means of achieving it. Means must match culture. Different cultures, different means. Among the means available for controlling family size and population are the following: sterilization, abortion, infanticide, civil penalties for over-large families, and delayed marriage associated with continence outside of marriage. Though it may not be obvious, polygamy also can reduce population growth. If one man has many wives (polygamy) it follows that many men have no wives. The wifeless men may patronize prostitutes, who are notoriously (and fortunately) relatively infertile, while wives gathered together in harems will not—despite all dreams of *machismo*—be as well serviced (to use the language

of animal husbandry) as they would be in a monogamous society.

68 Few among us would approve all these ways of reducing the rate of population growth, yet every practice listed is followed some place in the world today. We could hardly be expected to recommend to others a practice we are unwilling to follow ourselves; but must we go out of our way to disapprove of an effective means of population control used with approval by another culture? Unfortunately many among us do just that. There seems to be a growing sentiment toward promoting the idea of universal human rights. In practice, any nation that adopts this position defines its own version of human rights as the universal one. Universal human rights is an absolutist concept; basing international policy on this concept leads to ethical imperialism.

69 We will fail in our intention if, in encouraging another nation to assume responsibility for the control of its own population, we are so arrogant as to dictate the means. Different means fit different cultures. Furthermore, we may even be mistaken in the means we adopt in our own society, a truth we will discover sooner if we encourage varied practices throughout the world and then observe the varied successes to see what we can learn of benefit to ourselves. Tolerance of differences is a virtue that recommends itself to altruists, but it has merit for egoists as well: those who admit that they may not have all the best answers can improve their ethics through vicarious experience.

STUDY QUESTIONS

1. Why, after beginning by discussing American foreign aid, does Hardin launch into a lengthy discussion of animal populations in paragraphs 9–27? Could you defend that segment of his essay as something other than a digression, or diversion from the point?
2. What is the meaning of *carrying capacity* as Hardin uses the phrase? Why does he consider it a vital concept, and how do its implications challenge traditional American ways of thought?
3. What is Hardin's answer to the absolute commandment "Thou shalt not kill"? On what grounds would you agree or disagree with that answer?
4. In the total strategy of Hardin's essay, what do you consider to be the importance of paragraph 28?
5. We sometimes hear the claim made that the United States could reconstruct its social and industrial system after a nuclear war. What is Hardin's view of such a claim? Do you find him persuasive? (See paragraphs 33–36.)
6. Think of one or two standard arguments against population control. How do you suppose Hardin would reply to them? What values lie behind his position?

7. In paragraph 40 Hardin claims that "it would be foolish for other nations to accept responsibility for keeping alive millions of people the procreation of whom they had nothing to do with." In what way would that action be "foolish"? Do you agree? Be prepared to defend your position.
8. Why does Hardin recount the story of the Andes survivors (paragraphs 49–50)? Is this an effective means of making his point?
9. How do you think Hardin would reply to the following three charges?

   (a) Your argument treats human populations as if they were no different from animal populations.
   (b) Your argument is an elaborate means of concluding that the rich nations, such as your own, are justified in keeping all the wealth to themselves.
   (c) You recognize no universal norms of right conduct—not even the principle that killing babies is wrong.

   Are you satisfied with the answers you have provided in Hardin's behalf? Why, or why not?

ARGUING BY IMPLICATION

James Herndon

Since the 1950s James Herndon has been associated with the San Francisco literary community. During much of this period he has also taught junior high school at the school in Daly City that he whimsically renames "Tierra Firma." His unconventional responses to that experience have gone into two acclaimed books, *The Way It Spozed to Be* and *How to Survive in Your Native Land* (1971), in which "The Dumb Class" forms a chapter.

THE DUMB CLASS

1 One afternoon during our free seventh period someone looked around and said This faculty is the Dumb Class.

2 It was so. Given the community or the entire country as a school —reversing the usual image of the school as mirror of society to make society the mirror of the school—and given that community as one which is tracked or ability-grouped into high, high-average, average, low-average, high-low, low and low-low, the faculty or faculties, teachers, *educators,* are the dumb class.

3 We are the dumb class because we cannot learn. Cannot achieve. Why not? Cannot concentrate, have a low attention span, are culturally deprived, brain-damaged, nonverbal, unmotivated, lack skills, are anxiety-ridden, have broken homes, can't risk failure, no study habits, won't try, are lazy . . . ? Those are the reasons *kids* are in the dumb class, supposing we don't say it's because they are just dumb. But the characteristic of the dumb class is that it cannot learn how to do what it is there to do. Try as one may, one cannot make the dumb class learn to do these things, at least not as long as it is operating together as a dumb class. Even if those things are completely obvious, the dumb class cannot learn them or achieve them.

4 Is it so that what the dumb class is supposed to achieve is so difficult that only superior individuals can achieve it, and then only with hard work, endless practice? Is it so mysterious and opaque that only those with intelligence and energy enough to research and ferret out the mysteries of the universe can gain insight into it? Eighth period I was involved with this dumb class which was supposed to achieve adding and subtracting before it got out of the eighth grade and went to high school. Could the class achieve it? No sir. Given an adding problem to add, most of the dumb class couldn't add it. Those who did add it hadn't any notion of whether or not they'd added it correctly, even if they had. They asked me Is this right? Is this right? This ain't right, is it? What's the answer? If you don't know whether it's right or not, I'd say, then you aren't adding it. Is this right? screamed four kids, rushing me waving papers. Boy, this dumb class can't learn, I'd say to myself. Not a very sophisticated remark, perhaps.

5 For a while I would drop in on the Tierra Firma bowling alley, since Jay and Jack° were always dying to go there. One day I ran into the dumbest kid in the dumb class. Rather, he came up to us as we were playing this baseball slot machine. Jay and Jack were not defeating the machine, to say the least, and as a result had to put in another dime each time they wanted to play again. Well, the dumb kid showed us how to lift the front legs of the machine in just the right way so that the machine would run up a big score without tilting, enough for ten or so free games, all by itself. After it did that, he told us, you could go ahead and really play it for fun. Jay and Jack were pretty impressed; they thought this dumb kid was a genius. Those big kids in your school sure are smart, was how Jack put it.

6 Well, as Jay and Jack happily set out to strike out and pop-up to the infield on the machine for those free games, the dumb kid and I walked around and watched the bowlers and had a smoke and talked. In the end, of course, I asked him what he was doing around there. He was getting ready to go to work, he told me. Fooling around until five, when he started. What did he do? I keep score, he told me. For the leagues. He kept score for two teams at once. He made fifteen bucks for a couple of hours. He thought it was a great job, making fifteen bucks for something he liked to do anyway, perhaps would have done for nothing, just to be able to do it.

7 He was keeping score. Two teams, four people on each, eight bowling scores at once. Adding quickly, not making any mistakes (for no one was going to put up with errors), following the rather complicated process of scoring in the game of bowling. Get a spare, score ten plus whatever you get on the next ball, score a strike, then ten plus whatever you get on the next two balls; imagine the man gets three

---

[5] **Jay and Jack:** Herndon's two sons

strikes in a row and two spares and you are the scorer, plus you are dealing with seven other guys all striking or sparing or neither one . . . The bowling league is not a welfare organization nor part of Headstart or anything like that and wasn't interested in giving some dumb kid a chance to improve himself by fucking up their bowling scores. No, they were giving this smart kid who had proved to be fast and accurate fifteen dollars because they could use a good scorer.

8 I figured I had this particular dumb kid now. Back in eighth period I lectured him on how smart he was to be a league scorer in bowling. I pried admissions from the other boys, about how they had paper routes and made change. I made the girls confess that when they went to buy stuff they didn't have any difficulty deciding if those shoes cost $10.95 or whether it meant $109.50 or whether it meant $1.09 or how much change they'd get back from a twenty. Naturally I then handed out bowling-score problems and paper-route change-making problems and buying-shoes problems, and naturally everyone could choose which ones they wanted to solve, and naturally the result was that all the dumb kids immediately rushed me yelling Is this right? I don't know how to do it! What's the answer? This ain't right, is it? and What's my grade? The girls who bought shoes for $10.95 with a $20 bill came up with $400.15 for change and wanted to know if that was right? The brilliant league scorer couldn't decide whether two strikes and a third frame of eight amounted to eighteen or twenty-eight or whether it was one hundred eight and one half.

9 The reason they can't learn is because they are the dumb class. No other reason. Is adding difficult? No. It is the dumb class which is difficult. Are the teachers a dumb class? Well, we are supposed to teach kids to "read, write, cipher and sing," according to an old phrase. Can we do it? Mostly not. Is it difficult? Not at all. We can't do it because we are a dumb class, which by definition can't do it, whatever it is.

10 Yet what we are supposed to do is something which, like adding, everyone knows how to do. It isn't mysterious, nor dependent on a vast and intricate knowledge of pedagogy or technology or psychological tests or rats. Is there any man or woman on earth who knows how to read who doesn't feel quite capable of teaching his own child or children to read? Doesn't every father feel confident that his boy will come into the bathroom every morning to stand around and watch while the father shaves and play number games with the father and learn about numbers and shaving at the same time? Every person not in the dumb class feels that these things are simple. Want to know about Egypt? Mother or father or older brother or uncle or someone and the kid go down to the public library and get out a book on Egypt and the kid reads it and perhaps the uncle reads it too, and while they are shaving they may talk about Egypt. But the dumb class of teachers and public educators feel that these things are very difficult, and they must keep hiring experts and devising strategies in order that they can rush these experts

and strategies with their papers asking Is this right? and What's my grade?

11 Yet, released from the dumb class to their private lives, teachers are marvelous gardeners, they work on ocean liners as engineers, they act in plays, win bets, go to art movies, build their own houses, they are opera fans, expert fishermen, champion skeet shooters, grand golfers, organ players, oratorio singers, hunters, mechanics . . . all just as if they were smart people. Of course it is more difficult to build a house or sing Bach than it is to teach kids to read. Of course if they operated in their lives outside of the dumb class the same way they do in it, their houses would fall down, their ships would sink, their flowers die, their cars blow up.

12 This very morning in the San Francisco *Chronicle* I read a scandalous report. The reporter reports the revelations of a member of the board of education, namely that 45 per cent of the *Spanish-surname children* (that is how we put it in the paper these days) who are in mentally retarded classes have been found, when retested in Spanish, to be of average or above-average intelligence. The board member thought that "the Spanish-speaking kids were shunted into classes for the mentally retarded because they did not understand English well enough to pass the examinations they were given." He figured that, just like if he was told that a bowler had a spare on the first frame and got eight on his next ball, he'd figure that the bowler's score in the first frame ought to be eighteen. Well, in this matter assume that the board member is the teacher in a dumb class. He's trying to tell the school administrators something obvious. Does the administrator learn, now he's been told it, that ten and eight are eighteen? No, the assistant superintendent for special services says that "the assumption was that they understood English well enough to be tested by the English versions of the Stanford-Binet and the WISC intelligence tests." He thought that "it wasn't so much the fault of the test as it was the cultural deprivation of the child at the time of testing" which caused these smart kids to be retarded. Asked if these smart retarded Spanish-surname kids were now going to be moved into the regular program, he *revealed* that no, that wasn't the case, for they were *"still working* with the elementary division to seek a proper *transitional* program, since these children were still *functional retardates"* no matter what their IQ.

13 The reporter, acting in his role as critical parent, found out that the tests *were* available in Spanish but that Spanish-speaking kids *weren't* tested, therefore, in Spanish (because of the above assumption). The tests *weren't* available in "Oriental," and the "Oriental" kids *weren't* tested, therefore, in "Oriental." Well, that made sense, so the reporter pried out the information that the school district got $550 extra a year for each kid in mentally retarded classes. The reporter implied cynically that they were doing it for the money and that if they let all these bright

retarded Spanish kids out there might be a shortage of $550 kids to be retarded.

14 But it is the dumb class we are concerned with. Here this administrator is told something obvious, told to learn it, told to achieve this difficult knowledge that them Spanish-speaking kids are only dumb if they are tested in a language they don't understand. But being in the dumb class, he don't learn it. He may be the smartest man in the world, able to keep score for league bowling, read The Book of the Dead,° go water skiing, make bell curves. But in the dumb class he can't learn anything, and there is no reason to expect that he ever will as long as he is in there.

STUDY QUESTIONS

1. In the headnote we have characterized Herndon as "unconventional." What do you find unconventional about him? Be prepared to cite examples.
2. Why does Herndon do without quotation marks in representing conversation? Apart from momentarily confusing you, what effect does he get from this device?
3. Herndon occasionally violates standard English usage, or what many people call "good grammar." Find several instances, and ask yourself whether they show a faulty command of usage on Herndon's part. If your answer is *no,* why do you think he has deliberately risked the disapproval of purists?
4. Herndon is highly sensitive to "educationese," or the language of the educational bureaucracy. Try to find several instances of that language, and be ready to discuss its usefulness for Herndon's purpose.
5. "Is adding difficult?" asks Herndon. "No, it is the dumb class which is difficult" (paragraph 9). What does he mean?
6. What is the thesis of Herndon's implied argument? What practical measures might be considered by a school administrator who agreed with Herndon's point?

14 **The Book of the Dead:** a collection of ancient Egyptian texts, customarily placed inside tombs to help the deceased combat the dangers of the underworld

Pauline Kael

Pauline Kael, who has written regularly for *The New Yorker,* is one of the most uncompromising of American film critics. The present review-essay comes from one of her several collections of pieces, *Deeper Into Movies* (1973).

HIGH SCHOOL AND OTHER FORMS OF MADNESS

1 Movies sometimes connect with our memories in surprising ways. My vocabulary loosened up during my freshman year at Berkeley, and I was quite pleased when my mother remarked that the more educated I got the more I sounded like a truck driver. When I was a sophomore, a group of us went on a trip to Los Angeles, and our car broke down in Oxnard; we were huddled there in the garage at night when two garage mechanics got into an argument and started swearing at each other. As the rhythm of their fury and venom built up, those words that I had been so free with sounded hideous. I hadn't understood their function as swear-words—hadn't understood that they were meant to insult the person receiving them, that they were a way of degrading another person. That night at Oxnard came back when I saw Frederick Wiseman's *Law and Order*° on N.E.T.: the police were cursed constantly by thieves and drunks. I had assumed that the police, coming from stricter and more religious backgrounds, didn't understand that college kids use the words in that liberated way that empties them of degradation or any real power; I hadn't considered that they hear that kind of talk so much they probably just can't stand it anymore. They're drowning in obscenity. College students are sometimes contemptuous of the cops for fearing *words,* but in the film those words really *are* weapons—often the *only* weapons of angry, frustrated people—and they're directed against the police all the time. *Law and Order* was the most powerful hour and a half of television that I've seen all year, and, since it won an Emmy, one might suppose that it would stir up interest in Wiseman's other films, but the New York Film Festival, which featured so many mindless forms of "artistic" moviemaking in the main auditorium, tossed some of the best new American pictures into the two-hundred-seat hall, and among them was Wiseman's *High School,* in its first New York showing.

---

[1] **Frederick Wiseman's Law and Order:** See paragraphs 2 and 3 for Wiseman's career, which also includes films about slaughterhouses, primate research, boot camp, and a monastery.

2 There's a good deal to be said for finding your way to moviemaking—as most of the early directors did—after living for some years in the world and gaining some knowledge of life outside show business. We are beginning to spawn teen-age filmmakers who at twenty-five may have a brilliant technique but are as empty-headed as a Hollywood hack, and they will become the next generation of hacks, because they don't know anything except moviemaking. Wiseman is a law professor and urban planner turned filmmaker, a muckraking investigative journalist who looks into American institutions with a camera and a tape recorder, and because he doesn't go in with naïve and limiting concepts, what he finds ties in with one's own experience.

3 Many of us grow to hate documentaries in school, because the use of movies to teach us something seems a cheat—a pill disguised as candy—and documentaries always seem to be about something we're not interested in. But Wiseman's documentaries show what is left out of both fictional movies and standard documentaries that simplify for a purpose, and his films deal with the primary institutions of our lives: *Titicut Follies* (Bridgewater, an institution in which we lock away the criminally insane), *High School* (a high school in a large Eastern city), and *Law and Order* (the Kansas City police force). Television has been accustoming us to a horrible false kind of "involvement"; sometimes it seems that the only thing the news shows can think of is to get close to emotion. They shove a camera and a microphone in front of people in moments of stress and disaster and grief, and ram their equipment into any pores and cavities they can reach. Wiseman made comparable mistakes in *Titicut Follies,* but he learned better fast.

4 *High School* is so familiar and so extraordinarily evocative that a feeling of empathy with the students floods over us. How did we live through it? How did we keep any spirit? When you see a kid trying to make a phone call and being interrupted with "Do you have a pass to use the phone?" it all floods back—the low ceilings and pale-green walls of the basement where the lockers were, the constant defensiveness, that sense of always being in danger of breaking some pointless, petty rule. When since that time has one ever needed a pass to make a phone call? This movie takes one back to where, one discovers, time has stood still. Here is the girl humiliated for having worn a short dress to the Senior Prom, being told it was "offensive" to the whole class. Here it is all over again—the insistence that you be "respectful," and the teachers' incredible instinct for "disrespect," their antennae always extended for that little bit of reservation or irony in your tone, the tiny spark that you desperately need to preserve your *self-*respect. One can barely hear it in the way a boy says "Yes, sir" to the dean, but the dean, ever on the alert, snaps, "Don't give me that 'Yes, sir' business! . . . There's no sincereness behind it." Here, all over again, is the dullness of high-school education:

TEACHER: What on the horizon or what existed that forced labor to turn to collective bargaining? What was there a lack of?
GIRL: Communications?
TEACHER: Security, yes, communications, lack of security, concern for the job. The important thing is this, let's get to the beginning. First of all, there was the lack of security; second of all, there was a lack of communication. . . .

5 The same old pseudo-knowledge is used to support what the schools think is moral. The visiting gynecologist in a sex-education class lectures the boys:

> The more a fellow gets into bed with more different girls, the more insecure he is, and this shows up actually later in all the divorce statistics in America. . . . You can graph right on a graph, the more girls fellows got into bed with or vice-versa the higher the divorce rate, the greater the sexual inadequacy. . . .

6 And there's the beautiful military doubletalk when it's a question of a teacher's incompetence or unfairness. A boy protests a disciplinary action against him by a teacher, and after he has explained his innocence, the dean talks him into accepting the punishment "to establish that you can be a man and that you can take orders." The teachers are masters here; they're in a superior position for the only time in their lives, probably, and most of the petty tyrannies—like laying on the homework—aren't fully conscious. They justify each other's actions as a matter of course, and put the students in the wrong in the same indifferent way. They put a student down with "It's nice to be individualistic, but there are certain places to be individualistic," yet they never tell you where. How can one stand up against such bland authoritarianism? The teachers, crushing and processing, are the most insidious kind of enemy, the enemy with corrupt values who means well. The counsellor advising on college plans who says "You can have all your dream schools, but at the bottom you ought to have some college of last resort where you could be sure that you would go, if none of your dreams came through" certainly means to be realistic and helpful. But one can imagine what it must feel like to be a kid trudging off to that bottom college of last resort. There's a jolly good Joe of a teacher staging a fashion show who tells the girls, "Your legs are all too heavy. . . . Don't wear it too short; it looks miserable." And she's not wrong. But, given the beauty norms set up in this society, what are they to do? Cut off their legs? Emigrate? They're defeated from the legs up. Mediocrity and defeat sit in the offices and classrooms, and in those oppressive monitored halls.

7 We went through it all in order to graduate and be rid of passes forever, and once it was over we put it out of our minds, and here are the students still serving time until graduation, still sitting in class staring out the windows or watching the crawling hands of those ugly

school clocks. So much of this education is part of an obsolete system of authority that broke down long ago, yet the teachers and administrators are still out there, persevering, "building character." *High School* seems an obvious kind of film to make, but as far as I know no one before has gone into an ordinary, middle-class, "good" (most of the students go to college) high school with a camera and looked around to see what it's like. The students are even more apathetic than we were. Probably the conflicts over the restrictions come earlier now—in junior high—and by high school the kids either are trying to cool it and get through to college or are just beaten down and sitting it out. We may have had a few teachers who really got us interested in something—it was one of the disappointments of the movie *Up the Down Staircase* that, treating this theme, it failed to be convincing—and, remembering our good luck, we could always say that even if a school was rotten, there were bound to be a few great teachers in it. This movie shows competent teachers and teachers who are trying their best but not one teacher who really makes contact in the way that means a difference in your life. The students are as apathetic toward the young English teacher playing and analyzing a Simon & Garfunkel record as toward the English teacher reciting "Casey at the Bat," and, even granted that as poetry there might not be much to choose between them—and perhaps Casey has the edge —still, one might think the students would, just as a *courtesy,* respond to the young teacher's attempt, the way one always gave the ingénue° in the stock company a special round of applause. But it's very likely that high schools no longer *are* saved by live teachers, if hostility and cynicism and apathy set in right after children learn their basic skills. The students here sit on their hands even when a teacher tries. That's the only visible difference between this school and mine. I think we would have responded appreciatively to obvious effort, even if we thought the teacher was a jerk; these kids are beyond that. So the teachers are trapped, too. The teachers come off much worse than the police do in *Law and Order. High School* is a revelation because now that we see school from the outside, the teachers seem to give themselves away every time they open their mouths—and to be unaware of it.

8 At the end, the principal—a fine-looking woman—holds up a letter from a former student, on stationery marked "U.S.S. Okinawa," and reads it to the faculty:

> I have only a few hours before I go. Today I will take a plane trip from this ship. I pray that I'll make it back but it's all in God's hands now. You see, I am going with three other men. We are going to be dropped behind the D.M.Z. (the Demilitarized Zone). The reason for telling you this is that all my insurance money will be given for that scholarship I once

---

[7] **ingénue:** the innocent young female lead

> started but never finished, if I don't make it back. I am only insured for $10,000. Maybe it could help someone. I have been trying to become a Big Brother in Vietnam, but it is very hard to do. I have to write back and forth to San Diego, California, and that takes time. I only hope that I am good enough to become one. God only knows. My personal family usually doesn't understand me. . . . They say: "Don't you value life? Are you crazy?" My answer is: "Yes. But I value all the lives of South Vietnam and the free world so that they and all of us can live in peace." Am I wrong? If I do my best and believe in what I do, believe that what I do is right—that is all I can do. . . . Please don't say anything to Mrs. C. She would only worry over me. I am not worth it. I am only a body doing a job. In closing I thank everyone for what they all have done for me.

And the principal comments, "Now, when you get a letter like this, to me it means that we are very successful at [this] high school. I think you will agree with me."

9 It's a great scene—a consummation of the educational process we've been watching: They are successful at turning out bodies to do a job. Yet it's also painfully clear that the school must have given this soldier more kindness and affection than he'd ever had before. There must be other students who respond to the genuine benevolence behind the cant and who are grateful to those who labor to turn them into men. For those students, this schooling in conformity is successful.

10 Wiseman extends our understanding of our common life the way novelists used to—a way largely abandoned by the modern novel and left to the journalists but not often picked up by them. What he's doing is so simple and so basic that it's like a rediscovery of what we knew, or should know. We often want more information about the people and their predicaments than he gives, but this is perhaps less a criticism of Wiseman's method than it is a testimonial to his success in making us care about his subjects. With fictional movies using so little of our shared experience, and with the big TV news "specials" increasingly using that idiot "McLuhanite"[10] fragmentation technique that scrambles all experience—as if the deliberate purpose were to make us indifferent to the life around us—it's a good sign when a movie sends us out wanting to know more and feeling that there is more to know. Wiseman is probably the most sophisticated intelligence to enter the documentary field in recent years.

---

[10] **"McLuhanite":** referring to the theories of the Canadian social critic Marshall McLuhan, who has written several books about the way electronic media affect our perception of reality

STUDY QUESTIONS

1. Do you regard Kael's opening paragraph as a unified one? In what ways does it become relevant to the eventual emphasis of her essay-review?
2. What is Kael's unstated objection to television programs that attempt nothing more than to "get close to emotion" (paragraph 3)? What, in her view, distinguishes Wiseman's work from such programs?
3. Is Kael's main concern with the film *High School* or with certain experiences that most Americans have undergone? Be prepared to support your answer by citing parts of Kael's text.
4. What conception of public high school lies behind Kael's remark that students today are still "serving time until graduation"? How does that statement relate to other parts of Kael's essay-review? Judging from your own experience, do you find the statement warranted?
5. Why does Kael save the incident of the letter from Vietnam (paragraphs 8–9) until she has completed her discussion of high-school routine? In other words, how does this item serve as a climax? What is Kael's response to that letter? Do you agree with her?
6. What is the tone or manner of this selection, and how is it conveyed? What impression do you have of the author's personality?
7. How would you sum up Kael's total attitude toward the typical American high school? If Kael could be the superintendent of a school district, what values would she want its high schools to foster?
8. In this example of "Arguing by Implication," what is the thesis of the implied argument? Could you make a case for classifying this piece under a different heading?

Jessica Mitford

Jessica Mitford, born in England but for many years a resident of California, specializes in exposing scandals—the more outrageous the better. The essay below is drawn from her best seller of 1963, *The American Way of Death,* a book which prompted many states to tighten their regulation of the "funeral industry."

AN UPSET VICTORY OVER DEATH*

1 The drama begins to unfold with the arrival of the corpse at the mortuary.

2 Alas, poor Yorick! How surprised he would be to see how his counterpart of today is whisked off to a funeral parlor and is in short order sprayed, sliced, pierced, pickled, trussed, trimmed, creamed, waxed, painted, rouged and neatly dressed—transformed from a common corpse into a Beautiful Memory Picture. This process is known in the trade as embalming and restorative art, and is so universally employed in the United States and Canada that the funeral director does it routinely, without consulting corpse or kin. He regards as eccentric those few who are hardy enough to suggest that it might be dispensed with. Yet no law requires embalming, no religious doctrine commends it, nor is it dictated by considerations of health, sanitation, or even of personal daintiness. In no part of the world but in Northern America is it widely used. The purpose of embalming is to make the corpse presentable for viewing in a suitably costly container; and here too the funeral director routinely, without first consulting the family, prepares the body for public display.

3 Is all this legal? The processes to which a dead body may be subjected are after all to some extent circumscribed by law. In most states, for instance, the signature of next of kin must be obtained before an autopsy may be performed, before the deceased may be cremated, before the body may be turned over to a medical school for research purposes; or such provision must be made in the decedent's will. In the case of embalming, no such permission is required nor is it ever sought. A textbook, *The Principles and Practices of Embalming,* comments on this: "There is some question regarding the legality of much that is done within the preparation room." The author points out that it would be most unusual for a responsible member of a bereaved family to instruct the mortician, in so many words, to *"embalm"* the body of a deceased

*Title chosen by editor

relative. The very term "embalming" is so seldom used that the mortician must rely upon custom in the matter. The author concludes that unless the family specifies otherwise, the act of entrusting the body to the care of a funeral establishment carries with it an implied permission to go ahead and embalm.

4 Embalming is indeed a most extraordinary procedure, and one must wonder at the docility of Americans who each year pay hundreds of millions of dollars for its perpetuation, blissfully ignorant of what it is all about, what is done, how it is done. Not one in ten thousand has any idea of what actually takes place. Books on the subject are extremely hard to come by. They are not to be found in most libraries or bookshops.

5 In an era when huge television audiences watch surgical operations in the comfort of their living rooms, when, thanks to the animated cartoon, the geography of the digestive system has become familiar territory even to the nursery school set, in a land where the satisfaction of curiosity about almost all matters is a national pastime, the secrecy surrounding embalming can, surely, hardly be attributed to the inherent gruesomeness of the subject. Custom in this regard has within this century suffered a complete reversal. In the early days of American embalming, when it was performed in the home of the deceased, it was almost mandatory for some relative to stay by the embalmer's side and witness the procedure. Today, family members who might wish to be in attendance would certainly be dissuaded by the funeral director. All others, except apprentices, are excluded by law from the preparation room.

6 A close look at what does actually take place may explain in large measure the undertaker's intractable reticence concerning a procedure that has become his major *raison d'être.* Is it possible he fears that public information about embalming might lead patrons to wonder if they really want this service? If the funeral men are loath to discuss the subject outside the trade, the reader may, understandably, be equally loath to go on reading at this point. For those who have the stomach for it, let us part the formaldehyde curtain. . . .

7 The body is first laid out in the undertaker's morgue—or rather, Mr. Jones is reposing in the preparation room—to be readied to bid the world farewell.

8 The preparation room in any of the better funeral establishments has the tiled and sterile look of a surgery, and indeed the embalmer-restorative artist who does his chores there is beginning to adopt the term "dermasurgeon"[8] (appropriately corrupted by some mortician-writers as "demisurgeon") to describe his calling. His equipment, consisting of scalpels, scissors, augers, forceps, clamps, needles, pumps,

---

[8] **"dermasurgeon":** surgeon of skin

tubes, bowls and basins, is crudely imitative of the surgeon's, as is his technique, acquired in a nine- or twelve-month post-high-school course in an embalming school. He is supplied by an advanced chemical industry with a bewildering array of fluids, sprays, pastes, oils, powders, creams, to fix or soften tissue, shrink or distend it as needed, dry it here, restore the moisture there. There are cosmetics, waxes and paints to fill and cover features, even plaster of Paris to replace entire limbs. There are ingenious aids to prop and stabilize the cadaver: a Vari-Pose Head Rest, the Edwards Arm and Hand Positioner, the Repose Block (to support the shoulders during the embalming), and the Throop Foot Positioner, which resembles an old-fashioned stocks.[8]

9 Mr. John H. Eckels, president of the Eckels College of Mortuary Science, thus describes the first part of the embalming procedure: "In the hands of a skilled practitioner, this work may be done in a comparatively short time and without mutilating the body other than by slight incision—so slight that it scarcely would cause serious inconvenience if made upon a living person. It is necessary to remove the blood, and doing this not only helps in the disinfecting, but removes the principal cause of disfigurements due to discoloration."

10 Another textbook discusses the all-important time element: "The earlier this is done, the better, for every hour that elapses between death and embalming will add to the problems and complications encountered. . . ." Just how soon should one get going on the embalming? The author tells us, "On the basis of such scanty information made available to this profession through its rudimentary and haphazard system of technical research, we must conclude that the best results are to be obtained if the subject is embalmed before life is completely extinct—that is, before cellular death has occurred. In the average case, this would mean within an hour after somatic death." For those who feel that there is something a little rudimentary, not to say haphazard, about this advice, a comforting thought is offered by another writer. Speaking of fears entertained in early days of premature burial, he points out, "One of the effects of embalming by chemical injection, however, has been to dispel fears of live burial." How true; once the blood is removed, chances of live burial are indeed remote.

11 To return to Mr. Jones, the blood is drained out through the veins and replaced by embalming fluid pumped in through the arteries. As noted in *The Principles and Practices of Embalming,* "every operator has a favorite injection and drainage point—a fact which becomes a handicap only if he fails or refuses to forsake his favorites when conditions demand it." Typical favorites are the carotid artery, femoral artery,

---

[8]**stocks:** locking boards to hold the hands and feet of criminals as a form of public punishment and humiliation

jugular vein, subclavian vein.° There are various choices of embalming fluid. If Flextone is used, it will produce a "mild, flexible rigidity. The skin retains a velvety softness, the tissues are rubbery and pliable. Ideal for women and children." It may be blended with B. and G. Products Company's Lyf-Lyk tint, which is guaranteed to reproduce "nature's own skin texture . . . the velvety appearance of living tissue." Suntone comes in three separate tints: Suntan; Special Cosmetic Tint, a pink shade "especially indicated for young female subjects"; and Regular Cosmetic Tint, moderately pink.

12 About three to six gallons of a dyed and perfumed solution of formaldehyde, glycerin, borax, phenol, alcohol and water is soon circulating through Mr. Jones, whose mouth has been sewn together with a "needle directed upward between the upper lip and gum and brought out through the left nostril," with the corners raised slightly "for a more pleasant expression." If he should be bucktoothed, his teeth are cleaned with Bon Ami and coated with colorless nail polish. His eyes, meanwhile, are closed with flesh-tinted eye caps and eye cement.

13 The next step is to have at Mr. Jones with a thing called a trocar. This is a long, hollow needle attached to a tube. It is jabbed into the abdomen, poked around the entrails and chest cavity, the contents of which are pumped out and replaced with "cavity fluid." This done, and the hole in the abdomen sewn up, Mr. Jones's face is heavily creamed (to protect the skin from burns which may be caused by leakage of the chemicals), and he is covered with a sheet and left unmolested for a while. But not for long—there is more, much more, in store for him. He has been embalmed, but not yet restored, and the best time to start the restorative work is eight to ten hours after embalming, when the tissues have become firm and dry.

14 The object of all this attention to the corpse, it must be remembered, is to make it presentable for viewing in an attitude of healthy repose. "Our customs require the presentation of our dead in the semblance of normality . . . unmarred by the ravages of illness, disease or mutilation," says Mr. J. Sheridan Mayer in his *Restorative Art.* This is rather a large order since few people die in the full bloom of health, unravaged by illness and unmarked by some disfigurement. The funeral industry is equal to the challenge: "In some cases the gruesome appearance of a mutilated or disease-ridden subject may be quite discouraging. The task of restoration may seem impossible and shake the confidence of the embalmer. This is the time for intestinal fortitude and determination. Once the formative work is begun and affected tissues are cleaned or removed, all doubts of success vanish. It is surprising and gratifying to discover the results which may be obtained."

---

11 **carotid artery, femoral artery, subclavian vein:** large artery (main blood vessel) carrying blood to the head; the main artery of the thigh, supplying blood to the leg; a blood vessel beneath the shoulder

15 The embalmer, having allowed an appropriate interval to elapse, returns to the attack, but now he brings into play the skill and equipment of sculptor and cosmetician. Is a hand missing? Casting one in plaster of Paris is a simple matter. "For replacement purposes, only a cast of the back of the hand is necessary; this is within the ability of the average operator and is quite adequate." If a lip or two, a nose or an ear should be missing, the embalmer has at hand a variety of restorative waxes with which to model replacements. Pores and skin texture are simulated by stippling with a little brush, and over this cosmetics are laid on. Head off? Decapitation cases are rather routinely handled. Ragged edges are trimmed, and head joined to torso with a series of splints, wires and sutures. It is a good idea to have a little something at the neck—a scarf or high collar—when time for viewing comes. Swollen mouth? Cut out tissue as needed from inside the lips. If too much is removed, the surface contour can easily be restored by padding with cotton. Swollen necks and cheeks are reduced by removing tissue through vertical incisions made down each side of the neck. "When the deceased is casketed, the pillow will hide the suture incisions . . . as an extra precaution against leakage, the suture may be painted with liquid sealer."

16 The opposite condition is more likely to present itself—that of emaciation. His hypodermic syringe now loaded with massage cream, the embalmer seeks out and fills the hollowed and sunken areas by injection. In this procedure the backs of the hands and fingers and the under-chin area should not be neglected.

17 Positioning the lips is a problem that recurrently challenges the ingenuity of the embalmer. Closed too tightly, they tend to give a stern, even disapproving expression. Ideally, embalmers feel, the lips should give the impression of being ever so slightly parted, the upper lip protruding slightly for a more youthful appearance. This takes some engineering, however, as the lips tend to drift apart. Lip drift can sometimes be remedied by pushing one or two straight pins through the inner margin of the lower lip and then inserting them between the two front upper teeth. If Mr. Jones happens to have no teeth, the pins can just as easily be anchored in his Armstrong Face Former and Denture Replacer. Another method to maintain lip closure is to dislocate the lower jaw, which is then held in its new position by a wire run through holes which have been drilled through the upper and lower jaws at the midline. As the French are fond of saying, *il faut souffrir pour être belle.* *°

* In 1963 *Mortuary Management* reports a new development: "Natural Expression Formers," an invention of Funeral Directors Research Company. "They may be used to replace one or both artificial dentures, or over natural teeth; have 'bite-indicator' lines as a closure guide . . . Natural Expression Formers also offer more control of facial expression."

[17] **il faut souffrir pour être belle:** one must suffer to be beautiful

18 If Mr. Jones has died of jaundice, the embalming fluid will very likely turn him green. Does this deter the embalmer? Not if he has intestinal fortitude. Masking pastes and cosmetics are heavily laid on, burial garments and casket interiors are color-correlated with particular care, and Jones is displayed beneath rose-colored lights. Friends will say, "How *well* he looks." Death by carbon monoxide, on the other hand, can be rather a good thing from the embalmer's viewpoint: "One advantage is the fact that this type of discoloration is an exaggerated form of a natural pink coloration." This is nice because the healthy glow is already present and needs but little attention.

19 The patching and filling completed, Mr. Jones is now shaved, washed and dressed. Cream-based cosmetic, available in pink, flesh, suntan, brunette and blond, is applied to his hands and face, his hair is shampooed and combed (and, in the case of Mrs. Jones, set), his hands manicured. For the horny-handed son of toil special care must be taken; cream should be applied to remove ingrained grime, and the nails cleaned. "If he were not in the habit of having them manicured in life, trimming and shaping is advised for better appearance—never questioned by kin."

20 Jones is now ready for casketing (this is the present participle of the verb "to casket"). In this operation his right shoulder should be depressed slightly "to turn the body a bit to the right and soften the appearance of lying flat on the back." Positioning the hands is a matter of importance, and special rubber positioning blocks may be used. The hands should be cupped slightly for a more lifelike, relaxed appearance. Proper placement of the body requires a delicate sense of balance. It should lie as high as possible in the casket, yet not so high that the lid, when lowered, will hit the nose. On the other hand, we are cautioned, placing the body too low "creates the impression that the body is in a box."

21 Jones is next wheeled into the appointed slumber room where a few last touches may be added—his favorite pipe placed in his hand or, if he was a great reader, a book propped into position. (In the case of little Master Jones a Teddy bear may be clutched.) Here he will hold open house for a few days, visiting hours 10 A.M. to 9 P.M.

22 All now being in readiness, the funeral director calls a staff conference to make sure that each assistant knows his precise duties. Mr. Wilber Krieger writes: "This makes your staff feel that they are a part of the team, with a definite assignment that must be properly carried out if the whole plan is to succeed. You never heard of a football coach who failed to talk to his entire team before they go on the field. They have drilled on the plays they are to execute for hours and days, and yet the successful coach knows the importance of making even the bench-warming third-string substitute feel that he is important if the game is to be won." The winning of *this* game is predicated upon glass-smooth handling of the logistics. The funeral director has notified

the pallbearers whose names were furnished by the family, has arranged for the presence of clergyman, organist, and soloist, has provided transportation for everybody, has organized and listed the flowers sent by friends. In *Psychology of Funeral Service* Mr. Edward A. Martin points out: "He may not always do as much as the family thinks he is doing, but it is his helpful guidance that they appreciate in knowing they are proceeding as they should. . . . The important thing is how well his services can be used to make the family believe they are giving unlimited expression to their own sentiment."

23 The religious service may be held in a church or in the chapel of the funeral home; the funeral director vastly prefers the latter arrangement, for not only is it more convenient for him but it affords him the opportunity to show off his beautiful facilities to the gathered mourners. After the clergyman has had his say, the mourners queue up to file past the casket for a last look at the deceased. The family is *never* asked whether they want an open-casket ceremony; in the absence of their instruction to the contrary, this is taken for granted. Consequently well over 90 per cent of all American funerals feature the open casket—a custom unknown in other parts of the world. Foreigners are astonished by it. An English woman living in San Francisco described her reaction in a letter to the writer:

> I myself have attended only one funeral here—that of an elderly fellow worker of mine. After the service I could not understand why everyone was walking towards the coffin (sorry, I mean casket), but thought I had better follow the crowd. It shook me rigid to get there and find the casket open and poor old Oscar lying there in his brown tweed suit, wearing a suntan makeup and just the wrong shade of lipstick. If I had not been extremely fond of the old boy, I have a horrible feeling that I might have giggled. Then and there I decided that I could never face another American funeral—even dead.

24 The casket (which has been resting throughout the service on a Classic Beauty Ultra Metal Casket Bier) is now transferred by a hydraulically operated device called Porto-Life to a balloon-tired, Glide Easy casket carriage which will wheel it to yet another conveyance, the Cadillac Funeral Coach. This may be lavender, cream, light green—anything but black. Interiors, of course, are color-correlated, "for the man who cannot stop short of perfection."

25 At graveside, the casket is lowered into the earth. This office, once the prerogative of friends of the deceased, is now performed by a patented mechanical lowering device. A "Lifetime Green" artificial grass mat is at the ready to conceal the sere earth, and overhead, to conceal the sky, is a portable Steril Chapel Tent ("resists the intense heat and humidity of summer and the terrific storms of winter . . . available in Silver Grey, Rose or Evergreen"). Now is the time for the ritual scattering of earth over the coffin, as the solemn words "earth to earth, ashes to ashes, dust to dust" are pronounced by the officiating cleric. This can

today be accomplished "with a mere flick of the wrist with the Gordon Leak-Proof Earth Dispenser. No grasping of a handful of dirt, no soiled fingers. Simple, dignified, beautiful, reverent! The modern way!" The Gordon Earth Dispenser (at $5) is of nickel-plated brass construction. It is not only "attractive to the eye and long wearing"; it is also "one of the 'tools' for building better public relations" if presented as "an appropriate non-commercial gift" to the clergyman. It is shaped something like a saltshaker.

26 Untouched by human hand, the coffin and the earth are now united.

27 It is in the function of directing the participants through this maze of gadgetry that the funeral director has assigned to himself his relatively new role of "grief therapist." He has relieved the family of every detail, he has revamped the corpse to look like a living doll, he has arranged for it to nap for a few days in a slumber room, he has put on a well-oiled performance in which the concept of *death* has played no part whatsoever—unless it was inconsiderately mentioned by the clergyman who conducted the religious service. He has done everything in his power to make the funeral a real pleasure for everybody concerned. He and his team have given their all to score an upset victory over death.

STUDY QUESTIONS

1. What do you take to be the thesis of Mitford's implied argument?
2. Mitford objects not only to certain practices of the funeral industry, but also to the kind of language that accompanies those practices. What instances of such language does she cite, and on what grounds does she find them objectionable? How is her implied critique of morticians' language related to the heart of her argument?
3. Mitford evidently expects us to respond not only to the content of her statements, but also to their manner of expression. Find several instances of "special effects" in her use of language. For each example, think about the way Mitford's phrasing helps to carry her point.
4. Why does Mitford go into considerable detail when explaining the gruesome processes of embalming and restoration? How would the impact of her presentation have been different if she had decided not to "part the formaldehyde curtain" (paragraph 6)?
5. Both in its development and in its conclusion, paragraph 17 typifies several aspects of Mitford's rhetorical strategy. What effects do you think such a paragraph has on a typical reader? Try to be as specific as possible in citing the text.
6. Why does Mitford go out of her way to quote a passage contain-

ing the phrase *intestinal fortitude* (paragraph 14) and then use the same phrase herself (paragraph 18)? What effect would have been created if she had used *intestinal fortitude* one or two further times?

7. Although the title of this selection was not chosen by Mitford, it echoes her own closing words. The football image is also developed in paragraph 22. What is its usefulness to Mitford? How does it help to convey her attitude toward embalming and restoration?
8. *The American Way of Death* was by no means the first book to attack the funeral business, but it has been incomparably the most influential one. On the basis of this excerpt from the book, how would you be inclined to account for that fact?
9. What sort of person do you take Mitford to be? For every adjective that forms part of your answer, try to find at least one illustrative passage.

Frances Fitzgerald

Frances Fitzgerald is an investigative writer who won a Pulitzer Prize and the National Book Award for her book about the Vietnam War, *Fire in the Lake.* More recently she has written *America Revised: History Schoolbooks in the Twentieth Century* (1979), from which the following selection is taken.

HISTORY AND HYPOCRISY*

1 Only in the nineteen-sixties did the textbooks finally end their rear-guard action on behalf of a Northern European America.° The civil-rights movement had shattered the image of a homogeneous American society and, for the first time in the twentieth century, raised profound questions about the national identity. The answer given by that movement and accepted as orthodoxy by most state and big-city school boards was that the United States is a multiracial, multicultural society. This formula, however, raised as many questions as it answered.

*Title chosen by editor

[1] **a Northern European America:** Fitzgerald's chapter up to this point has analyzed the textbook authors' neglect of blacks and their openly hostile references to the immigrant groups that arrived in the late nineteenth century.

Was the United States really like Yugoslavia—a country held together only by a delicate balance among ethnic and cultural groups? Or was there some integration of these groups? Was there a dominant culture —and was that a good thing? Was there some principle of unity that Americans ought to support apart from that of the state? The current texts show signs of struggle with these questions. The struggle has had no clear outcome, for the social portrait drawn by the texts remains divided and confused.

2 The current texts represent the United States as a multiracial society to the extent that they include some material on all the large racial and ethnic groups, and that their photographs show people of all colors (also of all ages and both sexes) and suggest that even white Americans come from different ethnic backgrounds. The books contain a good deal of social history on these groups. Most texts assert that the early settlers had African as well as European roots, and virtually all of them have sections on Aztec, Mayan, and North American Indian cultures. In one text, the account of colonization begins with the settlement of Puerto Rico by Ponce de León. Another text begins with a chapter on immigrants and includes a discussion of the migration of blacks from South to North after the Second World War. The texts also describe certain of the "problems" that minorities have faced in the United States, such as the internment of Japanese-Americans during the Second World War. But it's on the subject of these "problems" that the texts are still confused. They have succeeded in including all groups, but they have not succeeded in treating them all equally. There is, for instance, a remarkable disparity between their treatment of European ethnic groups and their treatment of all other ethnic minorities.

3 Most current texts discuss the European ethnic groups in two separate places—in their chapters on immigration and industrialization in the nineteenth century, and again in their chapters on modern-day life. Their nineteenth-century social history now includes a good deal of material that would have been labelled "too controversial" a decade ago. In place of the brief dismissive passages about toiling masses arriving in the land of liberty, the texts now describe in some painful detail the difficulties so many of the immigrants faced when they got off the boats: brutalizing labor in factories and mines, slum conditions in the cities, prejudice against them, and the shock of entering another culture. The so-called "inquiry," or "discovery," texts—which focus on a few topics and illustrate them with documents from primary and secondary sources—include portions of diaries or books by the newly arrived Europeans which present the experience from a perspective that was heretofore unthinkable: that of the immigrants themselves. In the sections on modern-day life, the texts make some attempt at consistency with this point of view. They describe not individual artists but working-class families that came originally from Poland, Greece, or Russia, and they contend that the European culture of these families has not

melted away—that they still have strong religious, culinary, and other traditions. But here the discussion ends. With two exceptions, they do not discuss the assimilation of European ethnic groups; they do not discuss the washout of European traditions in America or the fusion of various cultures. They insist—following Nathan Glazer and Daniel P. Moynihan's sociological study *Beyond the Melting Pot*—that the "ethnics" have not been assimilated but have separately added to the wonderful variety of life in America. There is some irony in this. The very fact that the texts can depict the horrors of life for the immigrants in the eighteen-eighties shows that some assimilation has occurred; otherwise, the texts would be accused of offending group sensibilities. A further proof is that a number of the authors of these American-history books are the children or grandchildren of such immigrants.

4 Still, even with this overstatement of the Glazer-Moynihan thesis, the treatment of European minorities is far more realistic than that of non-European minorities, whose sensibilities the publishers are anxious not to offend. The photographs in the mass-market texts rarely show a non-white person who is brutalized, dirty, or even poor—unless the photograph specifically illustrates "pockets of poverty in America." There are almost no pictures of black sharecroppers, or black laborers of any kind unless they are in integrated groups wearing hard hats. Except for Stokely Carmichael, other black militants, and the hardhat laborers, blacks pictured in current texts wear business suits or lab coats. The same goes for other non-white people. Most of them are smiling. You can find pictures of Chicano farmworkers, but the workers are always clean and look as if they're enjoying their work. They're always smiling at César Chávez. The Puerto Ricans are smiling and healthy. The Chinese are smiling at healthy-looking vegetable stands. Indeed, everyone is smiling so hard you would think that all non-white people in the United States took happy pills. (The Russians, by contrast, appear to be a sombre lot. Their grimness dates from a time in the fifties when a group of right-wing organizations made an enormous fuss about a photograph of smiling Russian children.) There are a few exceptions to this rule. But there are no exceptions to the rule of art. Many of the current texts overflow with examples of art by non-white people. In the first chapters, there are pages on which the printed word makes a few ant trails around huge color pictures of folk art: Mayan temples or Aztec masks, Iroquois blankets, Pueblo pottery (but no feather headdresses, for these are thought to be stereotypical). Later on, there are pictures of modern Mexican murals and disquisitions on black painters and writers, and occasionally on one or two black musicians. (One book includes a half-page reproduction of a painting in Hudson River school° style that

---

[4] **Hudson River school:** group of American painters who, in the mid-nineteenth century, specialized in romantic landscapes

happens to have been painted by a black.) Apparently the publishers have yet to find a Puerto Rican landscape painter or a Chinese-American poet, but one imagines that they are trying hard, since artists must now come from everywhere except Europe. In addition to artists, the non-white minorities seem to have hero figures and "leaders," while the European groups do not; and all of them are always said to be struggling to achieve full rights.

5 The publishers have mentioned the struggles of non-white peoples, but in order to sell books to a majority they sometimes refrain from mentioning what these groups are struggling against. Though most books delineate the social and economic institutions that made life so hard for the nineteenth-century immigrants, they do not always do the same for the non-white Americans in modern times. The Chicano farmworkers are struggling, but some texts fail to mention the growers. The American Indians are struggling in a void, there being no mention of the historical arrangements between private corporations and the Bureau of Indian Affairs for the exploitation of natural resources on the tribal lands. In regard to the civil-rights movement, there is often no discussion of institutionalized racism—not even that which was contained in the Southern school systems before Little Rock.° The books report at length on reform movements and reform measures but rarely tot up the results, thus giving little or no indication that many of the attempts at reform have failed. This is hardly surprising, since they usually fail to explain in any detail how or why the injustices came into being in the first place. As one critic has pointed out, the texts report that blacks fought in the Revolutionary War but not that the Framers of the Constitution, with the three-fifths compromise,° among other provisions, made slavery a part of the political system. Furthermore, only the most sophisticated of the inquiry books report any of the "struggles to achieve full rights" from the point of view of the strugglers.

6 The current version of the history of racial minorities in America represents the compromise that the publishers have made among the conflicting demands of a variety of pressure groups, inside and outside the school systems. The compromise is an unhappy one, and it is bound to change in the future, if only because its inconsistencies are so obvious. However, it is interesting to ask at this point what a truly "multiracial, multicultural" history text would look like. The question is an academic one, admittedly, but there are certain organizations, such as the Council on Interracial Books for Children, that do argue it, in an

---

[5] **Little Rock:** The capital of Arkansas was the scene, in 1957, of the first school desegregation showdown between state and federal officials.

[5] **three-fifths compromise:** a concession made to slaveholding states in the Constitutional Convention of 1787, whereby three-fifths of all slaves would be included in population counts, thus giving disproportionate power to those states in the House of Representatives

academic way, and that do give certain answers through their criticisms of current texts. To look at the council's very detailed and sophisticated criticism of the texts is to see that somewhere—far from where the texts are now—there is a real dilemma in the very notion of a "multiracial, multicultural" history. Let us take an example. In its list of twenty-six "stereotypes, distortions and omissions" that the history texts generally make about "native Americans," the council points to a passage from one of the more naïve of the texts—*America: Its People and Values,* by Leonard C. Wood, Ralph H. Gabriel, and Edward L. Biller. The passage reads:

> A friendly Indian named Squanto helped the colonists. He showed them how to plant corn and how to live on the edge of the wilderness. A soldier, Captain Miles Standish, taught the Pilgrims how to defend themselves against unfriendly Indians.

The council's objection to this passage is that it is Eurocentric to characterize native Americans as either "friendly" or "unfriendly." Squanto was actually assisting invaders, whereas the "unfriendly" Indians were defending their communities. "All nations define a 'patriot' as one whose allegiance is toward his or her own people," the council report continues. "Consequently, true Native American heroes are those who fought to preserve and protect their people's freedom and land."

7 The implications of that objection are far-reaching. To begin with, if the texts were really to consider American history from the perspective of the American Indians, they would have to conclude that the continent had passed through almost five hundred years of unmitigated disaster, beginning with the epidemics spread by the Europeans and continuing on most fronts today. Then, if the texts were really to consider the Indian point of view, they could not simply say this but would have to take the position of Squanto—if not that of his more patriotic fellows—and categorize Miles Standish as friendly or unfriendly. And ditto for the next four hundred years—while making sure, of course, to portray the diverse views of all the Indian nations, and their diverse relations with the white settlers. When you add to this, as the council would, the Chicano, Asian-American, African-American, Puerto Rican, and women's perspectives on events, American history becomes unbelievably complicated—as does the whole issue of what constitutes balance and fairness. But the inclusion of other perspectives is crucial to a multiracial or multiethnic history. Add to that the notion "multicultural" and there is yet another level of complexity involved, for culture, of course, is not the same as race, and (to raise a problem that neither the text writers nor their critics seem to have considered) some of the greatest cultural differences in the United States lie between Anglo-Saxon Protestant males. Conceivably, the publishers could make a book that would include all these perspectives—or, more realistically, they

could produce different texts for the different sections of society. But in either case the message of the texts would be that Americans have no common history, no common culture, and no common values, and that membership in a racial or cultural group constitutes the most fundamental experience of each individual. The message would be that the center cannot, and should not, hold.

8 The logical extreme of the "multiracial, multicultural" position is worth considering, if only because it clarifies the traditional ideology of the texts. At least since the eighteen-nineties, the school histories have focussed more or less narrowly on the development of the nation-state. To the extent that they dealt with social history, they have assumed a fairly homogeneous society, in which all differences could be justly compromised to suit all parties. In practice, this has meant taking the position of the ruling groups—whoever they happened to be at any given time—and suppressing the views of others. Since the nineteen-thirties, text writers have been lecturing children on the need for tolerance and respect for differences, but they have at the same time continued to minimize social conflicts and emphasize the similarities between Americans. The conflicts of the nineteen-sixties jolted only a small percentage of the texts out of this approach. The inquiry books, for extremely literate—and thus largely white, upper-middle-class—children, present cultural diversity and social conflict. The mass-market texts, for the less literate, picture people with "foreign-sounding" names and different-colored skin, but the message remains the traditional one: Americans are all alike, no matter what their color or their background.

STUDY QUESTIONS

1. Would you be able to tell that this selection—an excerpt from a book chapter—was not designed as a complete essay? Study the opening and closing paragraphs and ask yourself how they do or don't make an "essayistic" impression.
2. What is Fitzgerald's intended audience, and what tone does she assume in addressing that audience?
3. Why, near the end of her second paragraph, does Fitzgerald put the word *problems* within quotation marks? Where else in this selection does she develop the point that is implied here?
4. What is the main difference, according to Fitzgerald, between the textbooks' "treatment of European ethnic groups and their treatment of all other ethnic minorities" (paragraph 2)? What signs of that differential treatment does she mention? If her point is cor-

rect, what does it reveal about the attitudes of textbook makers?

5. How do "inquiry" textbooks differ from others? Is Fitzgerald in favor of them?
6. What is the "melting pot" thesis about American society, and what view of it does Fitzgerald take?
7. In what sense can this selection be considered an argument? How else might it be classified?

by Novelpress 77 S.a.r.l. English translation copyright © 1978 by Viking Penguin, Inc. Reprinted by permission of Viking Penguin, Inc.

Rachel Carson, "The Obligation to Endure," from *Silent Spring,* by Rachel Carson. Copyright © 1962 by Rachel L. Carson. Reprinted by permission of Houghton Mifflin Company.

Frank Conroy, "A Yo-Yo Going Down, a Mad Squirrel Coming Up," (retitled: "Conquering the Universe,") from *Stop-time,* by Frank Conroy. Copyright © 1965, 1966, 1967 by Frank Conroy. Reprinted by permission of Viking Penguin, Inc.

Aaron Copland, "How We Listen," from *What to Listen For in Music,* by Aaron Copland. Copyright © 1939, 1957, 1964 by McGraw-Hill Book Company. Reprinted by permission of McGraw-Hill Book Company.

Joan Didion, "Some Dreamers of the Golden Dream," from *Slouching Towards Bethlehem,* by Joan Didion. Copyright © 1966 by Joan Didion. Reprinted by permission of Farrar, Straus & Giroux, Inc.

Joseph Epstein, "Running and Other Vices," from *Familiar Territory: Observations on American Life,* pp. 149–163, by Joseph Epstein. Copyright © 1979 by Joseph Epstein. Reprinted by permission of Oxford University Press, Inc.

James Fallows, "Why the Country Needs It," from *The Atlantic Monthly* (April 1980), pp. 44, 85–90. Copyright © 1980 by The Atlantic Monthly Company, Boston, Mass. Reprinted by permission of The Atlantic Monthly Company.

Frances Fitzgerald, "History and Hypocrisy," from *America Revised: History Schoolbooks in the Twentieth Century,* by Frances Fitzgerald. Copyright © 1979 by Frances Fitzgerald. Reprinted by permission of Little, Brown and Company in association with The Atlantic Monthly Press. First appeared in *The New Yorker.*

Ben Funk, " 'Milking' Cobras for Cures," from *The New York Times Magazine* (August 3, 1978), pp. 68–70. Copyright © 1979 by The New York Times Company. Reprinted by permission of The New York Times Company.

Paul Fussell, "The Stationary Tourist," from *Harper's Magazine* (April 1979), pp. 31–38. Copyright © by *Harper's Magazine.* All rights reserved. Reprinted by special permission of *Harper's Magazine.*

Lois Gould, from *Not Responsible for Personal Articles,* by Lois Gould. Copyright © 1978 by Lois Gould. Reprinted by permission of Random House, Inc.

Dan Greenberg, "Scientists Wanted—Pioneers Needn't Apply; Call A.D. 2000," from *Smithsonian Magazine* (July 1976), pp. 60–67. Reprinted by permission of the author.

Garrett Hardin, "Ethical Implications of Carrying Capacity," from *The Limits of Altruism: An Ecologist's View of Survival,* by Garrett Hardin. Copyright © 1977 by Indiana University Press. Reprinted by permission of the publisher.

James Herndon, from *How to Survive in Your Native Land,* pp. 103–108. Copyright © 1971 by James Herndon. Reprinted by permission of Simon & Schuster, a Division of Gulf & Western Corporation.

Edward Hoagland, "A Low-Water Man," from *Red Wolves and Black Bears,* by Edward Hoagland. Copyright © 1976 by Edward Hoagland. Reprinted by permission of Random House, Inc.

Ada Louise Huxtable, "Houston," from *Kicked a Building Lately?* by Ada Louise Huxtable. Copyright © 1976/78 by The New York Times Company. Reprinted by permission of the New York Times Company.

Jane Jacobs, from *The Death and Life of Great American Cities,* pp. 50–54, by Jane Jacobs. Copyright © 1961 by Jane Jacobs. Reprinted by permission of Random House, Inc.

Pauline Kael, "High School and Other Forms of Madness," from *Deeper into Movies,* by Pauline Kael. Copyright © 1969 by Pauline Kael. Reprinted by permission of Little,

Brown and Company in association with The Atlantic Monthly Press. First appeared in *The New Yorker.*

Don B. Kates, Jr., "Against Civil Disarmament," from *Harper's Magazine* (September 1978), pp. 28–33. Copyright © 1978 by *Harper's Magazine.* All rights reserved. Reprinted by special permission of *Harper's Magazine.*

Martin Luther King, Jr., "Letter from Birmingham Jail," from *Why We Can't Wait,* by Martin Luther King, Jr. Copyright © 1963 by Martin Luther King, Jr. Reprinted by permission of Harper & Row, Publishers, Inc.

Maxine Hong Kingston, from *The Woman Warrior: Memoirs of a Girlhood Among Ghosts,* pp. 171–181. Copyright © 1975, 1976 by Maxine Hong Kingston. Reprinted by permission of Alfred A. Knopf, Inc.

Robin Lakoff, from *Language and Woman's Place,* pp. 19–25. Copyright © 1975 by Robin Lakoff. Reprinted by permission of Harper & Row, Publishers, Inc.

John Leonard, "The Only Child," from *Private Lives in the Imperial City,* by John Leonard. Copyright © 1976 by The New York Times Company. Reprinted by permission of The New York Times Company.

Enrique Hank Lopez, "Back to Bachimba," from *Horizon* (Winter 1967), pp. 80–83. Copyright © 1967 by American Heritage Publishing Company, Inc. Reprinted by permission of *Horizon.*

Alison Lurie, "Vulgar, Coarse, and Grotesque," from *Harper's Magazine* (December 1979), pp. 66–72. Copyright © 1979 by *Harper's Magazine.* All rights reserved. Reprinted by special permission of *Harper's Magazine.*

Peter Marsh and Rom Harré, "The World of Football Hooligans," from *Human Nature* (October 1978). Copyright © 1978 by Human Nature, Inc. Reprinted by permission of the publisher.

Mary McCarthy, "The Blackguard," from *Memories of a Catholic Girlhood,* pp. 87–101, by Mary McCarthy. Copyright © 1946, 1974 by Mary McCarthy. Reprinted by permission of Harcourt Brace Jovanovich, Inc.

John McMurty, "Kill 'em! Crush 'em! Eat 'em Raw!" from *Maclean's* (October 1971). Copyright © 1971 by *Maclean's* Magazine. Reprinted by permission of the author and the publisher.

Jessica Mitford, from *The American Way of Death,* by Jessica Mitford. Copyright © 1963 by Jessica Mitford. Reprinted by permission of Simon & Schuster, a Division of Gulf & Western Corporation.

George Orwell, "Shooting an Elephant," from *Shooting an Elephant and Other Essays,* by George Orwell. Copyright © 1950 by Sonia Brownell Orwell; 1978 by Sonia Pitt-Rivers. Reprinted by permission of Harcourt Brace Jovanovich, Inc., Mrs. Sonia Brownell Orwell, and Secker & Warberg Ltd.

Robert M. Pirsig, from pp. 107–111 (retitled: "The Rationality of Repair") in *Zen and the Art of Motorcycle Maintenance,* by Robert M. Pirsig. Copyright © 1974 by Robert M. Pirsig. Reprinted by permission of William Morrow & Company.

Richard Rhodes, "Watching the Animals," which originally appeared in *Harper's Magazine* (March 1980.) Copyright © 1970 by Richard Rhodes. Reprinted by permission of the JCA Literary Agency, Inc.

D. L. Rosenhan, "On Being Sane in Insane Places," from *Science,* 179, (January 19, 1973), pp. 250–258. Copyright © 1973 by the American Association for the Advancement of Science. Reprinted by permission of the author and the American Association for the Advancement of Science.

Frank Rowesome, Jr., "Apple and Beech, Birch and Oak," from *The Bright and Glowing Place,* by Frank Rowesome, Jr. Copyright © 1975 by Frank Rowesome, Jr. Reprinted by permission of the Stephen Greene Press, Brattleboro, Vermont 05301.

AUTHOR-TITLE INDEX

ABOUT THE AUTHOR

Frederick Crews, Professor of English at the University of California, Berkeley, received his Ph.D. from Princeton University. Throughout a distinguished career he has attained many honors, including a Guggenheim Fellowship, appointment as a Fulbright Lecturer in Italy, and recognition from the National Endowment for the Arts for his essay, "Norman O. Brown: The World Dissolves." His writings include highly regarded books on Henry James, E. M. Forster, and Nathaniel Hawthorne, the best-selling satire *The Pooh Perplex,* and a recent volume of his own essays entitled *Out of My System.* Professor Crews has published numerous articles in *Partisan Review, New York Review of Books, Commentary, Tri-Quarterly,* and other important journals. He has been Chairman of Freshman Composition in the English Department at Berkeley.